The Roeper School

ADVANCES IN CREATIVITY AND GIFTEDNESS
Volume 5

Advances in Creativity and Gifted Education (ADVA) is the first internationally established book series that focuses exclusively on the constructs of creativity and giftedness as pertaining to the psychology, philosophy, pedagogy and ecology of talent development across the milieus of family, school, institutions and society. ADVA strives to synthesize both domain specific and domain general efforts at developing creativity, giftedness and talent. The books in the series are international in scope and include the efforts of researchers, clinicians and practitioners across the globe.

Series Editor:
Bharath Sriraman, The University of Montana, USA

International Advisory Panel:
Don Ambrose, Rider University, USA
David Chan, The Chinese University of Hong Kong
Anna Craft, University of Exeter, UK
Stephen Hegedus, University of Massachusetts, Dartmouth, USA
Kristina Juter, Kristianstad University College, Sweden
James C. Kaufman, California State University at San Bernardino, USA
Kyeonghwa Lee, Seoul National University, Korea
Roza Leikin, University of Haifa, Israel
Peter Liljedahl, Simon Fraser University, Canada
Paula Olszewski-Kubilius, Northwestern University, USA
Larisa Shavinina, University of Quebec, Canada

Editorial Assistant:
Claire Payne

The Roeper School

A Model for Holistic Development of High Ability

Edited by

Don Ambrose
Rider University, Lawrenceville, New Jersey, USA

Bharath Sriraman
The University of Montana, Missoula, Montana, USA

and

Tracy L. Cross
College of William & Mary, Williamsburg, Virginia, USA

SENSE PUBLISHERS
ROTTERDAM/BOSTON/TAIPEI

A C.I.P. record for this book is available from the Library of Congress.

ISBN: 978-94-6209-417-8 (paperback)
ISBN: 978-94-6209-418-5 (hardback)
ISBN: 978-94-6209-419-2 (e-book)

Published by: Sense Publishers,
P.O. Box 21858,
3001 AW Rotterdam,
The Netherlands
https://www.sensepublishers.com/

Printed on acid-free paper

The following chapters have been reprinted with permission from the Roeper School which retains copyright of this material:
The Roeper Philosophy, George Roeper & Annemarie Roeper
and
"The Most Exciting Meetings": An Interview with Annemarie Roeper and A. Harry Passow, Denita Banks-Sims

All Rights Reserved © 2013 Sense Publishers

No part of this work may be reproduced, stored in a retrieval system, or transmitted in any form or by any means, electronic, mechanical, photocopying, microfilming, recording or otherwise, without written permission from the Publisher, with the exception of any material supplied specifically for the purpose of being entered and executed on a computer system, for exclusive use by the purchaser of the work.

TABLE OF CONTENTS

Acknowledgements   ix

Part I   Introduction

Facets on the Gem: Brilliance Shining Through a Special School for the Gifted   3
Don Ambrose

Part II   The History and Philosophy of the School

Constancy and Change in Progressive Education: The Roeper Philosophy of Self Actualization and Interdependence   21
Michele Kane

The Roeper Philosophy   43
George Roeper & Annemarie Roeper

Growing Deep Community Roots   51
Cathy Wilmers

Empowering the Gifted and Intense Child   57
Emery Pence

"The Most Exciting Meetings": An Interview with Annemarie Roeper and A. Harry Passow   69
Denita Banks-Sims

Nurturing the Gifted Child or Developing Talent? Resolving a Paradox   79
David Yun Dai

In Their Own Words: Students Reflect on the Roeper Difference   99
Susannah Nichols

How Is Roeper Different?   107
Dylan Bennett

Roeper Alumni Reflect on Lasting Lessons   111
Marcia Ruff

A Personal Tale of Development and Growth: The Inadvertent Influence of the Roeper School on a Scholar   123
Tracy L. Cross

TABLE OF CONTENTS

Part III   Curriculum and Programs

Differentiation in Action: The Integrated Curriculum Model   131
Joyce VanTassel-Baska

An Interdisciplinary Journey   145
Wendy Mayer

Social Justice in an Early Childhood Classroom   153
Nancy B. Hertzog, Megan A. Ryan & Nick Gillon

A View from the Preschool Classroom: The Child's Role
in Creating a Socially Just Community   171
Colleen Shelton

Standards and Balanced Assessments: Relationships to the Roeper
School's Philosophy and Practices   175
Susan K. Johnsen

College Counseling and the Gifted Student   193
Patrick O'Connor

Next Steps for Roeper School: Evaluation and Research   209
Carolyn M. Callahan

Part IV   Emergent, Democratic Leadership

Developing Leadership Capacity in Gifted Students for the Present
and the Future   225
Dorothy Sisk

Emerging Leaders: Believing in Children and Building Leadership
Capacity Over Time   259
Lisa Baker

Leadership at the Roeper School   265
Emery Pence

Leadership at the Roeper School Through the Eyes of an Insider   275
Alexandra Dickinson

Process and Voice   281
David H. Feldman

Observations on Governance at the Roeper School   285
Douglas Winkworth

Part V Looking Forward: A Most Unusual, Thought-Provoking, Time-Transcendent School

The Roeper School in the 21st Century: Trends, Issues, Challenges, and Opportunities   293
Don Ambrose

The Roeper School from 12 Years Out: Reflections of a 2001 Graduate   317
Daniel Faichney

Contributors   323

Subject Index   335

ACKNOWLEDGEMENTS

Pulling together a very large project involving many contributors from diverse locales is a lot like herding cats. Fortunately, all of our cats were highly intelligent and motivated so we are very proud of their contributions. A couple of individuals deserve special mention. Susannah Nichols, teacher of English at the Roeper School, served as the school-based point person during some crucial times in which the prospects for completion of the project were uncertain. Her diligence kept things afloat until we could establish sufficient momentum. Fortunately, Marcia Ruff, the school historian, stepped up and provided that momentum. In fact, she did such an amazing job finding and encouraging contributors from the school that the quality of a substantial portion of the book largely came from her efforts. We also wish to thank Merzili Villanueva, Valerie K. Ambrose, and Jenny Robins for their extensive, helpful copyediting in the final phases of the project. Finally, we thank our insightful contributors for their interesting and important perspectives on this unique school for the gifted. Contributions came from alumni, current students, faculty, administrators, a Board of Trustees member, and an array of leading thinkers in the field of gifted education.

The editors,
Don Ambrose
Bharath Sriraman
Tracy L. Cross

PART I

INTRODUCTION

DON AMBROSE

FACETS ON THE GEM

Brilliance Shining Through a Special School for the Gifted

After spending significant amounts of time observing in the Roeper school and interacting with its students and personnel one feels at a loss for words when trying to find ways to describe its essence. As a lover of metaphor, I tried to find ways to capture the spirit, philosophy, and dynamics of the school through engaging metaphors, selecting one, trying it out, and then tossing it aside to play with another, and yet another. Finally, I settled on the metaphor of a gleaming gemstone. While this metaphor also is lacking in some respects it does convey some of the most interesting attributes of the school.

We can think of the gemstone metaphor at two levels of analysis. At a macro-level it represents the school itself with individual students, faculty members, administrators, support personnel, board members, and alumni as facets on the gem. Each facet conveys and reflects brilliant light, and all of the individual luminosity taken together comprises the glowing brilliance of this unique school. In addition, the gem sits up high on its point striking a fine balance between the needs and rights of the individual and the needs and rights of groups, as well as the need for exquisite balance between long-range philosophical constancy and dynamic, context-sensitive change. A gemstone sitting up on its point normally could not maintain itself in that position, and that's the case with many other organizations that attempt to strike important balances. But the Roeper School has managed to maintain itself upright in this beautifully balanced position for decades. The strength of its philosophy and the purposeful sense of agency felt by everyone involved in the system are the reasons for that.

The gemstone metaphor also seems to work at the level of the individual. For example, each student is a highly promising rough stone with enormous potential when she or he enters the school. Over the course of time, through the guidance of the philosophy and the help of peers and educators in the school, the individual begins to purposefully trim away some of her or his rough edges, as with the cutting of a diamond. This creates potentially brilliant facets of intrinsic motivation, interpersonal acumen, higher-order thinking, ethical awareness, and talent discovery and development.

A carefully cut diamond is more valuable than one that is roughly crafted. Individuals with considerable latent ability can find themselves roughly crafted by external forces—for example, the mania of shallow, superficial test preparation that shortsighted, dogmatic policymakers and ideological hacks impose on most students throughout the United States (see Berliner, 2012; Ravitch, 2010). But individuals within the Roeper School do their own personalized, student-centred diamond cutting within a challenging but safe environment. Consequently, they tend to end up with exquisite polish and luminescent facets that allow their full potential to shine through.

As mentioned earlier, no single metaphor is adequate when it comes to conveying the essence of this school. A metaphor tends to capture some dimensions of a complex issue or phenomenon while ignoring or obscuring other dimensions (see Ambrose, 1996, 2012; Gardner & Winner, 1993; Lakoff & Johnson, 1980, 1999; Sternberg, 1990; Sternberg, Tourangeau, & Nigro, 1993). The facets-on-the-gem metaphor doesn't work very well when it comes to the emergent, organic nature of the Roeper School. The metaphor seems too rigid for that. So ultimately multiple metaphors should come into play. But there isn't space in this chapter for such explorations and we'll have to leave that for another time.

Another way to think big picture about a complex phenomenon is to look for perspectives from multiple disciplines. Interdisciplinary excursions sometimes turn up useful insights about intriguing, complex phenomena (Ambrose, 2005, 2009, 2012a; Ambrose, Cohen, & Tannenbaum, 2003; Ambrose & Cross, 2009; Gardner, 1988; Page, 2007; Sriraman, 2009; Sriraman & Dahl, 2009). Many insights from scores of academic disciplines could help us understand the school in more depth and detail. For example, neuroscience has the potential to tell us something about the cognitive processing involved in the intrapersonal self-discovery or altruism that the school promotes (see Martin & Monroe, 2009; Morishima, Schunk, Bruhin, Ruff, & Fehr, 2012; Rose & Abi-Rached, 2013). Historians and sociologists can pull back the socio-contextual curtains that obscure the reasons why clever, creative leaders can so callously initiate devastating wars (see Bacevich, 2010, 2012) or encourage dogmatic favoritism of particular identity groups while promoting oppression or even genocide when it comes to outsiders (see Chirot, 2012; Chirot & McCauley, 2006). Some economists can help us perceive the refined conceptions of merit that emerge from the achievements of Roeper School students and alumni and the juxtaposition of these conceptions with distorted notions of egocentric, hyper-materialistic, ruthlessly attained or effortlessly inherited *unearned merit* that prevail in societies dominated by the dogmatism of neoclassical economic theory (see Ambrose, 2011, 2012; Sen, 2000; Stiglitz, 2010, 2012). But exploring these constructs and others would require at least another book. For now, let's consider just a few more ideas from foreign disciplines.

Scholarly discussions of indigenous leadership and decision making drawn from indigenous studies and cultural anthropology can shed some interesting light on the dynamics of collaboration, problem solving, and leadership at the school. For example, Alfred (1999) showed how indigenous leadership sharply contrasts with stereotypical leadership in the mainstream Western culture. Predominant notions of leadership suggest that strong leaders are focused, forceful, manipulative, and egocentric. In fact, studies of psychopathy have revealed that corporate leadership is populated with a significantly higher percentage of psychopaths than the general population. Psychopaths who can dial back a few of their psychopathic traits just a little while leaving other traits running at full throttle tend to find success in organizations and societies that are based on ruthless competition (see Babiak, Neumann, & Hare, 2010; Dutton, 2012; Gao & Raine, 2010).

In stark contrast, according to Alfred (1999), effective leaders in indigenous cultures are inconspicuous, remaining behind the scenes to support other members of the group in non-manipulative ways. They develop skin "seven spans thick" to deal with criticism when they do step forward to take the blows aimed at their collaborators, as opposed to leaders from the mainstream culture who tend to step forward when it is time to claim credit for success. Indigenous leaders assume responsibility and set good examples while facilitating communication, inclusion, and decision-making consensus.

In another example of interpersonal processes from an indigenous culture, Bohm (1994) discussed the observations of an unnamed cultural anthropologist who joined a group of Native Americans during a collaborative decision-making meeting. The 30 plus members of the group sat in a circle and simply began a discussion. There was no apparent agenda for the meeting and there was no designated leader. The only hint at hierarchy came from somewhat more deference paid to the older members of the group. No minutes were kept. After a considerable time the group simply disbanded without summarizing any conclusions. Remarkably, everyone in the group left knowing what to do about the issues under discussion.

These examples of nonhierarchical leadership and unpredictable, bottom-up, emergent, collaborative decision-making look very much like what goes on in the school on a regular basis. But they don't capture everything. Somehow the school manages to blend these processes with a strong focus on individual self-discovery and self-determination. The collaborative leadership processes are helpful but they seem to be means to important ends with intrapersonal self-discovery and ethical considerations always prominent.

With the facets-of-the-gem metaphor and the potential of interdisciplinary borrowing to establish a big-picture context let us look more closely at the contents of this book. We have organized it into several sections that seem to represent some essential elements of the school. The section following this introductory chapter deals with the all-important history and philosophy of the school. Contributors shed light on the reasons for the creation of the school and the dynamics of its evolution over the course of time. They also address the Roeper philosophy in depth and detail. All of this provides a foundation for the remainder of the book. The next section includes discussions of programs and curriculum, both from the viewpoint of best practices in education as a whole and from the perspective of structures and processes within the school itself. The following section addresses the ways in which leadership emerges from the philosophy and dynamics of the school and provides important directional beacons for students' self-discovery and self-actualization. Finally, the concluding section provides some insights about how the school fits the unpredictable, globalized 21st-century environment. The remainder of this introductory chapter outlines the authors' contributions in each section.

The History and Philosophy of the School

In many institutions in today's world a philosophy statement seems to be not much more than an item on a to-do list. Philosophy and vision or mission statements tend to be crafted, printed, framed, and posted on office walls only to be neglected over the long term. The philosophy at the Roeper School is taken much more seriously. It is the living, breathing central core of virtually all that takes place in the system. It permeates the thoughts and actions of students, teachers, administrators, support personnel, board members and alumni. Moreover, it has provided directional guidance for the development of the school throughout the mid-late 20th century and now into the 21st. The section of this volume on the history and philosophy of the school includes contributions from the school's founders, current students, alumni, teachers and administrators, and some leading thinkers from the field of gifted education.

Michele Kane begins this section with some deep insights about the school's founding, purpose, and development. Michele has done extensive research into the social-emotional dimensions of high ability and is an expert on the Roeper philosophy. In her chapter, *Constancy and Change in Progressive Education: The Roeper philosophy of Self Actualization and Interdependence,* she illustrates the compelling power and impact of the school's belief system, especially the ways in which it leads to insightful self-discovery. More specifically, individuals and groups following the philosophy will emphasize the self as the curriculum; the dynamic integration of social, emotional, spiritual, and intellectual endeavors; and the crucial importance of developing a strong school community. Young people need a safe environment to support them in the difficult work required by multidimensional self-discovery and a vibrant, accepting school community can establish that safety. While describing the importance and interactions of all of these elements and dynamics, Michele takes us back in time through the development of the Roeper philosophy and the formational history of the school. She highlights important events, documents, and a helpful timeline of the school's development to show us how George and Annemarie wrestled with important educational ideas and plans and came to refine them. In essence, while creating and refining the school they pursued the same intrapersonally flavoured inquiry processes that they hoped all of their students would use in the development of their own life trajectories.

The voices of George and Annemarie Roeper are represented strongly in the chapter titled *The Roeper philosophy.* Marcia Ruff provided this material, which is derived from a 1981 document written by the Roepers to establish the essential belief system of the school. This is a panoramic ethical philosophy that brings together notions of individual and group responsibility, community building, the inseparability of education and real life, and a nonhierarchical, collaborative, egalitarian ethos aimed at counteracting the competitive, dog-eat-dog flavour of the ideological and cultural systems that tend to dominate the modern world. The Roepers believed that an excessively competitive culture leads to its own destruction because we don't fully use our collaborative abilities and ethical sensibilities. The learning environment they valued enables students to gain the inner strength necessary to engage in purposeful self-development, productive collaboration, and the betterment of the world over the long-term. Their philosophy supports the creation of a productive learning environment because it is based on complex replication of the real world within the structure and dynamics of the school, which also navigates a dynamic balance between constancy and change.

Demonstrating strong consistency with the philosophy, faculty member Cathy Wilmers addresses a core activity of the school in her chapter *Growing Deep Community Roots*. She provides some keen insights about the thoughtful, bottom-up, democratic approach to community building through painstaking but enjoyable student-centred processes in the school. She uses a specific example of community building through the work of a class full of purposeful, very young students who diligently worked on community building as a long-term project and then shared the results with a large number of older students at an assembly. A standing ovation from the older students put a strong punctuation mark on this work and left an indelible impression on all involved. Going even further, the students and their teacher employed impressive higher-order thinking to articulate the meaning of all of this.

Emery Pence, alumni relations coordinator at the school, gives us an entertaining, insightful look at the innards of the Roeper philosophy in action. In his chapter, *Empowering the Gifted and Intense Child,* he introduces the analysis with portrayals of hypothetical students based on composites of students he has worked with over the years. The intensity and the ability of these students to make intellectual and affective connections help them capitalize on and contribute to the student-centred dynamics of the school. Pence illustrates ways in which learning communities, service-learning opportunities, and the problem-based, inquiry approach to learning at the school enable students to develop authentic relationships, intellectual humility, and ownership of and authentic participation in the organic, bottom-up learning processes that characterize and distinguish the school. These dynamic processes permeate the school and enrich learning while providing important life lessons. Pence shows how enabling this kind of self-development is not easy and demands much of the students and adults involved; however, it is at the core of the Roeper philosophy and is well worth the effort.

In her chapter, *"The Most Exciting Meetings": An Interview with Annemarie Roeper and A. Harry Passow,* Denita Banks-Sims, director of development and publications at the school, illustrates important evolutionary steps taken by the school with a transcript of an interview she carried out with these two luminaries in the early 1990s. In the 1950s, the Roepers had been thinking about modifying the school to align it more with the needs of gifted children. They became aware of Dr. Passow's work and begin to interact with him. This eventually culminated in intensive conferences and other interactions at the school where the creative idealism of these visionary thinkers came alive. Dr. Passow was a leader in gifted education at the time. His strong ethical awareness combined with practical intelligence made him an ideal resource for the transformation of the school into a school for the gifted. Through this interview, Denita enabled Annemarie and Harry to describe the dynamics of this transformation, which combined Harry's broad and deep knowledge of education for the gifted with the Roeper's willingness and ability to design a school aligned with best practices and imbued with ethical sensibility. As if that isn't enough, the interview is flavoured with humour and intrapersonal insights from both Annemarie and Harry.

David Dai is one of the most perceptive, integrative thinkers in the field of gifted education. In his chapter, *Nurturing the Gifted Child or Developing Talent? Resolving a Paradox,* David begins with overviews of some conceptual trends and issues in the field of gifted education: most notably the dynamic tension between the whole child and talent-development approaches. He discusses the particular strengths of the Roeper School when it comes to the whole-child paradigm, which includes emphases on social-emotional development and intrapersonal intelligence. He goes on to craft an argument showing how the two paradigms can be integrated to create an education that develops talent and excellence within specializations while generating strong, intrinsic motivation and self-awareness. While recognizing that the school establishes exceptional learning systems that help young people discover and develop their abilities in very effective and efficient ways he makes some recommendations for future refinement. Essentially, he shows how the school is well designed and positioned to develop both the whole child and domain-specific talents.

Consistent with the Roeper philosophy, Susannah Nichols, a freelance writer and teacher of English at the school, turned the opportunity to participate in this project into a forum for some of her students to discuss their school experiences in their own voices. Her chapter titled, *In Their Own Words: Students Reflect on the Roeper Difference,* provides student insights by employing quotations revolving around important Roeper School themes. Based on a key question, which asked students what the "Roeper difference" is, their responses coalesced around a number of ideas pertaining to empowerment. Nichols distilled the responses nicely with the following comment: "these qualities (of the school) build a place where students have the courage and confidence to advocate for themselves and the camaraderie of peers and adults who share their love for learning." The students made it clear that the school is not a hierarchical institution and does not operate as a job-training factory. Instead, it emphasizes supportive relationships blended with high expectations, responsibility, and self-advocacy leading to self-discovery.

Although scholars from outside the school and professionals working within the school give us rich insights about leadership dynamics, often through the words of students and alumni, it is helpful to gain some perspective directly from an individual current student of the school. Fortunately, Dylan Bennett, a junior at the school at the time of this writing, gives us a current student's perspective on the dynamic experiences that take place in the Roeper environment. In the response piece titled, *How is Roeper Different,* he discusses the nuances of conflict resolution, which is a core process at the school in terms of enabling nuanced decision-making, artful collaboration, and effective self-actualization over the long-term. He discusses how nonhierarchical student-teacher relationships are key elements in the system. Interestingly, he also shows how conceptions of success in the school do not align with the extrinsic, competitive definitions of success in the larger society. Instead, students engage in interest-based quests for personal meaning, which ultimately lead to personalized definitions of success. The freedom, independence, and empowerment within the school setting enable all of this to take place.

Marcia Ruff, the school historian, provides some very interesting perspectives on the workings of the school through the voices of various alumni in her chapter, *Roeper Alumni Reflect on Lasting Lessons.* She begins the chapter with some insights from George Roeper and then provides interpretations of the meaning embedded in some direct quotes from alumni. In essence, the alumni consistently confirm that the habits of mind, values, and beliefs they gained from their experiences in the school were more important than the academic preparation although they certainly value the high-level academic work the school enabled them to do. The alumni voices she highlighted included people from very diverse backgrounds. For example, a musician and songwriter, an associate professor of mathematics education, entrepreneurs and public policy experts, business owners, artists, an engineer, a law student, and a lawyer all weighed in on what they gained from the school. An overarching theme in their comments is that the Roeper School helped all of them deal with the world in more nuanced, engaged ways than they otherwise might have expected from a different educational experience.

Putting a fine punctuation mark on this section, Tracy Cross tells a story of the long-term impact of the school on an insider/outsider in his chapter titled, *A Personal Tale of Development and Growth: The Inadvertent Influence of the Roeper School on a Scholar.* Tracy is a dynamic leader in the field of gifted education having (a) edited all of its leading academic journals, (b) provided exemplary leadership for several high-profile academic institutions, and (c) taken on the role of President of the National Association for Gifted Children. Consequently, he is well positioned to assess the attributes and impact of the school in both macro and micro ways. He does this here by describing his longstanding involvement with the school in various capacities and some ways in which purposeful, ethical individuals from the school shaped his thinking over the long term. An expert in the social-emotional dimensions of giftedness (among many other things), Tracy portrays the ways in which the school impacted his own social and emotional development as a scholar and how it inspired him to do his best work elsewhere. He makes it obvious that the influence of the school extends far beyond its geographic location in Michigan.

Programs and Curriculum

Most educational systems around the world place programs and curriculum at the center of what they do. Of course, these dimensions of education are crucially important. Interestingly, while the Roeper philosophy recognizes the importance of programs and curriculum these tend to take a backseat to intrapersonal discovery and collaborative ethical development. At the Roeper School, programs and curricula flexibly evolve according to the needs of students and often seamlessly intertwine with the intrapersonal and ethical aspects of education. This section of the volume includes some analyses of programming and curricula that are conducive to the development of gifted and talented individuals (e.g., curriculum integration, standards and assessment, program evaluation) while also highlighting ways in which the special version of student-centred dynamics at the school make these managerial aspects of education work in support of students instead of the other way around.

Joyce VanTassel-Baska is a preeminent scholar of curriculum in the field of gifted education. In her chapter, *Differentiation in Action: The Integrated Curriculum Model,* she describes the value of curriculum integration, the theoretical and research support for this approach to curriculum development and implementation, and some ways in which it aligns with some of the best practices found at the Roeper School. The integrated curriculum model (ICM) she developed emphasizes confrontations with advanced academic content, invigorates higher-order thinking, strengthens differentiation of instruction, and promotes interdisciplinary thinking. It also encourages real world, authentic learning and collaborative processes. All of these emphases nicely align with what the Roeper School does well. For example, the school excels in collaborative learning, meaningful, real world service-learning projects, promotion of higher-order thinking around interdisciplinary themes, embracing diversity, and strengthening the ethical dimensions of education. Faculty and students employing curriculum integration seem better able to avoid locking themselves within disciplinary silos. Given the complex problems in today's globalized world, silo-breaking approaches to learning, such as those embedded in the ICM, are particularly important.

Given that Joyce VanTassel-Baska highlights the importance of curriculum integration, it is fortunate that middle school science teacher Wendy Mayer illustrates some of the highly creative, inspiring aspects of interdisciplinary work in the classroom through her chapter, *An Interdisciplinary Journey.* Reacting to Joyce's chapter on curriculum integration, Wendy tells the story about how her students were centrally involved in the creation of a large-scale, collaborative, interdisciplinary, thematic unit plan on the important topic of climate change. As with many initiatives at the school this plan evolved out of faculty team meetings and a series of subsequent student meetings. Wendy describes how expansive thinking about the theme and the various relevant subject areas combined with diligent attention to detail made this plan come together. The overall plan attended to diverse subject areas and the diverse needs of learners while generating authentic tasks such as crafting ways that students could contribute to cutting carbon emissions. Throughout the process, students were deeply engaged with the development of the unit. This stands in contrast to the teacher-centred dynamics that occur in many other locales. Wendy concludes with some insightful reflections on the entire, invigorating process.

According to leading economists (e.g., Heckman, 2011; Madrick, 2008) national economies thrive when there are healthy investments in early childhood education. In addition, the 21st-century socioeconomic, ideological, and political environments are plagued by ethical dilemmas requiring attention to issues of social justice (see Ambrose & Sternberg, 2012; Stiglitz, 2012). Early childhood expert Nancy Hertzog and her collaborators, Megan Ryan and Nick Gillon, bring these two important themes together in their chapter, *Social Justice in an Early Childhood Classroom*. The authors connect the strong emphasis on social justice, which is embedded in the Roeper School's core philosophy and the dynamics of its early childhood education, with scholarly literature on social justice education. They explore some of the contentious issues surrounding this important but often ignored dimension of education. While perusing the literature on these topics they develop and refine their own conception of early childhood social justice education, which includes emphases on inequality and power structures, and then provide details about implementation.

The school doesn't hold back in the effort to develop impressive collaborative skills and ethical sensibilities so it should not be surprising that faculty member Colleen Shelton illustrates some advanced interpersonal and instructional dynamics that take place in an early childhood classroom. Her response piece titled, *A View from the Preschool Classroom: The Child's Role in Creating a Socially Just Community,* is a reaction to the more extensive scholarly treatment of social justice in early childhood education generated by Nancy Hertzog, Megan Ryan, and Nick Gillon. Colleen's analysis provides a practical illustration of some ways in which very young children can take charge of their own ethical development. The examples she uses highlight the time-consuming messiness of the processes involved in this ethical development along with the crucial importance of those processes.

The Roeper School exists within a rather foreign educational context—one currently characterized by a flurry of activity revolving around national standards, assessment, and accountability. With its emphases on purposeful, student-centred intrinsic motivation and initiative, and it's cautions about external, hierarchical, bureaucratic authority, the Roeper philosophy largely runs counter to these national trends; however, leading gifted education scholar Susan Johnsen shows how the philosophy and practice of the school aligns well with the more thoughtful sets of standards in the larger environment. In her chapter, *Standards and Balanced Assessments: Relationships to the Roeper School's Philosophy and Practices,* she shows how the school actually aligns well with the more visionary sets of standards and assessment practices in education today, especially with 21st-century skills frameworks and standards developed within the field of gifted education. Particularly interesting is an outline showing the particularities of alignment between the Roeper philosophy and both the Partnership for 21st-Century Skills and the NAGC Programming Standards. She goes on to describe in depth and detail a wide variety of thoughtful assessment practices that are conducive to creative and critical thinking and student-centred work. These descriptions confirm some of the strengths of the school while also giving it some options for future development of assessment work that is consistent with its philosophy.

Patrick O'Connor, past college counselor at the school, delves deeply into the college selection and admission processes students engage in during the latter phases of their time as Roeper students. In his chapter, *College Counseling and the Gifted Student,* he contrasts their thought processes and activities during this life-trajectory planning process with the superficiality of the college selection process that usually occurs in many other places. As with most other procedures in the school, college selection tends to occur in a nuanced manner with much less extrinsic motivation like that experienced by most students elsewhere. College selection for students at Roeper tends to be driven by self-reflection, which O'Connor nicely captures with the phrase, "college is a natural but exciting next step in the student's deeper understanding of self." He illustrates the results of this more nuanced brand of college selection and admission through examples of the decisions past students have made and the results they experienced. Overall, college and career planning for upper-level Roeper students mirrors the exceptional intrapersonal awareness they develop through their time at the school.

Carolyn Callahan, a prominent scholar in the field of gifted education, concludes this section on curriculum and programs by helping the school look into its future. She discusses the need for and nature of program evaluation for the school in her chapter, *Next Steps for the Roeper School: Evaluation and Research.* Program evaluation requires a detailed description of the program and collection of input from key stakeholders. Drawing from various sources, including a recent accreditation self-study, she also outlined the perceived strengths of the school and the challenges it currently faces. After that, she brings into play the set of research-based standards from the National Association for Gifted Children and discovers that these standards highlight the considerable strengths of the school while also suggesting some areas for future focus. Recommendations include more attention to academic student outcomes and clarification of important terminology pertaining to the goals of the school. She concludes with a recommendation that the school align its future program evaluation with the guidelines in this chapter in order to continue its own improvement and to establish the bases for research that would guide the field of gifted education more effectively over the long term.

Emergent, Democratic Leadership

Leadership is a very strong theme at the Roeper School. The founders, George and Annemarie Roeper, had seen and viscerally experienced the dark side of leadership in the ascendance of Nazi Germany and wanted to do all they could to turn leadership into a more positive force in the world. Their philosophy addressed that issue by promoting the notion of bottom-up, democratic leadership as opposed to its more pernicious, authoritarian versions. The section of this volume on emergent, democratic leadership begins with a comprehensive overview of leadership theory and research and then moves into the subtle nuances and enormous strengths of Roeper-style leadership. As always, student growth and ethical awareness are at the forefront.

Dorothy Sisk's chapter, titled *Developing Leadership Capacity in Gifted Students for the Present and Future,* represents an expansive, in-depth look at leadership in general, which includes detailed presentations of findings pertaining to the leadership dimensions of high ability. Dorothy is a go-to expert in the field of gifted education on the topic of leadership so her panoramic overview of leadership covers all the bases extending from the thoughts of Greek philosophers, to theory and research about leadership in various disciplines and fields, to the extent to which leadership is included in definitions of giftedness. She also explores issues pertinent to the identification of leadership in gifted students. Sisk provides examples of practical leadership lessons drawn from a model she created. Throughout, her chapter is permeated with discussions of ways in which leadership emerges spontaneously and productively through activation of the philosophy of the Roeper School. She nicely summarizes the highly productive form of leadership at the school with the words: "relational, transformative, process-oriented, learned, and change-directed," which also characterize her refined conceptions of this important phenomenon.

An administrative leader of the school herself, Lisa Baker provides a response to Dorothy Sisk's extensive treatment of leadership and substantially grounds that work in the everyday realities of the school. In her response chapter titled, *Emerging Leaders: Believing in Children and Building Leadership Capacity Over Time,* she employs many examples drawn from the rich variety of activities in the school, and the voices of students, alumni, and teachers, to illustrate ways in which this leadership is nonhierarchical and emergent in nature, and how it is consistent with the Roeper philosophy. One of the most interesting of these consistencies is the dispersal of leadership throughout the student body to the extent possible. Instead of seeking out and developing a few promising leaders the school attempts to develop leadership talent and inclination in all students. Moreover, this development begins in the students' early years. The school does not wait until students reach adolescence for them to think about their own leadership abilities. In Baker's view, the students feel comfortable navigating between roles as leaders, followers, and collaborators depending on topic and circumstance.

In his chapter, *Leadership at the Roeper School,* Emery Pence gives us a ground-level view of some ways in which leadership emerges and evolves in the school setting. He develops an operational definition of giftedness, guided by his rich experiences as a professional leader in that school setting, to frame the discussion of leadership. Also, as with some other chapters in this volume, he provides a synopsis of the Roeper philosophy as it comes alive in the leadership dimensions of the school.

In wise, rather Zen-like statements Emery captures the essence of this dynamic when he says, "The Philosophy is something we not only *have* but *do.*" And "our only non-negotiable is that we have to negotiate." In this chapter, he finds ways to drive home the important point that leadership isn't about egocentrism. Instead, it is an emergent phenomenon that works in a bottom-up fashion to provide students with rich opportunities for self-discovery and ethical collaboration. Finally, he describes some of the attributes that are necessary for a leader to be successful at the school and discusses some challenges that lie ahead when it comes to keeping the Roeper philosophy alive in a complex 21st-century environment.

In the response piece, *Leadership at The Roeper School Through the Eyes of an Insider,* alumna Alexandra Dickinson gives us another up-close view of the unobtrusive leadership style fostered by students, teachers, administrators, and board members at the school. She details a number of ways that nuanced yet energetic conversations brought about problem resolutions and new directions for individuals and groups during her time as a student. Through the use of intriguing examples such as arguments over possession of a playground fort, dealing with the Columbine tragedy, and student representation on the Board of Trustees during the selection of a new head of school, she captures the spirit and practice of leadership at the school with the term, "leadership by conversation." She illustrates ways in which leadership emerged from multiple players in the system as opposed to lodging itself at the apex of a reified hierarchy. In her view, the success of this approach largely resides in the ability of skillful individuals and groups to listen carefully and to structure conversations artfully. Alexandra closes with some commentary about the ways in which the lessons she learned about leadership have stayed with her in the adult "real world," much to her benefit.

Anyone who has served as the principal of a school or the superintendent of a school district knows the feeling of angst when a group of students pushes the boundaries with a well-intentioned initiative that can be viewed as controversial. David Feldman, the current Head of the Roeper School, uses one such incident to illustrate the uniqueness of the school in his response piece, *Process and Voice.* He describes how he viewed an upper-school theatre production that included highly provocative, sensitive, and mature themes. Interestingly, the students and faculty involved did not back away from the inflammatory content but instead used it to "engage the community in important conversations." And they didn't stop there. Having gained the attention of the audience they asked for support and involvement with the purpose of improving the lives of deprived and desperate people. In essence, they took risks to seamlessly integrate an artistic performance with purposeful service learning. Feldman discusses the way in which these high levels of student engagement and the trust and empowerment provided by the adults involved represent impressive examples of engaged learning that are rarely found elsewhere.

In his reaction piece, *Observations on Governance at The Roeper School,* former chair of the Board of Trustees Douglas Winkworth enables us to see within the Roeper School system through yet another intriguing lens. Serving as board chair for a school can be challenging but it's even more so when that school is saturated with a distributed, democratic, emergent leadership ethos. Fortunately, Doug's intelligence and dispositions enabled him to excel in this and in other roles throughout his affiliation with the school. Not surprisingly, Doug views the role of board chair as that of supporting and preserving a flexible, nurturing environment for the important student-centred work that goes on in the system. He captures this work with the term "guardians of the philosophy." He also articulates some indispensable characteristics of the work done by the board and several ways in which the board deliberately sacrifices organizational efficiency to sustain the all-important philosophy of the school.

Looking Forward

Our final section consists of a chapter analyzing the fit of the Roeper School with the demands of the highly complex 21st-century context, and a response chapter to this piece from an alumnus. It is fitting that the book ends with a portrayal of the school as time-transcendent. Based on these analyses, the philosophy, structure, and dynamics of the school are at least as relevant in the 21st century as they were in the mid-20th century.

In the chapter, *The Roeper School in the 21st Century: Trends, Issues, Challenges, and Opportunities,* Don Ambrose engages in a wide-ranging interdisciplinary excursion to develop a panoramic portrayal of big opportunities and enormous problems in the 21st century. He uses this portrayal as a framework highlighting the knowledge, skills, and dispositions required for success in the 21st century and then employs the results of that analysis to analyse how the philosophy and dynamics of the Roeper School align with 21st century demands. During this process he draws insights from repeated visits to the school along with findings from the school's strategic plan and accreditation study to develop a picture of the school's attributes. His conclusions are that this school, which was conceived within the turbulence of mid-20th century disasters and ethical problems, is at least as well suited to the demands of the even more turbulent and problem fraught 21st century. Among many other connections he shows how the knowledge, skills, and dispositions individuals develop through their experiences in the school will help them grapple, as individuals and as collaborative citizens, with 21st-century macroproblems such as climate change and increasing socioeconomic inequality. Macroproblems are so large and complex that they cannot be solved from within a single academic discipline or within the borders of a single nation. He also shows how graduates of the school are well positioned to capitalize on unprecedented, 21st-century macro-opportunities.

In a final reaction piece, *The Roeper School from 12 Years Out: Reflections of a 2001 Graduate,* alumnus Daniel Faichney, a law student at the time of this writing, gives us an insider's response to Don Ambrose's analysis of the 21st-century context that surrounds and influences the Roeper School. Faichney selects some key themes from the 21st-century analysis (prevalence of macroproblems; emphases on justice, equity and altruism; emphasis on the whole child; appreciation for cognitive diversity) and uses them as lenses for interpretation of his own experiences as a student and alumnus of the school. At one point he illustrates some ways in which a group of Roeper alumni reacted to the September 11th tragedies by relying on the acute perceptivity, creative thinking skills, and ethical sensibilities they had developed while at the Roeper School. His reflections reveal a high level of nuanced judgment to which the nation's policymakers would do well to aspire.

We hope you enjoy reading this volume as much as we enjoyed pulling it together. Consistent with the Roeper philosophy, this has been a work like no other. It has been enriched by the insights of leading scholars from the field of gifted education. But the conceptual and emotional glue that holds the project together comes from the students, alumni, faculty, administrators, and board members who contributed their perceptive responses and insights. As editors for the project, we conclude that the Roeper School truly is a luminous gemstone that can shed light on gifted education and, more broadly, on the development of a more creatively intelligent, humane society.

REFERENCES

Alfred, T. (1999). *Peace, power, righteousness: An indigenous manifesto*. Toronto, Canada: Oxford University Press.

Ambrose, D. (1996). Unifying theories of creativity: Metaphorical thought and the unification process. *New Ideas in Psychology, 14*, 257–267.

Ambrose, D. (2005). Interdisciplinary expansion of conceptual foundations: Insights from beyond our field. *Roeper Review, 27*, 137–143.

Ambrose, D. (2009). *Expanding visions of creative intelligence: An interdisciplinary exploration*. Cresskill, NJ: Hampton Press.

Ambrose, D. (2011). Dysmorphic capitalism and the aberrant development of creative intelligence. In E. N. Shelton (Ed.), *Capitalism in business, politics and society* (pp. 119–130). Hauppauge, NY: NOVA.

Ambrose, D. (2012a). Finding dogmatic insularity in the territory of various academic disciplines. In D. Ambrose & R. J. Sternberg (Eds.), *How dogmatic beliefs harm creativity and higher-level thinking* (pp. 9–25). New York, NY: Routledge.

Ambrose, D. (2012b). The not-so-invisible hand of economics and its impact on conceptions and manifestations of high abiliy. In D. Ambrose, R. J. Sternberg & B. Sriraman (Eds.), *Confronting dogmatism in gifted education* (pp. 97–114). New York, NY: Routledge.

Ambrose, D., Cohen, L. M., & Tannenbaum, A. J. (2003). *Creative intelligence: Toward theoretic integration*. Cresskill, NJ: Hampton Press.

Ambrose, D., & Cross, T. L. (Eds.). (2009). *Morality, ethics, and gifted minds*. New York, NY: Springer Science.

Ambrose, D., & Sternberg, R. J. (Eds.). (2012). *How dogmatic beliefs harm creativity and higher-level thinking*. New York, NY: Routledge.

Babiak, P., Neumann, C. S., & Hare, R. D. (2010). Corporate psychopathy: Talking the walk. *Behavioral Sciences & the law, 28*, 174–193.

Bacevich, A. J. (2010). *Washington rules: America's path to permanent war*. New York, NY: Metropolitan.

Bacevich, A. (2012). Next time victory. In D. Ambrose & R. J. Sternberg (Eds.), *How dogmatic beliefs harm creativity and higher-level thinking* (pp. 29–32). New York, NY: Routledge.

Berliner, D. C. (2012). Narrowing curriculum, assessments, and conceptions of what it means to be smart in the US schools: Creaticide by design. In D. Ambrose & R. J. Sternberg (Eds.), *How dogmatic beliefs harm creativity and higher-level thinking* (pp. 79–93). New York, NY: Routledge.

Bohm, D. (1994). *Thought as a system*. London, England: Routledge.
Chirot, D. (2012). Dogmatism and genocide. In D. Ambrose & R. J. Sternberg (Eds.), *How dogmatic beliefs harm creativity and higher-level thinking* (pp. 33–36). New York, NY: Routledge.
Chirot, D., & McCauley, C. (2006). *Why not kill them all? The logic and prevention of mass political murder*. Princeton, NJ: Princeton University Press.
Dutton, K. (2012). *The wisdom of psychopaths*. New York, NY: Scientific American.
Gao, Y., & Raine, A. (2010). Successful and unsuccessful psychopaths: A neurobiological model. *Behavioral Sciences & the Law, 28*, 194–210.
Gardner, H. (1988). Creativity: An interdisciplinary perspective. *Creativity Research Journal, 1*, 8–26.
Gardner, H., & Winner, E. (1993). Metaphor and irony: Two levels of understanding. In A. Ortony (Ed.), *Metaphor and thought* (2nd ed., pp. 425–443). New York, NY: Cambridge University Press.
Heckman, J. J. (2011). The economics of inequality: The value of early childhood education. *American Educator, 31*. Retrieved from http://www.aft.org/pdfs/americaneducator/spring2011/Heckman.pdf.
Lakoff, G., & Johnson, M. (1980). *Metaphors we live by*. Chicago, IL: University of Chicago Press.
Lakoff, G., & Johnson, M. (1999). *Philosophy in the flesh: The embodied mind and its challenge to Western thought*. New York, NY: Basic Books.
Madrick, J. (2008). *The case for big government*. Princeton, NJ: Princeton University Press.
Martin, A., & Monroe, K. R. (2009). Identity, moral choice, and the moral imagination: Is there a neuroscientific foundation for altruism? In D. Ambrose & T. L. Cross (Eds.), *Morality, ethics, and gifted minds* (pp. 73–87). New York, NY: Springer Science.
Morishima, Y., Schunk, D., Bruhin, A., Ruff, C., & Fehr, E. (2012). Linking brain structure and activation in the temporoparietal junction to explain the neurobiology of human altruism. *Neuron, 75*, 73–79.
Page, S. E. (2007). *The difference: How the power of diversity creates better groups, firms, schools, and societies*. Princeton, NJ: Princeton University Press.
Ravitch, D. (2010). *The death and life of the great American school system: How testing and choice are undermining education*. New York, NY: Basic Books.
Rose, Nikolas, & Abi-Rached, J. M. (2013). *Neuro: The new brain sciences and the management of the mind*. Princeton, NJ: Princeton University Press.
Sen, A. (2000). Merit and justice. In K. Arrow, S. Bowles & S. Durlauf (Eds.), *Meritocracy and economic inequality* (pp. 5–16). Princeton, NJ: Princeton University Press.
Sriraman, B. (2009). Interdisciplinarity and mathematics education: Psychology, philosophy, aesthetics, modeling and curriculum. *ZDM-The International Journal on Mathematics Education, 41*, 1–4.
Sriraman, B., & Dahl, B. (2009). On bringing interdisciplinary ideas to gifted education. In L. V. Shavignina (Ed.), *International handbook on giftedness* (pp. 1235–1256). New York, NY: Springer Science.
Sternberg, R. J. (1990). *Metaphors of mind: Conceptions of the nature of intelligence*. New York, NY: Cambridge University Press.
Sternberg, R. J, Tourangeau, R., & Nigro, G. (1993). Metaphor, induction, and social policy: The convergence of macroscopic and microscopic views. In A. Ortony (Ed.), *Metaphor and thought* (2nd ed., pp. 277–303). New York, NY: Cambridge University Press.
Stiglitz, J. (2010). *Free fall: America, free markets, and the sinking of the world economy*. New York, NY: W W Norton.
Stiglitz, J. (2012). *The price of inequality: How today's divided society endangers our future*. New York, NY: W. W. Norton.

PART II

THE HISTORY AND PHILOSOPHY OF THE SCHOOL

MICHELE KANE

CONSTANCY AND CHANGE
IN PROGRESSIVE EDUCATION

The Roeper Philosophy of Self Actualization and Interdependence

An alternative model of education called, "Self Actualization and Interdependence" (SAI), sees education as a global, all-encompassing process of growth.

—Annemarie Roeper

The Roeper School was co-founded by Annemarie and George Roeper in 1941 soon after fleeing Nazi Germany. This immigrant pair remained at the school and developed a progressive and innovative educational framework which they refined until their retirement in the early 1980's. Currently, as one of the pre-eminent schools for gifted education in the United States, The Roeper School remains a sanctuary for the social, emotional, spiritual and intellectual growth of gifted children.

The heart of the work that Annemarie and George Roeper developed for over forty years resulted in a concept which they deemed a *Philosophy of Self-Actualization and Interdependence (SAI)*. Together, they distilled the essence of their educational beliefs, described as "an idealistic philosophy of life based upon self-actualization, interdependence, diversity and human rights" (Roeper, A., & Roeper, G., 1981). Within this philosophical framework, the growth of the Self of the child is paramount and there is a deep recognition of the complexity of his/her inner life with all the unconscious drives and characteristics that comprise it.

The *SAI* philosophy presents parents and educators an alternative lens through which to view the education of children. With *SAI* there emerges a different purpose and goal of education. The emphasis in *SAI* is on learning from the inside out and following the inner agenda of the Self. In doing so, the Self recognizes the interdependence that is common to all humanity and the effect that each Self has on the other. Therefore, in this nontraditional model of education, the goal is to honor the Self by providing opportunities for self-actualization and interdependence.

This educational approach is humanistic and child-centered and embodies the concept of social-emotional learning. The growth of the self is the curriculum. This curriculum that emerges emphasizes all aspects of the developing Self including social, emotional, and spiritual, as well as intellectual experiences. The school community is of equal importance in this model. Accordingly, the Self in relationship to community is also a vital educational component for the evolving child. Educational goals become more easily accomplished within this supportive and nurturing context.

According to the Roepers (1981), the community is the context that provides the safe harbor for the child to explore his place in the world. Relationships become critical for self-development. In community, students begin to identify with each other and exchange their ideas and feelings honestly. Children are able to relate in ways that are not superficial. In such an environment of encouragement, learning <u>does</u> evolve from the inside out when based on the inner agenda of each child. Emotion is not divorced from intellect. The mutual respect for Self, other individuals, and the community fosters academic growth, which is a by-product of the educational process, not the main goal.

FROM THEORY TO PRACTICE

Crisp, cool air fluttered through trees that had only just begun to lose their scarlet and orange leaves. It was a typical fall day at the Birmingham, Michigan campus of the Roeper School. Yet, October 12, 2003 was not just an ordinary school day. Hundreds of people had gathered to celebrate the eighty-fifth birthday of co-founder Annemarie Roeper.

Inside the auditorium were rows of guests, tightly packed. Students scrambled to find more chairs as latecomers arrived. Five members of the Forensic Team had assembled amidst a stage set under construction. Center stage was Annemarie Roeper, the school's co-founder and co-author of the piece that the students were about to perform. This choral presentation of the Roeper philosophy, the educational philosophy of *Self-Actualization and Interdependence* that provided the framework of the Roeper School, was a gift from the students to Annemarie.

The team, under the direction of teacher Dan Jacobs, began the piece. In unison, the students began sharing core elements of the philosophy:

"Our philosophy is a way of life…"

"To develop skills of cooperation…"

"Not a hierarchy, rather interdependence"

"Equal human rights"

"Our promise to children"

Together, in pairs and individually, the group continued to thread the key points that shape the Roeper philosophy. The performance was a demonstration of the philosophy-in-action as it unfolded. Its vital spirit was reflected in both the content conveyed as well as the process itself.

Seamlessly, each student either blended in with the others or remained silent. The phrasing only served to underscore the coming together in community as well as the rights of each person to maintain individuality. Even when a student stumbled over lines or rushed through a phrase, it simply showcased that all is co-mingled and enfolded into the whole. These miscues served to enrich rather than diminish the piece. The teacher stood in the wings and was clearly visible, supportive, and available—but not intrusive. This performance highlighted one of the key tenets of Annemarie and George Roeper's general mindset that "a philosophy is only as valid as its implementation" (Roeper, 1990, p. 19). This performance was a clear indication that their educational philosophy was valid in theory and in practice.

DEVELOPING AN ALTERNATIVE EDUCATIONAL MODEL

Annemarie has further outlined the Roepers' beliefs in *Educating Children for Life: The Modern Learning Community*. The book was published in 1990, after their retirement from Roeper School, and illustrates how the approach is a departure from traditional education. In the forward of the book, Annemarie states that only after retirement were she and George able to see their philosophy as one of uniqueness rather than universality. She then articulates the philosophy on behalf of the couple with the intention of moving their philosophy beyond the school walls and into the general educational community. Although George influenced the writings tremendously, it was Annemarie that translated the ideas into the written word. Many of the extant publications regarding the Roeper philosophy were compiled by Annemarie; yet, it is essential to understand that these writings typically reflect the combined ideas of the pair.

This vision of education is nestled in the arms of Max and Gertrud Bondy, Annemarie's parents. They were both progressive educators and founded several schools in Germany. From Max, her father, she came to know the importance of community; from Gertrude, her mother and a Freudian psychoanalyst, she learned the importance of the inner world. George was student at her parents' school and was similarly imbued with these ideas. In this milieu, the Roeper philosophy of George and Annemarie emerged.

Drawing on a strong foundation, the Ropers were able to create, change, hone, and implement this philosophy both as educators and administrators. Annemarie and George were active participants and practiced their theoretical beliefs just as they had been modeled for them. In *Educating Children for Life: The Modern Learning Community*, Annemarie begins by sharing the dilemma of modern education:

> Humanity has made two promises to its children. The first is to prepare a world, which accepts them and provides them with opportunities to live, grow and create in safety. The other is to help them develop their whole beings to the fullest in every respect. Education is the vehicle through which we try to keep these promises. (p. 3)

The remainder of *Educating Children for Life: The Modern Learning Community* examines what is described as the three components of education: namely, the goals and philosophy of education, the characteristics of the students and finally, from the interaction of the first two components, the third component, which is the process of education. The first component is discussed here to give an overview of the philosophy and the resulting framework of this educational model.

At the core of the book are simple questions: what is the philosophy and goal of education? The Roepers believed that many models of education answer this question with varying conventional formats and with student achievement and student success as the answer. These frameworks replicate outdated approaches and ignore the impact of modern society and child psychology. Many educators continue to perpetuate the old thinking and do not grapple with the fundamental issues regarding the purpose of education, nor do they respond to a changing and interdependent world. In this worldview, the education of children is linear. That is, the system educates for elementary school, then for middle school, then high school, and then college or the world of work.

The successes and failures of the national educational system continue to wax and wane as the purpose of education is uncritically examined. Education becomes divorced from life. The experiences of the children become fragmented as the relevance of these experiences to Self and to their world seem inconsequential and disconnected.

In general, the Roepers believed that the philosophies and subsequent goals of education have not been explored in a meaningful way. Administrators far removed from classrooms often impose time-honored methods of teaching and assessments, while ignoring the real needs of learners. The current national testing frenzy has created an atmosphere where teaching to accomplish testing benchmarks is the focus of most teaching and learning. In a hierarchical structure, the learning needs of the student are directed from above rather than emerging from the needs of the child. The Roepers' ideas are a contrast to these traditional perspectives. Annemarie stated:

> Out of the SAI concept develops a different model of education; the growth model as opposed to the success model. In the growth model, the Self is seen as healthy, not pathological. It wants to grow and learn, and not to be fixed. The tasks of learning and teaching are seen from a different perspective. A child's inner agenda is seen as part of reality, therefore, defines that reality in a different manner. We must respond to that. (Unpublished article, 1999)

The differences are further explicated in Table 1.

An ecological worldview is an essential component of the Roeper philosophy. A global perspective is one that was familiar to George and Annemarie. They had first-hand experience of being involved in global events that affected all of humanity. They perceived the innate struggles of self-preservation and self-integration in a world that both welcomes and frightens. Yet, their overriding beliefs in the goodness of man and the need for each individual to find meaning and purpose continued to refine their core beliefs. According to Annemarie (1990), the *Philosophy of Self-Actualization and Interdependence*:

Table 1. Conceptions of success comparison (from Roeper, unpublished document, 1999)

SAI/GROWTH	TRADITIONAL/SUCCESS
Who am I?	What can you do?
Self-evolvement	Fulfill expectations
Growth	Success
Learning	Teaching
Free will imposed	Limitations
Power of self	Power of society
Never bored	Boring
Inner agenda	Empty vessel
Active learner	Passive learner
Interdependence	Hierarchies
Mutuality	Survival of the fittest
Many causes and effects	Cause and effect
Self as power	Self ignored, unknown
Education: from inside out	Education: from outside in
Relationships	Strategies
Include the unknown and the mysteries making the unknown known	Conquering life,
Long-range view	Short-range view
No winners or losers; a circle of interdependence	Belief in victory
Support of the ecology	Support of hierarchy

[This philosophy] originates from a combination of an idealistic commitment to equal rights and a realistic view of the limitations of power by our mutual interdependence. It provides a unifying principle. It is based on the following realization: there is neither absolute power nor complete dependence or independence. The fact of interdependence or human ecology becomes more and more apparent in today's world. (p. 15)

This leads to the following philosophy of learning and life, "We are concerned with the whole impact of life on the young person and the impact the person will make on society. We are concerned with the development of the 'Self' and the interdependence of all 'Selves'" (Roeper, 1990, p. 15). This worldview within in an educational setting has tremendous implications for all involved. Each of the participants; students, teachers, administrators, parents and community members are therefore instrumental in the growth of the "other." It is not only the students who are the learners.

Annemarie has since expounded on her philosophy of life. Reflecting on aspects she remembered as important in the creation of the school, she stated:

> It was a school based on a principle to which I gave a name much later on, but which was functioning all the way through, which I called *Self-Actualization and Interdependence (SAI)*. The goal of education was to help the child to become who he was, which included all the academic work and everything that was needed to help this particular person. It is a mistake to think that if you think about the Soul, academic work is not a part of it. It is a very important part of it, but the goal is a different one. The goal is to help the Soul rather than to get into college. So we tried to create the kind of school that allowed children to do that. (personal communication, 2006)

It follows then that the goals evolve from the philosophy of education. Annemarie and George believed that both goals and philosophy must be aligned so that cooperative action of all members of the school community becomes the ultimate moral goal. These closing words authored by Annemarie and George in the 1981 *Roeper philosophy* represent the culmination of their work together and demonstrate their belief in the organic nature of their philosophy. To the Roepers this concept represented the living, evolving, developing and intricate aspects of their "philosophy of life."

This philosophy is not a vague and sentimental idea of warmth and understanding. It represents not just a desire for happiness and a good life, although in a much broader sense these hopes are part of it. It actually is a relentlessly demanding concept, for its consequences are most complex, intellectually, emotionally, and practically.

One is always in danger of contradicting it or losing it altogether without realizing it, by making small compromises, which have a tendency to grow and yet may only solve the problem apparent at the moment. They may exclude more difficult solutions within the philosophy, which are not found because they are not looked for.

Built into this philosophy are both constancy and change. Its inherent goals remain constant while the implementation may change as life and times require. If constancy is not maintained or change is not occurring, it will result in a philosophy that is either mere lip service, irrelevant, or non-existent.

Their beliefs allow for the growth of the ideas and the changes as they may emerge while simultaneously situating their approach with goals that didn't waver. Tracing the evolution of the ideas from the early beginnings provides a means of looking back as well as forward. It follows from the philosophy that some aspects will reflect change while a sense of certainty and constancy is at the core.

FROM HUMBLE BEGINNINGS TO BROAD VISTAS

George and Annemarie arrived in Michigan at the behest of family friends and psychoanalysts, the Sterbas. The Sterbas wished to create a school based on psychoanalytic principles and the newly-wed Roepers answered the call. The first school was in a rented house in Highland Park, Michigan and named the Roeper Grade School and Editha Sterba Nursery School. In remembering the early days it was noted, "There were only a few parking spaces and we would have to take turns every few hours and run out to move our cars because the traffic police would put stripes on the tires" (personal communication, 2005).

Musical cars were only one of the challenges the Roepers faced. The family lived and worked in the same facility and some of the students were boarders. Cooking, cleaning, and care giving coupled with the education of these children was an awesome responsibility. This was the only time that the Roeper School would include children other than the Roeper's own children in residence. George and Annemarie wanted to ensure that their children would have all the attention of their parents, at least for part of the day. For that reason, the Roeper School never entertained the idea of becoming a boarding school.

In addition to the underlying foundation of Freudian principles, which were embedded in the Roeper School from its inception, there was another dynamic in play. Central from the very beginning was the vision of creating a school community that rests on principles of the interconnectedness or interdependence of the members. The influence of Max and Gertrud Bondy in the development of the school is unmistakable. Max provided his knowledge of the importance of building community and Gertrude shared her knowledge of the emerging field of psychology. The Self in relationship to community is a theme that is repeated as the school grows and changes—while the paradox of constancy and change also repeats.

George and Annemarie were involved with the daily operations of the school as administrators in addition to their role as teachers. George remained the leader within the Roeper Grade School while Annemarie provided the direction for the Editha Sterba Nursery School. In 1942, the school moved to 668 Pallister Avenue in Detroit and it continued to grow. It was also a time of growth for their family. Each summer the couple would return to Vermont and help with the summer camp at the Windsor Mountain School. It was there that son Tom was born at the end of camp in 1943.

In September 1944, the Roepers bought a house at 8634 LaSalle Blvd., nearby in Detroit, and moved there to make more room at Pallister for students and to gain some privacy. The Editha Sterba Nursery School and the Roeper Grade School remained in the house at the Detroit location. Eventually, two other teachers joined them. In the Holocaust Oral History Project in 1995, Annemarie had this to say about those early days:

> The basic principle was that it was a very open, progressive type school based on psychoanalytic theory, where we thought about, talked about, and taught the teachers about unconscious motivation and about what really made a person be what they are. We worked very closely with the Sterbas all during that time. We participated in psychoanalytic theory as well as humanistic philosophy. (p. 101)

By 1946, Annemarie and George were ready to make a major move and with the help of friends and loans they purchased the property at 2190 N. Woodward Avenue in Bloomfield Hills, Michigan (Roeper, 1966). The property had been known as the Stephens Mansion, which was situated on four and one half acres, large enough for children to roam and with enough room for eventual expansion. The Roeper family reflected this expansion with the addition of another new child. Peter Roeper was born on the day that the property was scheduled to close in 1946 and it was a time of great joy. A new era was ushered in as the school name was changed to City and Country School of Bloomfield Hills. The Roepers moved to this new facility and lived in the upper floor of the home while the lower floor was used for the nursery and grade school. Later, in 1949, daughter Karen arrived, which completed the Roeper family constellation in Michigan.

The name was changed to Roeper City and Country School in 1966 to celebrate the school's 25th anniversary. During this time in Bloomfield Hills, the enrollment saw a sizeable increase beginning with 90 students in 1946 and growing to over 500 student in 1979–80 when the Roepers retired in June, 1979 (George) and June, 1980 (Annemarie). Each decade that followed the move to Bloomfield Hills would bring noteworthy change to The Roeper School. Each change was in response to the social and political climate of the times. During a speech to parents on May 16, 1972, Annemarie had this to say,

> Every school is a living organism with a soul of its own. It is more than the sum of its parts, but it looks different from each individual's point of view. Each person is part of it, be it a teacher, a driver, a child, a parent.

These words are very important because they underscore the administrative belief that the school is a living system that acts and reacts to the environment. It has a *soul*, which means it has a unique identity that emerges from the interaction of the members. Each member has an individual perspective that is valued regardless of the status of the member. Together, in community, the school is not only whole but more than its membership could ever be singly. Such a vision of a school requires that the threads of constancy and change are kept in balance. Constancy, in that there is a clear vision of what is essential for growth and evolution, yet adaptable to the inevitable change in the external landscape. The spirit of Roeper School mirrors that of its membership.

It would be difficult to share the most noteworthy events that occurred over the almost 40 years that the Roepers were involved with Roeper School. However, there is an alternative means to chronicle the significant markers during this time span. When asked by interviewer Constance Shannon (1989) to describe the innovations that occurred at Roeper School over the years, Annemarie replied:

> What you really could say was there was a series of landmarks. Each one meant the risk of losing children and community support. The first one was racial integration of the school; the second was the introduction of the gifted

child program; the third one was the introduction of the instructional open classroom; and the fourth was the introduction of the participatory democracy into the administrative structure of the school community—moving from a hierarchical system to a cooperative one. This meant involving teachers and other staff in decision-making—such as the hiring of new staff members— wherever the results of the decision would affect them. Each one of these landmarks at the time was a complete innovation. (p. 31)

Annemarie reflected that at first when the family came to the United States they were unaware of the racial prejudices that existed and they had always planned that the school become a world in miniature. This meant that all racial, ethnic, and religious groups would be represented. There were obstacles that were not anticipated. In further conversation with Constance, Annemarie related the following:

> Years later, in the early 50s, after we had our citizenship, we received an application from a black family for their little boy. No private school had black children. It was unheard of at the time.... We told the parents that we couldn't take their son immediately, that we would have to wait until the following year. And in the meantime we would have to do some groundwork. What we did was to write a letter to all the parents stating that we believed in the principle of integration and that we were going to integrate our school. (pp. 31–32)

Although there was a risk that students would leave, not a single student was withdrawn. The racial tensions continued to simmer in the city of Detroit and erupted in the summer of 1967. There were the difficulties of living through the race riots in Detroit during that turbulent time. White students comprised only 40% of the student population in Detroit city schools at the time of the riots. This contrasted with the 80% of white students in city schools in 1946, the year that the Roepers moved their school to Bloomfield Hills (Mirel, 1993 in Muchmore, 2005). Racial tensions erupted in many large cities that year.

The transformation that occurred after the integration of the school provided opportunities for all members of the school community to participate in a world that more accurately reflected the world in which they lived. It provided opportunities for expanded viewpoints and consequently for more understanding.

Another event of particular note took place in the 1950s. When the Russians launched the first space satellite in 1957, Americans began looking in earnest for ways to make public schools more academic, more competitive, and more concerned with the identification and development of the gifted. It was the age of curriculum reform. Just before the Sputnik event, City and Country School proposed to reorganize as a school for gifted children. The school brochure (1956), which described the proposed changes, had endorsements from Eleanor Roosevelt and the Michigan Governor at the time, G. Mennen Williams. A *Gifted Child Institute* was held under the direction of Dr. A. Harry Passow of Columbia University, who chaired the project. The institute was held at the school from June 18 to June 22,

1956 and included Annemarie and George and a host of other luminaries in the field of education. The purpose was to coordinate the available information on gifted children, create a definition, suggest identification measures, chart curriculum and suggest psychological methods to enhance personality development (p. 21). Annemarie recollected:

> It was actually my husband George who became interested in gifted education when there was a series of articles in the New York Times. There was a real interest in the gifted, and it struck him that the work that we were doing, which always in the end was trying to help save the world, would be more understood by gifted people. Also, that we would be able to understand the gifted and that their need for self-fulfillment was different and maybe stronger, than many others and that we would help them because we needed them to help the World. And so, I think early in the 1950s we began to be interested in gifted education. It was at this time that George met Harry Passow, and Harry put a group of experts together to design a program for gifted children. We spent a week at our school in Michigan just designing this program.

Instead of focusing on competition, the literature of the time focused on the cooperative and inclusive aspects of a gifted community. For example, the brochure specifically stressed that the education of gifted girls, particularly in math and science, should be encouraged. It stressed that curriculum would be designed to match the needs of the child including his emotional development and, might include subjects not typically found in traditional schools. Later, Passow would remember:

> But, here we were being asked by the Roepers to design a school of our dreams! And dream we did that week as we explored every aspect of what a school for the gifted student should be—from its guiding philosophy, to the selection of its student, to its curriculum design and instruction; strategies, to its staffing to its overall ethos and climate.

We made our plans—fully expecting that George and Annemarie would implement them, and we were not disappointed. The City and Country School became—and still is—a remarkable school with a program guided by a unique philosophy of what education should be (Passow, in *Educating Children for Life*, 1990, Preface).

This early work by George, Annemarie, and their colleagues, as they worked together in community, changed the world of gifted education as a result. The Roeper Legacy is mentioned by Delisle (2000) as one of the top 10 events that took place in gifted education in the last century. He says, "Indeed, [the Roeper School] is arguably the best school for gifted children in America" (p. 28). Furthermore, he stated, "Through the social, educational, and political upheavals of three generations, the vision of George and Annemarie Roeper has been a constant beacon of light for the entire field of gifted child education" (p. 29).

As City and Country School made the transition to a school for gifted children there were more changes ahead for the Roepers. The traditional classroom arrangement no longer suited the needs of these gifted students. The next two decades would reflect the Roeper's responsiveness by adopting an open classroom model as well as a participatory democracy administrative model.

These critical landmarks, described to Constance Shannon, would require that they continued to develop their notions about the best way to guide students to assure that they would participate in their own destiny. In 1962, George delivered these words during a lecture on *Learning and Creativity*:

> We know that a large part of the occupations of today did not exist twenty-five and fifty years ago. It is reasonable to assume that our children today will have in twenty-five years many occupations which do not exist today and of which we do not know what they are like. What kind of education shall we provide in this world where our knowledge of science, chemistry, techniques, resources, changes so rapidly that it appears useless to teach today what we believe are facts today and not facts tomorrow?

Creating, formulating, developing, implementing, and refining these innovative approaches to education would occupy the remainder of their years at Roeper School.

CURRICULUM IN ACTION: CONNECTING LEARNERS AND COMMUNITY

> A philosophy of education is only relevant if it exists within a philosophy of life.
>
> —Annemarie Roeper

Scanning the busy classroom, there are bursts of activity in every corner of the room. Some of the children are cuddled up in a corner busily thumbing through stacks of picture books. Another group of three or four are gathered around a teacher who is showing them a cocoon and some leaves. Two children sit at tables engaged in a world of their own; one lifts her head with eyes tightly closed and then writes long sentences pausing only briefly to stop and think. The other child has pieces of brightly colored paper that he is arranging and gluing into a pleasing pattern. Classical music is playing quietly in the background and another group of six or seven children appear to be re-enacting a fantasy story that they are reading. Two children, one with a scowl and another without emotion are sitting facing each other while a teacher monitors the interaction from a supportive yet private distance.

This is Stage II (four- to six-year-old children) at The Roeper School in 2005. Groups of children still gather to work together in similar fashion more than six decades after the doors first opened. These students are actively engaged in an *open classroom* approach to teaching and learning. The *Open Classroom* was the third major milestone that Annemarie mentioned as an important change in the direction of the school (Shannon, 1989). The fourth significant turning point, which is closely related, is the implementation of the *participatory democracy model of administration*, which was a style of leadership closely aligned with the Roeper philosophy.

A Philosophy Comes of Age: A Personal Statement for Independent Schools Association of the Central States (ISACS), which Annemarie wrote in the early seventies, outlined the stages of development that took place before the introduction of the *Open Classroom.* However, it was noted that this new approach was predicated on the underlying humanistic philosophy of education that has been constant since the inception of the school. This statement embodied the beliefs at the time:

> A philosophy is only as good as its implementation. In order to implement a philosophy, one must be conscious of one's commitments in dealing with every detail of one's life and work. There are many examples of where people believe deeply in certain ideas but do not take the steps to realizing these beliefs. This, then creates a discrepancy between the philosophy and its realization. The philosophy, in that case, has little impact. To create this impact is often difficult and involves risk taking. How did our philosophy fare during the past thirty years?
>
> Our philosophy has not basically changed since the school was first founded. The fact is the school was founded because of our philosophical beliefs. I would say that most of our work could be described as an eternal search for implementing what we held to be true. (p. 1)

The inner agenda of the child was always at the center of every decision made about identification and curriculum frameworks. However, the manner in which the programs were delivered reflected the trends of the time. In the document, four distinct periods are described:

Period of progressive education. Progressive education and psychoanalytic development theories greatly influenced programs in many educational settings. Misunderstandings and contradictions within the progressive movement led to a backlash. Structure and tradition replaced progressivism in mainstream educational settings.

Traditional education. The Roeper School was deeply influenced by the traditional trend and added more grades and more children in lock-step fashion. The first priority was preparing students to be successful in college—preparing for life became an added feature. Academic focus with gifted students allowed them to become highly proficient in academics yet underdeveloped in emotions. The gap was getting wider and hierarchical advantages were becoming more pronounced. It became clear that it was an advantage to be a boy, to be white, to be older, to be a teacher and not a bus driver, and to be obedient rather than have internalized moral virtue. The school was drifting from the philosophy and was in search of an approach that was better suited to match the philosophy.

Non-graded education. In 1968, a pamphlet was developed that described this plan; it was called *The Continuous Progress Program.* The influence of Piaget is evident and the brochure details how a child differs emotionally, academically, physically and socially. The concept of asynchrony is not labeled but thoroughly detailed. The brochure described the difference between teaching and learning and demonstrated a renewed interest in the social-emotional aspects of learning. The emphasis had shifted to individual instruction within a group setting. Suggestions for enhancing the emotional climate as well as the intellectual climate are outlined in the remainder of the brochure. Students are grouped in age clusters to facilitate teaching skills, which are based on needs of the children.

Open classroom. In 1969–70 after attending workshops and reading about the concept of Open Classroom it was decided that this approach would best embody the humanistic point of view held by the Roepers. This was also the perspective of the teachers that were at the school, although the form and structure of this approach was entirely new. It meant that the educational goals were defined by each child instead of decided by the institution. It also required teachers that were willing to work to fit the subject matter to the children. The long-range goal would be that this learning environment would provide opportunities for students to develop skills and self-confidence and make positive contributions to society (pp. 1–4).

There were some risks involved that were made quite clear when this proposition was suggested to the staff, the parents, and Board of Trustees. It was acknowledged that change creates some discomfort since things are not as familiar. The teachers were given some flexibility in making the transition and some made it quickly and some more reluctantly; however, there was ongoing communication at every stage of implementation and therefore there were no major disruptions.

In Immediate Steps to Open Up a Traditional Classroom (1970), Annemarie expanded these ideas:

> The very first step to open up a traditional classroom is to recognize the fact that it requires a completely different frame of reference, one that is foreign and therefore, somewhat threatening to our traditional concept of education, to our traditional priorities, to the traditional role of teacher, and to the expectations of parents. (p. 1)

In the same article, she continued:

> Education does not really come in steps. Education in its natural form moves and flows and spreads and circles, it jumps and rests, it slopes and rises, it spirals and only occasionally, it also steps. Traditional education was built mostly on steps; lockstep from grade to grade, age to age, achievement level to achievement level, test result to test result, sequence to sequence. Every year in the fall the six year olds all over the United States assembled at the foot of the mountain of education and climbed it step by step at the same time over the same territory, in the same manner, and lo and behold, twelve years later, in the spring, they were all expected to reach the top at the same time. How many were left by the wayside because it was too fast, too slow, the wrong method, the wrong road, the wrong mountain? Too many, and this is why change is imperative. What then does it take to open up a classroom if not steps? (pp. 1–2)

The Roepers concluded that what was necessary was *people*. People who are willing to listen to the child and determine his/her needs, to serve as role models and to be emotionally and intellectually in synch with the child so that the subject matter can be related in the best way possible. Out of this change comes a different learning environment. Consequently, another shift during this time period was from a focus on teaching to a focus on *learning*. Learning is an activity that children are naturally motivated to experience. Learning takes place at a different pace and in a different manner for each child as well. Each child learns with his own learning style and the role of the teacher is to guide the child in exploration and discovery (pp. 4–5).

Parents, teachers, and children still work cooperatively in the Roepers' arrangement but the focus shifts from the needs of the school or the needs of society to the needs of the children. The writings stated that the shift represented "institutions in the service of human beings" (p. 7). Learning is the by-product of these interactions. In the current educational milieu, some of these ideas may seem mainstream; however, these ideas were very radical for the time. It was not clear that the Roeper school community would adopt them readily.

"Understanding the characteristics of the learner and how the self develops is another key aspect of this model" (p. 27). It is imperative that the Self sees that he is a member of the community and has a relationship with all other Selves so that he is better able to develop empathy. When adults are able to provide a healthy model, then the tiny Self becomes secure in his self-understanding and self-image. However, one of the first tasks of the new Self is to be separate. He learns that the caregivers leave and he is alone. Being separate and learning to live without caregivers and yet remain attached is a lengthy process. The other task that happens simultaneously is to interact with others. The Self must navigate the space between these two boundaries (p. 29).

George and Annemarie came to know children deeply, particularly gifted children, and their viewpoints reflected what they learned. They learned that it is essential to understand these tasks not only from the adult point of view but also the perspective of the child. It is necessary to know what tasks are critical in developing a healthy Self. If, in fact, the goal for the child is to grow and learn during his schooling experience, then it becomes imperative that there is an understanding of his needs from the inside out and that they are not imposed from the outside.

Gifted children are extremely sensitive to the moods, the emotional tone, and relationship that they have with their teacher. Sensitive to environmental stimuli, physical, sensual, psychomotor and emotional, the children may respond unevenly depending on how they are affected by what is happening in their school world.

One result of these observations resulted in a major paper that was published in *Roeper Review* in 1982. Titled *How the Gifted Cope with Their Emotions*, this article was based on the Roepers' work with children at the Roeper School. Annemarie wrote:

> Interest in gifted children is primarily focused on their intellectual and creative characteristics rather than on their emotional nature. There is, however,

an awareness of the dichotomy between their intellectual and emotional development, the intellectual viewed as advanced and the emotional viewed as normal or slow.

I believe this model to be inaccurate and detrimental in planning for the gifted child. A child is a total entity; a combination of many characteristics. Emotions cannot be treated separately from intellectual awareness or physical development; all intertwine and influence each other. A gifted five-year-old does not function or think like an average ten-year-old, nor does this child feel like an average ten-year-old, nor does this child feel like an average four- or five-year-old. These children's thoughts and emotions differ, and as a result, they perceive and react to their world differently (p. 21).

The role of the teacher also changes in the *Self-Actualization and Interdependence Model* (1990, p. 37). The child's development of a sense of security and empathy is paramount, and the teacher must be selected in order to ensure the best fit possible.

Depending on the developmental path of both teacher and student, there may be times when it would be better not to make a match. Unfortunately, in many school situations, a hierarchical framework is in place and the success of each child is needed for the success of the group. For example, it may be important for children to test well so that it appears that the teacher is doing a good job. If the teachers are all successful then the principal will look successful. It is clear in such a system that it is impossible to know which children are learning holistically and which are not. In this traditional model, the growth of each child is not as important as the perceived growth of the group.

Changing the goal of education and changing the role of the teacher necessarily changes the educational process. In a child-centered approach, the teacher goes back to the child over and over to gather information about how to guide the child in his learning. Throughout the learning process, the children will be grouped and regrouped depending on need and interest. The resulting curriculum is not dependent on particular disciplines but is a *Curriculum of the Self* (1990, pp. 37–40).

The teacher must also facilitate the needs of the children within the group. As situations arise that cause emotional or intellectual challenges, the teacher may need to guide the children through to an acceptable resolution of a problem. This process is not one that can be hurried, and it is important that opportunities be given to explore ethical and moral situations. Such investigations may help provide the gifted child with the insight needed to come to a more informed decision. In such an environment, the children are able to recognize their needs and develop the social skills needed to live cooperatively and with mutual respect (1990, pp. 41–44).

Even within this structure, there need to be learning experiences available and accessible for children. Another aspect of programming in the *Open Classroom* depended on the belief that experts were needed in content areas. For example, children who wanted to learn art or music were taught by specialists in those areas. Other curricular areas were available for children within a conceptual framework.

Since gifted children are such global learners, it is necessary for them to understand conceptual frameworks to create meaning. These broad areas provided some of the entry points into learning experiences:

Table 2. Learning experiences to build a conceptual framework

Concept of Family and Home	Concept of Animate and Inanimate Objects
Concept of School	Concept of Earth
Concept of Geography	Concept of Universe
Concept of Natural Science	Concept of Physical Science
Math Concepts	Current Events
Concept of Literature	Concept of Daydreaming
Concept of Psychology	Concept of Beauty
Concept of Play	Concept of Creative Expression
Concept of Physical Education	Concept of Psychology

In opening the classroom, the children shared in the responsibility of selecting learning opportunities. Although the classroom might look as if the students were merely playing, each child selects his work with the guidance of the teacher. Individual and group spaces are available for work, and children are grouped not by single grade but in *stages* with groups of age peers (1990, pp. 48–61). These elements combined to form the process of education. The educational philosophy and goals combined with the learner characteristics lead to the learning experiences that become the essence of the educational process. Necessarily, within a school, this process occurs in community.

During this time, Annemarie and George became aware of another dynamic in play. Annemarie presented their ideas:

> I realized that one of the outstanding characteristics of gifted children is that they, maybe even more than other children, need to be in charge of their own destiny and are in charge of their own destiny. When I thought about that, all of a sudden it became clear to me that the structure of the adults, how the teachers function, was a hierarchy. In addition, that was in contradiction to the way these children function and the way we understood that children needed freedom. I have a feeling that we first reorganized the lower school into giving up the grades and stages and free choice and so on and then realized that the structure around the children was one of self-actualization but that the staff was organized according to our hierarchical principle and was at that point that we thought we can't have that contradiction. (personal communication, 2005)

There must be some framework for communication, rules, regulations, and discipline within an educational institution. The *SAI* model represented an alternative to a traditional model of governance and focused on cooperation instead of competition. This new model of interdependence arose from the awareness that neither total independence nor dependence was desired. To create a governing structure that embodied this framework would not be an easy task. A hierarchical, top-down management style was the only form of school governance that most school community members had known. Annemarie mused:

> How can teachers help children function in that way so that they can make changes when they don't know how to do it themselves? It was so much of a structure that I had to make many of the decisions. I don't know, you find it to be true, but it was a very two-sided sword. Not only did I have the responsibility for everything but I was also being blamed for everything. Finally, what brought the new idea to me was a situation with a teacher. She was very unpopular and none of the other teachers wanted to teach next to her. They came to me and told me that I needed to fire her. It took me another year before I had reached that same conclusion. I didn't believe in firing anyway—there are different ways of doing this in a participatory democracy. When I finally realized that she was not going to learn and that she needed to leave, I asked her to do so and the teachers sided with her and told her how unfair I was. That's when I felt I'd had enough of that. (personal communication, 2005)

This realization led to the fourth landmark that Annemarie had shared with Constance Shannon, which was introduction of the participatory democracy into the administrative structure of the school community. The school community began to reflect these changes as well. An article in *Roeper Review* (1986) described some of the results of the nonhierarchical structure. The article titled, *Participatory vs. Hierarchical Models for Administration: The Roeper School Experience*, explained how each stakeholder was responsible for outcomes that occurred within the governance of the school. The first changes occurred with the Board of Trustees as some staff members, students, and alumnus were given voting rights. Placement decisions and staffing decisions were made jointly with the teachers involved. An administrative council was formed that allowed for open meetings. Teacher evaluations were ongoing and input from staff, especially specialists, was solicited for the purposes of encouraging growth (pp. 8–9).

The school community participated in multiple administrative tasks. Teachers and staff members were asked to help in the screening and selection of students who had applied to the school. Different from a public school, a school for gifted children considers many pieces of information before a decision is made. Since teachers were able to participate in the process, they were more likely to make a commitment to a child who might have otherwise lacked a strong endorsement.

Parents were also more invested in what happened in the classroom. They would communicate with the teachers and more readily share their children's interests so that the teachers were able to craft lessons around these interests. Both parents and teachers became more secure in negotiating differences.

In this system, the homeroom teacher guided the child in the areas of math, social studies, and reading. Of equal importance was the growth of the child in social, emotional, and creative expression because the focus was on learning for life, and not just for academic success. The system was not perfect. Teachers in such an environment must be secure in their own abilities and feel capable regardless of the feedback from the school leaders. In an environment where the change is radical, it is reasonable to expect that fears and problems might arise that would have to be resolved in a timely fashion. This is an organizational structure that takes time to implement and time must be set aside for tackling issues and not settling for a quick fix.

A benefits committee was formed to look at issues of sick leave, salary, and medical leave. Recommendations from the committee were sent to the board. Staff evaluations were also conducted by committee. Parent input, student input, and observations from members of the school community were solicited.

Each staff person that was to be evaluated was responsible for the selection of the members that would conduct the evaluation. Hiring and team selection was another area that was done by consensus. Every member would have ownership of new members that were added or of ones that were released. Every member of the school community had an equal voice through these democratic practices (1986, pp. 8–10). These practices were more evidence of translating philosophy into action.

The convictions and beliefs of the Roepers were able to flourish, in part, because of the ability to see multiple perspectives and to approach new ideas by incorporating all points of view. They were able to facilitate change while maintaining the constancy of their core beliefs. Annemarie summarized their perspective; "It was our hope that children who grew up in a specific community, where equal human rights were valued, would carry the same perception of people into the world" (1986, p. 123). The Roepers provided a model for a learning community that encourages growth and makes adjustments to modernity while resting on rock solid principles that are comprehensive and fully articulated. The physical presence of George and Annemarie are long gone from Roeper School but their legacy lives on. The doors of The Roeper School are still open. Stop by for a visit if you would like to see the Roeper philosophy in action—it is certain that those who are interested in observing their "philosophy of life" would be welcome.

REFERENCES

Delisle, J. R. (2000b). *Once upon a mind: The stories and scholars of gifted child education.* Fort Worth, TX: Harcourt Brace Publishers.

Kane, M. (2006). *A life history of Annemarie Roeper: A view from the self.* (Unpublished doctoral dissertation). Loyola University, Chicago, IL.

Muchmore, J. (2001). The story of "Anna": A life history study of the literacy beliefs and teaching practices of an urban high school English teacher. *Teacher Education Quarterly.* Retrieved December 30, 2005, from LookSmart database.

Roeper, A. (n.d.). *A philosophy comes of age: A personal statement for Independent Schools Association of the Central States (ISACS).* Unpublished manuscript.

Roeper, A. (2011). *Beyond old age: Essays on living and dying.* Berkeley, CA: Azalea Art Press.

Roeper, A. (1999). *Self-actualization and interdependence*. Unpublished manuscript.
Roeper, A. (1995). Annemarie Roeper: Selected writings and speeches. Minneapolis, MN: Free Spirit Press.
Roeper, A. (1990). Educating children for life: The modern learning community. Monroe, NY: Trillium Press.
Roeper, A. (1986). Participatory vs. hierarchical models for administration: The Roeper School experience. *Roeper Review, 9*, pp. 4–10.
Roeper, A. (1982). How the gifted cope with their emotions. *Roeper Review, 5*, 21–24.
Roeper, A. (1972). *Parent newsletter*. Unpublished manuscript.
Roeper, A. (1968). *Continuous progress program at Roeper City and Country Lower School*. Bloomfield Hills, MI: Roeper School.
Roeper, G. (1962). *Learning and creativity*. Unpublished manuscript.
Roeper, A., & Roeper, G. (1981). *Roeper philosophy*. Unpublished manuscript.
Roeper City and Country School. (1956). *Roeper School* [Brochure]. Bloomfield Hills, MI: Author.
Shannon, C. (1989). Hand in hand: An interview with Annemarie and George Roeper. *Advanced Development, 1*, 27–40.

APPENDIX A: TIMELINE OF THE ROEPER SCHOOL

1910: George Alexander Roeper is born in Hamburg, Germany, on September 7.

1918: Annemarie Martha Bondy is born in Vienna, Austria, on August 27.

1920: Max and Gertrud Bondy, parents of Annemarie, establish their first school in Bruckenau, Germany, in partnership with Ernst Putz.

1923: The Bondys part ways with Putz and establish a school of their own in Gandersheim, Germany. George Roeper arrives as a 13-year-old student in 1924.

1929: The school moves to Marienau, near the village of Dahlenburg, outside Hamburg.

1937: Max Bondy is forced by the Nazi regime to sell Marienau because he is of Jewish heritage; the family operates a school in Gland, Switzerland, called Les Rayons, for several years.

1939: The Bondy family sails to the United States, where they join George Roeper, who had come ahead in November 1938 to find property for the Bondys to start a school. The Bondys' school, Windsor Mountain School, opens in Windsor, VT, in 1939, moves to Manchester, VT, in 1940, and finally settles in Lenox, MA, in 1944, until it closes in 1975 due to financial difficulties.

1941: George and Annemarie Roeper, now married, move to Detroit. Annemarie begins as Director of the Editha Sterba Nursery School (founded 1939) on Woodward Ave. in Highland Park; George founds the Roeper Grade School in the same building. They begin the year with 9 students and end with 30.

1942: The school outgrows its Highland Park building and moves to 668 Pallister Ave., in the New Center area of Detroit.

1946: The Roepers purchase a house and 4 acres in Bloomfield Hills in April. In September the school opens in the new location, under the name of City & Country School of Bloomfield Hills (incorporating the Editha Sterba Nursery and the Roeper Grade School) with 90 students through 6th grade.

1947: First season of summer camp.

1952: Roepers purchase 8 more acres in Jan 1952 to complete the Bloomfield Hills campus.

1955: The Roepers integrate the student population when Sheila Tanner Cain joins the school as a two-year-old. The school had already had an African-American teacher, Hattie Wyatt, since 1942.

1956: In June, the Roepers convene the Gifted Child Institute, chaired by A. Harry Passow of Columbia University, to develop a curriculum for gifted children. In September, the school opens as the nation's second elementary school exclusively for gifted children.

1960: Four classrooms of the Middle Building open in September, expanding the school beyond Hill House.

1961: Middle Building expansion provides four more classrooms.

1964: The first 9th grade is formed.

1965: The previous year's 9th graders all go on to other high schools, but this year's 9th grade will become the Class of 1969. The Quad Building opens.

1966: The school is renamed Roeper City & Country School in honor of the school's 25th anniversary. The first 10th grade is formed and new students are accepted into the Upper School.

1969: The Domes open in September; dedicated as the Martin Luther King, Jr., Domes in May 1970.

1972: Duplex Science Building opens.

1977–78: The Roeper Review is established as a quarterly professional journal; George and Annemarie receive honorary doctorates from Eastern Michigan University in spring 1978.

1979: George retires in June 1979.

1979–80: Annemarie and Phillip Parsons direct the school; Annemarie retires in June 1980.

1980–81: No single Head; Pam Dart Head of LS and Phillip Parsons Head of US.

1981–82: Pam Dart named Head of School; Birmingham building is purchased and Grades 6–12 move there. Grade 6 (which had been part of Lower School) and

Grades 7 & 8 (which had been part of the Upper School) are formed into the school's first Middle School.

1988–89: Linda Chapin named Head of School; leaves midyear and Board Chair Rennie Freeman serves as Head for the rest of the year.

1989–90: Libby Balter-Blume named Head of School; leaves midyear and LS Director Lorene Porter and US Director Chuck Webster serve as co-Heads for the rest of the year.

1990: Chuck Webster becomes Head of School.

1993: The school changes its name to The Roeper School.

1998: Ken Seward becomes Head of School.

2001: Birmingham building renovations completed by start of school

2003: Swim Center opens for 2003 camp season; Steward Classroom Building opens in September 2003.

2004: Randall Dunn becomes Head of School.

2007: Community Center is completed in the spring of 2007.

2011–12: Philip S. Deely serves as Interim Head; the Children's Library opens in the spring.

2012: David H. Feldman becomes Head of School.

GEORGE ROEPER & ANNEMARIE ROEPER

THE ROEPER PHILOSOPHY

When George and Annemarie Roeper founded their school in Detroit in 1941, their educational philosophy was rooted in the psychoanalytic and humanistic approach used by Annemarie's parents, Max and Gertrud Bondy, in their schools in Germany. Over the years, the language and concepts they used in memos, speeches and philosophy statements evolved as the school changed and grew. When George and Annemarie retired, they wanted to write down in one place the most current and complete description of their educational philosophy. They completed their statement in April 1981, and the school's Board of Trustees adopted it in January 1982. Although new philosophy statements have been written over the years, often as part of accreditation processes but also to try to make key principles more accessible, the 1981 statement remains the foundational expression of the school's philosophy.[1]
—Marcia Ruff, School Historian

THE ESSENCE OF THE PHILOSOPHY

The following are its guiding tenets:

- Making equal human rights for all people a priority.
- A complete commitment to justice rather than power.
- A willingness to allow the child to participate in the shaping of his [or her] own destiny and to consciously prepare him [or her] for it.
- To prepare this future generation to deal with the unknown.
- To view the needs of each child independently.

OUR PHILOSOPHY OF EDUCATION IS A PHILOSOPHY OF LIFE

We are concerned with the whole impact of life on young people and the impact they will make on society. Ours is a philosophy of basic human rights for all. We expect them to learn to control and direct themselves rather than depend on adults only. As they develop controls from within, outer controls must recede. They must learn the process of decision-making along with the academic skills and concepts. We cannot teach subject matter separate from life.

THE PHILOSOPHY IS A WAY OF LIFE

This philosophy is a universal one. It is a way of life. It is not limited to the school or the children in it. It is based on a concept of human rights, not in theory only, but in daily living. It embraces a principle of responsibility and support for each other, a principle of helping those who are in need because they are entitled to it, not because of charity. It includes the notion that even a little bit more love and mercy would make this world a better place to live in. It is a goal, which, although it can never be quite realized, is only as good and as real as its honest attempts at implementation. It does not exist for the school only, but the school exists because of it. It is the framework for living and learning within the school.

IT REPRESENTS A BASIC DEPARTURE FROM THE USUAL

If we look at it carefully, we find that it represents a basic departure from the usual view of human interaction and the approach that usually governs human affairs, yet it is not at all unique to this school. Examples of it and striving toward it can be found in many institutions and theories in history and in the present. There are a number of schools, colleges, and other organizations, that today function under the same principle.

IT ORIGINATES FROM A COMBINATION OF IDEALISM AND REALISM

This philosophy originates from a combination of an idealistic commitment to justice and a realistic view of the limitation of power by our mutual interdependence. It provides a unifying principle. It is based on the following realization: there is neither absolute power nor complete dependence or independence. The moment a child is born, he or she becomes part of the network of interdependence. Although it appears as though children are powerless, they bring with them power over our lives; they change them. And of course we have power over theirs. As they grow, they continue to be part of this network forever. We are all caught in it, although it is invisible and easy to forget.

Actually, the fact of interdependence, of human ecology, becomes more and more apparent in today's world. All parts of the globe depend on each other economically, culturally, and emotionally. All this, if followed through logically, translates into the compelling need for cooperative action. Yet most of our skills and beliefs are based on confrontation and competition. Most people function as though there were a hierarchy of human rights and human life-structures. There is a top to be reached by the few, built on a hierarchy supported by the many. Therefore, people feel justified and safe to use each other as stepping stones to success. Their value is measured in terms of their usefulness to those in apparent power. This state of affairs soon becomes intolerable to those at the bottom and they become aware of the bottom power of the many as opposed to the tower power of the few. And so the battle never ends.

We live in a dog-eat-dog world, where might makes right. It is obvious to all that this has brought us to the brink of destruction. We are teetering at the edge of it and yet we continue to teach children to live in the same way. We are raising children to function in a manner that has created our present state of life. Why? Because we use our real ability of cooperation only in certain areas of endeavor. We have not yet incorporated in our emotions and thoughts a belief in mutual responsibility or a concept of human interdependence or ecology. We believe in victory and our perceptions are short term. We are aware of the consequences of the moment, not the long-range chain reaction of our behavior. We do not remember that if we accept stealing as a way of life we have to guard against others stealing from us. If we kill, we create the possibility of being killed, even if we do it for justice or revenge. All of this is obvious and yet we have not found other methods of dealing with each other.

A philosophy that tries to develop the skills of cooperation and looks at this as the ultimate moral and realistic, not illusionary, goal, may be the only true approach that might keep the world from destruction. Of course, we are aware that we will not be able to change the world but we might make a slight impact and at least help the members of this community to live a different life. It may also serve as a model for others. It shows that it can be done.

ITS IMPLEMENTATION REQUIRES AN APPROPRIATE GOVERNANCE STRUCTURE

To implement this philosophy in our school community, which is a society in microcosm, requires the creation of a living and learning environment, which proves that it is possible while teaching how to do it. It requires a structure of administration, an educational program and attitude which is in every respect based on the philosophy, not separate from it. It requires a structure that protects the rights of each individual, a structure truly based on a concept of justice and interdependence. It requires a structure that tries to pursue the following goals:

Specific Goals

Consistent with the essential tenets of the philosophy, the following goals guide actions within the school:

1. To protect the equal rights of each member within our specific community: children, maintenance and all support persons, teachers, administrators, parents, board, etc.
2. To find ways to do this in times of conflict, in times of change, in times of stress and in the face of human frailty. To find ways to do this even in the face of failure and guilt of the individual. To find ways to protect the rights of those who have no spokesperson and those who are no longer useful to the community. To accept this as our mutual responsibility and to find a balance to all rights that is just and acceptable.

3. To create opportunities to develop the skills, attitudes, techniques, and emotional acceptance of the concepts of cooperation and interdependence. To realize that these are radically different from those of competition and power to which we are accustomed. To make this part of the process of education.
4. To keep the unspoken promise made by teachers and parents to their children and to fulfill their unspoken expectations of us. And in order to do this, to create a living and learning environment which supports their inner strength to cope with the world and to make an impact on it.

Specific Skills and Attitudes

What are the attitudes and skills required?
- To develop a vision of the whole, not just a part of it.
- To develop an understanding of one's rights and obligations within the community.
- To see the community as a circle of interdependence rather than a hierarchy of dependency.
- To see peers and other community members as cooperators rather than competitors. This includes trusting and supporting the expertise of others.
- To see oneself as a member of the community in four important ways: to have a stake, to have a voice, to have responsibility, and to fulfill a specific task: to see the participation in the community as a whole, indeed, as a part of this task.
- To see oneself as a valuable and valued member of the community.

This also means an obligation to make responsible judgment openly and honestly, not secretively and anonymously. Anonymous opinions tend to be irresponsible because they do not have to be defended. It means on the one hand an identification with the needs of others, an expectation of mutual goodwill, and on the other hand a realization of human limitations and that even though one should strive for it, there can be no perfection of judgment, expertise, behavior, and action.

It means a realization that the individual's protection becomes increased by cooperation, but also that no individual or community can provide absolute protection without risk. One attraction of the hierarchical structure is the illusion of absolute protection to be given by those in power to those under them. It means: daring to take risks for one's own convictions while attending to the following:
- that the concept of obedience is replaced by a concept of responsibility.
- that the end does not justify the means.
- a commitment to trust in others, rather than distrust.
- the realization that we can go far in learning these skills and attitudes but that we will never be perfect, and therefore never be satisfied.
- an understanding that the processes of cooperation are complex and difficult, time-consuming, emotionally taxing, but allow the individual more freedom to grow in all directions, and at the same time have more real awareness and commitment to his or her immediate community and the world community of people.

THE ROLE OF LEADERSHIP

Within this structure, not only the role of the members of the community, but also that of the leadership (board of trustees, administrators) becomes differently defined. The trustees are the guardians of the philosophy: the administrators, its chief implementers. This also requires different types of skills and attitudes on the part of the leadership. For this leadership is not based on the authority vested in the power on the top of the hierarchy but rather on the confidence of the community in the expertise and goodwill of the leaders. It requires the skills to establish open communication and respect in the constituency, as well as their legitimate participation in decision-making. Only those who are affected by a decision, experiencing its consequences, should participate in reaching it in some form and to the extent that they are able. It includes the obligation to be continually aware of the rights of each individual and maintain a balance between all of those individual rights.

It requires leadership that sees the members of the community as models for the children and sees the living environment and the overall atmosphere as part of the educational program for the child. It includes a commitment to mutual responsibility and therefore a realistic system of mutual accountability and evaluation. Such a philosophy can only function if it is expressed in the attitudes and feelings of the members of the community. These can only grow and develop if the governmental structure represents the philosophy. It includes a commitment to a pluralistic society, which means that the constituency, the leadership and the staff represent all racial, religious, and economic groups. It means carefully working toward a goal, which diminishes economic restrictions as far as realistically possible.

OUR PROMISE TO CHILDREN

The philosophy is a universal one but in our community it is applied specifically to the education of children and among them the gifted. What are the reasons for this?

A. Children are in many ways underprivileged because they are not able to speak for themselves and therefore need advocates. Such advocacy is an integral part of the philosophy of the school. This means a concern for the unconscious misuse of children by society, by certain educational approaches and within this imposed structure, by teachers and parents. In other words, society's expectations of children are not prompted by the child's real abilities and needs but by arbitrary goals set by the outside. Our school tries to set goals appropriate to the individual. Advocacy also includes awareness that the child is not an island, and that bridges and connections need to be rebuilt without hurting his/her individuality.

B. It is even easier to misunderstand gifted children and to take advantage of them.

C. Children are our only hope for a brighter future and the future depends on them. Gifted children who have a global point of view might make even more of an impact on the future. Every educator and every parent makes an unspoken promise to children and every child has unspoken expectations. The promise and the expectations are to give and receive the help to learn to cope with life, to learn to support and respect their environment and to enter a world that supports and respects them. Yet, as we look at the child and the world, we wonder about the future of both. How can they help each other survive? And the outlook is overwhelming, for each is too complex for us to really understand. Do we leave to fate the unpredictable happenings of life? How can we prepare them for the unknown future? The future will not be anything like the future which is now our present and past and for which we were so woefully unprepared in many ways.

FULFILLING THE PROMISE

How can we really fulfill our promise? How can we keep it when confronted with such complexity? We must be aware that all we can do is to make the honest attempt to give it the best we can and never to forget either the complexities or the extent of our promise. That promise means that we can never separate education and life; that we are always aware of their interdependence.

This, then, is a basic departure from the usual goal of education. Even though they profess otherwise, in most educational institutions life and education are considered two completely different things. This has limited the goals of education. Parents educate for entrance into school, first grade teachers educate for second grade, high school for college, and colleges for careers. In order to do this, educators have long ago created a curriculum separate from life. As the child moves through school, certain aspects of this curriculum have been designated to be appropriate for preparation for the "next step." These have been lifted out and taught and tested and children become defined in terms of their achievement in these areas. We are aware of their learning. Yet, while they learn they live and life becomes the hidden curriculum.

Does traditional education help the student deal with these dilemmas? No. The priorities are elsewhere and in the meantime we break our promises and truly disappoint the children. How can we keep the promise? By taking the curriculum of life out of hiding.

The best preparation for life is living. Therefore, the children should live in an environment where they can learn the skills of cooperation, where they can participate in decision-making and become aware of their complexities, where their point of view is respected, where they can take a risk, where there are channels of interaction, where they become aware of the power within the chain of interdependence. They also need to be able to trust in the goodwill and expertise of the adults. They need adults who can be their models and show them how to live in the world. And again, in order to do this the adults around them need to provide them with a well thought out philosophy of life and a living-learning environment that reflects it.

The children also need adults who are experts in their field, and who know how to help them learn the skills necessary to live in this world and stimulate them to develop their potential and interest in any direction for their future. They need a flexible learning environment, which allows them to grow in their own style and manner within a framework of expectations adequate to their individual needs; they need open communications with the adults. Children need adults who are sensitive to the needs and interests of the individual, who value creative expression and physical development as much as academic and intellectual pursuits, adults who are informed and knowledgeable about child developmental phases, adults who help them cope with the world as it is and equip them with skills, self-esteem, and motivation to change it.

Among many other typical traits, many gifted children have a strong sense of justice. They often have an unexpectedly accurate perception of life situations, but great difficulties dealing with them. They react to limitations, secretiveness, and deception. They need to learn in an atmosphere that is open and supportive. This means a realization of the fact that the individual teacher does not educate the child alone, but also through the impact of the whole environment. It can be called milieu education.

THE PHILOSOPHY REFLECTED IN THE PROGRAM

In order to be effective the philosophy must permeate all dimensions of the school. We note its influence in the school's program design in the following ways:

A. the creation of the opportunities for children to participate in their destiny to the extent they are developmentally able.
B. seeing the child as a valid member of the community and respecting his or her rights and responsibilities, perceptions and thoughts.
C. emphasizing all aspects of learning and growing, by not lifting out certain areas as more important and thus making others less important. If, for example, evaluation is indicated, all areas of growth should be evaluated, not only academic, because that immediately gives them priority, for they are being measured.
D. creating a program rich in opportunities for all kinds of growth: academic, creative, physical, social, moral, and opportunities for joy.
E. using an approach that stresses a global point of view and mutual responsibilities.
F. building into all subject matters an emphasis on complexities of life and the fact that every experience, every action, every perception has many causes and many effects; that in truth life is not a linear progression but an all-encompassing development in all directions.
G. including in all subject matter confrontations with moral decisions, which grow out of our increased technical knowledge and our commitment to humanism.
H. emphasizing that the future is theirs to create.

I. emphasizing all areas of communication: openness, mutual understanding, verbal (language, literature, writing), nonverbal (dance, art, music), first-hand experience (travel, contact with people from different walks of life, off-campus jobs and instruction for older students, etc.). By involvement in the events of the moment: political, social, and cultural.
J. looking at the school as the world in microcosm where all of the conflicts, problems, solutions, interdependence, and chain reactions exist in a small way that one finds in the world at large. To use these opportunities to create learning experiences for the children and to enhance the scope of the community by letting students make an impact through student government structures and other channels.

One might argue that living in our community does not prepare for the so-called real world, which is in most part competitive and not cooperative. However, individuals who grow up in a cooperative world where they feel supported and respected develop a positive self-image and an understanding of who they are and their own strengths and potentials as well as weaknesses. They develop an understanding that even though they live in a competitive world they will not be defined by it. A person developing in such a world will be able to cope with it better, bring with her/him more internal resources than anyone who has never had a chance to make an impact and whose self-image depends only on climbing the ladder of success.

IN CONCLUSION

This philosophy is not a vague and sentimental idea of warmth and understanding. It represents not just a desire for happiness and a good life, although in a much broader sense these hopes are part of it. It actually is a relentlessly demanding concept, for its consequences are most complex – intellectually, emotionally, and practically. One is always in danger of contradicting it or losing it altogether without realizing it, by making small compromises, which have a tendency to grow and yet may only solve the problem apparent at the moment. They may exclude more difficult solutions within the philosophy, which are not found because they are not looked for. Built into this philosophy are both constancy and change. Its inherent goals remain constant while the implementation may change as life and times require. If constancy is not maintained or change is not occurring, it will result in a philosophy that is either mere lip service, irrelevant, or non-existent.

NOTE

[1] Minor wording changes have been made to the original document in order to "modernize" the text (e.g., changing "he" to "he or she" or the plural "they" to provide gender balance).

CATHY WILMERS

GROWING DEEP COMMUNITY ROOTS

At Roeper we talk about our Homeroom communities, our Stage Communities, our Lower School Community, our All School Community, our Parent Community, and so on. They are all vitally important to our school, yet creating each of those communities takes time, respect, careful work, tenacity, and a willingness for tolerance at all levels.

Recently we were challenged by the arrival of a new child from out of state coming into our homeroom of 7- and 8-year-olds (Stage III) four months into the school year. Our class had been working together, laughing together, supporting each other, even had been crying together, and this brilliant child needed us to facilitate integrating him into Roeper and our homeroom community. Of course, at the beginning of the fall our homeroom (as most do) created a list of agreements about how we were going to be together for the upcoming school year. Examples of these were "Listening respectfully to each other" and "Raise your hand to share as we all want to hear." It became apparent that it was now time to discuss again what being a community meant, but in a deeper and more specific way. What did being collectively together as a homeroom really mean minute by minute and day to day? What did it look like? What did it feel like? How was community really established?

When the project was introduced, the children were asked if they were interested in spending their time trying to generate a list of possibilities for what our community really looked and felt like. After a resounding "Yes!" the discussions began as children tried to articulate what it meant to be together. The work was sincere, very personal and at times difficult. One child described waiting for another child to catch the bus and said, "I wait for others, even if they are slow." Another child described the importance of what carrying ladders from our maintenance shed did for the group, so it was decided "Carrying heavy things" was important to building our community. Idea after idea emerged. "Understand that we are not at our best each day"; "Seek to forgive"; "Smile often". Each idea would be listed, discussed, changed, and challenged by the children until each phrase reflected the true meaning of their ideas. Then the language was revisited on succeeding days.

It was an exciting project to work on and children were engaged in the ideas, interested in articulating their experiences, and pleased to be working together. There were a great deal of comments during the other parts of our day as the ideas in our working document began to reoccur within our homeroom. Once the list was finished, it was left to percolate and then revisited to ensure that everyone felt it was complete and made sense. The list was then turned into a poster using a variety of fonts (as surely each idea was unique and personal), placed on a large flat piece of wood (8 feet high), and each of the children who worked on it was pleased to sign her or his name.

For over a month this piece held a prominent place in our homeroom and was referred to often by the children. Everyone was pleased that so much of it was so relevant throughout our school days.

Another turning point of the project came a month later when the Director of the Upper School asked if our children (perhaps a few) would be interested in sharing their work of Building Community with the Upper School students at an upcoming assembly. This idea was brought to our homeroom and the children decided that they would like to do this, but instead of only a few children going, they decided that everyone should go because everyone had written it together. (Ownership was essential and very present.) Work began on what the presentation should be like. How could we best convey all of our ideas? We began to revisit and talk about some of the work we had done previously. The children decided some of the words would be performed altogether while others would be done in small groups or partnerships. The result was a performance piece with everyone having input and a voice. The children worked on presenting, giving each other feedback about being heard, mumbling, etc. All the while they tried to make sure their presentation was interesting – after all it was going to be performed in front of 200 9th through 12th graders! The children were purposeful, industrious and clearly excited about the project.

The day of the presentation arrived. The children boarded the bus to go to the Roeper Upper School with their tall stools. The poster was lovingly carried by several children. There were no groans, no 7-year-old children complaining about carrying tall awkward stools onto the bus, or how difficult it was to manoeuvre the board. There was an air of excitement, nervousness and pride – they clearly owned and were pleased to be a part of this element of the project! The children were focused, ready and so very proud to be invited to share their work at the Roeper Upper School.

After a brief run-through in the theatre, the children were ready to begin. The room began to fill as the children sat confidently, yet apprehensively on stage. The eyes of our children grew bigger as they observed just how many people were coming to see and hear what they had created.

With a nod of her head from the Upper School Director, the children began. Several children carried our huge wooden poster across the stage and began explaining that *"Carrying heavy things together created community."* The presentation had begun. One by one, group by group, partnership by partnership, children in loud, clear strong voices presented their ideas. *"Show appreciation for others,"* *"Smile often,"* and *"Wait for people even if they are slow."* The audience was hushed. *"Notice if someone is left out."* Imagine a room full of students and faculty glued to the stage, listening and riveted to every word 7- and 8-year-old children were performing.

GROWING DEEP COMMUNITY ROOTS

"Talk to people; you get to know them." "Understand that we are not always at our best each day." "Turn up the music." Their voices were clear, easy to hear (even though the children were not using microphones) and their expressions during the performance spoke to the conviction of the children. *"Be loud together."*

Show appreciation for others
Clap, listen and enjoy other people
Smile often
Respect others' time
Tell jokes
Be loud together
Wait for people, even if they are slow
Being different is interesting
Listen to others' opinions
Notice if someone is left out
Greet people
Look up when walking
When in a group, try to contribute
Turn up the music
Turn down the music
Sing together
Share your strengths
Try your best
Talk to people, you get to know them
Be patient with others
Bake or make extra and share
Start traditions
Help carry heavy things together
Understand that we are not always at our best each day
Read books out loud
Be aware of sadness in others
Listen to birds
Fix it even if you didn't break it
Seek to understand
Share what you have
Take time to help others
Know that some people need more time to think through ideas
Dance together
Have fun together
Know each other's names
Seek to forgive
Seek to find good things in others
Be polite

Partway through the presentation, everything stopped and a group of children together said, *"Learn each other's names"* and, with this, the children who were comfortable with it (not everyone felt that they could go into the audience) got up off the stage, introduced themselves to some of the Upper School students in the audience, learned their names and then sat back on the stage. The presentation continued. *"Listen to the birds." "Turn down the music."* Several minutes later in the performance, those same children waved hello from their stools using the names of the students they had just met previously. The faces on the Upper Schoolers showed surprise as they realized that our children actually paid attention to them as they met them and even remembered their names! They were in awe of the children and only recovered because the presentation continued. The experience of being known was realized through 7- and 8-year-old children!

Once the presentation was complete, the Upper Schoolers spontaneously gave our children a standing ovation and many students later declared that it was one of the best assemblies all year. What happened next was magical as we asked the audience if they had any questions for the children. There were two parts in particular that, as the writers of the piece, we knew were confusing: The idea of turning *up* the music and turning *down* the music seemed contradictory, and what does listening to the birds have to do with community? Our children responded with clarity and thoughtfulness. They explained that sometimes in our homeroom it is fun to turn up the music and dance together while at other times it is as great to turn down the music and relax and read. It is the quietness of the gentle music that brings us peace, a certain mellowness that allows all of us to "chill" and read uninterrupted. "Listen to the birds" is about taking time to slow down and notice things around you. When we are outside and rush around, many things go unnoticed. In the same way, rushing by people can create a community that doesn't know each other. It was joyful the way the children articulated their understandings and were so proud talking and speaking from their hearts. Our children all felt the strength of the experience. It is one thing to perform a piece, but it is quite another to defend the work in front of so many *teenagers*!

Because the children stay in one homeroom for two years, this year half of the class that worked on the project last year are still in the homeroom. They continue to quote from the project, truly making it their own. Whenever the ladder is needed (as it often does in a homeroom that is continually evolving), children quote *"Carrying heavy things together builds community"* as a group of children heads off to gather the ladder. One child in particular loves the *"Being different is interesting"* idea. In another school, in another place, in another time, looking different from all of her peers would be difficult for her, but here as the result of many experiences (and I would like to think the above project had a little something to do with it) she glows with pride as she happily states, "Being different is interesting!"

I recently asked a parent to reflect on what the experience meant to her daughter. "I believe that presenting such personal work at our Upper Campus opened their eyes and gave them a bigger community and a bigger world responding to them."

When children from our homeroom were asked to think back on the project, the huge grins and excitement were a good indicator of its impact. Here are some of their responses:

- "At Roeper we are all teachers—it doesn't matter what age you are, you can always teach and always learn."
- "I remember signing our names because it was so important that we all worked on it. It's funny but we kept on building a stronger community when we were thinking about how to say what we meant."
- "We took so much time on it because it was good to learn even more about each other."
- "I still remember that the person's name I met was Elisa."
- "I remember that one of the lines was about listening to the birds and it means that you should look around and think outside of yourself. Don't be selfish."
- "I remember that being different is interesting because if we were all the same it would be boring."
- "Going to the Upper School was a little scary because the kids were so big, but they gave us a standing ovation. We all felt really honored because the Upper School thought we did an amazing job."
- "I liked signing my name because I felt important."

From a teacher's perspective, the sense of community; and care, support, and encouragement for each other is ever-present. (Of course, we do many other things throughout the day to promote community as well.) Opportunities for growth sprouted up all over this project. Some children gained a deeper understanding of what being in a community really meant. Other children were able to articulate personal feelings, take risks and as a result move others along a continuum of understanding themselves better and what being together means. Clearly the child who always waited for a slower child and the child who suggested the idea of being left out were taking risks in sharing and resulted in others being more respectful and thoughtful. Each time children revealed a little more about themselves, we became a closer group. Oftentimes in education there can be a great deal of pressure to complete units, cover material, and in essence put on blinders to the possibilities of the natural flow of what is important. Deliberate work in areas such as community-building, developing personal strengths, going beyond one's comfort zone and talking about ideas and feelings that may be uncomfortable, are all elements that breathe air and life into a homeroom.

Creating community first respects individuals and their unique views of their world. When they are valued for who they truly are in every aspect – their strengths and their vulnerabilities – then they are ready to understand, reach out, and embrace others. This is part of our mission at The Roeper School: to facilitate children to become people who can accept themselves first and then look beyond and bring richness to a community and their world.

EMERY PENCE

EMPOWERING THE GIFTED AND INTENSE CHILD

> "In order to believe in justice, the child must be raised with justice. In order to trust others, he must be trusted. He must be expected to understand, not only to obey. As he develops controls from within, outer controls must recede. In order to be able to shape his own destiny, the child must learn the process of interaction with other people—a process based on justice, not power, and he must learn the process of decision making along with all academic skills and concepts."
> —George and Annemarie Roeper

When I started to plan this chapter I wanted to make it a scholarly treatise based on the research. But over a Tony Packo's lunch of sausage and sauerkraut, Larry Coleman of the University of Toledo gave me some wise advice. In effect, he said:

> You are not an academic. You are a practitioner. You have worked with gifted kids for a long time so speak from your experience of who they are and what works for them. What you say will help and maybe inspire other educators out in the trenches.

Wise words for which I thank Larry.

> Two typical students represent many who have attended Roeper. Julie is a hypothetical nine year old in Stage IV (fourth and fifth grades). Because she is extremely sensitive, her parents sometimes wish that she not watch the news as the injustice and pain in the world can cause her to tailspin into sadness and worry. Feeling connected to and responsible for the world has, at times, overwhelmed her.

Jacob, similarly a composite, is twelve years old, in 7th grade, and is, to say the least, an intense young man. Although the following description has softened some since he came to us, the personality traits which made his life in his public school so hard and lonely still are a big part of who he is at Roeper. Focusing like a laser on what he wants to know, Jacob can almost feel physically sick if he doesn't understand something. He wants to make sense out of things. So with topics or problems that he can figure out and understand (even if he has developed an incorrect answer or model of reality), Jacob has a passion and willingness to gain knowledge. But he tends to avoid topics and problems that are messy and/or that are hard to solve. Once in middle school when faced with speculating on motives of a character in a novel, he withdrew from the discussion as he felt he had no clue why someone would act like that. Jacob also doesn't like working with others as his ideas are so important to him that compromise and open-mindedness are akin to intellectual treason. He can quibble and bicker over a few small points. As a young adolescent, he feels some loneliness as he doesn't easily connect to others but takes comfort in a world of history and geography and a pride in knowing more than other students about these fields. He has a tendency to discount his fellow students as stupid and not useful as sources of information.

What both of these students share is an intensity and an ability to make connections. In Julie's case, the connections can be painful as each connection reminds her of a world not as it should be. With Jacob, if the ends can't all be tied up neatly, the world doesn't make sense so he retreats.

Annemarie and George created Roeper to be a safe place, emotionally and physically so children could work on their academic, emotional and social development but also recognize the interdependence of us all. How can we offer a refuge for children like Julie and Jacob to grow and still prepare them to make the world a better place?

In Julie's case, do we want a Prince Siddhartha gilded cage to protect students from knowing about human suffering? At times, *yes,* as we need to protect students from exposure to what they are able to intellectually grasp somewhat but not emotionally handle. But, no one lives completely cut off from the world and certainly no one will be living on the Roeper campus forever. Siddhartha seeing an elderly man and realizing that people grow old and die took the first necessary step in his spiritual journey.

In Jacob's case, do we want to help him build an isl.and of pure intellectual learning and mental exercises cut off from the world like the province Castalia in Herman Hesse's *The Glass Bead Game (Magister Ludi)*? Does he need an ivory tower that safely removes him from ideas and experiences that are troubling and hard for him to neatly and easily understand? At times, we do need to allow Jacob to pursue his passions and control what he learns. But we do him a disservice if we don't help him (push him?) to be able to deal with a messy, incoherent world and with others who may disagree with him or fail to live up to his standards.

So what to do, what to do? I propose that some of the answer lies in creating a better sense of control and safety in three areas:

- General atmosphere, milieu and philosophy of a true learning community
- Service-learning curriculum
- A problem-based, inquiry approach

GENERAL ATMOSPHERE OF A TRUE LEARNING COMMUNITY

As mentioned earlier, Roeper tries to be a *safe* place but to understand what that means in the broadest sense, we must define it as safe to admit mistakes, to be confused, to confess to others and one's self that one just doesn't know, to change one's mind, to hold two contradictory beliefs until a synthesis can be achieved, and in general to have the intellectual integrity to be humble and secure enough to accept cognitive dissonance. What is necessary for such a culture of the open mind to flourish?

Educators Must Be Aware of the Emotional Intensity of Their Gifted Students

I remember that as middle school director, I attended a meeting with a set of parents who too easily identified their child as "lazy" because he had just started avoiding doing his math after years of being a successful math student. Perhaps not being very open-minded myself, I thought to myself that the "lazy" answer was "lazy." It didn't take much of a conversation with that student to learn he was scared because for the first time, math didn't come easily. Teachers need to ask questions, refrain from making quick judgments, and remember that human beings are not easy to sum up. Educators should be emotionally secure themselves so they are able to detach a bit while retaining empathy. Being able to laugh a lot helps a lot. I remember the time as middle school director, a student came in, did an exorcism ceremony and left. What could I do but laugh? Only by committing to and working towards these qualities will an educator be able to give each student the respect all humans deserve and gifted kids absolutely require in order to thrive.

Respect Is Both Necessary for and an Outcome of Close Authentic Relationships with Our Students

A teacher can't solely treat kids as a monolithic bloc such as "gifted," nor as a developmental stage, nor as racial group, nor as anything but as individuals. Such "lenses" with which to view students are perhaps, at best, hypotheses to use but not to reify. With open dialogue and by listening without filters and prejudices (as much as possible), adults can ask students rather than stereotype them, learn from talking to them rather than trying to read their minds, and involve them more as owners of their education rather than as objects upon which to act. If adults have authentic, honest relationships with students so as to know them well, they will not only know when to push and challenge and when to back off, they will have the trust of their charges. With teachers, coaches and administrators "having their backs," intense learners will be more likely to transcend their comfort levels, to be willing to try new activities, to accept not knowing the answer for a while, and to rebound after a perceived failure.

Teachers and Other Adults in the Child's Life Have to Be Models of Intellectual Humility

Why can't we say "I don't know; how can we find out?" or "I was wrong." The students will respect a person this emotionally strong and will appreciate that no one is trying to fool them with a veneer of knowledge. We are all works in progress and that's okay.

It Is Important to Downplay Competition as a Motivator

In many schools, students are motivated by external forces like grades and parental disapproval. Even at Roeper these forces have power and sometimes do "work" as immediate motivators. But the more we can help students trust us and be internally motivated, the more the emphasis will be on learning instead of playing the game. If students are encouraged to be responsible for their educations, the more likely they will become life-long learners, able to cope with a rapidly changing world. One of my favorite Roeper stories was when a panel of Roeper upper school students was addressing a group of AIMS (Association of Independent Michigan Schools) administrators about creating a true learning community. One of the administrators asked, with skepticism, how such an ethos of non-grade-grubbing and non-"Is it going to be on the test?" mentality could be achieved. Senior Ariella Eis looked him straight in the eye and the following interchange ensued:

Ariella: Do you rank your students?

Administrator: Yes.

Ariella: Don't. Do you have a valedictorian and salutatorian?

Administrator: Yes

Ariella: Don't. Are students' GPA's common knowledge around school?

You get the picture. I wouldn't say students at Roeper never cheat or worry too much about grades or avoid taking a desired class because they want to take another one that might help them get into an Ivy. But the emphasis is more on learning and pursuing one's passions.

Students Should Be Constantly Reflecting on How They Are Doing in Relation to Their Own Goals and Those of Teachers and Parents

Pupils need to be involved in the evaluation and assessment process. I know that you can take portfolios too far and end up spending more time polishing the finished product than in learning what the product is supposed to reflect. But what better way to make the students responsible for learning and to show they are trusted enough to have input into educational process than to have them set goals for the semester for the class, to be at conferences, and to do self-evaluations?

Cooperation, Good or Bad for Gifted Kids?

There have been some in the gifted education community who think that collaborative learning is a dead end for the gifted learner. He or she may get stuck doing all the work, may be held back by slower students or may be marginalized by group members who can't understand what he/she is saying or trying to do. All of these are real risks if the educator in charge of the learning environment doesn't understand the gifted student or slavishly adopts group work without fully appreciating the pitfalls. Even at Roeper, a school for the gifted, we have such a wide range of abilities that intense group work is not without problems. We don't lack conflict resolution teachable moments.

Given these challenges, why teach cooperation? There is no way that any student or individual is ever going to be working totally alone. Strong interpersonal and communication skills are necessary to accomplish almost anything. In addition, gifted kids may appear, at times, lost in their own little worlds, seemingly impervious to loneliness, but are they?

At Roeper, which is a school for the gifted with a tradition of tolerance and safety, going solo might be easier than in more mainstream institutions but no matter, somehow, someway, all students are going to be better off if they can work with others when necessary. So start early, do conflict resolution when teachable moments arise, give some opportunities for kids to pursue their own passions individually, refrain from pitting pupils against each other, don't be too upset when kids don't get along, and some day you will be surprised at how even crazy-smart people can work together.

Students Need to Be Taught About the Diversity of Learning Styles and Strengths and They Need to Be Able to Identify These for Themselves

Saying "I'm dumb" at math is a cop-out. Saying "I'm a visual learner and I need pictorial representations" or "I'm scared silly of math" are steps towards becoming an empowered math scholar.

Giving Them Choice over What They Learn Will Give Students More of a Sense of Control

Obviously, the professionals know what the student needs to do well in the field of study. Obviously, the parents are paying the bills and are worried about where the kid can get into college. But more obviously, children who are allowed some choice in what they learn from an early age feel more confident about, and responsible for, their cognitive and skill development. They are better able to direct their own learning later on in college and beyond. By offering many electives, optional class offerings, and extracurriculars, and by allowing students choices within a class, Roeper creates the opportunity for students, teachers, and parents to negotiate a balance of everybody's desires and needs. As we face a rapidly changing world with too much information coming at us, don't we want to help develop people who can pursue their passions and are self-motivated to learn? Allowing genuine choice is not easy for anybody. It means more work for the educator, more worry for the parents and more mistakes and frustration for the student but also a better likelihood of confident life-long learners.

Service Learning

Students need to feel like they have some control over what bothers them be it a pesky little brother or global climate change. If they don't, they feel weak and helpless. Students learn best with real problems as they can see the importance and relevance. Since they make connections anyway, why not help them connect with the real world in a controlled, safe environment? Then they will learn that life isn't as scary and unfathomable as it might seem. Or, at least, it won't overwhelm and depress them into isolation and despair. Being active beats being passive.

At Roeper, service learning involves problem-solving projects that address authentic issues or needs. Through these projects, students identify, research, and address real community challenges, using knowledge and skills learned in the classroom. They assess the project during its implementation and after its completion. What we want to avoid are projects that are unrelated to learning and that are directed by adults. Deep understanding of the problem and the confidence to engage in sustained effort are preferred to short-term, superficial feelings obtained with one-shot charity events.

The following are necessary components of good service learning at the school:

- Emphasis on Student Ownership: Students share in decision making with adults, and adults share in learning with students—acting as partners and coaches rather than experts and decision makers. The biggest problem is keeping adults from taking over, especially when students are floundering and when adults think they could do better. More about this problem later.
- Reliance on a Process Model: In service learning students discover problems and needs in their school and/or community, investigate the causes and effects of the problems they identify, research various solutions to the problems, evaluate the pros and cons of each solution and decide on the actions to take, create an action plan and timeline to implement ideas, implement the plan, and evaluate the results of actions. Much of the process is ongoing and overlaps as opposed to being strictly sequential. But the model is referred to, discussed, and kept ever-present in everybody's focus.
- Proper Teacher Role: Before and during the linear steps listed above, educators also create a collaborative environment to foster teamwork; facilitate on-going reflection (make connections between learning and the project); connect the service-learning project to the curriculum; with students, reach out to parents and the public; and celebrate successes along the way.

I'm currently teaching a Stage IV (grades 4 and 5) class called Leadership and the Roeper philosophy in which students consider and discuss fundamental questions about being a leader (Why do people want to be leaders? How do leaders lead; what do leaders do? What are the sources of leaders' influence and power? What are the downsides of leadership? and more). They also work on communication skills and goal setting as necessary to becoming better leaders. Finally, they take on service-learning projects of their choice. To prevent them from too quickly jumping on an activity (Let's have a bake sale) or personal cause (I love puppies) without properly considering other alternatives, I introduce the concept of establishing and using criteria by asking, "What would a good project look like?" The brainstormed responses usually include that it must,

- be safe (no picking up trash on the median of a highway);
- help someone or solve a problem (no petitions to get a day off from school);
- be worthy enough to take up our time and energy (no throwing an ice cream party for the class);
- be an opportunity to learn something (no working on something we have already done before unless there is something new about it);
- be doable and realistic (no trying to eliminate world hunger in two weeks);
- be something we kids can do with a minimum of adult help (nothing where a teacher or parent has to do most of the work);
- give us a chance to lead others (no working only with ourselves without reaching out to others);
- educate others (no bake sale without at least a poster about the problem and what we and others can do about it).

As a class, we constantly refer to these criteria as we decide on a project and we carry it out. Then students are to identify five problems or causes and then brainstorm three to five different ways they can work on each problem. They get ideas by looking around (There is litter on campus), asking mom and dad (Have you heard about Asian Carp possibly getting into the Great Lakes?), or by personal connection (A friend of the family at Temple died of cancer last month).

The worksheet for one child's first item might look like the example in Table 1:

Table 1. Example of a worksheet used for generating initial ideas for a service-learning project

PROBLEM	WHAT WE MIGHT DO
1. Cancer kills a lot of people	– Raise money by a bake sale. (You can't keep a good bake down.) – Research cancer so we can educate people on how to help avoid it or get early treatment. – Convince people to donate to the American Cancer Society.

Students explain as their ideas are put on the whiteboard. Then they have to prepare short, persuasive pieces on why one of problems/causes (and its accompanying possible strategies) should be adopted by one of our groups.

After everything is presented, students confer among themselves and form teams. Amazingly, teams often are not based on friendship. Also, sometimes causes are divorced from their originally proposed strategies and remarried with others. For example, an afterschool movie series to raise money for the Humane Society morphs into a film festival for the space committee to get people dreaming of being on the first manned mission to Mars.

Students meet with me to devise action plans, which include goal setting, marketing steps, assignment of duties and some sort of crude evaluation procedure. Because the course often ends before the project is completed, student teams from previous sign-ups meet with me at lunch or recess once a week. Some projects have become embedded into the culture of the school. The 2010 Bagel Sale for Haiti morphed into the 2010–11 Bagel Sale for Pakistani Flood Relief, into the 2011 Bagel Sale for the Red Cross into Japan, and next year is being passed on to younger students for whatever they think needs our help. The community has grown to expect and rely on bagels once a week along with a pamphlet or fact sheet. Some of the projects these 4th and 5th graders have taken on include the following:

- saving axolotl habitat;
- stopping Asian Carp from getting into the Great Lakes;
- helping the Humane Society;
- stopping puppy mills;
- helping fund cancer research;
- investigating the negative effects of winter salting on our campus and environment and trying to lessen them;
- teaching a college education class about gifted education at Roeper;
- gathering school supplies for Afghanistan and Iraq;
- supporting Special Olympics with a swimathon;
- getting people excited about space again;
- building positive perceptions about the City of Detroit;
- educating folks about why they should buy Fair Trade chocolate;
- supporting a homeless shelter.

Many of these projects have reaped benefits beyond the initial cause. The young lady who started showing afterschool movies for komodo dragon preservation (I'm not making this up) has created a greater sense of community for kids and families.

What is very positive is that students not in this class (or not in this class anymore) have started proposing and carrying out projects on their own (with me as the unofficial advisor). Our biggest problem is that we actually have too many events going on. We used to worry about one-shot deals. Now we worry about groups that want to continue forever. We need to be careful about initiatives starting to bump into each other causing community confusion and fatigue.

Service learning doesn't have to be part of a separate class like Leadership and can be integrated into content-specific areas as well. Gym classes have done Jump Rope for Heart (physical exercise to raise money for the Heart Association). The art teachers and Stage IV homeroom teachers hold an Empty Bowls event every year to benefit The Lighthouse to help feed hungry people. Everybody makes a bowl and at a dinner, students run the event and explain the problems Lighthouse is working on. In our Upper School, a homeroom has had a six-year tradition of holding a spring talent show. For the first few years it was to raise awareness and money for Darfur and recently it has supported Detroit Alternative for Girls and other local cuases. This labour-intensive project builds community, showcases Roeper talent, gives students a chance to organize and lead, informs our community about some problems (for example, students gave presentations and showed videos about the situation in Darfur) and most importantly, shows that we all don't have to be depressed or overwhelmed, but empowered. The Julies are energized and the Jacobs learn how to work the light and sound equipment and realize that working with others can be fun.

Don't Let the Adults Take Over

Students have to be given legitimate control over what they take on. I personally didn't think axolotl habitat was the most serious problem facing us but a young lady did and she convinced three other kids. She has developed a real interest in amphibians and has made friends with an upper school student who owns two axolotls.

We adults have to let the kids go down silly routes, make mistakes, and create unpolished events. Parents invariably get involved and on the day of the after-school lemonade sale, you have to watch for them manning the cash box as opposed to teaching the student how to make change. A little pre-event talk goes a long way to prevent "parent creep."

Sometimes administrators in the school prefer that everybody adopt the same project. It is true there is a certain efficiency when everybody is working together and it can build community. But with such large events, a few people, often adults, by necessity become the organizers; as a result, student choice and individual passion are frequently overlooked. But with a little caution and a lot of behind the scenes prep work, a fine balance can be achieved. We are presently planning a schoolwide event, which students are leading. The Stage IV homerooms voted to get involved with the Lighthouse Walk Against Hunger not only by getting pledges and walking themselves but also by mobilizing the Roeper community. They convinced the MS/US Student Government to be co-sponsors. They are making posters for both campuses. They are creating YouTube videos. They are researching hunger in Oakland County and how Lighthouse fights it. They are addressing Stage III, the MS and the US to encourage other walkers. They are writing newsletter articles about the event. Not all kids are marching and not all kids are working hard to get others involved. Also, I must admit that at times I do too much but I try not to forget that the role of adults is to strive constantly to empower the kids. I have to constantly remind myself to remember that these events are important not only to help a cause but also to open the students to new experiences and to show them they can have some say in what happens in the world.

Question

There wasn't much problem with taking a stance on Darfur (giving money to anti-genocide organizations) since Roeper was started with the goal of preventing future Holocausts. But what do you do when what the students want to do is "political?" Recently, one of the school's staff members told me we should have the Leadership and Roeper philosophy kids take on the fight for NPR funding and protest cuts. The 5th sign-up students will be looking for projects. Most people don't define service learning as involving political fights but I wonder why not.

If, after I mentioned the topic, some students wanted to research what is going on with Congress cutting funds to public radio and they wanted to start a petition or run an advertising campaign to drum up resistance to the cutting, would that be wrong? If the teacher was helping the students gather information from different sides and was not proselytizing then could we move into political disputes so the kids become advocates? Perhaps, in addition to or in lieu of advocacy they could be the ones sponsoring the discussion forums or arranging for the school newspaper to investigate.

"Getting political" is much more controversial than students setting up a system to take their pets to visit a retirement home on Saturday morning. Fear of captive kids being brainwashed and the huge amount of time and energy necessary to prevent "one-sidedness" makes me somewhat relieved we haven't moved much into political controversies, especially on the elementary school level. But...

Students need to go beyond the superficial. I'm glad that probably 100 or more Roeperians soon will take part in a Walk Against Hunger but shouldn't we be asking why there is so much hunger in our community to begin with? What role should the government play in preventing it? What is the moral obligation we have to feed the less fortunate? Perhaps problem-based learning can offer us ways for students to go deeper.

STUDENT-CENTRED, PROBLEM-BASED INQUIRY

There is another way to give students a heightened sense of control. What if we built into everything we taught some way that students were always looking for answers to their questions? What if before they read the chapter, they skimmed it and jotted down questions to answer by a more careful reading? What if each question answered led to another question? What if every experience was prefaced by brainstorming what we didn't know and debriefed by asking what we found out and what we now still had to investigate?

If schools really structured their curricula based on student questioning, we adults would have to give up some control of what students learned, at least with regard to content but maybe less so with skills and concepts. It would be a tremendous amount of work supporting and guiding students and would require master teachers who could never really relax from evaluating individuals and making decisions to jump in and jump out, help out and step back.

Obviously, students need direct instruction to acquire certain basic knowledge and skills. But think of how empowering and reassuring it would be if students knew they had some control over what they studied. What would happen if teachers rewarded good questions more than right answers? What if students constantly were asking, "What do I want to know; what do I have to know; and how am I going to find out?" In addition, what if learners had to share what they had learned? Having to teach something is a great way to master it. Teaching requires heavy amounts of preparation, use of the executive function of the brain, and advanced communication skills.

With students asking more questions and directing their own educations, the Julies would proceed at a pace they could handle, especially if we have taken steps to help them understand themselves. The Jacobs could delve into a topic very deeply but also would be able to share their work and gain recognition for their expertise. No more having to wait for a teacher to tell them what to learn; students could fly (actually fly, fall, walk, fly, stumble, fly, rest…)

Transferring These Ideas from Roeper to Other Environments

The three areas we are advocating, *a safe general environment, service-learning programs, and inquiry-based learning,* are tougher in public schools with larger classes, parents less tolerant of the ambiguity and messiness of student control, and the "Sword of Damocles" (AKA state testing), among other things. But even at Roeper we have parents and students anxious about college, overworked teachers and administrators looking for easier ways to teach and manage, and students reluctant at times to step up to take responsibility.

So there are challenges everywhere. Teachers, students, parents, and administrators in all schools have to look for windows of opportunity through which the emphasis can be changed from competition to cooperation, from grades to learning, from external motivation to intrinsic motivation, from accepting the world for what it is to changing it to what it should be, from being an object to being an actor, from superficial familiarity to deep understanding, from receiving information to questioning and devising research strategies; in short, moving toward being empowered to take over one's own education. The key is to focus on where we want to go while not getting discouraged by the realization that we have a long way to go. In essence, we always are guided by the question—how can we develop strong life-long learners who work towards bettering themselves so they can better the world?

DENITA BANKS-SIMS[1]

"THE MOST EXCITING MEETINGS"

An Interview with Annemarie Roeper and A. Harry Passow

Roeper School co-founder George Roeper once wrote, "The truly gifted person, it appears likely, is one who is capable of revising what is known, exploring the unknown, and constructing new forms. He will tend towards the novel and the speculative, in addition to having the ability to learn the known, the problems already solved, and the answers known to be acceptable."[2]

In 1993, I had the privilege of interviewing Annemarie Roeper and A. Harry Passow, who gave me a peek into the motivation and vision of those who so expertly "explore the unknown." Harry had been a collaborator of George and Annemarie's since 1956 when George asked him to help assemble and chair a panel of experts to write a new curriculum the school could use as it converted to a school for the gifted.

At the time, Harry Passow was one of the best-known figures in both urban education and gifted education. He began his pioneering work when he was named director of the Talented Youth Project in 1954. He was involved with two influential publications that emerged in 1955. One was a book called *Planning for Talented Youth: Considerations for Public Schools,* which described a framework for educated gifted students. The other was an article titled "Are We Short-Changing the Gifted?" that appeared in *School Executive* magazine. This article became one of the most talked-about and widely reprinted pieces of the era, particularly after October 1957, when the Russians launched the Sputnik satellite and Americans felt an urgency about educating their most gifted students, especially in science and mathematics.

George Roeper first became interested in gifted education in the 1950s through the articles of Benjamin Fine, the education editor of the New York Times. Through his research, George quickly became aware of A. Harry Passow at Teachers College, Columbia University, and his pioneering work in gifted education. Harry's prominence caught George's attention and he contacted him to ask for a meeting. They quickly realized they shared similar philosophies about a humanitarian pedagogy, and Harry agreed to chair the panel, which they called the Gifted Child Institute. Harry and his wife came to Michigan in June 1956 for a week that led to a lifelong friendship with the Roepers.

The opportunity to document a conversation and "peek at the motivation" came in 1993 when Harry joined Annemarie in a visit to The Roeper School. Almost forty years had passed since the Gifted Child Institute, and The Roeper School was now a leader in gifted education. A remarkable vision had been realized. At the time of his visit, Dr. Passow had retired two years earlier; George and Annemarie's house had burned to the ground in the Oakland Firestorm of 1991; and George Roeper had passed away the previous year. With these reminders of time passing, my journalism background—coupled with my interest as a Roeper parent—compelled me to conduct the following interview and capture the memories of those so crucial to the school's development. The admiration I have for George, Annemarie, and Harry is a present and constant motivator for ensuring that their individual and collective legacies thrive in the embodiment of The Roeper School.

A BRIEF HISTORY OF THE GIFTED CHILD INSTITUTE

George, Harry, and Annemarie shared the same dreams for education. They were all idealists who wanted to create schools that would fit the needs of children, rather than the other way around, and extend quality education to all children. Harry spent much of his career identifying and investigating ways to ameliorate the effects of poverty on children's ability to learn. He famously disagreed with Admiral Rickover in 1958 over the Admiral's plan to create 25 elite high schools to train young people who were especially talented in math and science, calling it a "perversion" of democracy: "It goes against the basic idea of American education, which is to give all children an equal opportunity for the best possible education."[3]

At George and Annemarie's school, Harry found many of the best qualities already in place. The school was multi-racial and multi-ethnic, at a time when most of the country was struggling to implement desegregation after the Supreme Court decided *Brown v. Board of Education* in 1954. The school already was focused on the whole child, with a rich arts program, a discovery-based curriculum, attention paid to healthy psychological development, emotionally engaged teachers, an open admission program that sought out children regardless of ability to pay, and a democratic atmosphere.

Harry agreed to help assemble and chair a group of educators and psychologists to create a program to convert City and Country School to a school for the gifted. He asked his colleague, Dr. Miriam Goldberg, a professor of psychology and education at Teachers College and his co-author in the writing of "Planning for Talented Youth" to join the group. He also called on Marie Spottswood, who had been Headmistress for many years of the Fieldston School in Manhattan, a Dewey-based progressive school. She had just left in 1954 to lead the Oakwood School in North Hollywood, at the time a new and struggling progressive school that had been founded by a group of left-leaning parents in the movie industry. She provided a great deal of specific input based on activities in a progressive classroom.

Other members of the group were Dr. Robert DeHaan, chairman of the psychology department at Hope College; Dr. Anton Brenner of the Research Staff of the Merrill-Palmer Institute in Detroit, known nationally for its research into child development and early childhood education; Dr. Marie Skodak, head of psychological services for the Dearborn Public Schools; and Dr. Elizabeth Drews, associate professor of education at Michigan State and a member of the MSU Gifted Child Committee. George and Annemarie were, of course, part of the panel, and some Roeper faculty attended some of the meetings. Invited but unable to attend because of prior commitments were Dr. Gertrude Hildreth of Brooklyn College, Dorothy Harris of the Cleveland public schools, and Dr. Margaret Neuber of Penn State University.

The group, which called itself the Gifted Child Institute, met in Hill House at City and Country School in Bloomfield Hills, Michigan for a week in June 1956. City and Country School at the time ran from nursery through 8th grade, although the upper grades were sparsely filled, with combined 5/6 and 7/8 classrooms. One of the key interests of the group was to design a program for the early elementary years because they were so critical to nurturing gifted children's love of learning and knowledge of self. Others who were interested in gifted children, such as Admiral Rickover, concentrated on the secondary grades, intensifying and accelerating academic programs for gifted youth. The Roepers, Passow, and the others believed that if you waited that long to identify gifted children, you would miss some students whose talents had withered away earlier, and you would have failed to help them develop a well-adjusted personality.

Another key interest was focusing on the meaning of the learning. In one discussion comparing the curriculum they were developing with the curriculum of the elite gymnasium schools of Europe, the report noted that,

> the difference lay in the fact that the gymnasium put the emphasis on the acquisition of facts and information *for its own sake*, while the School would put the emphasis on the acquisition of facts and information *as a means* for interpreting and understanding the present and predicting the future...Hence social values and service values should accompany the training in science. Experiences in other areas such as art and citizenship should keep the child always in touch with the realities of the complex world about him.[4]

The organizing, integrating aspects of the curriculum the group developed focused on two areas as they applied to gifted children: motivation (how to nurture a love of learning) and self-awareness, which meant that personality development would be a key component. In addition, instilling a sense of morality was imperative. "The development of the personality," the group concluded, "should also entail the growing desire of the child to develop his talents for their own sake (the need for self-understanding and self-fulfillment because of the talent he has) coupled with a sense of responsibility for the application of his talents for the benefit of society and the service of mankind."[5]

These organizing principles were summarized later as a curriculum that studies "people and their problems of living."[6] Students would study a wide range of cultures past and present in a holistic way – incorporating myths, culture, technology, aesthetics, and employing skills of writing, experimentation, critical thinking and physical manipulation – to acquire a broad understanding of how the world works and how to contribute to it. The group also called for special attention to helping gifted girls see themselves as making important contributions to society, in addition to those of motherhood and homemaking and family living.[7]

In September 1956, City and Country School became only the second elementary school in the country at the time to be exclusively devoted to gifted education, using the curriculum devised by the Institute. Students already in the school were allowed to stay as long as they wished. All the children were tested, however, and 60% had IQs of 130 or above (the level recommended by the Institute), which wasn't surprising given the school's attractiveness to well-educated, progressive parents in the area.

Although the group as a whole didn't reconvene to follow the progress of the school as it implemented its program for gifted children, the Roepers maintained close ties with several of the members, frequently drawing on their expertise, including Harry Passow. – Marcia Ruff, Roeper School Historian

THE INTERVIEW WITH ANNEMARIE ROEPER AND HARRY PASSOW ON 11/12/1993[9]

Denita Banks-Sims: This morning I am speaking with Dr. Harry Passow and Dr. Annemarie Roeper. We're going to discuss the advent of gifted education to start. As I was thinking about this—and feel free to discuss this among yourselves—I was wondering about your relationship, because that seemed to evolve, Harry, from the school changing over to gifted education. Is that true?

Harry Passow: Yes, sometime in the spring of 1956. I remember the date because my daughter, my youngest child, was two years old when we came out here. George Roeper had written me and asked if he could see me. I'm not sure where he had gotten my name, but he came into the office and we talked. He talked about the school, and he talked about his dream for the school, for it to become a school for gifted children. He asked if I could come out for a week and chair a group to convert the school to a school for gifted.

Denita: Was that like a task force?

Harry: I guess you could call it a task force. In those days we just called it a meeting. In June of 1956, I drove out here with my wife and three children and we stayed at a Pontiac motel called the St. Christopher. We had about 10 people meeting for a week. I was at Teacher's College at Columbia. I had started a talented youth program in 1954. One of my colleagues, Miriam Goldberg, came out, and I remember Bob DeHaan was at the meeting. I think Elizabeth Drews was at the meeting. And then there was somebody from the Merrill Palmer Institute. I can't remember his name, but he was German. He even had dueling scars! We met at the only building, which is, what do you call it?

Annemarie: Now we call it the Hill House, but at that time it was the Main Building.

Harry: We had just the most exciting meetings because this was sort of an opportunity to create and live your dreams—if, IF, the *Roepers* did it. (laughter) These were our ideas about giftedness. These were our ideas about the fact that it had to be multi-racial and multi-ethnic. We talked about how to identify kids. We talked very early about how to identify minority kids who are gifted and bring them in. We talked about the curriculum. The curriculum was essentially what George and Annemarie believed in. We just put a little patina on it.

Annemarie: Except we tried to do something that then later on we never actually carried out. It was really a wonderful dream that the first three years we could teach them (gifted children) all the skills. They'd learn how to read and write and whatever else came, and then after that, for the rest of the time we would offer everything else. We could really educate the children, all creativity.

Denita: Was there any research at that time or were you creating something at this point?

Harry: There had been research but not of this kind; there was relatively little empirical research.

Annemarie: There was a series of articles that had been written in the *New York Times*.

Harry: Yes, Ben Fine had written some articles.

Annemarie: And really, that's what really gave George the idea. That's what caught his attention. And that's when we felt that the school needed to be identified more. We had children from all sides, including some children who were almost retarded, because people wanted to send their children to a school with our philosophy. We did at the time also have many gifted children.

Denita: At what point did you think that this population was being underserved?

Annemarie: We noticed it mostly because of those articles that Ben Fine wrote in those days.

Denita: Is Ben Fine still around?

Harry: No, he died a long time ago. He eventually left the *New York Times* and opened up a school for the gifted called Sands Point.

Denita: What were the plans after your initial set of meetings? Did you establish a set of goals?

Harry: We established, if you will, a complete plan. What the school should try to achieve. How we would identify gifted students. What the curriculum might look like, what the special aspects of it might be like, even how it might be evaluated. I must confess that, after that week, in a sense we consultants said, here, George and Annemarie, here's the big idea, now you work out the detail. Because the school was essentially George and Annemarie implementing with their own ideas the actual conversion of the school and the development of the school and so forth.

Shortly thereafter I became a consultant to the Wayne Intermediate School District. I used to come out two or three times a year and often I would spend an evening with the Roepers or add a day and come out. It was mostly to sort of talk to George and Annemarie. They were doing the work; they were developing the school. And I could come out and occasionally speak to parent groups and so forth.

Annemarie: It seems to me that one of the points was that we wanted to stress areas that were not the usual curriculum. We were very concerned with art and music.

Harry: Right, they were talking about creativity before it became fashionable, before Torrance and others were.

Denita: What characteristics did you see in George and Annemarie that made you think it would be a good match?

Harry: I really didn't know when I first met George. He was a complete stranger. And then I came out. I remember driving up here on a Sunday afternoon, I think it was, because we drove out at that time, thinking it would be a good vacation, and meeting Annemarie for the first time. And then we began on Monday morning. What you felt was that these people, George and Annemarie, were not only listening, they were *hearing*. What's more, they were participating in the discussion as actively and more intelligently than us. Because they had been running a school for, what was it, about 10 years?

Annemarie: No, it was more than that. It was 1956 and we started the school in 1941, so 15 years.

Denita: Were there political overtones that you can recall? There were some obvious things that were happening in this country—the civil rights movement, and the Cold War...

Harry: It was right after Brown vs. Topeka in 1954. But even without Brown, George and Annemarie, their values were such that if we hadn't suggested it (integration), it wouldn't have made any difference, they would have done it. But they may have brought it up. (laughter)

Annemarie: Actually, the people that Harry assembled were all people that had some experience with gifted children, had done some research, were experts. The person that we finally spent a great deal of time with, and who participated in the school a lot, was Elizabeth Drews, because she was in Lansing at the time.

Harry: Very good, very insightful. She was a secondary-school person to begin with, but the study for which she is still remembered had to do with high-school gifted students in language arts and English.

Annemarie: She also did what I am still missing in the gifted movement: she combined it with value education.

Harry: Right, very much so.

Denita: Is she still living?

Harry: No, she died of a brain tumor many, many years ago. She was quite young. It was a real shame, a real loss.

Annemarie: I had a lot of very beautiful letters from her. She was really a good, a poetic writer. A very important person to the school. You continued to see her?

Harry: Oh, yes, I continued because the NEA academically gifted and talented project was started after Sputnik in 1958. Conant (Dr. James Conant, president of Harvard University) called a national conference that he chaired. Elizabeth attended that and I still remember her participating and giving a speech.

Denita: That was the government trying to respond to the Russians beating us?

Harry: That was a whole other story. Yeah, the government passed a National Defense Education Act, they tried to improve math and science and foreign languages. Eventually that spilled over into all subject areas.

Annemarie: But the stress was math and science, science education. It made the schools really responsible for Sputnik getting up there. And what I remember, and you might not remember it like that, is that because in those days the boys still had a different position than girls, gifted girls didn't really enter the picture.

Harry: That's right.

Denita: Annemarie, if you could do a composite of what you and George thought your students or your school would look like, on that spring day in 1956, what would it look like?

Annemarie: It is very hard for me to try to remember what I thought then, forgetting what I think now.

Harry: What you should do, Annemarie, is say what you think now and attribute it to what you thought then. (laughter)

Annemarie: In a way, what I think now *is* what I thought then.

Harry: She's been persistent! Persistent *and* consistent!

Annemarie: Persistent and consistent, yes! Namely, that we wanted, actually what we felt was that the gifted simply weren't being served. That was the main thing. And we always felt that what we wanted to do was serve those who needed help. Also, we just began to be very excited about these children who offered so much and who were so verbal and were educating us. But I think that from the very beginning we thought that the gifted have a big role to play in this world and that they might be the ones that maybe bring about change. In all of our thinking, we never did forget about our experience in Germany with the Nazis. That is still as vivid to me today as it was then.

Denita: It seems that there is such a formalized approach—I don't know if that's necessarily bad—to cultural diversity. But what you had intended in the beginning was simply to bring children…why don't you describe it? Because it seems now that Roeper, and not just Roeper but everyone, are wrestling with how to make an environment culturally diverse where you respect all the differences.

Annemarie: I don't know that we really knew how to do that very well, because we were still adapting to America. Something I always thought was that instead of trying to bring some of the things we had experienced, we were becoming Americans. Although I do think that the school has always had a European flavour. We couldn't help that.

Harry: That is true, I'm sure, and I think that's a positive aspect of it because many people in the '50s, after getting into *desegregation*, really had, I think, no idea what *integration* meant. So they thought if they got some kind of racial balance that was desegregation—which, in my view, is not integration. They (George and Annemarie) may not really have been conscious of that distinction because they were still adapting, but they were doing what they thought, in their value structure, was the right thing. They had lived through discrimination; they had lived through that kind of thing. They were, in a sense, doing it from the heart, when many of us were doing it from the head, and I think that's a big difference.

Annemarie: You know the actual integration happened later on, but what did happen in those days was that we actually still went through a period of segregation, of anti-Semitism, which actually was a great surprise to me because I never thought I'd find that here. But we were living in segregated areas. There was a certain area of Detroit where all the Jews lived. And out in the suburbs, Jews were not welcome. Just as later on it was that way with Afro-Americans. You had to go to a certain area and the different buses would pick up certain people.

Denita: Did you purchase your house in Franklin at this time?

Annemarie: No, we were outside Franklin. No Jews were in Franklin. It's a little bit better now.

Harry: How about buying the Hill House?

Annemarie: That wasn't a problem so far as I remember. But when we were negotiating the contract, Bloomfield Hills wanted to put in the contract that we would not take any black students.

Harry: That's what we called a gentleman's agreement.

Annemarie: We said that we knew that was not legally right and we refused to do that. But they wanted to put that right in the contract. That was really something.

Harry: Although I was not intimately connected with the implementation, I had opportunities to keep my friendship with George and Annemarie over the years.

Annemarie: What is it, 40 years now?

Harry: Yes, and it's a friendship that I treasure. And also it has been for me a real pleasure to be able to see something that you dreamed aloud —and they did it.

Annemarie: It's been very mutual. We couldn't have done it without Harry. We have had his support over all these years as he rose in the ranks. (laughter)

NOTES

1. Denita Banks-Sims carried out this interview at the Roeper School on November 12, 1993. She edited the original transcript to produce this chapter and co-authored the introduction to the chapter with Marcia Ruff.
2. Roeper, George A., Changing concepts of giftedness, delivered October 1962, p. 3. *George A. Roeper Papers, Record Group 2, Box 1, The Roeper School Archives*, Bloomfield Hills, MI.
3. Stout, David. "A. Harry Passow, 75, Dies; Studied gifted pupils." *The New York Times*, 29 Mar 1996.
4. "Summary of the proceedings of the gifted child institute, City and Country School of Bloomfield Hills, June 18–22, 1956," pp. 12–13. *The Roeper School Archives*, Bloomfield Hills, MI.
5. "Summary of the proceedings," p 8. *The Roeper School Archives*, Bloomfield Hills, MI.
6. "Summary of the proceedings," p. 16. *The Roeper School Archives*, Bloomfield Hills, MI.
7. "Summary of the proceedings," p. 21. *The Roeper School Archives*, Bloomfield Hills, MI.
8. Banks-Sims, D. "Interview with Annemarie Roeper and A. Harry Passow." *The Roeper School Archives*, Bloomfield Hills, MI.

REFERENCES

Passow, A. H. (1955, September). Are we short-changing the gifted? *The School Executive, 75,* 54–57.

Passow, A. H. (1955). *Planning for talented youth: Considerations for public schools, volume 1.* New York, NY: Teachers College.

DAVID YUN DAI

NURTURING THE GIFTED CHILD OR DEVELOPING TALENT? RESOLVING A PARADOX

[T]he yeast of education is the idea of excellence, and that comprises as many forms as there are individuals to develop a personal image of excellence. The school must have as one of its principal functions the nurturing of images of excellence.
—Jerome Bruner

Success often comes to those who are too busy to look for it.
—Henry David Thoreau

THE PROBLEM

I had the pleasure of visiting the Roeper School twice in the mid-2000s during my tenure as a member of the Advisory Board of the *Roeper Review*. Meeting with the faculty and students there was a refreshing experience to me, especially when I saw many interesting ways in which the school structures student learning, and teachers work with students. I still remember an interactive session Marci Delcourt and I organized with a group of students on academic motivation. We discussed a range of issues from interest development to persistence in the face of setbacks. I found the atmosphere of the school conducive to the free spirit of the students, ready to explore the world and self, and open to new possibilities.

In this chapter, I discuss an issue that has lingered in the field of gifted education for a while and has not been well addressed, an issue that the Roeper School also faces if it is to further improve its quality of services to students. What I refer to is a tension between two approaches to gifted education. One approach focuses on the "whole child": how the uniqueness of each child should be valued and how his or her educational and social-emotional needs can be met in the service of his or her optimal personal growth (e.g., Roeper, 2006; Silverman, 1993). The other approach focuses on talent development: what kinds of talent students demonstrate and how we go about identifying and developing these talents based on what we know about the trajectories of talent development and eminent accomplishments in adulthood (e.g., Subotnik, Olszewski-Kubilius, & Worrell, 2011; Subotnik & Rickoff, 2010). The Roeper School has shown much strength using the first approach. For example, a recent accreditation study based on a summary Don Ambrose created and distributed to all contributing authors at the beginning of this project, identifies the following strengths:

- Attention to the whole child; integration of the cognitive, social, emotional, motivational, and physical aspects of the student.
- Special attention to the social and emotional development of students.

Intrapersonal intelligence: learning one's own strengths, weaknesses, and motivations and then using that self-knowledge to guide one's own future development; students' individual interests as driving forces for motivation and learning.

The question is will this whole child education naturally lead to optimal talent development? There is no doubt that an intrapersonal focus on inner growth is a necessary condition for optimizing one's development for the benefits of society as well as the person involved. In this sense, the child-centred approach (e.g., Piechowski & Grant, 2001) is a viable approach to maximizing individual potential for living a productive and fulfilling life in an individual's own terms. In fact, my recent work on talent development (Dai, 2013; Dai & Speerschneider, 2012) treats talent development as a fundamentally fully personalized enterprise with a mission of finding one's own niche or destiny rather than conforming to certain external standards of success. In this regard, the Roeper School has been right in its educational philosophy. Is the child-centred or whole-child education approach sufficient to fulfill its goal when it comes to technical support and instructional guidance? Advocates for the talent development approach argued that it may not be sufficient (e.g., Coleman & Cross, 2005). The above-mentioned accreditation study, which identifies a need for improvement, provides evidence that a child-centred approach does not necessarily guarantee high motivation and self-initiative for talent development. For example, the report suggests that the School:

- find ways to balance faculty autonomy and student choice with the need for consistent academic excellence, and
- address some apathy that remains in the student body in spite of the school's student-centred philosophy and initiatives.

Taken together, there is a need to find a way in which the School can provide opportunities, structures, and support that ensure not only personal growth but also advanced talent and skill development in students' chosen areas (Dai & Coleman, 2005). In other words, how can we find a way to ensure that the pursuit of excellence in their chosen areas become part of students' intrinsic needs and that talent development becomes the right vehicle for their personal growth.

MY OWN JOURNEY

My research career started with a focus on motivation of gifted students (Dai, 2000; Dai, Moon, & Feldhusen, 1998). In these early years of my professional career, I fully embraced Gagné's (2005) Differentiated Model of Giftedness and Talent

(MDGT), and considered motivation as a critical catalyst for translating natural gifts to highly developed talents. While working as a post-doctoral fellow at the National Research Center on the Gifted and Talented at the University of Connecticut, I ran into an article published in *Gifted Child Quarterly* by Grant and Piechowski (1999), who expressed concerns that a talent development focus would lead to "measuring a child's worth in terms of his or her accomplishments, rather than on the basis of the child's inherent worth" (p. 8). They argued for a child-centred gifted education that honors and respects children's own developmental agendas. At the time, the idea that gifted education should not be based on a utilitarian model with an exclusive focus on the instrumental value of talent resonated with me, but I was wary of the idea that children can somehow discover their own "inner agendas" or hear their own calling without significant social mediation, including adult-structured activities and adult guidance. More pertinent to the topic of this chapter, I wondered whether the affect and motivation conducive to talent development itself is socially mediated. In a response to their article (Dai & Renzulli, 2000), Joe Renzulli and I suggested an alternative possibility or direction for gifted education: integrating personal growth and talent development.

But let me be clear about what I mean by talent development and personal growth. Talent development is a process involving prolonged formal and informal learning in one or multiple domains, with highly committed efforts, deliberate practice, and extended problem solving and self-improvement, resulting in a unique set of specialized knowledge, skills, and dispositions. Taken together, these efforts facilitate (a) performance in domains requiring execution of advanced skills and problem solving (e.g., piano virtuoso, neurosurgery, or computer troubleshooting), (b) production of new and useful ideas and products (e.g., composing a piece of music, invention of a robot, or development of a scientific theory), and (c) major contributions to a particular line of human endeavor (Ericsson, 2006; Subotnik & Rickoff, 2010; Tannenbaum, 1997; Weisberg, 2006). The talent development focus in gifted education has the ultimate goal of developing "gifted leaders—people who make a positive, meaningful, and enduring difference to the world" (Sternberg, Jarvin, & Grigorenko, 2010, p. 53). It is quite natural that achievement, success, even eminent accomplishments are highlighted in such an orientation.

Personal growth, at its basic level, involves a developmental process of individuation in terms of behavioral, emotional, and intellectual autonomy. At a higher level, it can also mean the development of ever refined understandings of the world and self, and the growth of interests, passions, values, commitments, and beliefs that transcend self-interests and ego-centrism (Dabrowski, 1964; Maslow, 1970), and potentially enhance the vitality of a society (e.g., constituting an important part of social and cultural capital; Renzulli, 2009). Personal growth is largely an affective agenda of education, treating personal meanings and aspirations as the basis for a good life.

It became clear to me in those early years that talent development entails personal growth, which is consistent with Grant and Piechowski's (1999; Pichowski & Grant,

2001) position. I also believe in *differential development* by which the child's own strengths, interests, and preferences are harnessed and organized to maximize their developmental potential and chances of success in adulthood. In our response to Grant and Piechowski (1999), we (Dai & Renzulli, 2000) quoted Annemarie Roeper's (1996) following remarks to reinforce this position: "Do we want the child to achieve and succeed according to our homogenized standards or do we educate for self-growth and their success within it?" (p. 19). Clearly, forces driving one toward the goal of excellence should come from within rather than from without. However, I differed and still do differ from Grant and Piechowski on one count. I believe that the relationship between talent development and personal growth is a two-way street: they reciprocate. Talent development, when properly facilitated and guided, enhances and promotes personal growth. In this regard, personal excellence reflected in socially recognized achievement and success can be an important part of personal growth. This position is supported by the research by Amabile and her colleagues (e.g., Hennessey, 1997), who modified their early position on intrinsic and extrinsic motivation (see Dai & Renzulli, 2000 for a discussion).

About the same time, I was getting interested in a more general issue: the nature of intellectual functioning and development. I espoused a conviction through my anecdotal observations that highly accomplished individuals are the most passionate about their own work, but not necessarily the smartest. An email exchange with Robert Sternberg concerning the lack of research attention to this matter eventually led to a major effort (an edited volume) aimed at integrating motivation, emotion, and cognition in understanding intellectual functioning and development (Dai & Sternberg, 2004). In this volume, a wide range of perspectives enriched our understanding of the nature of learning, thinking, and performance, for example, the distinction between maximal performance and typical intellectual engagement (Ackerman & Kanfer, 2004) the role of self-beliefs on attentional and cognitive processes (Dweck, Mangels, & Good, 2004), the dispositional aspect of good thinking (Perkins & Ritchhart, 2004). These more nuanced understandings of intellectual functioning in real life rather than contrived testing contexts made me rethink the nature of giftedness. When I looked back at the founding fathers of the field, they did not separate the intellect and affect as we often do. To quote Francis Galton (1869) from his famous *Hereditary Genius*:

> By natural ability, I mean those qualities of intellect and disposition, which urge and qualify a man to perform acts that lead to reputation. I do not mean capacity without zeal, nor zeal without capacity, nor even a combination of both of them, without an adequate power of doing a great deal of very laborious work. (p. 33)

In a comment on Gagné's (2005) DMGT theory, I started to question Gagné's definition of giftedness as some form of "pre-existing" ability to be realized by catalysts such as motivation, because there is an inherent value judgment in such a definition, built on the shaky assumption of test scores as indicating an invariant capacity. "I would venture to argue," I (Dai, 2004b) wrote, "that passion for knowledge and dogged persistence are essential qualities (not just catalysts), sometimes even more important than whatever *initial ability level* one brings to learning situations, if one is to be highly successful in academic fields" (p. 160, italics original). In retrospect, I might add that ability types and thresholds for particular domains may differ, and developmental processes by which gifted potential develops and manifests itself are more dynamic (see Dai & Renzulli, 2008); also, there are multiple ways leading to high talent achievement (Gottfried, Gottfried, & Guerin, 2006). A more contextual, functional, and developmental definition of giftedness serves us better than a static, ability-centric one (see Dai, 2010).

In more recent years, my focus has shifted to broader conceptual foundations of gifted education, including the nature-nurture debate (see Dai & Coleman, 2005). I continued the line of work I started in collaboration with Robert Sternberg, focused on developing an integrated approach to intellectual functioning and development that puts learning, thinking, and performance *in situ*, comprised of (a) the individual person as an agent who is capable of feeling, thinking, and acting in effecting changes (and experiences oneself as such); (b) a world of immediate or cognitively mediated (represented) objects, practices, tools, and systems, with distinct meanings and valences to the person; and (c) a community of learners who have their shared and unique dispositions and positional identities. This is a general framework, but nevertheless applicable to precocious and advanced development.

More specific to talent development, I proposed three key concepts crucial for understanding the processes of talent development: selective affinity, maximal grip, and staying at the edge of chaos, as three main facets of gifted and talent development in context (Dai, 2010; Dai & Renzulli, 2008). *Selective affinity* refers to the way individuals selectively attend to and choose certain aspects of their environments in cultivating their developmental niches or niche potential. *Maximal grip* refers to a process of striving for mastery of a practice or system that cognitively and affectively further propels individuals toward differential development (niches, trajectories, and pathways). *The edge of chaos* refers to critical points where individuals experience a psychological tension between the known and unknown, the old and new, or two systems of thought, and have to make decisions in dealing with opportunities, risks, and uncertainties engendered by such occasions. These central concepts represent an attempt to preserve the functional integrity, unique individuality, and the contextual dependency of human functioning while making generalizable claims about talent development. They integrate cognitive, emotional, and motivational processes at a particular juncture or moment of talent development, and help us design curriculum in a similarly integrated way to foster talent development.

It is important to note that these concepts are state or process constructs, not trait constructs; the latter are used by Gagné (2005) in his DMGT model. Trait models and state or process models have differing practical utilities: Trait models are good at classifying people and predicting long-range outcomes (e.g., using traits to predict long-term developmental outcomes in the longitudinal studies of mathematically and verbally precocious children; Lubinski & Benbow, 2006). In comparison, state or process models are good at micro-level descriptions and explanations, including elucidating conditions and proximal processes necessary for achieving a particular outcome, thus more useful for curricular and instructional planning and interventions. For example, after reviewing the literature, and particularly in light of the integration of affect and personal knowledge development, I proposed six principles for curriculum design for talent development: the principles of a) optimal challenge, b) deep intellectual engagement, (c) relevance, (d) continuity of curriculum experiences, (e) balancing breadth and depth, and (f) integrating cognitive and affective experiences (Dai, 2010, pp. 237–239). A curriculum that treats knowledge and skill development not as a technical matter of acquisition but as an intimate process of building personal and social connections (e.g., Folsom, 2006; Tomlinson et al., 2002) would enhance the personal relevance and meaningfulness of the curriculum, hence deep intellectual engagement and personal growth.

To put this discussion of talent development and personal growth in a larger international or global context, I was struck most recently, as probably many American parents were, by a Wall Street Journal article entitled "Why Chinese Mothers Are Superior" (Chua, 2011). The article clearly struck a nerve on the American psyche in view of the fact American students don't compare favorably in international comparisons, and a kind of parenting style we find egregiously authoritarian is claimed to produce wonder kids that excel in academics and arts (see Paul, 2011 for a balanced account). Although the notion of tough parenting with high expectations producing excellent kids is oversold in this article, the story of this "tiger mom" is revealing with respect to some important cultural differences regarding general child development with an emphasis on developing talent. The Western values of freedom and self-exploration to find one's true self or "inner agenda" is confronted with the Eastern values of self-discipline and self-perfection; the Western style of child-centred parenting and education that values children for their intrinsic worth is confronted with the Eastern style of adult-centred parenting and education that attempts to prepare the child for the tough, competitive world out there; and the development of whole child as a educational doctrine confronted with academic competition to "race to the top."

I am obviously biased in favor of the Western approach, despite the fact that I was born and raised in China. However, the notion that the Chinese culture assumes strength and the Western culture assumes fragility in children (see Paul, 2011) struck me as an important insight regarding cultural folk beliefs about the child and child development. Cultural differences aside, we should ask ourselves that, for the sake of both talent development and personal growth, do we need to push our students harder, sometimes out of their comfort zones in order for them to grow? My answer is yes. I feel the same way as Carol Dweck (2006) does that Americans are not doing well in this category. A related question is: Do we need to give our children or students sufficient space for self-explorations and development of personal interests and identities? My answer is a definitive yes. I believe Americans are doing better in this category than, for example, China. To me, it is a matter of balancing discipline and freedom in education, and knowing when we need discipline and when we need freedom.

RESOLVING THE PARADOX

If a talent development orientation is compatible with a personal growth orientation, then what does it mean for curriculum and instruction? There are two main implications. The first is that specialization at appropriate developmental conjunctures is needed as a way to foster deep engagement and help students gain deep experiences (Subotnik & Coleman, 1996). This is why Whitehead (1929) claimed that "in education wherever you exclude specialism you destroy life" (p. 10). Renzulli (2009) sees "romance with a topic or discipline" as a necessary condition for talent development, whereby children are expanding their personal horizons and developing life themes that are bigger than themselves. In this sense, a talent comprises not only a set of cognitive skills, but attitudes and values as well; developing a talent is to experience a way of social practice of thinking, talking and acting that carries distinct values and meanings (Gee, 2003). Only through deep engagement can one truly develop insights into a domain, and consequently a firm commitment to the values and visions of the world it embodies. Besides, there is also clear importance in timely special training in technical domains, such as mathematics and computer science, as it usually takes 10 years to develop high-level expertise in skill domains (Ericsson, 2006). Early specialization can enhance a person's chance of an early debut of a creative career (Simonton, 1999). Specialization in any pursuit does not mean that one cannot change interests and career aspirations once a commitment is made. Rather, specialization is intended to produce transformational experiences for the person, regardless of how these experiences will benefit one's future development. Some may hear one's calling from doing a major science project, others may find the experiences beneficial in broadening their intellectual horizons. Some individuals are more single-minded in their pursuits, and others are pursuing talent development on several fronts, changing gears when new opportunities emerge. Either way, it is likely to benefit both talent development and personal growth.

The second implication has to do with structured environments and the role of adults (teachers and parents) in talent development. The editors of a recent volume on "social-emotional curriculum" concluded that while children should be encouraged to develop self-direction and take personal initiatives in talent development, "without the critical and appropriate involvement of adults important in each child's life, there is ample reason to believe that development approaching optimum in *both* the cognitive and affective domains is unlikely" (Cross, VanTassel-Baska, & Olenchak, 2009, p. 365). From an affective point of view, talent development provides a context for development of affective and motivational characteristics deemed necessary for sustained talent development, in terms of taking a particular structured path to gaining expertise and demonstrating excellence by professional standards. Learning the hard part of a discipline can be challenging to even the brightest minds, and development of tenacity and persistence is part of personal growth that would not be developed "automatically" but can be nurtured through rigorous training in talent development. Thus, talent development demands character building along with skill development. To meet these challenges, teachers need to take a proactive role in nurturing students' coping skills and positive attitudes in the face of setbacks, rather than taking a laid-back attitude, accepting mediocrity in the name of protecting student autonomy or a sense of self-worth. Resilience is a virtue that can be nurtured through talent development for the sake of children's long-term development and happiness.

One major socializing role of adults (teachers and parents) is to help children better understand the world and themselves and negotiate a path to a productive and happy life. Personal excellence (to give one's best) should be the expectation we hold for our most promising students, while granting much flexibility and freedom for them to choose paths deemed promising and productive for them. Some might opt to do technology work, and others arts, and still others writing or helping the socially disadvantaged. Striving for excellence is an important way, if not the only way, to self-actualization (Maslow, 1970).

What if high standards of excellence are not valued and stressed? Will children spontaneously develop high standards for themselves? I strongly doubt it. For most educators, a gifted education program should be held accountable for whether it provides a challenging curriculum that is commensurate with the capabilities of a particular group of gifted learners, and whether it is effective in achieving its goals and standards. A problem with the argument that children should be allowed to set up their own standards is that children may not be in a position to tell whether they are exceeding or falling short of what is needed for advancing their talent to the next level. For example, a student aspiring to build intelligent robots in the future needs to be told what levels of mathematical and computer skills he or she needs to possess. Left to their own devices, children may fail to realize the importance of certain necessary steps needed to be taken to measure up to the challenge until it is too late. This is a cognitive reason, of course, why teachers need to take a proactive role. However, similarly important is the affective agenda of helping students realize the significance of a particular line of work in which they are engaged. For that matter, an important part of education is to figure out a way to kindle interests and motivations within the child through an affective curriculum that promotes high personal standards for excellence.

TOWARD AN AFFECTIVE CURRICULUM FOR TALENT DEVELOPMENT

My position is quite clear by now: I am advocating a gifted education that aims at talent development and excellence (i.e., the primacy of the domain excellence criterion in gifted education), but with a distinct personal touch; that is, the sources and impetuses should come from within the child, and we now know much about how to nurture and cultivate this affective part of talent potential along with the cognitive one to promote personal excellence.

Typically, a school has an explicit curriculum that emphasizes academic skills and knowledge. But rarely is there an explicit affective curriculum along with the academic one. If our understanding of the close connections between personal growth and talent development is correct, then the personal growth side should be more distinct and explicit in our curriculum, and how talent development engages the affective and motivational development needs to be better articulated. Following the commonly accepted practice, affective characteristics in the curricular context include any emotions, attitudes, values, desires, aspirations, and personal dispositions (e.g., resilience) that either move students forward or hold them back (e.g., negative affects or flat affect). In the following section, I (Dai, 2013; Dai & Speerschneider, 2012) delineate an affective Cope-and-Grow curriculum model that has implications for the scope and sequences of curricular and extracurricular activities, as well as pedagogical strategies aimed to promote personalized talent development.

Cope and Grow: A Model of Affective Curriculum

The Cope-and-Grow Model is based on a dual process theory of expanding one's personal agency and horizon (Grow) while dealing with stressful events and negative emotions (Cope) (Boekaerts, 1993; Dai, 2004a; Dweck, 1999). Coping and growing are flip sides of the same coin of responding to environmental opportunities and challenges, depending on how individuals construe their experiences (see Figure 1). To illustrate this point, an activity can be perceived by one person as opening a new horizon but perceived by another as too much to handle. Specifically, the Cope-and-Grow Model is based on the following three interrelated arguments:

Proposition 1. Human beings as active agents experience the world in terms of personal meanings and valences (e.g., opportunities and threats), and experience themselves as a form of personal agency capable of effecting changes (or for that matter as lacking in agency). This dynamic of personal meaning and effectiveness is the main source of positive and negative affects.

Corollary: An affective curriculum should be a cyclical process of action and reflection that promotes the human agency and the potential for growth (Grow) and supports coping efforts (Cope).

Proposition 2. The dual process of expanding oneself (open to the opportunity to expand one's personal agency and horizon) and preserving oneself (the need to maintain positive affect and self-worth, sometimes even at the cost of learning and growth) plays an important role in human development. Successful coping with stressful situations and negative affects can become a growth experience in terms of gaining personal strength.

Corollary: An affective curriculum should turn coping efforts into growing experiences (i.e., Cope to Grow) and expand coping resources by helping students cultivate inner strength (i.e., Grow to Cope).

Proposition 3. Highly able students have an advantage in expanding their personal horizons and building their personal visions and life ambitions (i.e., more inner resources to work with, more potential for Grow), but they also have to cope with issues related to their personal ambitions, such as high expectations, more performance pressure, and negative affects, such as alienation from others and discontent with the world and self-doubts and dissatisfaction with oneself (more issues to Cope with).

Corollary: The focus of an affective curriculum for talent development should be on cultivating personal strengths and promoting personal visions (Grow) as well as addressing their extra burdens of coping: (a) living up to one's high personal standards and goals, (b) ward off social pressure of varied sorts, and (c) dealing with the fundamental instability (negative affect) of inner life (Cope).

In short, an affective curriculum is meant to optimize personal dynamics for talent development through *enhanced growing experiences* and *supported coping experiences*. Thus, an affective curriculum is by nature growth-oriented, rather than deficit-oriented (cf. Peterson, 2009).

As illustrated in Figure 1, the enactive self (I-Self) is engendered through guided personal actions, such as guided self-explorations and interest development, through which a sense of agency will be gained, life themes will emerge, cross-validation of ideals and ambitions will take place, and a sense of purpose will be crystallized. Developmentally, the enactive self is initially more spontaneous (e.g., sustaining an interest for a prolonged period of time) and then becomes increasingly deliberate (e.g., executing and keeping track of a plan for a science or art project). In contrast, the reflective self (Me-Self) is enhanced through guided self-reflections, problem-based versus emotion-based coping with setbacks and negative emotions, and through the evolution of self-identity from simple self-perceptions to deeper self-understandings of feelings and emotions about the world and self.

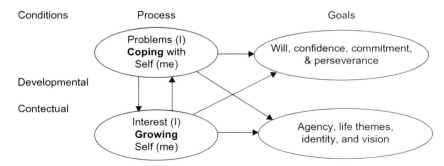

Figure 1. A schematic representation of the Cope-and-Grow Model.

Detailed description of the Cope-and-Grow Model can be found elsewhere (see Dai & Speerschneider, 2012). Regardless of what models one prefers, several developmental principles that guide the integration of talent development and personal growth should be observed.

Three Guideposts: Age, Domain, and Developmental Considerations

An affective curriculum should be commensurate with the cognitive and affective changes and transitions at particular points in development. Age-appropriate meaning-making and exposure to various areas of human activity is important as children of different ages perceive and feel about domain experiences differently. When to usher a child into a realm of meaning and valence is an important decision; building a rocket or cleaning a river may be highly meaningful to an 8 year old, but building a technique to move molecules around or creating artistic expressions that are meant to shock instead of pleasing our senses may not. Sometimes it is social, cognitive, and affective maturity, and sometimes it is not age per se, but constraints in experience and knowledge that go with particular ages.

There are domain considerations, namely, how to provide the kind of domain experiences that develop deep interests, personal meaning, and commitment. For example, social studies and language arts can afford personal appreciation of certain cultural values (e.g., empathy or social justice) more directly than, say, mathematics can. Motivationally speaking, arts are more expressive and can provide more immediate reward and gratification (i.e., positive affect) than sciences, which are more instrumental than expressive and entail epistemic motivation and intellectual curiosity (i.e., cognitive motivation). Thus, each domain has its own unique affordances in terms of affective rewards and motives. Domain considerations also include situations that pose challenges, constraints, and barriers. What if a child is interested in engineering but not interested in mathematics, or interested in becoming a public servant but dreads public presentation? How do we build the child's self-efficacy and interests to optimally develop the skill set necessarily for a particular line of talent development? These are questions that should be used to guide curriculum decisions.

Besides age and domain, there are developmental considerations that can be used to guide an affective curriculum: Talent development can be seen as negotiating one's pathway through *developmental corridors,* which are the structured spaces and paths open to individuals, through which students traverse and developmental trajectories are formed. This does not mean the paths of talent development are fixed; rather, it means that talent development is constrained by what is offered and supported in the environment over time. For example, the current curriculum structure at the Roeper School attempts to provide individualized developmental corridors within the constraints of faculty expertise. Developmentally, it is the range of learning experiences we provide to students at different junctures of development with their unique sets of sensitivities and sensibilities that eventually shape the way a person develops. The notion of developmental corridors fits Feldman's (1994,

2009) notion of universal and unique development: developmental corridors can be as wide as accommodate most people initially; however, as one moves toward one's unique niche in talent development, developmental trajectories become increasingly unique (i.e., increasingly differentiated interpersonally and intrapersonally).

When one traverses through a developmental corridor, milestone events will occur. *Developmental milestones* are significant or critical events that shape one's self-perceptions, interests, and commitments. For example, successfully overcoming internal and external barriers, successful completion of a major project, winning an achievement-related award or science competition, getting to know a mentor, can all become significant turning points in one's life. Connecting these proverbial footprints of traveling through developmental corridors, we will find longitudinal patterns and meaningful sequences of developmental events. The term *developmental trajectory* means that talent development follows a tractable pathway in an orderly fashion. For example, one cannot develop commitment without first developing interest/self-efficacy, and one cannot develop advanced skills without significant foundational knowledge, so on and so forth. Sometimes issues and conflicts in early development (e.g., self-doubts) can resurface at the later stage to disrupt higher-level development (e.g., relinquishing a commitment), very much like how Erikson (1968) characterized personal development: new properties at each stage build on developed components in the previous development but are also constrained by these components.

Delineation of an Affective Curriculum by Stage

The proposed Cope-and-Grow Model is based on extensive research on talent development (Bloom, 1985; Ciskzentmihalyi, Rathund, & Warren, 1993; Gottfried, Gottfried, & Guerin, 2006; Lubinski & Benbow, 2006; Subotnik & Coleman, 1996). Given that talent development goes through stages and transitions, the model specifies four stages, each having its own major opportunities and challenges.

In the following section, I delineate an affective curriculum of talent development. For pragmatic as well as developmental reasons, I discuss curriculum provisions in the context of stages of development, based on a multi-level theory of talent development I described in my book (Dai, 2010) as well as the Cope-and-Grow Model discussed earlier (Dai, 2013; Dai & Speerschneider, 2012).

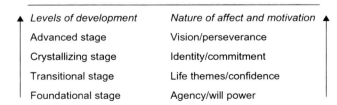

Figure 2. *Developmental stages and major psychosocial themes in affective development.*

The foundational stage. For the Foundational Stage, which roughly covers preschool and most part of elementary school years, during which children still develop their basic mental instruments (e.g., 4Rs: reading, writing, arithmetic, and reasoning), their behavioral patterns are still relatively spontaneous rather than deliberate, and they are still developing emotionally. During this stage, we emphasize the enactive aspect (I-self) of affective growth. Specifically, the focus for this stage is Agency and Will ("I can," "I will"). A sense of agency is promoted through a variety of meaningful activities (Grow), and children's willpower, is fostered by helping children cope with and overcome *internal barriers* such as fear and anxiety, instant gratification and lack of persistence (Kuhl, 1985; Mischel, Shoda, & Rodriguez, 1989), as well as *external barriers* such as peer pressure, lack of stimulation, and support (Reis, 2006).

A curriculum of talent development at this stage should encourage five forms of agency: expressive, technical-inventive, intellectual, social, and psychomotor. *Expressive agency* is expressed in activities involving writing, drawing, imaginative play; *technical-inventive agency* is expressed in activities involving making, building, modeling things; *intellectual agency* is expressed in activities involve reasoning, understanding, explaining, theorizing; *social agency* is expressed in activities involving communicating, negotiating, collaborating, and leading; and *psychomotor agency* is expressed through coordinating body movements to accomplish complex tasks. Cultivation of a variety of artistic, instrumental, intellectual, and social excitabilities and life themes through exploratory activities should be the mainstay of the curriculum. Children not only develop and demonstrate respective capacities (talents) through these activities; they also *experience* personal agency and positive affect through these activities, which is an important source of intrinsic motivation to expand the self. Specific "growth" activities to generate such experiences include the following:

- thematic units of personal and social relevance;
- mini-projects that engage personal agency and initiative;
- a variety of enrichment activities to induce "romance with a topic";
- a range of books to expand the intellectual horizon; and
- group or enrichment cluster activities to cross-validate their experiences.

Through the "growth" experiences, "habits of mind" can be nurtured in formative years, such as intellectual playfulness, intellectual risk taking, tolerance and high thresholds for frustration, coping with anxiety and fear of failure, and reflection. In the Cope-to-Grow model, gifted children particularly need challenges and experiences of setbacks to develop coping skills and will power (e.g., normalization of "failures;" developing an incremental mindset; Dweck, 2006). When the sources of obstacles are mainly external, how to instigate aspirations and a sense of personal agency through empowering experiences becomes essential (Olenchak, 2009).

The transitional stage. (Roughly starting in middle school and continuing in high school years). Compared to the Foundational Stage, the Transitional Stage features more formal learning of disciplinary knowledge and more systematic development of academic skills, such as critical reading and scientific methods. Developmentally, children are making an important transition from other-direction to self-direction, with increasing autonomy and responsibility. The period is marked by the onset of puberty, heightened reflectivity, the increased ability for self-direction, and affective vulnerability. Stable peer groups start to form in school and neighbourhood, and popular media become a distinct competing attraction; through social comparison and group identification, self-categorization takes place, leading to distinct patterns of self-efficacy appraisals, self-concepts, interests, and value orientations (i.e., a more differentiated sense of self). Interests and self-efficacy appraisals take on a new level of reflective consciousness in the face of increasing intellectual challenges. Gender differences and gender roles emerge as a significant force differentiating girls and boys' interests and preferences (Dai, 2002).

Educators designing an affective curriculum at this stage should seriously consider early teens' emergent strengths as well as their uncertainties about themselves and vulnerabilities, and design activities accordingly. The priorities of an affective curriculum of affect at this stage include building high self-efficacy or agency beliefs, coping skills, and resilience, coupled with opportunities for developing more differentiated and deeper expressive, technical-inventive, intellectual, social, and psychomotor interests or enduring life themes. It is important to offer enrichment and extracurricular activities to encourage self-initiative (Larson, 2000) and opportunities and support for developing personal interests (Barron, 2006). Social-emotional issues such as achievement-affiliation conflicts, perfectionism, and the big-fish-little-pond-effect can occur as students are coping with the new academic and social challenges. Guidance and counseling for promoting self-awareness and self-understanding and developing coping skills may also supplement these efforts. Curricular and extracurricular activities can include:

- activities that encourage risk taking and endeavors that are out of one's comfort zone;
- projects that expose students to frontiers of knowledge and technology;
- field trips that expose students to new horizons and possibilities;
- reading of biographies that provide role models for aspiring students;
- focus groups on sharing affective experiences and forming support groups; and
- training coping skills and developing resilience.

Both integrated approaches and independent sessions can be organized, and school counselors can collaborate with classroom teachers or gifted specialists in developing a coherent plan. For more detailed recommendations, see Hébert (2009), Kitano (2003), Moon (2009), and Peterson (2009).

The crystallizing stage. (high school and onward). For most gifted and talented students, this is a period of development of advanced knowledge and skills. It should be a period marked by a heightened sense of personal meanings of knowledge pursuits, commitment, and identity, leading to a clear sense of self and future (Dai, 2010). If early stages are characterized by more or less spontaneous, self-organized patterns of "characteristic adaptation" to the curriculum offerings, this stage shows more deliberate self-direction; typically, commitment is deliberately made to pursue advanced knowledge and skills that most peers would not have (e.g., challenging electives, Advanced Placement classes). Self-motivation is apparent, often sustained by participation in a scholarly or expert community, and can be both expressive (playful enjoyment) and instrumental (driven by skill improvement). Internal barriers such as the big-fish-little-pond-effect, perfectionism, and self-doubts still can occur, particularly when highly challenging materials are introduced and peer groups are also highly competent (Dai & Rinn, 2008). However, personal meaningfulness of a particular pursuit is of more concern. Providing opportunities for advanced level projects, mentorship experiences with experts, and encouragement of personal initiatives and leadership should be on the affective agenda. Curricular activities for this stage can include:

- taking challenging AP classes and honor-level classes;
- independent or team projects that deal with authentic problems and have a real impact;
- mentorship experiences with experts in a one's chosen field;
- participation in summer residential and networking with kindred spirits through local organizations and Internet; and
- career counseling programs to facilitate crystallizing experiences and career planning.

Although many occasions can generate "crystallizing experiences" (Walters & Gardner, 1986, p. 307), this stage is the most important for developing a clear sense of direction and purpose, or a personal niche (Dai & Renzulli, 2008; Olenchak, 2009). Commitment and identity formation mark the important milestone events. Characteristically, a personal vision of one's future will not fully develop until one has done significant amounts of advanced work in a domain, as in the case of finalists of the Intel Talent Search Program.

The advanced development stage. (college and onward). By advanced stage, we mean students having already made their choice on a particular career path, and invested their energy and time in a professional endeavor (e.g., starting a company, or pursuing a college degree and beyond). Although there are exceptions, typically students will not enter this stage until college, even graduate studies. Concerns in this stage are about successful completion of advanced training and the ability to make creative contributions to a domain in which individuals chose to work. The goal of affective curriculum in this stage goes beyond identity and commitment: it is to develop a personal vision of how one can make professional contributions in a domain (Shavinina, 2009) and to develop effective ways to cope with setbacks and failures, frustrations and self-doubts (i.e., building perseverance).

Mode of Delivery and Pedogocial Strategies

As can be seen, an affective curriculum for talent development/personal growth does not need to be a separate one but can be integrated into curricular activities meant to develop capacities or talents. Moon (2009) distinguishes between direct and indirect forms of an affective curriculum, direct instruction of affective knowledge and skills, and indirect methods of creating climates and conditions for optimal affective experiences and motivations. The best way to carry out an affective curriculum, in my opinion, is through various non-didactic, "non-intrusive" methods, such as mutual validation of the importance of the curriculum, sharing affective concerns among peers, modeling by the teacher or peers, and biographic methods. The Cope-and-Grow Model specifies two modes of curriculum: *enactive* and *reflective*; the former is experiential and the latter uses personal experiences as an object for reflection or "processing" (Peterson, 2009). Both are non-didactic, using strategies to induce affect, meta-affect, and self-understandings rather than teaching students what they should do and how they should feel (see Moon, 2009 for a distinction between indirect and direct teaching). We specify three main tools and resources to support the curriculum delivery: (a) Engage students in structured activities for *experiential* gains, (b) organize *social* group activities for cross-validation and perspective taking, and (c) use *media* (books, videos, Internet sources) to help build a broad vision of the world and life. A counseling component is warranted whenever there is a need for addressing specific problems, including internal and external barriers for talent development and personal growth.

CONCLUSION

The Roeper School has been a pioneer for the kind of formal schooling that is tailored to individual students' developmental needs rather than ignoring these needs for the sake of administrative convenience. I submit that the School also can be an even more promising venue for integrating talent development and personal growth, wherein both diversity and excellence are promoted and honored. It already does this admirably but it's also known as an institution striving for continuous improvement; consequently, it will not shy away from opportunities for refinement. I envisage a curriculum structure that provides "developmental corridors" wide and flexible enough to allow students to excel and succeed in their own ways and rigorous and challenging enough to ensure that its graduates will rise to the challenges ahead of them after they leave the school. Building capacities, developing passions, and nurturing good habits of mind are all important and should be parallel goals of education aimed at producing leaders in various areas of human endeavor, leaders who are not only well equipped with high talent, but also determined to make a positive difference to the world. For that matter, an affective curriculum seems imperative.

REFERENCES

Ackerman, P. L., & Kanfer, R. (2004). Cognitive, affective, and conative aspects of adult intellect within a typical and maximal performance framework. In D. Y. Dai & R. J. Sternberg (Eds.), *Motivation, emotion, and cognition: Integrative perspectives on intellectual functioning and development* (pp. 119–141). Mahwah, NJ: Lawrence Erlbaum.

Barron, B. (2006). Interest and self-sustained learning as catalysts of development: A learning ecology perspective. *Human Development, 49*, 193–224.

Bloom, B. S. (1985). *Developing talent in young people.* New York, NY: Ballantine Books.

Boekaerts, M. (1993). Being concerned with well-being and with learning. *Educational Psychologist, 28*, 149–167.

Bruner, J. (1979). *On knowing: Essays for the left hand.* Cambridge, MA: Belknap Press of Harvard University Press.

Chua, A. (2011). Why Chinese mothers are superior. *Wall Street Journal*, Jan. 9.

Coleman, L. J., & Cross, T. L. (2005). *Being gifted in school: An introduction to development, guidance, and teaching.* Waco, TX: Prufrock Press.

Cross, T. L., VanTassel-Baska, J., & Olenchak, F. R. (2009). Creating gifted lives: Concluding thoughts. In J. VanTassel-Baska, T. L. Cross & F. R. Olenchak (Eds.), *Social-emotional curriculum with gifted and talented students* (pp. 361–372). Waco, TX: Prufrock Press.

Csikszentmihalyi, M., Rathunde, K., & Whalen, S. (1993). *Talented teenager.* New York, NY: Cambridge University Press.

Dabrowski, K. (1964). *Positive disintegration.* Boston, MA: Little, Brown.

Dai, D. Y. (2000). To be or not be (challenged), that is the question: Task and ego orientations among high-ability, high-achieving adolescents. *Journal of Experimental Education, 68*, 311–330.

Dai, D. Y. (2002). The self in cultural context: Meaning and valence In D. McInerney & S. Van Etten (Eds.), *Research on sociocultural influences on motivation and learning* (Vol. 2, pp. 3–21). Greenwish, CT: Information Age Press.

Dai, D. Y. (2004a). Putting it all together: Some concluding thoughts. In D. Y. Dai & R. J. Sternberg (Eds.), *Motivation, emotion, and cognition: Integrative perspectives on intellectual functioning and development* (pp. 419–431). Mahwah, NJ: Lawrence Erlbaum.

Dai, D. Y. (2004b). Why the transformation metaphor doesn't work well: A comment on Gagne's DMGT model. *High Ability Studies, 15*, 157–159.

Dai, D. Y. (2010). *The nature and nurture of giftedness: A new framework for understanding gifted education.* New York, NY: Teachers College Press.

Dai, D. Y. (2013). Naturalizing and contextualizing self: Self-in-action and self-in-reflection in differential development. In D. M. McInerney, H. W. Marsh., R. G. Craven, & F. Guay (Eds.), Theory driving research: New wave perspectives on self-processes and human development (pp. 183–204). Charlotte, NC: Information Age.

Dai, D. Y., & Coleman, L. J. (2005). Introduction to the special issue on nature, nurture, and development of exceptional competence. *Journal for the Education of the Gifted, 28*, 254–269.

Dai, D. Y., Moon, S. M., & Feldhusen, J. F. (1998). Achievement motivation and gifted students: A social cognitive perspective. *Educational Psychologist, 33*, 45–63.

Dai, D. Y., & Renzulli, J. S. (2000). Dissociation and integration of talent development and personal growth: Comments and suggestions. *Gifted Child Quarterly, 44*, 247–251.

Dai, D. Y., & Renzulli, R. S. (2008). Snowflakes, living systems, and the mystery of giftedness. *Gifted Child Quarterly, 52*, 114–130.

Dai, D. Y., & Rinn, A. N. (2008). The Big-fish-little-pond effect: What do we know and where do we go from here? *Educational Psychology Review, 20*, 283–317.

Dai, D. Y., & Speerschneider, K. (2012). Cope and grow: An affective curriculum for talent development. *Talent Development and Excellence, 4*, 181–199.

Dai, D. Y., & Sternberg, R. J. (Eds.) (2004). *Motivation, emotion, and cognition: integrative perspectives on intellectual functioning and development.* Mahwah, NJ: Lawrence Erlbaum.

Dweck, C. S. (1999). *Self theories: Their role in motivation, personality, and development.* Philadelphia, PA: Psychology Press.

Dweck, C. S. (2006). *Mindset: The new psychology of success*. New York, NY: Random House.
Dweck, C. S., Mangels, J. A., & Good, C. (2004). Motivational effects on attention, cognition, and performance. In D. Y. Dai & R. J. Sternberg (Eds.), *Motivation, emotion, and cognition: Integrative perspectives on intellectual functioning and development* (pp. 41–55). Mahwah, NJ: Lawrence Erlbaum.
Ericsson, K. A. (2006). The influence of experience and deliberate practice on the development of superior expert performance. In K. A. Ericsson, N. Charness, P. J. Feltovich & R. R. Hoffman (Eds.), *The Cambridge handbook of expertise and expert performance* (pp. 683–703). New York, NY: Cambridge University Press.
Erikson, E. H. (1968). *Identity: Youth and crisis*. New York, NY: Norton.
Feldman, D. H. (1994). *Beyond universals in cognitive development* (2nd ed.). Norwood, NJ: Ablex.
Feldman, D. H. (2009, August). Giftedness and development: What kind of theory? Paper presented at the annual meeting of *American Psychological Association*, Toronto, Canada.
Folsom, C. (2006). Making conceptual connections between gifted and general education: Teaching for intellectual and emotional learning (TIEL). *Roeper Review, 28*, 79–87.
Gagné, F. (2005a). From gifts to talents: The DMGT as a developmental model. In R. J. Sternberg & J. E. Davidson (Eds.), *Conceptions of giftedness* (2nd ed., pp. 98–119). Cambridge, England: Cambridge University Press.
Galton, F. (1869). *Hereditary genius: An inquiry into its laws and consequences*. London, England: Macmillan.
Gee, J. P. (2003). Opportunity to learn: A language-based perspective on assessment. *Assessment in Education, 10*, 27–46.
Gottfried, A. W., Gottfried, A. E., & Guerin, D. W. (2006). The Fullerton Longitudinal Study: A long-term investigation of intellectual and motivational giftedness. *Journal for the Education of the Gifted, 29*, 430–450.
Grant, B. A., & Piechowski, M. M. (1999). Theories and the good: Toward child-centred gifted education. *Gifted Child Quarterly, 43*, 4–12.
Hébert, T. P. (2009). Guiding gifted teenagers to self-understanding through biography. In J. VanTassel-Baska, T. L. Cross & F. R. Olenchak (Eds.), *Social-emotional curriculum with gifted and talented students* (pp. 259–287). Waco, TX: Prufrock Press.
Hennessey, B. A. (1997). Teaching for creative development: A social-psychological approach. In N. Colangelo & G. A. Davis (Eds.), *Handbook of gifted education* (2nd ed., pp. 282–291). Boston, MA: Allyn and Bacon.
Kitano, M. K. (2003). What's missing in gifted education reform. In J. H. Borland (Ed.), *Rethinking gifted education* (pp. 159–170). New York, NY: Teachers College, Columbia University.
Kuhl, J. (1985). Volitional mediators of cognition-behavior consistency: Self-regulatory processes and action versus state orientation. In J. Kuhl & J. Beckmann (Eds.), *Action control: From cognition to behavior* (pp. 101–128). Berlin, Germany: Springer.
Larson, R. W. (2000). Toward a psychology of positive youth devepment. *American Psychologist, 55*, 170–183.
Lubinski, D., & Benbow, C. P. (1992). Gender differences in abilities and preferences among the gifted: Implications for the math-science pipeline. *Current Directions in Psychological Science, 1*, 61–66.
Lubinski, D., & Benbow, C. P. (2006). Study of mathematically precious youth after 35 years. *Perspectives on Psychological Science, 1*, 316–345.
Maslow, A. H. (1970). *Motivation and personality*. New York, NY: Harper & Row.
Mischel, W., Shoda, Y., & Rodriguez, M. I. (1989). Delay of gratification in children. *Science, 244*, 933–938.
Moon, S. M. (2009). Theories to guide affective curriculum development. In J. VanTassel-Baska, T. L. Cross & F. R. Olenchak (Eds.), *Social-emotional curriculum with gifted and talented students* (pp. 11–39). Waco, TX: Prufrock Press.
Olenchak, F. R. (2009). Creating a life: Orchestrating a symphony of self, a work always in progress. In J. VanTassel-Baska, T. L. Cross & F. R. Olenchak (Eds.), *Social-emotional curriculum with gifted and talented students* (pp. 41–77). Waco, TX: Prufrock Press.

NURTURING THE GIFTED CHILD OR DEVELOPING TALENT? RESOLVING A PARADOX

Paul, A. M. (2011). The roar of the tiger mom. *Time*, Jan. 20.

Perkins, D., & Ritchhart, R. (2004). When is good thinking. In D. Y. Dai & R. J. Sternberg (Eds.), *Motivation, emotion, and cognition: Integrative perspectives on intellectual functioning and development* (pp. 351–384). Mahwah, NJ: Lawrence Erlbaum.

Peterson, J. S. (2009). Focusing on where they are: A clinical perspective. In J. VanTassel-Baska, T. L. Cross & F. R. Olenchak (Eds.), *Social-emotional curriculum with gifted and talented students* (pp. 193–226). Waco, TX: Prufrock Press.

Piechowski, M. M., & Grant, B. A. (2001, November). Talent development versus personal growth. Paper presented in the annual convention of the *National Association for Gifted Children*. Cincinnati, Ohio.

Reis, S. M. (2006). Talent development in women who achieve eminence. *Korean Journal of Educational Policy, 3*(2), 29–54.

Renzulli, J. S. (2009). Operation houndstooth: A positive perspective on developing social intelligence. In J. VanTassel-Baska, T. L. Cross & F. R. Olenchak (Eds.), *Social-emotional curriculum with gifted and talented students* (pp. 79–112). Waco, TX: Prufrock Press.

Roeper, A. (1996). A personal statement of philosophy of George and Annemarie Roeper. *Roeper Review, 19*, 18–19.

Roeper, A. (2006). *The "I" of the beholder: A guide to an essence of a child*. Scottsdale, AZ: Great Potential Press.

Shavinina, L. (2009). A unique type of representation is the essence of giftedness: Toward a cognitive-developmental theory. In L. Shavinina (Ed.), *International handbook on giftedness* (pp. 231–257). New York, NY: Springer.

Silverman, L. K. (1993). *Counseling the gifted and talented*. Denver, CO: Love.

Simonton, D. K. (1999). Talent and its development: An emergenic and epigenetic model. *Psychological Review, 3*, 435–457.

Sternberg, R. J., Jarvin, L., & Grigorenko, E. L. (2011). *Explorations in giftedness*. New York, NY: Cambridge University Press.

Subotnik, R. F., & Coleman, L. J. (1996). Establishing the foundations for a talent development school: Applying principles to creating an ideal. *Journal for the Education of the Gifted, 20*, 175–189.

Subotnik, R. F., Olszewski-Kubilius, P., & Worrell, F. C. (2011). Rethinking giftedness and gifted education: A proposed direction forward based on psychological science. *Psychological Science in the Public Interest, 12*, 3–54.

Subotnik, R. F., & Rickoff, R. (2010). Should eminence based on outstanding innovation be the goal of gifted education and talent development? Implications for policy and research. *Learning and Individual Differences, 20*, 358–364.

Tannenbaum, A. J. (1997). The meaning and making of giftedness. In N. Colangelo & G. A. Davis (Eds.), *Handbook of gifted education* (2 ed., pp. 27–42). Boston, MA: Allyn & Bacon.

Tomlinson, C. A., Kaplan, S. N., Renzulli, R. S., Purcell, J. P., Leppien, J., & Burns, D. (2002). *The parallel curriculum: A design to develop high potential and challenge high-ability learners*. Thousand Oaks, CA: Corwin Press.

Walters, J., & Gardner, H. (1986). The crystallizing experience: Discovering an intellectual gift. In R. J. Sternberg & J. E. Davidson (Eds.), *Conceptions of giftedness* (pp. 306–331). Cambridge, England: Cambridge University Press.

Weisberg, R. W. (2006). Modes of expertise in creative thinking: Evidence from case studies. In K. A. Ericsson, N. Charness, P. J. Feltovich & R. R. Hoffman (Eds.), *The Cambridge handbook of expertise and expert performance* (pp. 761–787). New York: Cambridge University Press.

Whitehead, A. N. (1929). *The aims of education*. New York, NY: The Free Press.

SUSANNAH NICHOLS

IN THEIR OWN WORDS

Students Reflect on the Roeper Difference

Just what is it that makes Roeper different? That, for me, is a fairly easy question to answer: I am a human being here.
—Connor G., Jr.

In examining any educational program, the core indicator of success is the effect on the student. The Roeper School prides itself on its philosophy and its willingness to diverge from the expected shape of a traditional education. The 2010 Philosophy Statement promises a "safe, rigorous, and joyful learning environment" and an understanding that "each person, child and adult [is] a whole human being, worthy of respect and recognition, deserving every opportunity to fulfill his or her potential."

But does it work? And how are these ideas manifested in the day-to-day life at the school? When several teachers asked Upper School students to reflect on what the "Roeper Difference" is—what they have gained by being at Roeper that might not have been possible elsewhere—the answers continually circled back to four intertwined threads: relationships, opportunities, trust, and freedom. These qualities build a place where students have the courage and confidence to advocate for themselves and the camaraderie of peers and adults who share their love for learning.

There is a respect and trust among students, often built on both a mutual excitement for knowledge and deep sense of compassion for others. When students see their peers succeed, the instinct is for celebration rather than competition. When someone new arrives, the instinct is to include. Jessica F., a sophomore, remembers the first time she attended High Performance basketball camp—her first Roeper-related event. "I didn't know anyone there, and an older student walked up to me and told me all the coaches' names and where to go. You can't find that in many places. Trust me, I know." Joanne O., a sophomore, sees this same respect and welcome each day: "The Roeper Difference is going to school with people who are very different, but at the same time just like you in terms of wanting to succeed and become someone important in the world. The Roeper Difference is the welcoming 'good morning' and warm smile on those dreary mornings when the last place you want to be is at school."

"The students at Roeper are some of the nicest people I have met," shares Jake F., a freshman. He goes on to say,

> They are kind people who are always happy to interact with people across grades, and that can be helpful when new to the school or entering the Middle/Upper school campus. (Students in grades 6–12 attend classes in the same building.) In fact, a sixth-grader can ask a senior for help finding a class, and not only will he or she tell them where to go, but sometimes the senior will even lead the sixth-grader to the class.

The reflections of the current students echo the sentiments expressed by George Roeper in a letter he wrote welcoming new students to the 1970–71 school year:

> Here are a few things I would like you to know even before you come, but you will get to know them better the longer you are with us. We all know that everybody is good at something and everybody is not so good at something else. We don't look down on the other fellow if he is not as good at spelling because we know he is very good in science. We don't think that the one who is good in arithmetic is a better person than the others, just because of that. This is the way we look at each other as friends. If somebody is your friend, he stays your friend even though he might not throw the baseball as far as you or even though he might jump higher than you do.

Such compassion can be written off easily as nonessential in a world where achievement and advancement are most highly prioritized, but the importance of this unflinching kindness should not be trivialized: it provides the emotional safety people need to grow into the best versions of themselves. Ethan R., a sophomore, articulates the way his time at Roeper has shaped him:

> I don't want to overstate it, and I don't think this is, but Roeper changed my life. Prior to coming to Roeper, I was a loner, and I reveled in that. But there was always that nagging feeling that I wanted to be accepted and have an opportunity to express myself to people who really understood where I was coming from. I had lots of unaccessed potential, and still do, and the reason I've been able to and will be able to access it is because of the support, and even the love, of everyone in the community of Roeper. I feel like I belong now, like I have a purpose, and Roeper helped me realize that. Something that is only offered at Roeper is a true sense of community and belonging, and to be able to be a part of that showed me that yes, I do leave a mark on this earth, and with help from Roeper, I know it'll be a good one.

Maha H., a freshman, considers that she might have grown into a different person without the support of the Roeper community:

> I came to Roeper in 6th grade as a very shy girl. When I first arrived, I was in a class called Forensics, where you perform a piece. . . . I used to be terrified

to talk to new people or present to talk to new people or present to a class. Roeper has made it comfortable for me to give speeches or perform in front of the school. Without Roeper, I would now be a shy high-schooler afraid to speak to people. I am glad that I can act and dance in front of crowds without worrying about anything.

Liam G., a junior, shares a story about how the structure of Roeper is instrumental in the way that people at the school interact and treat one another:

As a sophomore in high school, I befriended a middle-schooler who impacted my life very deeply. Though we did not have a lot in common on the surface, we discovered that we shared many of the same struggles and experiences. We learned to see the world through each others' eyes and both grew as people in unexpected ways. This friendship would not have been possible without Roeper.

Most schools, public or private, are hierarchical institutions. Administrators sit at the top of the pyramid and run roughshod over the will of the teachers and students. Rules are put into place with no input from those who have to follow them. From where they sit in class to what types of classes are required to whether or not chewing gum is permitted, every aspect of a student's life at school is controlled. Replacing child labour in the factories of the industrial era, many schools operate as 'job training factories' with no regard for the inherent rights of all who study and teach there. Mirroring their superiors, students create their own complex social orders based on exclusion and prejudice.

Codified in Roeper's philosophy is equality in relations between all members of our community—students, teachers, and administrators. The result is that the barriers created by arbitrary formalities or fear of punitive action are removed, and unanticipated bonds flourish. This is not just limited to the mutual respect between teachers and students that create incentive for students to take an active role in the classroom—it extends to how students treat each other. Most students at Roeper are eager to welcome someone new. They treasure diversity and abhor discrimination. While these generalizations certainly do not apply to everyone in the Roeper community, they are the values held by the majority.

Only in this environment could my unconventional friendship be realized. I was able to reach out to someone in spite of an age division because I had been taught inclusion. Empowered through advocating for myself in front of teachers and administrators in the past, I knew I had the strength to stand up to ridicule.

A key component of developing both a strong sense of self and supportive relationships is trust—among students and between students and faculty. "The teachers here at Roeper put trust in me and my classmates to hand in homework, do classwork, say what we feel," shares Ben K., a freshman. "Also, another factor of this trust is the fact that Roeper tries not to pressure you. They know that you'll do the right thing for you."

While freedom always comes with the danger of abuse, most Roeper students responsibly use their liberties—free blocks, off-campus privileges, and lack of constant supervision. Adam S., a junior, explains ways that Roeper students use these freedoms for good: "the trust that is bestowed upon us is an excellent thing that would be frowned upon at other schools, like allowing the jazz trio I play in to practice after school in a room without a teacher."

The relationships between community members don't just make life more pleasant; they also create better learning environments. Students are invested in the material, eager to push the limits of what they can discover, and keen to the complexities of any subject matter, from literature to chemistry to the mechanics of fishing-rod construction. This delight stems from a sense that the student-teacher relationship is supportive rather than adversarial. As Meagan S., a freshman and long-time Roeper student shares,

> Having smaller classes and being on a first-name basis with teachers can really help break down the student/teacher barrier. Roeper has a lot of respect for the students' opinions. No matter how old you are, an adult or faculty member will always listen to what you have to say.

Abena S., a senior, further explains,

> It's not that those sort of relationships don't exist at other schools, but Roeper allows room for those relationships, and there is a mutual respect between students and teachers, which not only cultivates an excellent learning environment, but also a comfortable community where I can confide in friends who otherwise would be revered as my superiors.

Rosie D., a senior, similarly sees a link between the genuine student-teacher relationships and the quality of the learning environment:

> Roeper makes education personal. This is kind of a 'well, duh' thing when it comes to the question of what makes good education, but the teachers care and are rooting for the students' success. They have high expectations and make that clear from day one, and they do their best to be open and engaging. Kids are asked to think about and debate huge issues ranging from global politics to the school philosophy. And they do! Largely due to the standard here that says they ought to.

Rebecca B., a junior, articulates that part of this personalized education comes from not only investment on the part of the teacher, but from a teacher's awareness that he or she is a learner as well as an expert:

> I have been challenged academically and inspired by my teachers and classmates to care about what I'm learning because they are engaged and caring, too. I have close relationships with my teachers, and when I ask questions they don't know the answers to, they explore it with me instead of dismissing it.

Julia M., a freshman in her first year at Roeper, reflects on the benefits of being able to play an active role in one's classroom experience:

> Being someone who has gone to public school and has seen how your average school is run, I can see a big difference at Roeper. At Roeper the classes are

much more interactive, which for me makes it easier to pay attention. I'm not just an audience member to the teacher, but a contributing actor. I no longer feel the information is just being shoved down my throat. I have a voice in how I want to learn, and I actually have choices in how I can absorb information best.

For many students, this environment allows them to view school as a genuinely productive and positive experience, rather than a rote and meaningless one. Andy R., a freshman, explains:

> I consider Roeper to be my sanctum sanctorum. Roeper is a place where I can be myself and express my own opinions. The teachers at Roeper understand me and are aware of the way I learn and how my brain functions. The small class sizes create more opportunities for one-on-one teaching, a luxury that students in other schools really don't receive. These personal learning experiences have helped me to develop my skills and the constructive criticism I have received, especially in the case of my writing, has transformed me into a strong academic. The Roeper teachers have been very accommodating, have allowed me to learn at an accelerated pace, and have permitted me to take courses that students of my age at other schools would not be offered. Roeper has changed my life and has privileged me with wonderful friends and peers, an exhilarating learning environment, and a place that I can call home.

Many students share Andy's lifelong zeal for learning, but for some adolescents, the process of discovering themselves as a scholar is a slower one. Sophomore Matt M. explains how Roeper's approach to academics helped him engage more thoroughly in his own education:

> At other schools, I had no drive to learn. At other schools there is a great emphasis on grades while looking past learning and retaining knowledge. I think this might have to do with class size, teachers, and involvement. Rather than lectures and worksheets, we learn from class involvement and conversation. I never cared for schools or learning, but since I've been here, I've had a desire to learn and progress, making the grades come easy.

As a result of this dynamic classroom environment, students learn more than just skills and content—they learn responsibility and self-advocacy. Danielle Y., a freshman, shares:

> I have discovered a love for 'un-required' learning. If I don't understand or know something, I'll take it upon myself to go and learn it. I've never had that kind of drive before. It really helps that the teachers want you to learn and succeed. They will do their best to help students achieve their goals.

Justin F., a senior, was able to capitalize on his ambition and excitement in math thanks to both the support of his teachers and his own willingness to speak up for himself:

Over the past four years, I have been empowered to believe in myself, to take risks that pay off, and to take control of my future. Coming from a middle school somewhat lax in the fields of math and science, I entered Roeper in 9th grade behind many of my classmates, feeling ashamed at my inferiority. Never before having been exposed to rigorous math, I didn't identify much with the subject. But even starting where I did, on the lower end of the math spectrum, I discovered a new passion in the subject. I itched to accelerate, to take as much math as possible during my short few years here.

I have trouble imagining that a public school bureaucracy would have accommodated my crazy ambition to take two math courses at once, by myself, over the summer, and come back the next year three math courses ahead of my original trajectory. But Jamie, my wonderful math teather, knew me well enough in a small classroom setting to recognize my motivation and commitment. She believed in me and helped me through that summer. The payoff was outstanding: my endeavor could have ended in disaster, but as it turned out, I gained a new passion for the subject and a sense of accomplishment that would not have been possible any other way. I owe my sense of identity largely to Roeper.

The opportunities for growth and advancement aren't limited to the classroom. Roeper's no-cut athletic policy means that any student, regardless of ability, has the chance to participate in sports, even at the high-school level. For many students who love sports, a lack of sheer talent might prohibit them from participating in something they love. Max W., a sophomore, recognizes that while his soccer talent might have been enough to get him on a team at another school, he "would most likely not be playing basketball to this day," if he were not at Roeper. And rather than just providing students with a sense of inclusion or opportunity to participate, athletic participation has tangible payoffs as well. Senior Amy R., a three-sport Varsity athlete, speaks to the skills of time-management she's gained from sports: "my involvement in athletics has helped me keep my grades up."

There's perhaps no better example of the benefit of allowing students to pursue their athletic passion than Abe H., a senior varsity basketball captain who recently brought a packed crowd to its feet when he nailed a buzzer-beater shot in a late-season game. Basketball has played a major role in shaping Abe as a leader at Roeper, in part because it allowed him to maximize his capabilities:

> Roeper has a no-cut policy for sports, so the team accepted me with whatever skill level I had. If I went to [my local high school], I either would not have made the team or I would have sat on the bench the entire time and not set foot on the court during game time. Roeper gave me the opportunity to play my favorite sport and excel at it while others at [local high school] didn't even get the chance. Also, with the awesome athletics program, I was coached very well here and have become the best player I can imagine myself being at this age.

The same story can be heard when talking to students about their experiences in music, Model UN, forensics, theatre, or even a subject area in which they might have initially doubted their abilities. You never know what you're capable of unless you take the chance—and at Roeper, you often have the opportunity to do so.

If Roeper is, as Connor said, a place where a student truly can be a human being, it is also a place where students can determine who they want to be and who they are capable of becoming. "Roeper has helped me discover myself by letting me be who I want to be until I'm able to find out who I am," reflects junior Sammiey J. And sophomore Rory N. adds, "in all, I'm happy here because I get to be me. Sounds cliché as hell, but it's really true."

DYLAN BENNETT

HOW IS ROEPER DIFFERENT?

Imagine an environment where a 38 year-old dude and a 16 year-old guy talk about the highs and lows of last Saturday night. Simultaneously, a principal (head of school) converses with a 12th grader about potential career paths, a student plays Sinatra tunes on the piano, a sixth grader (who is trying to find his place in his new Upper School community) attempts to max out his weight limit on the bench press in the weight room, and a Harvard law graduate teaches the dimensions of the Constitution to eager upper classmen. This is none other than The Roeper School. Although Roeper has had some very successful graduates—a co-founder of Microsoft, a winner on Jeopardy, the world's most decorated Ice Dancer—the Roeper student doesn't have to fit into a preexisting mold. The mold each Roeper student wishes to create is filled with challenging but enjoyable courses, the power to have influence in school policy and the mindset that there is no right or wrong path to life after Roeper. Every Roeper student's mold prepares the said student for how the world should be rather than its current state, thus empowering her or him to have the will and desire to change it.

SUCCESS

Success is measured much differently at Roeper than at a traditional college prep school and most other learning institutions. We have no academic honor awards, top-of-the-class distinctions, or student ratings. Success is measured by the student and by the student only. The mold the Roeper student creates establishes an environment designed for success by permitting the student to explore areas of potential interest. These areas of potential interest are found within the school's plethora of extracurricular activities. Students use these extracurricular activities as a medium for success, such as winning the district tournament in Varsity Basketball or winning states in a forensics category. That said, some students might choose to create their own medium for success rather than join an already established one. One of my classmates has taken on the entrepreneurial task of becoming a graphic designer and another has entered and continues to win international rocketry competitions. Students such as these would not be able to use these activities as mediums for success if it were not for the freedom, independence, and empowerment that exist within the non-formulaic view of success at Roeper. At Roeper, what one student accomplishes doesn't set a standard for others. It only creates an environment where success is achievable by different kinds of students, through various mediums providing each student the ability to chart her or his own course in a given situation.

STUDENT-TEACHER RELATIONSHIPS

A role model, a friend, an advisor and a confidant all describe relationships Roeper students have with their teachers. The unbound environment allows students to act as they would around their closest peers and family. Because the student and the teacher feel they can act freely around each other, they are each on equal footing. There is no hierarchy. Yes, as in all schools there are certain things students need permission for, but in the everyday school scene at Roeper, a student might engage with a teacher or administrator just as often and regarding the same topics as he or she would with a classmate. Another advantageous result of this unique student-teacher setting is that the teachers get to know their students extremely well academically and socially. This is beneficial in many ways. For example, if a student is having trouble in a certain class, the teacher will understand how the student having forensics practice after school each day might be affecting her/his study habits and may suggest an alternate study plan based on that student's academic and social needs. Having a free and liberated teacher-student environment allows for each student and teacher to act as they would around their same aged peers, translating into a more comfortable and beneficial learning environment making things easier when problems and conflict arise.

CONFLICT RESOLUTION

Deliberation at Roeper is truly a unique asset that makes The Roeper School one of a kind. Conflict resolution at Roeper can be comedic, such as a disagreement among a few students regarding whether there is such a thing as left and right socks—or whether or not wearing shoes should be required in the school building. The shoe debate was a contentious issue, as many students felt that not wearing shoes was a way to express themselves in Roeper's free and accepting environment. On the other hand, opposing students felt that by not wearing shoes, students were exposing themselves and their classmates to health risks and were disturbing students simply because they had no shoes.

The contention among the student body sprouted from the fact that students should be able to have the freedom to express themselves, but to what extent? Roeper has no dress code, but opposed students thought no shoes went beyond this policy. I have been told by 50-year-old Roeper alumni that the issue came up in the 1970's as well and was never put to rest. Well, just last year, our head of school held an assembly regarding the issue in which various students voiced their opinions. The assembly did not resolve a great amount but what it did create was casual, student-led, unorganized, and instantaneous debates in hallways, the weight room, or the moments leading up until class in the biology room. Roeper students simply talked out the shoe debate in impromptu settings, something that could be considered a

"Roeper thing." Whether or not there was a winner in the debate is not important, what it important is how the issue and debate was handled. The students took it upon themselves to discuss (with students of the opposite opinion) why requiring or not requiring shoes was important to them.

This method of conflict resolution is how many things become resolved at Roeper. An issue literally bounces off the halls of The Roeper School and is worked out among the voices of the students. Various debates have been worked out using this "Roeper method," and it is not uncommon to see this method put to work on a monthly basis. For instance, the talk of the hallways recently has been whether or not having a Black Student Union, only open to African-American students, should be allowed on campus. This issue has yet to be solved but is currently making its way through the halls and classrooms at Roeper hearing the voices and opinions of the Roeper students. At Roeper, internal conflict is handled respectfully, maturely and uniquely. Conflict resolution at The Roeper School is simply another aspect of how the school evolves constantly and creates critically thinking students.

IN CLOSING

The day-to-day "operations" at one of the world's most unique gifted institutions are always changing based on the motivation and innovation that the student body presents. The Roeper environment induces constant learning, constant experience, and constant interaction, and this is why there is never a dull moment.

A junior at The Roeper School at the time of this writing my motivation to write this brief essay on my school sprouted from my brain's full capacity of observations, observations that range from secret conversations to how students and teachers act in the same habitat. My Roeper observation bank has reached its limit and my Roeper observations deserve to be shared with the world of gifted education. Here is my chance.

MARCIA RUFF

ROEPER ALUMNI REFLECT ON LASTING LESSONS

When George Roeper spoke to the school's parents about an upcoming landmark for the school, its first high school graduating class, he outlined his understanding of his task. "We prepare our youngsters for college. This is a matter of course," he said. "But I consider preparation for college as half of our job. We also want to help our students to be amply prepared for this world in a social and human sense."[1]

When he addressed the Class of 1969 on graduation day, he went into more detail about the balance between academic preparation and character preparation:

> While I look at you, a thought flashes by. What are you going to be like in 10 years from now? You may be married, you may have children, you will have a job. You may have been immensely successful, you may have failed. But regardless, you will have an outlook towards life that is open-minded, progressive, more understanding and accepting of differences among human beings. You'll be intolerant of ruthless, inhuman cruelty and I hope intolerant of violence of any kind. You will feel passionate about justice and rights of the individual and fight injustices, racism, and narrow-minded bigotry. Of course, it is taken for granted that we also hope for the full development in use of your talents and capabilities. However, I think this is less predictable than your likely attitudes towards life.[2]

These beliefs reflected George's own experience of life and its uncertainties. Born in 1910 into a wealthy family in Hamburg, Germany, at the height of his nation's power, he had no reason not to expect a well-ordered life of accomplishment. But World War I, the post-war economic and social chaos, and the rise of Nazism turned every assumption on its head. George discovered that the most valuable lessons were the ones he learned at Marienau, the progressive boarding school he attended that was founded by Annemarie's parents, Max and Gertrud Bondy. The intellectual flexibility, open-mindedness, self-awareness, and respect and appreciation for others that the Bondys nurtured proved most critical to his ability to escape from Germany and build a happy life in the United States.

When we asked Roeper alumni to reflect on their experience at the school and to identify the elements that had made the most impact on the course of their lives, they responded much as George predicted. While the academic preparation has been critical to their careers, it was certain habits of mind and values learned at Roeper that had the greatest impact on the shape and happiness of their lives.[3]

D. Ambrose et al., (Eds.), The Roeper School, 111–122.
© 2013 Sense Publishers. All rights reserved.

Phred Brown '03 is now the Music Director for Bruno Mars, writing songs and arrangements and leading the band backing this Grammy Award-winning musician. When Phred looked back at Roeper, he remembered the freedom from having to fit into a mold, and the power of being surrounded by an atmosphere that encouraged him to build his own success.

> I wanted my adult life to feel like the 13 years I spent on the benches of Roeper's halls and the couches of its classrooms. Roeper's landscape is vast. Its campus may be small, but Roeper has created a world within its grounds that extends far beyond any boundary. I can point to memories—school assemblies, band concerts, sporting events, theatre performances—that make for great examples of a cultivating environment. But it's the spaces in between those moments that really stick with me.
>
> I came out of Roeper with an optimism that inspires everything I do because the school's community is uplifting in every aspect. Everything I was a part of while I was there encouraged my peers and me to continue upward and find the next level. Band class was first offered as an elective in Stage IV. As a 9-year-old, I spent one semester in Beginner Band playing snare drum. The following semester I moved into the Advanced Band on snare and went back to Beginner Band to learn saxophone. At the end of the year, I asked to take a trombone home for the summer. By the time school started back up, I was ready to play the trombone in the Advanced Band. My teachers noticed this passion and always opened doors for my talent and curiosity to flourish.
>
> Roeper is a place where kids don't have to fit molds. Students explore and develop and rediscover themselves through interactions and growing together. There's so much to take in at Roeper that I think the greatest method of learning is to just stop, observe, and take note. That open-minded focus is one of the greatest gifts Roeper gave me. Being able to stay the course while remaining aware of—and open to—the periphery has been essential to navigating life after Roeper. There's no template for building a career in the music industry. You have to make your own, step by step, and it takes creativity and logic.

Mahvish Rukhsana Khan '97 pointed to the power of the school's emphasis on empathy and human justice. While a law student at the University of Miami, the Pashto-speaking Khan volunteered to assist defence attorneys representing clients incarcerated at Guantanamo Bay. She eventually published a book, *My Guantanamo Diary: The Detainees and the Stories They Told Me*.

> My Roeper education helped structure and hone so much of what I value today. Aside from solid critical thinking and communication skills, my teachers instilled an integral sense of human justice, a sense of inner strength, self-motivation, and a belief that authority—of all kinds—must be checked. These principles compelled my involvement at Guantanamo Bay and later allowed

me to shed light on the gross violations of human dignity and constitutional law that I witnessed. My Roeper experience also furthered a deep sense of empathy. This allowed for a greater understanding and appreciation for the struggles of the prisoners I got to know at Guantanamo. It helped me form a close rapport with prisoners who have perhaps forgotten that they still could trust.

Melissa Sommerfeld Gresalfi '95, Associate Professor of Mathematics Education and Learning Sciences at Vanderbilt University, found that her Roeper education influenced her research focus: how to design learning environments that promote opportunities for all students to engage meaningfully with complex mathematical ideas.

> It seems like a modest goal: to design curricula that encourage students to engage "critically" with information. Critical engagement involves being intentional about the disciplinary tools you use to resolve a problem, and being able to reflect on how that tool (as opposed to another), enables you to achieve the end you had in mind. The decision you finally make is based on the tools you used and what you personally value. This is what expertise is really about—not blindly following a procedure, but making intentional decisions about how to approach a problem, what tools to bring to bear on it, and how to convince others that we are doing something reasonable.
>
> In my research, I argue that critical engagement should be a primary goal for education, but despite the seemingly obvious benefits, it is unfortunately not a typical educational outcome. There are some funding agencies who agree this is a worthwhile goal to pursue, but it continues to be shocking to me how much effort it takes to convince some people that fostering critical engagement is a reasonable—and attainable—learning goal.
>
> My befuddlement stems, no doubt, from the fact that until I started graduate school, I took it for granted that everyone thought that the purpose of education was to be able to engage in a good debate. This conviction developed from my own educational experiences, which have dramatically shaped my expectations of what education can and should be. Specifically, having attended Roeper for 14 years, I was quite accustomed to being asked what I thought about something, and then having to explain why I thought I was right. I was fortunate to be surrounded by a lot of other students who ALSO had ideas and opinions about things, and were equally passionate about persuading others that THEY were right. And we were quite privileged to have teachers who helped us to transition from simple debates based on opinion to reasoned arguments that leveraged disciplinary evidence to support our claims.
>
> When I look at the careers that my peers from Roeper have chosen, which range from law, to the arts, ecology, engineering, medicine, engineering, writing, and beyond, the clear thread that cuts through their work is a commitment to using

their expertise to critically engage the world. It is one thing to be an attorney; it is quite another to use one's law degree to advocate for children in poverty. It is one thing to study community art; it is quite another to leverage that experience to design programs where children learn to advocate for their own futures.

What we learned at Roeper was the importance of taking a stand; what our classes provided for us was a way to engage content so that it could be a tool to use to support those stands. In the short term, this approach to teaching fostered an interest in learning that could be seen in heated debates, frantic study sessions, and creative independent projects. In the long term, this approach fostered so much more: a commitment to look at the world not as it is currently is, but as it could be, and a sense of ourselves as people who are expected, obligated, and entitled to make those changes.

Alexandra Dickinson '04, now working at Beekeeper Group, a Washington, DC, public affairs company specializing in community-based social media, also valued the emphasis on critical thinking at Roeper and uses often the lessons in collaboration gained from being part of an active community.

The passion for thinking critically and learning about the world that Roeper instilled in me has become a valuable resource and has helped me in my career. When I think about it now, I realize that a lot of that came from being a part of the Roeper community as a whole and not just the classes I went to or the activities I participated in.

People who attend Roeper have a wonderfully unique sense of what community means. In fact, it occurred to me recently that for many Roeper alums, community and Roeper are pretty much synonymous. The reason for that is plain and simple: the Roeper experience is more than a typical education—it is an education for life. Roeper teaches you to think critically about what it means to be a citizen of the world and how to work with others—a helpful skill for surviving in Washington! Roeper also teaches you that respect for others coupled with an open mind are some of the best assets a person can have in this world.

Most importantly for me personally, Roeper teaches you how to listen and what you can gain from listening. From my earliest days in the Lower School all the way through my senior year, I saw firsthand that the best way to learn is by listening to other people and appreciating the stories they share. So whether it was listening to a teacher speak passionately about material for a class, or an assembly about a current political issue, or a rehearsal for a play, or even just spending time on the sidelines of a soccer game cheering on my friends, Roeper helped me grow to really love learning in every sense of the word.

Carolyn Graham Tsuneta '78 found that Roeper has enriched her personal life in ways she didn't anticipate.

Given that so many Roeperians leave the school and go on to become quite famous, it's easy to assume that more ordinary lives would not necessarily be of interest, but the truth is that my "ordinary" life feels quite extraordinary to me, and so much of what drives me and inspires me comes directly from my experience at Roeper. It astonishes me that I graduated from Roeper 35 years ago. I still identify so strongly with the 18-year-old girl who left Roeper to go to Northwestern University, but when I look in the mirror, the woman who looks back at me is the mother of three grown sons and the grandmother of three.

What I have observed in my 30 years of parenting and grandparenting is that my Roeper education informs everything that I do with regard to my children and grandchildren. While I was at Roeper, I learned the importance of questioning everything, remaining open to possibility, asking for clarification if something was confusing. I learned that everyone has different gifts and that we are each obligated to share those gifts with the larger community. I learned that learning something quickly didn't have any more merit than learning something slowly. It is not the speed of comprehension that determines its importance. I learned that there is not *one way* to learn. I saw that my friends with dyslexia had to learn by *hearing* words, not *seeing* words on paper and that their memories were much stronger as a result of not being dependent on the written word.

I learned that being sensitive was a blessing and a curse, but that it was definitely part of being highly intelligent. I learned that the secret to having an interesting life is to be a lifelong learner and that not all education happens in schools. I learned that it was okay to be passionate about ideas and to have strong opinions, that dialogue and even argument have merit when people are trying to understand each other. I learned that humour was a great diffuser of tension and that being able to laugh at myself was crucial to my sanity. All of my children and grandchildren have been and are being raised with these principles.

Britt Harwood '05 graduated from Brown University with a double major in Comparative Literature and Public Policy and is now at the University of California, Berkeley School of Law. She has relied on skills learned at Roeper for academic success and a sense of being grounded in her values.

As a Roeper student, you have to question everything, think for yourself, and make connections. Inquisitiveness is the single most important part of academia. When I went to college I brought intellectual rigor and curiosity with me, because I grew up in an environment that fostered it.

Roeper engages students in a constant dialogue about values. It's an idealistic place, but its ideals are grounded in the principle that people's actions can shape the world around them. As a student I always had to examine what kind of person I wanted to be, what kind of society I wanted to live in, and what I could do to move toward that vision. When I face major decisions about my education and career today, I am guided by my Roeperian values to make choices that position me to help others and create social good.

Finally, Roeper students learn remarkably deep compassion and tolerance at a young age. When I describe Roeper, I can't capture the environment properly without talking about the bust of Dr. Martin Luther King, Jr. at the entrance to the Lower School or the student-painted portraits of both MLK and Mahatma Gandhi inside the doors of the Upper School. I am so grateful that I was raised on a diet of liberal humanism and taught to respect each individual for his or her unique worth. That's probably the most important lesson I took away from my 16-year education.

Choice is another core element of a Roeper education. The Roepers considered the ability to make good decisions a key life skill and so, beginning in kindergarten, students are given steadily increasing opportunities to make their own choices. Jeff Deutsch '94, an entrepreneur who has been living in China for eight years and is the CEO and Co-Founder of Frobark Laboratories, transferred into Roeper at high school and found the freedom a little shocking but transformative.

When I arrived at Roeper, I found that it was a completely different environment from what I had experienced before. The teachers were generally not so concerned with having absolute authority over the students—and we, the students, were given a scary amount of freedom. Healthy debate with teachers was encouraged. We got a liberal amount of leeway when it came to what we researched and wrote about. Students negotiated scheduling and school policy with staff. We even got off-campus privileges! It totally blew my mind.

I didn't always use my freedom for the powers of good. Mostly I was still a little punk, and my bad habits persisted. Thankfully, the reaction I got was different from my other schools. My classmates (especially kids who'd been at Roeper since Lower School) didn't find my behavior amusing, and teachers and staff didn't give me the punishments I had gotten before either. In fact, their punishments were far worse. They would let me know how disappointed they were in me because, although I was being given all the support I could ever want, instead of appreciating it, accepting it, and learning, I was still rebelling.

Strangely, living <u>without</u> the freedom to do what you want is a very comforting thing. Your job is to follow and consume. If you follow with any kind of effort and still don't succeed, you get none of the blame. Blame is reserved for the teachers, your parents, the school district's policies, the school lunch, society, the economy, and so on. This is what I have seen in Chinese schools, too.

Having freedom, on the other hand, is extremely unnerving. You are expected to lead and produce. When you fail, the blame falls on YOU. This is especially true when you have the kind of unconditional support we got at Roeper. Even though I didn't realize it back then—and even though I don't think it was by design—the freedom and support Roeper provided put us all under an immense amount of pressure.

However, I believe that pressure is a good thing, because it forces you to rise to the challenge. While it took me many more years to attain the level of personal responsibility I needed to accomplish what I have here in China, the lessons I learned at Roeper are what put me on the path.

One of the most radical notions at Marienau, the German school that gave The Roeper School its roots, was that the teachers and administrators in the school should share their thoughts and passions authentically with their students, providing a model of lifelong learning. LeeAundra Keany '86* found that her life has been shaped dramatically by her teachers.

In 1982, the new English teacher, Nancy Hopkins, asked to speak at our assembly about a new school activity. Even for Roeper, it was strange. Competitive public speaking? What was that and why was it called "forensics"? Thirty years later, I laugh at my confusion. Nancy had, in that moment, introduced me to a lifelong passion and my eventual livelihood.

That is one reason I have to be grateful for my time at Roeper. But in fact, there were so many moments during my four years there that were truly life-defining. For the past 15 years, I have owned my own communications coaching business where I am honored to work with the most fascinating executives, authors, actors, scientists, politicians, and entrepreneurs. All because Nancy started a forensics team at Roeper.

I now get to spout off on political rhetoric as a pundit on television and radio because Kate Millet said the State of the Union was important and no matter how boring it was I must watch it every year.

I answered the Final Jeopardy question, "What is a filibuster?" correctly and became a Jeopardy champion because Frank Blondale's history lectures were so indelible I remembered that the American filibuster was first used when Congress was debating the Kansas-Nebraska Act.

I am a writer for *Discover Magazine* in spite of the fact I am not a scientist nor a journalist because Sandy Lash was so excited about the first space shuttle launch happening on her birthday, I couldn't help but think it was cool. I should also mention that the number one requisite for a science journalist, keep asking "Why?" until everybody hates you, was encouraged by every science teacher I ever had at Roeper.

I am married to a brilliant actor and the most wonderful man in the world because Dean Acheson taught me enough about three-act structure that I was able to carry on a conversation during our first date.

I volunteer for a number of humanitarian causes because George Roeper once told me about his escape from Nazi Germany and instilled in me a lifelong respect for the rights, dignity, and life of all humans.

I am a (reasonably) confident, functioning member of society instead of a scared, insecure misfit because in Annemarie Roeper's "Who am I?" class, I learned about Barbara Bartz's former life as a nun and saw for the first time, the richness and worth of difference.

If I have had some measure of conventionally defined success in my adult life, it is because of Roeper. More important, the parts of me I like the best are also because of Roeper.

I am now watching my stepson go through the paces of his public school's version of a gifted program. While he is no doubt getting a superb "education," I look at his "accelerated" curriculum, his "development plan" (for a six-year-old?), and children not too much older than he being tracked for Ivy League, and I am reminded anew of how lucky I was to have Roeper. Roeper served the whole child, all of me. It put my happiness before base achievement, personal fulfillment before society's metrics, giving before individual ambition.

For me, Roeper was a "school for the gifted" not just because the students were gifted but also because we received life gifts every day from our teachers, from the other kids and, of course, from George and Annemarie.

If Roeper had a motto, it would probably be George Roeper's oft-quoted line, "Where there is freedom, there is responsibility."[4] As Rachel Ratchford '09 reflected during her senior year at Brown University, she saw that concept as core to her undergraduate success.

I feel that the phrase "With freedom comes responsibility" accurately sums up my entire academic experience at Brown. Roeper did a fabulous job instilling in me a sense of independence and responsibility regarding my academics. The ability to balance a schedule and extracurriculars became increasingly more important in college. In my first year, it was easy to become overwhelmed, but Roeperians learn early on how to juggle their responsibilities. Coming from a school that gave me so much freedom prepared me to enter one that gave me even more choice and control over my academic career. I have appreciated the opportunity to design my schedule at Brown and was glad to have learned at Roeper the importance of pursuing your passions while accomplishing what is necessary. I am proud to say that I have been able to have academic success while involving myself in experiences that have allowed me to give back to the greater Providence community.

A signature element of a Roeper education is the time and space to discover what is important for oneself. Even the youngest children have the chance to feel unobserved and in charge of their own lives. Kristin Clark Taylor '76*, a writer, former journalist, and, during the George H.W. Bush administration, the first woman of colour to serve as White House Director of Media Relations, found her life's direction in a tree house at Roeper.

Writing has been my pride and passion for as long as I can remember. In fact, I wrote my first poem—as a very little girl—in a tree house on Roeper's beautiful campus. Along with a large, loving family and an unquenchable thirst to write, it was Roeper that truly nurtured this powerful passion, very early on in my little life.

Everything about the school radiated love, and the people within it showered me with comfort and confidence. It was a magical place, with a pulse and a spirit. Some of my first written words took shape there, sprawled out in a tree house with the sky and the leaves as my backdrop. It will be forever etched in my heart.

I began Roeper in kindergarten, and I stayed for a decade. During the 10 years I was there, I could feel my own emotional, spiritual, and intellectual maturity begin to rise up within me, growing stronger with each passing year. My time at Roeper was indeed a journey towards self-discovery; a dynamic, never-ending journey that I still walk to this very day.

When I think back on my years at Roeper, my mind automatically catapults itself back to one powerful, pivotal moment that occurred early in my childhood. It was a soulful, singular moment in time that crystallized the person I was to become.

I was in kindergarten; happy to have good friends, a great learning environment and, like most kindergartners, an overactive imagination. The moment itself unfolded late one afternoon, as I was preparing for the long ride home (I lived in Detroit, which seemed, back then, like a thousand-hour ride from Bloomfield Hills.) I remember plundering through my book bag, searching for something to prepare me for the long ride home.

As I burrowed through my book bag, my little hands brought up several, vital items: an apple (I was always hungry by the end of the day), my Raggedy Ann doll (much-loved and well-worn), and—wonder of wonders—a book! I looked at the book for a few seconds. Since I didn't yet know how to read, the book felt a little off-balance in my hands, like a stranger coming to visit, or a new and wonderful friend whose name I did not yet know. I decided to open it up. The moment I opened the book, I opened up my world as well. In that one split second, my soul seemed to expand. I looked down at the words (which had always been, to me, a confused jumble of disparate letters all bunched up together, in one line!).

As I continued to study the words, something happened. I could literally feel my mind telling my brain (which, in turn, told my heart), that I actually recognized a word! And as I continued looking at the word, I noticed that I also understood the meaning of the word right beside it!

Slowly, miraculously, as I sat there in the afternoon sun, those few words had transformed themselves into a sentence—and the sentence grew into an actual idea. It was an idea that I could see, hear, feel, and taste! I was reading! It took me a moment, but very quickly the stark realization set in. For the very first time in my young life, I was actually reading!

Magically and miraculously, my mind had expanded. My heart just about leapt out of my little chest. Needless to say, the ride home on that magical afternoon seemed particularly long. I was itching to share this earth-shattering news with the people I loved: my parents and my six siblings! The moment I arrived home, I was so excited that I tore through the entire house, shouting for all to hear: "I can read! I can read! The words turn into sentences! Can anybody hear me??? I can read!"

Throughout our home, all six of my siblings and both of my parents quickly found their way to me, as I stood hollering through our kitchen. Hugs and kisses all around, and from that moment on, words, writing and all things conceptual (if it can fit onto a printed page) have been the centre of my life.

Robyn Scott '00, an artist and visual arts teacher at a small private school in California, imbues her teaching with the Humanistic perspective that George and Annemarie Roeper espoused: "to live by trusting each other, being able to confide in each other, to be open to each other and to be open-minded, to rely on each other, to respect the individuality and humanness of each other, to accept differences without value judgments, and to see each other truly as equals."[5]

Although most people I come across are not knowledgeable of Humanism, I have found that incorporating its teaching into each child's life to be an essential part of educating a child or teenager to grow into an ethical, responsible, and happy adult. I am amazed at how interested my students can become in subjects as dry as test prep when they are given a say in their education. Self-control and self-guidance are two important life skills I learned at Roeper. I remember how shocked I was to be allowed to choose my own literature classes as an upperclassman, and how much more I cared about my own learning process when I was given constructive guidance.

More than 10 years later, I am thrilled to be passing these ideals on to my students. My most crucial emphasis as an educator is the idea of happiness and that it is not a goal but a state of mind. Each student is on his or her own path and the journey to happiness is not defined by a specific grade or a completion of a task, but rather the ideas or activities that help a child's (or adult's) inner essence be in line with an intangible part of the human spirit for which no word yet exists. I call it happiness.

Before becoming a teacher, these skills also helped me survive the "sink or swim" climate of the University of California system, as well as to have the courage to drop everything and move abroad to further my studies. Being accepted as an individual helped me to navigate the culture shock of living in another country. I can appreciate how patient my teachers at Roeper were, as well as their unusual ability to adapt to my learning style. Now with the tables turned, I can see that many of my current students have a ways to go before appreciating their own education, but I can see that little sparkle in their eyes that lets me know I have started to reach them.

Nurturing true empowerment means allowing students to make choices that are self-created, not just responses to safe, school-generated choices. Marko Slusarczuk '70, an engineer and lawyer who is a defence analyst and entrepreneur, was liberated by this opportunity to take risks.

I came to Roeper from a parochial school where my class had 54 students— in one classroom. The nuns demanded severe discipline and out-of-the box thinking was not tolerated. A teacher punished me once for completing the "Think and Do" book in the first week of school—it was to last all year. I did not follow the rules. All too often rules exist to make the job easier for the teacher and the administration—not at all considering the student.

Roeper and its environment gave me the tools to make difficult decisions and choices—something that a more-structured environment could not. Because of the confidence this gave me, as an undergraduate at MIT I had no fear in challenging rules. I performed my undergraduate thesis off campus—at the IBM Watson Research Centre, something expressly prohibited at MIT. My research was IBM confidential material until I published it, also prohibited. I was paid for doing the work—also prohibited. My transcript shows courses as substitutes for required courses even though the curriculum at the time expressly indicated that they were not acceptable substitutes. Why did I get away with this? Because I had learned at Roeper not to accept rules at face value, but that if you present a credible and well-thought-through argument, rules might become merely guidelines.

After the Vietnam War, which I opposed, ended, I joined ROTC in graduate school. When time came to attend the officer's basic course, I saw it as a total waste of time. Another MIT graduate and I convinced a 2-star general that our technical skills could better be used elsewhere in the military. When the commanding colonel of my unit received orders to assign us to technical intelligence analysis at Fort Meade, his response was "How in the h*ll did you do that? Everyone must attend the officer's basic course!" Roeper gives students a belief that they are in charge of their destinies and a sense of confidence they can change the world.

NOTES

1. George Roeper, "PTFA Speeches," October 15, 1968. Record Group 2, George A. Roeper Papers, Box 5. Housed in The Roeper School Archives, Bloomfield Hills, MI
2. George Roeper, "Graduation and Farewell Remarks," June 1969. Record Group 2, George A. Roeper Papers, Box 4. Housed in The Roeper School Archives, Bloomfield Hills, MI
3. Extended versions of these remarks can be seen on The Roeper School Website at http://www.roeper.org/netcommunity/page.aspx?pid=1349. Accessed February 19, 2013.
4. George Roeper, "Graduation and Farewell Remarks," June 1964. Record Group 2, George A. Roeper Papers, Box 4. Housed in The Roeper School Archives, Bloomfield Hills, MI
5. George Roeper, "Excerpt from Comments to the PTSA," Oct. 1, 1974. Published in Parent Communication, Fall 1974. Housed in The Roeper School Archives, Bloomfield Hills, MI

---

* Indicates that the person attended Roeper but graduated from elsewhere.

TRACY L. CROSS

A PERSONAL TALE OF DEVELOPMENT AND GROWTH

The Inadvertent Influence of the Roeper School on a Scholar

Since the early 1990s, I have had the opportunity to serve the Roeper Community in several roles, both official and unofficial. For example, I was on the Editorial Advisory Board and the Manuscript Review Board of the *Roeper Review*. I also served as the editor of the journal. I served on the Education Committee, the Roeper School Board of Trustees, the Roeper Institute, and the Roeper Institute Development Board. Moreover, I had a friendship with three headmasters and numerous members of the Roeper Community. In sum, I have worked with and on behalf of the larger Roeper School community for over 20 years. Ironically, the one person I never knew as well as I would have liked was Annemarie Roeper. This was primarily due to the fact that Annemarie had moved from Michigan to California a few years before I became involved with the community. Our interactions were limited to us landing at the Roeper School at the same time and occasional telephone calls. We also visited at conferences. I regret not having the close personal relationship with her that I have enjoyed with so many others from the Roeper Community.

My limited relationship with Annemarie, notwithstanding, my affinity and appreciation for the Roeper Community, have proven to be a major influence on my personal and professional life. Consequently, I wanted my contribution to this book to reflect my experiences. I hope to do justice in this homage. To begin, I will go to the end.

On a beautiful October morning about 2 a.m., as the fog rolled in on my drive across Central Michigan, I came to question my long-term involvement with the Roeper School. I had left the campus of the Roeper School after a two-day visit including a long Board of Trustees meeting that ended late. I decided that I would make the 5-hour drive back home rather than stay another day away from my family. As I drove faster and faster, anxious to get home, I came upon the five-mile patch of dense fog. I slowed to about 70 miles per hour and then I heard and felt a loud, deep, low rumbling. I could only see about 10 feet in front of my car. Finally a group of about 20 bikers rumbled past, driving at well over 100 miles per hour. It sounded like a jet engine but much lower and louder. The entire event only lasted about one minute, and when it was over I questioned whether it had actually happened. I knew that I was fatigued and then confused. I slowed to about 60 miles per hour for the remainder of the trip and thought about how easily I, or any of the bikers, could have been killed. That led to my pondering my 20-year experience with the Roeper School and whether I should stay involved. My role with the Roeper School at this time was primarily as a Board of Trustees member and a member of the Roeper Institute, meaning that I travelled from Muncie, Indiana to the suburbs of Detroit five times a year. I had made these trips for several years by the night of fog and bikers. Is there something so valuable that it is worth being away from your family and risking your life to boot?

To get to the reasoning behind the doubt, I must go back to the beginning. As a young academic, I was invited to sit on the *Roeper Review* (the longstanding journal sponsored by the school) Editorial Advisory Board (EAB). I did not know what this was. I knew of the journal but knew little about the school. I felt honored to be considered and agreed to serve. I was expected to provide guidance on behalf of the journal, which was then run by the venerable editor Ruthan Brodsky. We met once a year at the school and had an evening event at the Roeper House, a grand old house that was part of the old Bloomfield Hills campus for the younger students. A person from the Board of Trustees of the school provided a brief welcome, an Editorial Advisory Board member spoke, and then we had dinner with the students. The next day we met for eight or more hours, trying to deal with specific issues regarding the journal.

During the first night as a spry 30-something, I found myself standing in the food line between Harry Passow and Nancy Robinson. These academics were like gods to me. My first impression after the initial shock of realizing I stood between them, was that each of them seemed relatively diminutive. This could not be—they were giants—and I had already met John Feldhusen, who was a giant literally and figuratively. Most surprising was that they could not have been nicer to me. (For the many years that I served on this board, I met different fascinating and committed people.) To this day, I am so thankful that somehow I was elected to the EAB.

The next day at my first EAB meeting was amazing. Everyone was so collaborative and thoughtful. I met many leaders in the field of gifted education inside and outside of NAGC and TAG. At the end of the day, it was time to go through the process for nominating new people for the EAB. This was such a positive learning experience for me.

Also during the day, we met with Doug Winkworth, the President of the Roeper School Board of Trustees. Doug was a fascinating person whose intellect and curiosity were keen and focused. He was quite serious about helping the students at the school. I also spent some time with the Headmaster of the school, Chuck Webster. For reasons I have never understood, we hit it off and he spent considerable time with me talking about ideas. In addition to all this attention feeling heady, it was nice to test my mettle with such a distinguished group. Later, when Chuck left the Roeper School to begin a new school called University High School in Indianapolis, we stayed friends and colleagues, and I served in a similar capacity on the school's board of trustees.

The EAB spent the second day presenting at a conference held at the upper campus located a few miles away in Birmingham, Michigan. This event included teachers from the Roeper School and teachers from around Michigan. It was described as an effort to give back to the community: to share the wealth. During these three days I learned that Giftedland is a vast group of people far beyond our national organizations; that the most significant thinkers in the field were kind to younger academics; that caring required intensive thought and community action; that opportunities come from hard work; that disagreements are a necessary part of the process; and that the Roeper School was a special place. I also learned that the Roeper School was guided by a philosophy that was regularly consulted and reviewed by the school's Board of Trustees.

For several years (8–10) I served on the EAB of the *Roeper Review*. I immediately appreciated and respected Ruthan Brodsky's editorial work and her worldview. The Roeper School was clearly operating on the goal, as I heard Annemarie say many times, "to prevent another holocaust." This created a very interesting relationship between the Roeper School and the *Roeper Review*. Annemarie had retired to California a few years before I began my involvement with the school. The EAB, led by Ruthan Brodsky's vision, often pondered the difficult question of what the role of the journal should be in relation to the school. Many hours of discussion across the years were spent on this question. How to make the journal a benefit to both the employees and students of the school, and the ever-growing outside readership was also part of the conundrum.

One of the most exciting parts of our meetings was when Annemarie Roeper would visit. She would stay anywhere from a few minutes to half a day. She brought her charm and inquisitiveness to each session.

It is very clear as a long-term inside supporter of the school that there is a very strong community that makes up all aspects of the Roeper School. Ruthan had been the editor for most of the *Roeper Review's* years as a journal. Late in my second term, Ruthan retired from the editorship and I was asked to follow her, serving as the next editor. Trying to find a person to follow her, given the very strong philosophy that the school is operated on, was very worrisome to the Board of Trustees. They were quite compelling when they approached me about the journal editorship. Because I was at that time the current editor of the *Gifted Child Quarterly*, beginning my final year in that role, I was very circumspect about trying to serve in both roles. I had a strong affinity for the Roeper School and the people who made up its community, plus I had served on the EAB of the journal for approximately a decade. I approached a representative of NAGC with my quandary and was berated as a turncoat and traitor. Worse things were said and I was told that I could not accept the role. I tried to explain the community issues and the longevity of the prior editor and the differences between the two journals, but to put it mildly, the response I received was by far the most foul and ugly diatribe that I had ever heard. (Please note that this person has not worked for NAGC for quite some time.) Of course, this treatment guaranteed my acceptance of the role as editor of the *Roeper Review*.

From this experience I learned that some people in the field see our roles as helping gifted children, while others see everything in terms of winners and losers. This second group seems to believe that you strive for control of resources and the winner takes all. This juxtaposition helped to codify my belief that if everyone associated with the field of gifted education worked at 100% capacity, we would still be far too few to help all those in need. About this time, a sage person in the field told me that being in leadership is risky. The higher up the pole you go, the more your rear end hangs out and the more criticism you will receive. I thank Sandy Kaplan for that wisdom. I have reflected on it many times. The essence of the Roeper School is its goal to create a better world. To that end we have to work together. Our careers cannot be about zero-sum gains; they have to be about collaboration. The Roeper community has provided me a 20-year object lesson in collaboration for the good of society.

During my time as editor of the *Roeper Review*, we continued much of the approach taken by Ruthan Brodsky. We added a section called "According to Jim" as a vehicle for Jim Gallagher, a leading figure in the field of gifted education, to be able to offer a regular essay on the field. We fired up the "Point/Counterpoint" feature and had some interesting dialogues between thoughtful professionals. We kept the book review section and the dissertation reviews. We encouraged philosophically based manuscripts and invited increasing numbers of international authors to write for the journal. Every year the EAB grappled with the intersection between the journal and school. To that end we produced a special issue wherein faculty from the Roeper School drafted real life case stories, and two invited academics per story offered ideas for successful resolution. Margie Kitano guest edited this issue and did a masterful job. The years I edited the Roeper Review were my most challenging and, in some ways, rewarding as an editor.

After several years of editing the *Roeper Review*, I stepped down. My friends in the Roeper Community were concerned about finding an editor who shared the valued Roeper qualities. Second only to improving the world by preventing a holocaust, the school had a longstanding commitment to global citizenry (my word). I had been fortunate to know Don Ambrose, the consummate gentleman and interdisciplinary scholar, and recommended him with great enthusiasm. Don met with the Roeper Community and the rest has been magical. Don took over the editorship of the *Roeper Review* and has done an incredible job of moving the journal forward. Our field is fortunate to have him at the helm.

About this time, Chuck Webster invited me to serve on the Roeper School Board of Trustees. He told me that I would be helpful to them and that I could also help the education committee do its work. The Board of Trustees had decided to create the Roeper Institute, a nonprofit organization, to help with the development side of the school's needs. I was on that board as well. I was an active member in the Roeper School's development activities that led to improving facilities and creating a new one. I learned a great deal about fundraising, a skill that I am increasingly asked to use. I have felt great personal reward by helping bring to light resources for the school on both campuses. This skill set was created out of a commitment to the people making up the Roeper Community.

On the job front, I was midway through my nine years serving the Indiana Academy for Science, Mathematics, and Humanities as its Executive Director. I also was honored with the George and Frances Ball Distinguished Professorship of Psychology and Gifted Studies at Ball State University. My trips to the Roeper School were helpful to me in both capacities as I tried to make the Academy as good a school as possible, wherein the students would thrive. I came to appreciate and value the Roeper School environment so much that I tried to import aspects of its philosophy to the Academy. The second Roeper School head I worked with, Ken Seward, came to visit the Academy partly to provide me ideas for moving the Academy culture in a Roeper direction. At this time, I came to appreciate that the structural differences were too many and too strong to allow us to create the same sort of intimate environment that the Roeper School enjoys, but we learned through this process to use advantages that we had such as our 24-hour-a-day community. Improving the world as a goal for the school was a reasonable one to take on, but we had to adapt to make it happen. My involvement with the Roeper School, its leadership and community, helped the evolution of the Academy in Indiana.

The commitment to giving back, and the wisdom and humility to request the opinions of others is an important life lesson from the Roeper community. What they do is for the betterment of society, including the students and their large community. The community gives of itself and provides a considerable number of scholarships for impoverished students. The Roeper Community clearly could avoid this step, leaving poor students to make their own way, but they do not. They work harder to raise additional money to help a broad, diverse group of students. In other words, they welcome everyone who can qualify academically and they do their best to gain these students entrance and affordability. Unlike those who see the world as a zero-sum game, where everything is a competition, where most people will have to lose so a few can win, the Roeper School community is committed to improving the world for everyone. They collaborate, bringing together great minds, and continue working to improve a school that already has impacted the lives of thousands of people. In a nutshell, the startling experience of the 100-plus miles per hour biker gang at 2 a.m. in the blinding fog, plus the overwhelming awareness of possible death, does not compare to the myriad life lessons I have learned by working in a community with so many virtues. Doing good for others in the quiet moments, away from any attention or recognition, is a wonderful way to lead one's life. I am very thankful that George and Annemarie created the Roeper School and later turned it into a school for gifted students. I am thankful that I was invited to work with the Roeper Community to try to help others. I am thankful that my colleagues thought highly enough of me to tell me when I was wrong. To this day, some of my best friends corrected me during our many discussions at the Roeper School. I am thankful for my 20 years as a member of the Editorial Advisory Board, Editorial Review Board, Education Committee, Roeper Institute, and Board of Trustees. I am a better person as a consequence.

A good way to end this chapter is to describe the Roeper School graduation I attended. Because the graduations were not held at the same time as the board meetings, I had never seen one. Several of my Roeper Community friends, including Linda Kohlenberg, Lori Lutz, and Susan Learman, invited me to attend. I was warned to plan for a long day and to wear comfortable clothes. I drove the five hours and observed the following. The event was held outside on the grounds of the lower school in Bloomfield Hills. Each student had asked one person to be his or her advocate/representative. One by one the students and advocates would come to the stage and the advocate would recount meaningful stories about the student. Because the school is K-12, many of the stories cut across the student's school life. Sometimes materials or products were on display, but mostly it was storytelling, smiles, and hugs. The emphasis was on the nature of the student and how the Roeper Community benefitted from the student's participation, or character. The pairing of each child with his or her chosen advocate revealed a considerable amount about each of them. The stories ranged from about five minutes to 20 minutes or so. This made for an emotional and endearing event. It also meant that the ceremony lasted for over four hours, and this was with a graduating class that was quite small, less than 35. I felt like I knew the students well when it was over. Each child got to shine and the descriptions did not pull punches, making for some interesting and awkward moments. The commitment to a personal education was true all the way through graduation. The candor was part of the celebration and seemingly quite appreciated. The students, teachers, administrators, support staff, and parents were celebrating each child, not merely their favorite. The Roeper Community deserves considerable credit for keeping an ideal going that focuses the attention on the development of children for the betterment of the world. Remaining true to their commitment is difficult and requires vigilance. I am confident that the Roeper Community is up to the task.

PART III

CURRICULUM AND PROGRAMS

JOYCE VANTASSEL-BASKA

DIFFERENTIATION IN ACTION:
THE INTEGRATED CURRICULUM MODEL

Differentiation for the gifted student in curriculum, instruction, and assessment requires attention to the adaptation and modification of the core curriculum in important respects. It requires a clear sense of what needs to be changed in the core, based on the characteristics and needs of these learners. It also requires a sense of the ways in which curriculum design can be tailored at each level of analysis, from goals and outcomes to activities, strategies, materials, and assessment levels of the process. The Integrated Curriculum Model is one approach found to be helpful in executing the process of differentiation in each subject area, integrating the content, process, and product dimensions to make them more balanced in the learning process that students experience.

This model also fits well with the philosophy, spirit, and operational work of the Roeper School, a haven for gifted children for over 50 years. Since a school for the gifted is required to provide differentiation for gifted learners in a comprehensive and articulated way, it has a special fit with the dimensions of the ICM, which values the integration of learning across disciplines as its most important tenet. This tenet is well integrated into the Roeper philosophy where interdisciplinary learning is a part of the mission carried out by a committed faculty. Engaging gifted learners in meaningful real-world projects is another tenet of the ICM, manifested in the service learning component at The Roeper School where action projects in real-world settings are the norm. The ICM also places great value on collaborative learning, with gifted students working with their peers in dyads, triads, and quads to solve a problem or address an issue or debate an argument. Roeper clearly applies this approach in its dealing with students, encouraging their collaborative potential through multiple modes of communication.

An account of the ICM model, its evidence of effectiveness, and key descriptors follow. In the final analysis, curriculum for the gifted must respond to student characteristics and needs through providing inquiry-based learning that motivates and inspires. The Roeper School offers a unique setting for such work to be carried out.

OVERVIEW OF THE ICM MODEL

The Integrated Curriculum Model (ICM) was first proposed in 1986, based on a review of the research literature on what worked with gifted learners, and further expounded upon in subsequent publications (VanTassel-Baska, 1986, 1998, 2011). The model is comprised of three interrelated dimensions that are responsive to different aspects of the gifted learner:

1. *Emphasizing advanced content knowledge that frames disciplines of study.* Honoring the talent search concept, this facet of the model ensures that careful diagnostic-prescriptive approaches are employed to enhance the challenge level of the curriculum base. Curricula based on the model would represent advanced learning in any given discipline.
2. *Providing higher-order thinking and processing.* This facet of the model promotes student opportunities for manipulating information at complex levels by employing generic thinking models like Paul's Elements of Reasoning (Paul & Elder, 2001) and more discipline-specific models like Sher's Nature of the Scientific Process (Sher, 1993). This facet of the ICM also promotes the utilization of information in generative ways, through project work and/or fruitful discussions.
3. *Organizing learning experiences around major issues, themes, and ideas that define understanding of a discipline and provide connections across disciplines.* This facet of the ICM scaffolds curricula for gifted learners around the important aspects of a discipline and emphasizes these aspects in a systemic way (Ward, 1981). Thus, themes and ideas are selected based on careful research of the primary area of study to determine the most worthy and important ideas for curriculum development, a theme consistent with reform curriculum specifications in key areas (American Association for the Advancement of Science, 1990; Perkins, 1992). The goal of such an approach is to ensure deep understanding of disciplines, rather than misconceptions.

These three relatively distinct curriculum dimensions have proven successful with gifted populations at various stages of development and in various domain-specific areas. Taken together, these research-based approaches formed the basis of the Integrated Curriculum Model (VanTassel-Baska, 1986, 1998; VanTassel-Baska & Little, 2011; VanTassel-Baska & Stambaugh, 2006). Figure 1 portrays the interrelated dimensions of the ICM model just described.

The Integrated Curriculum Model (ICM) curricular approach in the design and implementation process of working with learners in schools are united. Too often gifted learners end up with a curriculum diet that is composed of dabs of acceleration, dabs of project work, and dabs of higher-level thinking opportunities. The ICM organizes these features into one package, thus allowing gifted learners and others to experience a more integrated pattern of learning. This integrated approach also reflects recent research on learning. Studies have documented that better transfer of learning occurs when higher-order thinking skills are embedded in subject matter (Minstrell & Kraus, 2005; National Research Council, 2000; Perkins & Salomon, 1989), and teaching concepts in a discipline is a better way to produce long-term learning than teaching facts and rules (Marzano, 1992). Our understanding of creativity also has shifted toward the need for strong subject matter knowledge as

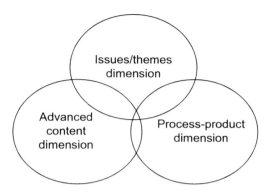

Figure 1. Dimensions of the ICM Model (VanTassel-Baska, 2003b)

a prerequisite (Amabile, 1996). Because the ICM is organized around the subject matter standards, it uses the content core as a basis for modification and integration.

Recent reviews of curricular interventions for the gifted have found the content modification features exemplified in the ICM have the greatest prevailing effect on an accelerative approach (Johnsen, 2000; VanTassel-Baska & Brown, 2007). The fusion of these approaches is central to the development of a coherent curriculum that is responsive to diverse needs of talented students while also providing rich challenges to all for optimal learning.

Theoretical Underpinnings

The theoretical support for the Integrated Curriculum Model comes primarily from learning theory and development. One source is the work of Vygotsky (1978). One aspect critical to the model is the zone of proximal development where learners must be exposed to material slightly above their tested level in order to feel challenged by the learning experience. This idea was expanded on by Csikszentmihalyi (1991) in his concept of flow where gifted learners demonstrated a broader and deeper capacity to engage learning than did typical students (Csikszentmihalyi, Rathunde, & Whalen, 1993).

A second aspect of this theory of learning is the view of interactionism, whereby the learner increases learning depth by interacting with others in the environment to enhance understanding of concepts and ideas. Ideas are validated and understood through the articulation of tentative connections made based on a stimulus such as a literary artifact, a film, a piece of music, or a problem. Learning increases as interactions provide the scaffolding necessary to structure thinking about the stimulus (Vygotsky, 1978).

A theory of constructivism whereby learners construct knowledge for themselves is also central to the instructional emphases within the application of the ICM. This theory is central to the tenets of the teaching and learning models found in the ICM curriculum and a central thesis to the model itself as students must be in charge of their own learning in respect to each dimension of the model, whether it be content acceleration, project-based learning opportunities such as PBL, or discussion-laden experiences in which concepts, issues, and themes are explored.

Another theoretical influence on the model was the work of Mortimer Adler and his Paedaeia Proposal (1984) that posited the importance of rich content representing the best products of world civilization coupled with the relevant cognitive skills to study them, appropriately linked to the intellectual ideas that spawned the work of the disciplines and philosophy. His world view of curriculum was highly influential in thinking about the role of academic rationalism in a curriculum for the gifted, even as cognitive science was the predominant force in the larger environment.

Finally, the theory of multiculturalism espoused by James Banks (1994a, 1994b, 2001) and more recently by Donna Ford (2005; Ford & Harris, 1999) speaks to the aspect of the ICM concerned with students making a better world through deliberate social action, whether through the resolutions brought to policy makers as a result of PBL work or the studies of technology use in researching issues or the concerns for censorship in the history of great literature. Moreover, this theoretical orientation also provides a major emphasis on the works of minority authors both in this country and abroad as well as an attempt to acknowledge multiple perspectives in student understanding of any content area, especially history.

Application

Current work in the ICM model for the gifted has continued to focus on a merger with the curriculum reform principles advocating world-class standards in all traditional curricular areas (VanTassel-Baska & Little, 2011). The major shift in thinking regarding this orientation is from one that looks only at the optimal match between characteristics of the learner and the curriculum to a model based on performance in various domains, thereby letting the level of functioning determine who is ready for more advanced work in an area rather than a predictive measure. Thus, differentiation for any population is grounded in differential standards of performance at a given period of time. Standards are constant; time is the variable. Such an approach holds promise for gifted students in that the level and pace of curriculum *can* be adapted to their needs, and the existing state standards call for the kind of focus that curriculum makers for gifted students have long advocated—higher-level thinking, interdisciplinary approaches, and an emphasis on student-centred learning.

Gifted students need high but realizable expectations for learning at each stage of development. Other students can also benefit from working to attain such standards. By the same token, gifted students can also benefit from a developmental and personal perspective on fostering their abilities at a close-up level, an emphasis requiring organizational models such as tutorials, mentorships, and small clusters to support it.

What types of students are best served using the ICM? The ICM model was designed for students who have strong intellectual abilities and/or strong academic aptitudes in the areas in which curriculum units have been designed. In the last several years, however, the research on effectiveness that has been conducted suggests that more students benefit from the curriculum beyond the population for whom it was intended (e.g., Swanson, 2006). Our collection of research on the units of study that used the ICM as the organizing framework have increasingly shown that the benefits of the units for all students is significant and important educationally in respect to achievement and motivation.

Because the units are content-based, students who are strong in only one area can benefit greatly from experiencing them. So, for example, strong readers can grow from exposure to the language arts units even if they are not identified as gifted since the readings in the unit can be used with strong readers and the other differentiation features of the units serve to enrich their understandings in key ways. Because the units employ opportunities for open-ended learning, higher-level opportunities to learn, and the use of multicultural literature, they work very well with promising learners from low-income backgrounds and children of colour. Moreover, the consistent use of instructional scaffolds becomes a critical aspect in elevating the level of learning for these groups. In the final analysis, the model has been useful in designing curriculum that can be used with all learners although the gains have suggested the greatest growth has occurred for promising learners, high-level readers, and students who are gifted in relevant subject areas of the curriculum.

Research on the Effectiveness of the Integrated Curriculum Model

Studies have been conducted over the past decade to discern the learning gains of gifted learners, promising learners from low-income and minority backgrounds, and typical learners exposed to the units of study based on the model. Both quasi-experimental and experimental designs have been employed to demonstrate differences among ability-similar groups of learners using curriculum based on the model compared to those who have not been exposed to such curriculum. An overview of these studies and their results in language arts, science, and social studies follow.

The Integrated Curriculum Model (ICM) has been tested substantially in the areas of science and language arts in particular, using quasi-experimental research designs that compared pretest-posttest performance of students participating in the Center for Gifted Education units in these areas with the performance of similar students who were not taught using the units. The presentation of claims for student learning in each area follows, demonstrating the results related to the specific curriculum, as well as supporting the notion of ongoing data-collection efforts to maintain high-quality curriculum development and implementation. In each content area, details and results of earlier studies are presented first, followed by discussion of more recent studies.

Science curriculum effectiveness data. The Center for Gifted Education's problem-based science curricular units for high-ability learners in grades 2–8 have been rigorously evaluated to ensure both effectiveness in promoting student learning gains and acceptance by teachers. Not only have the units and accompanying training materials undergone four major revisions in the course of their development but also the next-to-last edition of the units was field-tested across multiple school districts. The goals of the program across all of the units have consistently been threefold: (a) to develop student understanding of the concept of systems, (b) to develop specific content learning that is unit dependent, and (c) to develop scientific research processes. More specific learning outcomes have been delineated under each of these broad overarching goals, in keeping with the intent of the National Science Standards and the Benchmarks for Science Literacy that call for substantive content linked to high-level scientific processes and the understanding of meaningful scientific concepts (American Association for the Advancement of Science, 1990; National Research Council, 1996).

Evidence of effectiveness for Project Clarion. Although the PBL units discussed above address all three major goals in the science curriculum framework (i.e., the concept of systems and change, specific content learning, and scientific reasoning), the PBL curriculum studies focused explicitly on student application of scientific research and integrating students' understanding of science content and inquiry, reasoning, and problem-based reasoning skills. In the more recent units developed under Project Clarion, we addressed the development of curiosity in science, critical and creative thinking, as well as emphases on concept development in systems and change and the scientific research process. The PBL was part of the ICM units, not the lead feature. Goals and student outcomes are aligned to the National Science Education Standards. Each lesson includes instructions that detail the purpose, time needed, suggestions on how to implement the lesson, and ways to conclude and extend the lessons.

Language arts curriculum effectiveness data. The Center for Gifted Education's language arts curricular units have also been evaluated for effectiveness in terms of teaching literary analysis and interpretation and persuasive writing as language arts manifestations of higher-level thinking (VanTassel-Baska, Zuo, Avery, & Little, 2002). As such, the research findings contribute to our understanding of the importance of embedding higher-order skills into content and builds on prior understanding of effective research-based strategies for teaching writing (e.g., Burkhalter, 1995). Specifically, they suggest that gifted learners who deliberately receive instruction in literary analysis and interpretation and persuasive writing demonstrate significant and important growth when compared to equally able students not receiving such instruction. Each unit of study has 4–5 lessons that focus on the development of these skills, using short literary selections to buttress discussion and interpretation. Writing prompts are derived from the readings. After six weeks of classroom instruction, differential gains have consistently been recorded across units, teachers, and school types.

Evidence of effectiveness from Project Athena. Based on the growing research evidence on the use of The College of William and Mary's language arts units with gifted learners, the team at William and Mary began a three-year longitudinal study of using the curriculum in Title 1 schools and inclusive classrooms with all learners (VanTassel-Baska, Bracken, Feng, & Brown, 2009). The results of this five-year Javits project demonstrated the power of using more high-level materials with all learners, not just the gifted, as well as illustrating the importance of using multiple approaches to assess learning and multiple pathways for learning as the project team also developed a reading comprehension program, entitled Jacob's Ladder, to enable students to move to higher-level thinking, once comprehension has been attained.

Evidence of effectiveness from social studies curriculum. One comprehensive study has been conducted to date to examine the efficacy of the social studies units of study developed by the Center for Gifted Education under the Javits-supported Project Phoenix (Little, Feng, VanTassel-Baska, Rogers, & Avery, 2007). In a quasi-experimental study of using social studies units modeled on the ICM, conducted with Title I students in Grades 3–8, results suggested that significant and important learning gains were accrued for students in selected classrooms on the dimensions of content mastery, concept development, and higher-level thinking. Teacher results confirmed the unevenness of student learning as connected to implementation fidelity, although group analyses suggested that teachers enhanced their ability to use selected differentiation strategies as a result of the training and curriculum differentiation use designed into the units. Sub-analyses showed growth for both gifted and non-gifted students in the study and for low socioeconomic learners as well as minority students.

Research evidence for use of the ICM with special populations. Center studies of science and language arts curriculum effectiveness in heterogeneous Title I classrooms have shown that a curriculum written for gifted learners is also effective with non-gifted learners, given the use of proper differentiation, scaffolding, and flexible grouping techniques (VanTassel-Baska, Bracken, Stambaugh, & Feng, 2009; VanTassel-Baska, Feng, et al., 2008). Scaffolding may be in the form of a supplemental curriculum or specific differentiated strategies and pacing. In language arts, Jacob's Ladder was developed to provide additional scaffolding in reading to expose less-experienced students to models that bridge lower-level to higher-level thinking. Navigator novel studies were written so that students could have more choice in novel selections and differentiated activities at a given reading level. In science, specific models were developed to scaffold students' thinking in planning scientific investigations. Pacing of units as also modified within the regular classroom, and instructional grouping encouraged effective discussions.

The research evidence we have collected over multiple projects, as well as evidence collected by our colleagues (e.g., Swanson, 2006), suggests that the William and Mary units are effective with these special populations of promising learners. In fact, the data suggest that, given enough time, these students perform at comparable levels to more advantaged learners in selected areas like persuasive writing (VanTassel-Baska, Zuo, Avery, & Little, 2002). In Title I schools, all groups, including groups of diverse learners, showed significant and important growth in key areas of language arts, social studies, and science learning after using the units. The use of such curriculum, however, must be accompanied by faithful use of the teaching-learning models provided that scaffold instruction at higher levels of discourse and thought occurs, particularly for less-experienced learners in a subject area.

Examples of Curriculum and Instructional Modifications, using the ICM

The examples provided in Table 1 illustrate the major dimensions of the ICM and the translation of those dimensions into differentiated approaches in each major content domain. Each of these sketchy translations have been developed into full blown units of study with both pre and post assessments to assess the extent of student learning. Most units of study have also been judged exemplary by the National Association of Gifted Children (NAGC) annually since 1999 when the standards for curriculum were established.

The examples demonstrate the ways in which accelerated learning is promoted, the ways in which the higher-level processes of thinking, problem solving and research are exploited, the types of generative products that students create, and the conceptual foundation for given units of study. These dimensions then frame the units of study for each area of learning, with varying units by grade level that typically cut across two grades. The short hand table descriptions also suggest the nature of instructional approaches employed.

Each unit of study also has student outcomes that focus on content, process, product, and concept learning matched to unit-based assessments. For example, teachers may assess students within a unit on critical thinking, concept development, content acquisition, and product sophistication using the tools of instrumentation and rubrics provided. Exemplars also provide guidance for judgment regarding student performance.

Funded for 20 years by the United States Department of Education, these units of study were intended not only as models of exemplary curriculum but also as the basis for differentiation in classrooms. They have been successfully used in all states and 18 countries to provide the modifications needed for gifted learners

Assessment Approaches in the ICM

The ICM model employs pre and post performance-based assessments in each of its dimensions within each unit of study. Thus teachers can easily determine the baseline

Table 1. The Integrated Curriculum Model by subject area and dimensions of sample unit study

Content Area/Topic	Accelerative approaches	Higher level thinking/ problem solving	Product tasks	Concept theme
Science/ botany/plants	Pretesting and compacting, study of botany at primary level	Reasoning model, scientific investigation skills, questions	Logs, experimental designs, PBL resolution project and presentation	Systems: Understanding the elements, boundaries, interactions, inputs and outputs of cells, plants, and terrariums
Language Arts/ Autobiographies of writers	Reading selections calibrated 2 grade levels above	Reasoning model, literature web, persuasive writing, research project	Autobiographical project, with talent development markers	Change: The ways that change is everywhere, related to time, caused by people or nature etc.
Mathematics/ Study of animal populations	Advanced math skills in graphing, statistics, and estimation	Problem-based learning	Problem resolution in oral and written form for a real world audience	Models that are conceptual and physical applied to understand phenomena
Social Studies/Ancient Egypt	Emphasis on the systems of ancient civilizations that made them great	Emphasis on historical analysis, document study, and trends	Research paper on an historical issue	Patterns of change over time as chronicled by historical events within and across cultures

level of students in respect to content learning, capacity to engage in higher-level thinking tasks, and conceptual levels across subject areas via the use of a macro-concept assessment tool. The pre-assessment data may be used as an instructional tool to adjust the teaching needed in key areas of the units of study. These data may also be used to determine student outcome data after a unit has been taught, thus providing ongoing information for planning the next instructional module needed in a given subject area in respect to content skills, higher-level thinking, and concept development.

In addition to the use of pre-post assessments to document positive growth in learning overall, the units also use formative assessments for purposes of progress monitoring during the teaching of a given unit of study. This progress monitoring may involve the collection of activities designed to assess how well students are applying their understanding to new material in the areas of content, process, and concept dimensions of the curriculum. For example, as students study the concept of systems in science, they are asked to apply their understanding of systems to the social science system of state transportation. The activity, which they also illustrate and articulate to their peers, suggests their understanding of the concept at a level necessary for transfer to new applications. Such evidence of student performance provides the teacher the information necessary to modify instruction for individuals or groups of learners, based on the result. In several of our studies, we have found that students have difficulty transferring their understanding of boundaries as a part of a system. Consequently, teachers target that component of a system for further teaching.

The units also provide evidence from longer term individual products of the progress in learning that has accrued for students in all three dimensions of the model. Assessment forms are provided for teacher use to chart the extent to which the product meets the standards of higher-level thinking, problem-solving, and cross-disciplinary content expected.

Self, peer, and teacher assessment approaches are used for writing in both social studies and language arts in order to provide a way for all three groups to chart baseline and progress on important dimensions of the writing process and key models of writing. Journal writing may be examined by the teacher and the student to determine appropriateness to the prompt, fluency, and use of language devices.

How Is Differentiation Addressed in the Model?

At the most basic level, differentiation for the gifted is addressed through the construction of the ICM model to begin with. It was designed, based on the research evidence of 50 years of work with the gifted in multiple settings as to what has worked with them. Thus the dimensions of advanced content, the use of higher-level processes with a high quality product expectation, and higher-level concept development that allows for interdisciplinary connections distill that research base.

At the level of translation of the model into practical use, the units of study designed around the ICM also employ deliberate features of differentiation that include the use of acceleration, including pretesting and streamlining, complexity, depth, challenge, abstractness, and creativity. Each unit has designed activities and questions that incorporate these features in a systematic way. Question-asking is a major feature of the units, with questions designed around higher-level thinking models that frame the use of critical and creative thinking at levels of analysis, synthesis, and evaluation. The creation level of prompts is often included in the scaffolding. Other models of thinking are also used to provide openendedness in questions and depth of understanding.

CONCLUSION

The Integrated Curriculum Model represents one of only a few curriculum models designed for gifted learners in specific subject matter domains that have been fully developed into usable units of study at all stages of development K-12, have been piloted and field tested consistently across districts and states, and have demonstrated impressive growth gains for students in content, higher-level process skills, and concepts. The model has consistently demonstrated coherence in its design and development and fidelity of implementation in selected contexts. It has been enthusiastically received by teachers of the gifted as a powerful way to ensure challenge and sufficient differentiation for the gifted. It has proven to be a basis for motivating both students and their teachers to learn more at higher levels. In sum, it represents an important baseline for future work in curriculum for the gifted, work that provides both a model and its practical applications and demonstrates how our best learners can show significant and important intellectual growth through the process of systematic differentiation. As discussed earlier, the Roeper School provides a vibrant learning environment already richly imbued with curriculum integration. It also can enrich its ongoing evolution as an innovative school for the gifted by employing some of the ideas and processes from the ICM more directly.

REFERENCES

Adams, C. M., & Callahan, C. M. (1995). The reliability and validity of a performance task for evaluating science process skills. *Gifted Child Quarterly, 39,* 14–20.
Adler, M. (1984). *The paiedeia program.* New York, NY: MacMillan.
Amabile, T. (1996). *Creativity in context.* Boulder, CO: Westview Press.
American Association for the Advancement of Science. (1990). *Science for all Americans: Project 2061.* New York, NY: Oxford University Press.
Banks, J. (1994a). *Multiethnic education: Theory and practice* (3rd ed.). Boston, MA: Allyn and Bacon.
Banks, J. (1994b). *An introduction to multicultural education.* Boston, MA: Allyn and Bacon.
Banks, J. (2001). *Cultural diversity and education: Foundations, curriculum and teaching.* Boston, MA: Allyn and Bacon.
Bland, L. C., Kim, K. H., VanTassel-Baska, J., Bracken, B. A., Feng, A. X., Stambaugh, T. (under revision). Assessing science reasoning and conceptual understanding in the primary grades using multiple measures of performance: Project Clarion. *Gifted Child Quarterly.*

Brown, E., Avery, L., VanTassel-Baska, J., Worley, B., Stambaugh, T. (2006). A five-state analysis of gifted education policies: Ohio policy study results. *Roeper Review, 29,* 11–23.

Burkhalter, N. (1995). A Vygotsky-based curriculum for teaching persuasive writing in the elementary grades. *Language Arts, 72,* 192–196.

Cain, M. F. (1990). The diet cola test. *Science Scope, 13*(4), 32–34.

Center for Gifted Education. (1997a). *Acid, acid everywhere: A problem-based unit.* Dubuque, IA: Kendall/Hunt.

Center for Gifted Education. (1997b). *What a find!* Dubuque, IA: Kendall/Hunt.

Center for Gifted Education. (1998). *Autobiographies.* Dubuque, IA: Kendall/Hunt.

Center for Gifted Education. (2010). *Guide to teaching a language arts curriculum for high-ability learners* (2nd ed.). Dubuque, IA: Kendall/Hunt.

Csikszentmihalyi, M. (1991). *Flow: The psychology of optimal experience.* New York, NY: Harper Perennial.

Csikszentmihalyi, M., Rathunde, K. R., & Whalen, S. (1993). *Talented teenagers: The roots of success and failure.* New York, NY: Cambridge University Press.

Feng, A., VanTassel-Baska, J., Quek, C., O'Neil, B., & Bai, W. (2005). A longitudinal assessment of gifted students' learning using the integrated curriculum model: Impacts and perceptions of the William and Mary language arts and science curriculum. *Roeper Review, 27,* 78–83.

Ford, D. (2005). Integrating multicultural and gifted education: A curricular framework. *Theory into Practice, 44*(2), 125–138.

Ford, D., & Harris, J. J. (1999). *Multicultural Gifted Education* (Education and Psychology of the Gifted Series). New York, NY: Teachers College Press.

Garet, M. S., Porter, A. C., Desimone, L., Birman, B. F., & Yoon, K. S. (2001). What makes professional development effective? Results from a national sample of teachers. *American Educational Research Journal, 38,* 915–945.

Gentry, M., & Keilty, B. (2004). Rural and suburban cluster grouping: Reflections on staff development as a component of program success. *Roeper Review, 26,* 147–155.

Gubbins, E. J., Westberg, K. L., Reis, S. M., Dinnocenti, S. T., Tieso, C. L., Muller, L. M., et al. (2002). *Implementing a professional development model using gifted education strategies with all students.* (Report RM02172). Storrs: University of Connecticut, National Research Center on the Gifted and Talented.

Hansen, J., & Feldhusen, J. (1994). Comparison of trained and untrained teachers of the gifted. *Gifted Child Quarterly, 38,* 115–123.

Johnsen, S. K. (2000). What the research says about curriculum. *Tempo, 20*(3), 25–30.

Kaplan, S. (2009). The Kaplan grid. In J. Renzulli (Ed.), *Systems and models in gifted education.* Waco, TX: Prufrock Press.

Karnes, F. A., & Stephens, K. R. (2000). State definitions for the gifted and talented revisited. *Exceptional Children, 66,* 219–238.

Kennedy, M. (1999). Form and substance in mathematics and science professional development. *NISE Brief, 3*(2), 1–7.

Kim, K. H., VanTassel-Baska, J., Bracken, B. A., Feng, A., Stambaugh, T., & Bland, L. (manuscript submitted for publication). *Project Clarion: Three years of science instruction in Title I schools among K-third grade students.*

Little, C. A., Feng, A. X., VanTassel-Baska, J., Rogers, K. B., & Avery, L. D. (2007). A study of curriculum effectiveness in social studies. *Gifted Child Quarterly, 51,* 272–284.

Maker, J., & Schiever, J. (2009) *Curriculum development and teaching strategies for gifted learners.* Austin, TX: Pro Ed.

Marzano, R. (1992). *Cultivating thinking in English.* Urbana, IL: National Council for Teachers of English.

Matthews, D., & Foster, J. (2005). A dynamic scaffolding model of teacher development: The gifted education consultant as catalyst for change. *Gifted Child Quarterly, 49,* 222–230.

Minstrell, J., & Krause, P. (2005). Guided inquiry in the science classroom. In J. Bransford, A. Brown, & R. Cocking (Eds.), *How students learn: History, mathematics, and science in the classroom* (pp. 475–477) Washington, DC: National Academy Press.

National Assessment Governing Board. (1992). *Reading framework for the 1992 national assessment of education progress*. Washington, DC: U.S. Department of Education.

National Research Council. (1996). *National science education standards*. Washington, DC: National Academy Press.

National Research Council (2000). *How people learn*. Washington, DC: Author.

Parker, J., & Karnes, F. (1991). Graduate degree programs and resource centers in gifted education: An update and analysis. *Gifted Child Quarterly, 35*, 43–48.

Paul, R., & Elder, L. (2001). *Critical thinking: Tools for taking charge of your learning and your life*. Upper Saddle River, NJ: Prentice Hall.

Perkins, D. (1992). Selecting fertile themes for integrated learning. In H. H. Jacob (Ed.), *Interdisciplinary curriculum: Design and implementation* (pp. 67–75). Alexandria, VA: Association for Supervision and Curriculum Development.

Perkins, D., & Saloman, G. (1989). Are cognitive skills context bound? *Educational Research, 18*(1), 16–25.

Peterson, K. (2001, June). *Shaping school culture for quality teaching and learning*. Presentation to the National Leadership Institute, College of William and Mary, Williamsburg, VA.

Sher, B. T. (2003). Adapting science curricula for high-ability learners. In J. VanTassel-Baska & C. Little (Eds.), *Content-based curriculum for high-ability learners* (pp. 191–218). Waco, TX: Prufrock Press.

Swanson, J. (2006). Breaking through assumptions about low-income, minority gifted students. *Gifted Child Quarterly, 50*, 11–24.

Swanson, J. (2007). Policy and practice: a case study of gifted education policy implementation. *Journal for the Education of the Gifted, 31*, 131–164.

Tomlinson, C., Tomchin, E., Callahan, C., Adams, C., Pizzat-Timi, P., Cunningham, C., et al. (1994). Practices of preservice teachers related to gifted and other academically diverse learners. *Gifted Child Quarterly, 38*, 106–114.

Toulmin, S. E. (1958). *The uses of argument*. Cambridge, England: Cambridge University Press.

VanTassel-Baska, J. (1986). Effective curriculum and instructional models for talented students. *Gifted Child Quarterly, 30*, 164–169.

VanTassel-Baska, J. (2003). *Curriculum planning and instructional design for gifted learners* (2nd ed.). Denver, CO: Love.

VanTassel-Baska, J. (2008) *Assessment for gifted students*. Waco, TX: Prufrock Press.

VanTassel-Baska, J., Avery, L. D., Hughes, C. E., & Little, C. A. (2000). An evaluation of the implementation of curriculum innovation: The impact of William and Mary units on schools. *Journal for the Education of the Gifted, 23*, 244–272.

VanTassel-Baska, J., Bass, G., Ries, R., Poland, D., & Avery, L. D. (1998). A national study of science curriculum effectiveness with high-ability students. *Gifted Child Quarterly, 42*, 200–211.

VanTassel-Baska, J., Bracken, B., Feng, A., & Brown, E. (2009). A longitudinal study of reading comprehension and reasoning ability of students in elementary Title I schools, *Journal for the Education of the Gifted, 33*, 7–37.

VanTassel-Baska, J., & Brown, E. (2007). Towards best practice: An analysis of the efficacy of curriculum models in gifted education. *Gifted Child Quarterly, 51*, 342–358.

VanTassel-Baska, J., Feng, A., Brown, E., Bracken, B., Stambaugh, T., French, H., McGowan, S., Worley, B., Quek, C., & Bai, W. (2008). A study of differentiated instructional change over three years. *Gifted Child Quarterly, 52*, 297–312.

VanTassel-Baska, J., Johnson, D. T., Hughes, C. E., & Boyce, L. N. (1996). A study of language arts curriculum effectiveness with gifted learners. *Journal for the Education of the Gifted, 19*, 461–480.

VanTassel-Baska, J., & Little, C. (2011) *Content-based curriculum for the gifted*. Waco, TX: Prufrock Press.

VanTassel-Baska, J., & Stambaugh, T. (2006) *Comprehensive curriculum for the gifted*. Boston, MA: Pearson.
VanTassel-Baska, J., Zuo, L., Avery, L. D., & Little, C. A. (2002). A curriculum study of gifted student learning in the language arts. *Gifted Child Quarterly, 46,* 30–44.
Vygotsky, L. S. (1978). *Mind in society: The development of higher psychological processes*. Cambridge, MA: Harvard University Press.
Ward, V. (1981). *Educating the gifted: An axiomatic approach*. Ventura County, CA: Leadership Training Institute for Gifted and Talented?

WENDY MAYER

AN INTERDISCIPLINARY JOURNEY

How does the seed of a week-long interdisciplinary unit get planted? The origin of the unit plan started at one of our regular 8th grade team meetings. A group of four homeroom teachers and the middle school director gathered for our weekly lunch meeting to talk about students when the discussion spiraled into how to inspire students and help them connect to the curriculum in a deeper way. The conversation led to an enthusiastic agreement that a thematic interdisciplinary unit would be a fantastic addition to the 8th grade curriculum. The idea hung in the air with a lot of excitement as we all looked at each other. We loved the idea, but we could also see all the obstacles, too. Ignoring all the difficulties and running on pure vision, I decided I would take a run at it. Summer was rapidly approaching, so I did my best to quickly brainstorm with a few teachers and to flesh out a basic plan.

First, I needed a topic. I had completed a summer program a few years back on global climate change, and had been experimenting with different ways to integrate the unit into my regular 8th grade Science class. The topic lent itself very easily to the different subjects and provided real-world problem solving aspects that would give the unit more meaning. Our students heard so much about the problems in the world, and I wanted to create a unit that would allow them to provide well-reasoned, knowledgeable, and holistic solutions to a complex and urgent problem. I applied for and was awarded a summer grant from Roeper for professional development. The seed was planted and had begun to grow roots.

When attacking something that is amorphous and cumbersome, you have to pick a starting point. I started with the end. I knew what I wanted the kids to be able to do, and then I worked backward to determine what knowledge and skills they would need to be successful. I wanted 8th graders to work in groups to complete a cohesive, engaging presentation—a presentation that addressed country-specific problems and solutions for global climate change that were made with a holistic and educated perspective. I wanted to arrange the unit for the upcoming year to run for a week in January. Easy, right?!

Picking a time in the year to complete the unit was difficult. But after discussing it with my 8th grade team and a few others, it made the most sense to use our midterm week—a week in January when classes meet for two-hour blocks in order to take exams. Large exams are not really age appropriate for middle schoolers, so during this time, most teachers give a test and then find other activities to fill our block times. We all agreed that we could have the different climate change unit assignments count as a grade and just give our tests, if needed, before the mid-term week. We recognized that would be able to make much better use of our student's time.

Coordinating seven different departments (Math, English, Science, Social Studies, Communications, Fine Arts, Foreign Language) and 18 different teachers seemed like an overwhelming task. Luckily, at Roeper we have a wonderfully cooperative staff who embraced the unit with enthusiasm. To be considerate of everyone's time, and aware of the insights they would have, it was important to touch base with all involved parties and to give them time to ask questions and offer suggestions. To get teachers on board, I spoke with as many people as possible before the end of the school year and sent out an e-mail with a basic description and a request for input to teachers early in the summer. Once the new school year started, I reviewed and updated the plans at a few meetings and met up with teachers early in the school year. Each time I left my room, I made a habit of popping in on a teacher or two to catch up on progress, answer questions, and review the expectations. I knew communication was key.

A few days after summer officially began, with my suitcase hastily packed, I was heading off to Europe with a group of students and my colleague Mike Ruddy. Mike is a seasoned 8th grade Roeper social studies teacher, and was the perfect person to help me bring this idea to life. So I roped him into helping me. We spent hours on the bus from Spain to France, and then from France to Italy, planning different aspects of the unit. We sat over espresso in Piazza Della Signoria watching the people go by and taking in the shadow of the statue of David while discussing the key economic components of climate change. If you can ever integrate a fantastic setting on an incredible trip into your planning stages of a week-long unit plan, I highly recommend it!

Over the rest of the summer, I also worked out the crucial aspects the students would need to understand in science and social studies. They needed a refresher course on different types of economies, political systems, and governments so that they would understand all the terms they would encounter during their research. They needed to understand the important factors that create climate (e.g., latitude, proximity to water), the difference between climate and weather, a basic understanding of the multitude of ways scientists measure changes in climate, an understanding of the cycles that we know affect the global climate (e.g., continental drift, solar radiance cycles), the limitations of the future of fossil fuels, the carbon cycle, sources of greenhouse gas emissions, and alternative energy sources and other methods to reduce carbon emissions. I knew that global climate change was a complicated topic not only in terms of understanding all the factors, but also in overcoming some skepticism. The first task was to provide them with a deeper understanding, next to help them see the urgency to take action, and finally to provide them with realistic options for problem solving. I planned on kicking off the unit a week earlier in Science to provide all the needed background information. In the end, I put together PowerPoint presentations and videos to present the information. I also did some classroom flipping and assigned videos to watch on alternative energy sources as homework.

Skills and subject matter needed to be incorporated and synthesized across various departments in a way that didn't feel forced or contrived. Some aspects fit in easily. I often relied on the strengths of our teachers and only had to supply an overview on what I thought would fit, and they then fleshed out the full lesson. This was the case for our communication, music, and math teachers involved. I knew the kids needed a lesson on how to give an engaging PowerPoint presentation. I talked to Dan, who as a Forensics and Debate coach was the closest thing we had to a Speech teacher, about putting together some videos to critique, providing a "dos and don'ts" sheet, and then giving them a practice session within their groups. I asked our Statistics teacher, Christina, to create a presentation on the basics of understanding how graphs can be manipulated to mislead. I asked the Fine Arts teachers to design lessons about how music and art can be used to create awareness and send a message. They all took these ideas and put together engaging lessons for the students without much more from me. Some teachers took their own ideas and ran with them, and for a few others I helped to more thoroughly craft the lesson. Overall, we worked together like different parts of an assembly line to build a finished product. I'm not sure if they saw how all the pieces fit together, but each teacher understood their role in the outcome.

The plan was coming together, but including Foreign Language would be tricky. We had students in 4 different languages (Spanish, French, Chinese, and Latin) at different levels, a few students who take two languages, and a few taking no language. I worked with Mike to puzzle out country choices so as to provide a diverse range of countries. The students would be assigned a country that spoke the foreign language they were studying (Latin students studied countries whose current spoken languages have Latin roots, e.g., Italy). As a group they would research the climate, culture, government, and economics of their assigned country. We generated a list of questions for the students to research, and the language teachers gave them time in class to research during the week before we kicked off the unit. I met with the foreign language teachers as a group and brainstormed different ideas. Ultimately, we decided that the best way for each teacher to make use of the unit was to tailor what the students needed to do based on what fit the desired expectations for each level and language. This ranged from completion of the research questions to individual presentations on the different aspects they researched. The higher-level students even gave an introduction in their studied language and added interactive components to their presentations. In the end, each teacher was inspired by the process and had more ideas for how to modify and enhance the lesson in the next year, including adding a unit with some of the subject-specific vocabulary.

Math was a tricky piece because the kids were studying at so many varied levels (from Pre-Algebra to Pre-Calculus), and they had many different teachers. So I decided to include a general calculations sheet where they would have to apply some simple formulas after researching their country's annual carbon emissions,

GNP, and the main sources of energy for their country. They would then use that information to determine the energy changes they would recommend for their country based everything they had learned, including the key political players, type of economy, natural resources, social attitudes, and any other important aspects they had discovered during their research. Their recommendations would include construction costs and percentage of GNP for the construction. Their goal was to cut a minimum of 50% of the carbon emissions for their country by 2050, with four changes from the different energy sectors: Nuclear, Wind, Hydroelectric, Solar, Natural Gas, Geothermal, Biofuels, Tidal or Wave Energy, and Carbon Capture and Storage. Additionally, they would recommend other ways to reduce or offset their carbon output with methods like efficiency or reforestation. They would also research the main concerns for their country relating to global climate change based on year-2100 projections, with a focus on water-related concerns, temperature and precipitation changes, weather extremes, and changes in food supply. Their research would be included in the presentation and used to make a case as to why change is needed now. During the exam week, they would work as a group to complete the research and the calculation sheets, create the presentation, and to practice it to make sure they hit all the marks given in the speech lesson.

To incorporate English, we had the students compose letters to be e-mailed to local Michigan government officials about climate change concerns. Lisa, the English teacher, provided some examples and an outline for drafting letters that would be clear and make a case. We added an additional creative writing piece in which the students wrote a sci-fi short story about a possible future in which climate change had run amuck. "The year is 2100, and the temperature on Earth has risen 10 degrees. The Great Lakes are the last haven for fresh water"… could be a potential start.

I wanted to add some experiences from outside Roeper to enhance the experience, so we arranged for Dave Woodward, the Oakland County Commissioner, to speak to the group about his experiences with climate change and what obstacles and opportunities leaders had in initiating policy change. We also arranged for a half-day trip to the Detroit Zoo in which the students received a lesson on the benefits of biodiversity, and threats to and actions being taken to protect different plants and animals. We also had a little bit of free time and a docent tour.

One of the most difficult components was scheduling. We had to find times for different teachers to meet with the group, determine how much time each teacher would want for the lesson, and how to provide the group with time to study for the one exam they would still be taking: Math. At Roeper we personalize to student's needs, and that means very different schedules. I created a schedule that would work for most kids, but then I still had to work out what to do with the students who were taking Upper School Science classes, two languages, or two math classes. It took a lot of flexibility and creativity on the parts of many different teachers to make this work.

I knew it was also important to get the kids excited about the process, so I ran my ideas by my students from time to time to get feedback and take suggestions as I continued to develop the unit throughout the year. They were excited to be part of the process, and this really built up enthusiasm and gave them a chance to wrap their heads around doing something so different. They would have a unique schedule, go to different rooms, and have free time for independent group work. Our kids have free blocks and are given a lot of freedom as middle school students, but this week would raise the level of self-discipline and responsibility for them to a new height. Teachers would be available to help, but no one would be directly supervising the students.

Mike and I met for an additional day in November to go over the plan so far. Mike provided a second set of eyes on the schedule I had put together, and we also fleshed out the final Science and Social Study components to include. We were going to team teach the possible outcomes for different areas relating to climate change. We covered everything from environmental concerns to national security. I also began organizing a model presentation on Costa Rica to show the students, fleshed out the grading rubric, and compiled some on-line resources.

It is important to consider the age group for which you are designing the lessons. You want them to stretch their existing skills, gain new ones, and have high expectations. You want to provide them with a challenge and a chance to grow, but not to overwhelm them in the process. One area that I knew would be a challenge, but would provide them with an important lifelong skill would be how to work together as a team. Getting any group to work harmoniously can be a challenge, but middle school kids have a specific intensity and such varying levels of maturity that group work can seem impossible to them at times. I wanted to make sure everyone had to contribute and would be held accountable for their contributions. So, I gave them too much work for one person to do, stressed that they had to divide and conquer to get be able to complete the task, and showed them the self-partner evaluation they would complete at the end. I explained that they needed to find a way to negotiate each person's contribution so that no one took over and no one was left out. It was each member's responsibility to make sure they were doing their share of the work. I knew I was pushing some students to step up and be leaders, pushing others to control the urge to do everything, and hopefully providing them with a model for how to successfully navigate teamwork in the future.

To make all the papers and presentations available for the students while being environmentally aware, I made use of the website edmodo.com, which we began using as a school at the beginning of the year. I created a folder with all the documents where the students could post questions for me or each other. They had access to every presentation, the Costa Rica example, resources links, calculation sheets, the rubric, and more at school and at home.

With all this being said before the groups began, I knew they would have some conflicts. So I met with all the groups at the end of the first day to check in on their progress, help negotiate responsibilities, and make sure they felt good about their progress thus far. At the end of the first day, some groups were getting along swimmingly, a few had some bumps to smooth out, and a few had fallen into complete dysfunction. Some groups were experiencing personality conflicts, some were worried they would not have enough time to get all their work done, and some realized that they hadn't listened very well and had completed two hours of work that was unnecessary. It was then that I began to realize the additional role I would be taking on during the week: international conflict resolver. I have to admit the stress level was high for everyone at the end of the first day, but I relied on the trust my students had in me to not set them up to fail and the countless hours of planning I had put into the unit and pushed forward. I set a new rule that any group who felt they could not overcome their discord after a few minutes of discussion should come see me as a group to work out a plan. And we did, repeatedly.

I also had experience with students overcoming challenge in the past. I teach a few week-long summer science camps at Roeper. Each week has a theme and one of those themes is forces and water. It's called "Splish Splash Physics". I created many small activities for the week, but the big project was to build canoe-sized boats out of a few 2 by 4s and a piece of plywood. Each group of about seven kids would draw, cut, sand, drill, screw, glue and paint the boats for a few hours a day over the course of four days. The final day was the reward where we took the boats to the pool and tested them out. Many of the kids had never used tools and struggled with the process. At times they argued and looked miserable. I persevered and worked hard with them to get the boats completed. On the last day before we went to the pool, I asked the kids what I should change in the future. I started by posing the question of whether I should even include building the boat again, to which there was a cry of protest that the boat was the best part and that of course I should do it again. I learned a lesson along with the kids that week, which I already knew internally, but lost sight of: When you work hard, you might not enjoy all of the process, but in the end you take pride in knowing that you overcame obstacles and were able to do something that at some points in the journey you thought was impossible.

The next day, I made sure to get feedback on changes for the next year. By the end of the second day, spirits were improved, and they were feeling more confident about their groups and the work. The trip to the Detroit Zoo was a highlight. Hearing about the pressures placed on different animals and then being able to view the polar bears and arctic foxes right after that really made the concepts real. I only wish I had scheduled more time. As they came together as a group and saw their hard work manifesting into finished products, they were more able to enjoy the process.

In retrospect, I realized I did not take into account that they needed downtime. I thought scheduling the Fine Art lessons and other ungraded activities would be enough, but it was clear that when given challenging work, middle school students definitely need some time to blow off steam. I know that the next year, I plan to organize PE time, game time, or something else each day to give them a break. It was also clear that most groups needed assistance with the calculations sheet, so I plan to schedule a class with one of the Math teachers to provide them with more direct instruction. There were quite a few areas where tweaking and changing the lesson was needed for the next year. This is perhaps unsurprising, as I usually follow the "third time is the charm" rule with any lesson.

AN INTERDISCIPLINARY JOURNEY

The day of the final presentations was filled with excitement and anxiety for them and for me. Was it all going to come together? Was I clear enough in my examples and expectations? The first group presented, and they were superb. Their presentation demonstrated their deep understanding of the issues and provided logical and well thought-out recommendations. I was so impressed. At the end of the day, I had learned a lot and the students as fellow audience members who weren't presenting learned from each other, too.

Getting teachers working together can take a lot of patience, enthusiasm, and dedication, but the outcome for the students and the sense of community and connections made by students and teachers is fantastic. My years at Roeper have helped me build my confidence and learn to believe in myself. I knew I was taking on a very big project, but I had been trusted in the past to try out new ideas and to develop my own curriculum. To have your fellow teachers and your supervisors show faith in you and support you in a positive way, time and time again, makes you want to try out new ideas. Many of the obstacles like tremendous amounts of paperwork, red-tape, and the usual hoops to jump through are not an issue at Roeper, either. The environment at Roeper is so supportive and focused on the outcome that it truly fosters creativity and new ideas. Knowing that you can go from inspiration to green light within the day you have a new idea because your school trusts in your judgment and ability and will do their best to streamline your process is what makes you want to work hard to bring an inspired idea to fruition. The atmosphere that we have in our classrooms in which we encourage students' passions while providing opportunities to try out new things, make mistakes, and learn from them transfers to our teachers. We are allowed to try and to learn and to grow without fear.

NANCY B. HERTZOG, MEGAN A. RYAN & NICK GILLON

SOCIAL JUSTICE IN AN EARLY CHILDHOOD CLASSROOM

Equity and justice are the foundation of the Roeper philosophy as described and defined by the schools' founders, Annemarie and George Roeper. The Roeper School was founded to provide students an opportunity to learn together in an environment where they would be challenged to succeed. The school arose in response to the critical need for pupils to gain not only the knowledge and skills to understand the changing world, but also a social conscience to understand how to change it responsibly. In escaping the Holocaust to found their school, George and Annemarie Roeper responded to bigotry and hatred by providing a place where critical thinking and personal motivation would guide students toward social justice. The Roeper School's broader aim is to help students grow to be educated, aware, and capable to impact the world positively. In this chapter, we explore how young children may begin their path toward social justice and civic responsibility.

Three kindergarten boys are playing in the block area building a complicated airport scene. They excitedly share the blocks, and the toy airplanes and one of them begins to line the airplanes on the block runway that they just built when a fourth boy demands to use the airplanes for his play. An altercation breaks out and the teacher didn't know who started what, so she closed the block area for the rest of the morning. One child lamented, "That's not fair!" Did the children's voices get heard? Did the boys have equal access to the materials? Were the children equally verbally competent to express their opinions and solutions?

These scenarios play out daily in early childhood classrooms across the country. How are we teaching social justice in these settings? How are diversity, inclusion, equity, and justice actualized in early childhood classes? And how might classrooms across the country differ from those at the Roeper School, where educators focus on making the values of diversity, inclusion, equity, and justice integral to everything students do? Conceptually and practically, what does social justice look like in early childhood classrooms?

We know that what happens to children in their early years has a direct relationship to successful achievement in later years. Students younger and younger are given the formal skills needed to advance literacy and mathematics. We also know the importance of young children developing social competencies, including self-regulation of emotions, positive ways to interact with peers and develop friendships, and awareness of others' feelings. Children develop differently and at various rates.

Emphasis in early childhood education is placed on developing social competencies, but what about understanding the tenets of social justice? Shall we assume that the ways in which students experience social justice in early childhood classrooms also impact their future perspectives of social justice? Are early childhood classrooms meant to be the growing gardens of activism for justice? Can or should young children be taught to critically question authority, power, privilege, and prejudice? In this chapter, we will first present a literature review on social justice education and place those perspectives in an early childhood context. We conclude by suggesting appropriate strategies for enacting a social justice curriculum that would align with the Roeper School's philosophy.

LITERATURE REVIEW

What Is a Social Justice Curriculum?

A review of the research suggests that there are many lenses to describe and view social justice curriculum. Social justice education represents concepts, curricula, and practices in schools and teacher training colleges wherein students and teachers engage in dialogic communication with one another, the environment, and the curricula. Social justice education offers students and teachers opportunities to critically examine and thoughtfully reflect upon problems and causes that underlie societal symptoms of prejudice and inequity. At the root of all of the social justice literature is that not only do students learn about inequities; but they are taught to *question the root of those inequities*.

We searched online databases for social justice curriculum, social justice education, and social justice curriculum in early elementary school. Additionally, we examined an anti-bullying curriculum for preschool and used it as a means to investigate an exemplar of social justice curriculum.

Of the sixty most recently published articles in the last decade yielded by the ERIC search term "social justice education," 49 were relevant and were included in the literature review. Of these 49, 42 articles described qualitative studies of teachers trying to implement social justice curricula. Six described analyses of specific curricula and only one was a quantitative study. The preponderance of literature, however, reflected work with middle school or high school students.

To further probe articles that included early childhood or elementary students, we accessed the EBSCO and ProQuest databases, as well as Academic Search Elite and the University of Washington library itself. Key search terms included "early elementary AND social justice curricul," "early elementary AND social justice educat," and "early elementary social justice." We limited results to peer-reviewed articles. Overall, we found 28 articles either detailing narratives of teacher experiences with this type of curricula in their classrooms, or theoretical discussions of what recommended practices could exist. We also found books that informed our research, all of which were compiled works and teacher narratives. Of the articles we used, one was a mixed methods study, seven were theoretical discussions of social justice in education, three were narratives, and nine were qualitative studies. There were no quantitative studies.

Three studies looked explicitly at 5th through 8th grade students (Carroll, 2008; Miller, 2010; Zacher, 2007), five looked at elementary school students but did not explicitly state which grades were included (Carlisle, Jackson, & George, 2006; Johnson & Oppenheim, 2009; Picower, 2011; Theoharis & O'Toole, 2011; Wade, 2007) and only two looked at kindergarten and early elementary specifically (Araujo & Strasser, 2003; Burns, 2004). The books included one study on Kindergarten (Tenorio, 1997), one on 2nd grade (Hankins, 1999), and four on 4th through 8th grade (Blackburn, 1999; Michalove, 1999; Peterson, 1997; Taylor, 1999). Whether or not they expressly looked at early elementary children, each of these authors was helpful in clarifying definitions and explanations of social justice curriculum, and in providing useful frameworks for organizing our research.

Researchers that specifically addressed kindergarten and early elementary school found that young children have at least preliminary understandings of issues such as race and gender identity (Araujo & Strasser, 2003; Hankins, 1999; Tenorio, 1997). In Tenorio's (1997) account of working within a kindergarten classroom, she observed that her students had an understanding of the differences between races, and do use race both as a means to access power and to classify others as less powerful (Tenorio, 1997). Araujo and Strasser (2003) reached similar conclusions about their kindergarten class as well. Still further, other teachers, such as Hankins (1999), found through their experiences that second graders had relatively refined understandings regarding sexuality and sexual identity (1999). Because these teachers heard students using race and sexuality as a means to access and maintain power at these young ages, they concluded that it is appropriate to begin discussions about social justice issues with students in these grades. However, preparedness for and instruction about social justice education doesn't always lead to safer classrooms. Zacher (2007) concluded that students' readiness and learned expertise with labeling and categorizing classmates based on perceived differences also contributed to their increased efficiency in insulting and excluding peers in acts of social violence. Thus, simply providing students tools to recognize and discuss differences among us doesn't automatically lead them to understand how to act justly in light of those differences.

Ayers, Quinn, and Stovall (2009) characterized social justice education in its broadest terms as: "Relevant, Rigorous, and Revolutionary" (p. xiv). Dewhurst (2011) included three fundamental attributes of social justice education: (a) it is rooted in people's experiences, (b) it is a process of reflection and action together, and (c) it seeks to dismantle systems of inequality to create a more humane society. Zeichner (2003) offered it as one of three major approaches to teacher education reform. Murphy (1999) named social justice as one of "three powerful synthesizing paradigms" (p. 54) in educational leadership.

Although some consider social justice education in terms of curriculum content—including everything from racism (Araujo & Strasser, 2003; Blackburn, 1999;

Hankins, 1999; Miller, 2010; Taylor, 1999; Tenorio, 1997) to handicap awareness (Johnson & Oppenheim, 2009)—others approached it as a matter of pedagogy (Carroll, 2008; Moore, 2007). Still others deemed it a fusion of the two (Picower, 2011; Miller, 2010). There were differences in the definition of "social justice curriculum," and variations in the purpose of receiving such training, ranging from personal awareness to blatant activism. Furthermore, research related to social justice education included studies of students (Burns, 2004; Carroll, 2008; Miller, 2010; Zacher, 2007) and teachers (Gill & Chalmers, 2007; Picower, 2011; Stovall, 2010; Wade, 2007). They addressed both how teacher education programs may achieve a greater degree of attention to social justice, and how social justice curriculum may be successfully implemented within kindergarten through high school classrooms.

Hytten and Bettez (2011) suggested five main lenses through which to examine existing social justice literature. The philosophical/conceptual lens included those writings whose primary purpose is discussing the concept of social justice education, with the familiar rationale of needing a more solidified definition in order to better implement the concept. The practical orientation focused on outlining how social justice education could be successfully enacted within the classroom. Ethnographic and narrative literature focused on testimonies about social justice interactions and interventions, or perhaps more frequent, encounters with injustices. Theoretically specific literature was guided by specific agendas and as a result, frequently appeared in terms of curriculum content rather than pedagogy. Finally, democratically grounded social justice curriculum considered social justice education training for citizenship within a democratic society. Each of these types of writings have important bearing on directing social justice education, and provide an excellent framework through which to examine the existing literature and current practice in classrooms.

Of particular relevance to our understanding were the conceptual framings of social justice education by Hartlep (2010), Dover (2010), and the National Association of Secondary School Principals (1996). These articles described theoretical frameworks of elements common to social justice approaches to education. Dover's (2010) work characterized social justice education as unique in terms of three dimensions of educational practice: curriculum, pedagogy, and social action. Hartlep (2010) provided a list of seven elements across these dimensions that were common to social justice curricula: (a) cooperation and collaboration, (b) delivery with equal status, (c) unlearning common sense beliefs, (d) teaching of racial consciousness, (e) questioning of current education practice, (f) teaching of multicultural awareness, and (g) preparation for college.

Au (2012), Johnston (2008), Jaramillo (2010), Rozas (2009), and Picower (2011) build on these conceptual frameworks by emphasizing dynamics of power, privilege, access, and opportunity as they relate to equitable education. These authors contend that education for social justice necessarily extends beyond learning of human rights and their protections to include critical discourse from the perspective of marginalized populations intended to expose and redress issues of injustice in society. In early childhood, the environmental structure of the classroom represents the child's society. By distilling commonality of all definitions, we assert that social justice curriculum *is an emphasis on equality and includes a discussion about the power structures that either allow or cause inequalities.*

Most useful to the discussion of equality in early childhood classrooms was the examination of the meaning of equality: (a) equity of resources, (b) respect and recognition, (c) love, care, and solidarity, (d) power, and (e) working and learning (Hytten & Bettez, 2011). These five categories appear most clearly in terms of the environment in which students learn, the socially oriented aspects of the students' learning, the emotional impact and concentration of the curriculum, and the cognitive and academic focuses of schooling.

In early childhood education a focus on literacy is critical, but the role critical literacy places in early childhood education is still very much in question. As defined by Giroux and Aronwitz (1986), critical literacy "would make clear the connection between knowledge and power . . . [and] . . . would function as a theoretical tool to help students and others develop a critical relationship to their own knowledge" (p. 132). While on the one hand political, economic, and social realities of the wider world are beyond the everyday experiences of most 3–8 year olds, all young children challenge rules, *"Do I have to,"* *"I had it first!"* and *"You're not the boss of me!"* As early childhood educators we teach children to build knowledge from their questions; as social justice educators we teach children to question their knowledge. At a stage of schooling where literacy is a critical focus, questioning the focus on critical literacy and social justice education is "Relevant, Rigorous, and Revolutionary" (Dewhurst, 2011).

SOCIAL JUSTICE FROM THE YOUNG CHILD'S PERSPECTIVE

We turn now to discuss social justice from a young child's perspective. What is fair and equal to young children? How do they recognize equality, and what aspects of a social justice curriculum can be taught in a way that is *developmentally appropriate?*

Certainly one of the most important factors in discussing social justice with younger children is asking what material is and is not developmentally appropriate, both in terms of the severity and tone of the content, and also looking at the child's ability to actually grasp the meaning of social justice. From Vygotsky's (1978) research, we know that concepts develop gradually as a person becomes continually more exposed to the social world, and that children are capable of using a word in speech without fully grasping the extent of its meaning. The question, then, is at what age can children actually understand issues of social justice? In other words, when does "social justice" transfer between merely being words and being the key to an entire host of understandings?

Developmentally, between ages two and three, children begin to understand the world through physical attributes of the objects and people around them, and also consider themselves largely unique (Williams & Cooney, 2006; Piaget, 1969). Despite their beginning of categorization, they lack the ability to understand the larger implications of those attributes (Williams & Cooney, 2006; Piaget, 1969). Around this age, children also begin to develop a concept of a theory of mind (Flavell, 2000)—the ability to comprehend multiple points of view—and understand that the world does not exist only from their perspective (Flavell, 2000; Piaget, 1969). Consequently, by kindergarten most children have a preliminary sense of the fact that their actions and emotions can—and do—influence those around them (Flavell, 2000; Piaget, 1969; Harris, 1989), and that their own emotions are largely dependent upon the broader society (Harris, 1989). By the time children are between seven and eight years old, most have gained the understanding that they are part of a larger system of identity; they have refined the ability to classify both objects and people (Piaget, 1969; Williams & Cooney, 2006) and as a result, identify themselves with either one group of people or another. Furthermore, they understand that their actions and emotions have consequences in the larger world, which contributes to their ability to empathize and to understand larger conceptual ideas (Flavell, 2000; Harris, 1989).

This progression of emotional understanding is directly relevant for social justice educators because it helps gauge when children will be able to grasp larger social justice concepts. Explaining that one group or another is marginalized to children that still see the world from their own perspective would prove a difficult task. Although they may reiterate the words, they may not understand the concept of marginalized peers. We need to be intentional about discerning at what ages children actually understand and can critically question power structures. If we introduce these lessons too early, will we merely be teaching them empty words? Or will early exposure prime them for engaging in this type of thinking later in life?

The classroom itself remains one of the most intimate areas in which one can find instances to address imbalances of power that students can directly understand, and an opportunity to address social justice in terms of power dynamics and how those structures influence student access to resources (Hytten & Bettez, 2011). Although students might not understand larger racist trends, they can understand that their classmates' feelings were hurt from the way they were teased about their skin color. They can also understand how their peers were denied the chance to fully participate because of their various differences. They may iterate these understandings by saying *"it's not fair!" "that's mine!" "I don't want to do that now"* and so forth. Our research showed that teachers who intended to address social justice in terms of content based their conversations on situations that had arisen directly within their classrooms. As a result, the issues discussed varied widely, ranging between discrimination based on socioeconomic status (Zacher, 2007), race (Hankins, 1999; Tenorio, 1997; Michalove, 1999; Blackburn, 1999; Miller, 2010), various disabilities (Johnson, 2009), orientation (Taylor, 1999), intellect (Zacher, 2007), and appearance (Zacher, 2007), among other things. In each of these instances, the core of each conversation was spurred by events that had taken place within the actual classroom. By finding instances of imbalances of power within the children's lives, teachers can begin to make these concepts directly accessible to them.

Vivian Paley's books of children's stories, for example, *You Can't Say You Can't Play* (Paley, 1992) gave opportunities for children to explore concepts of inclusion and exclusion, or understand and value children's differences (*The Boy Who Would Be A Helicopter*; Paley, 1990). Teaching students to understand fairness within their classroom contributes to the process of creating just early childhood classrooms.

A JUST EARLY CHILDHOOD ENVIRONMENT

Creating Classroom Community

Teachers hold power and privilege in early childhood classrooms. Teachers also have the skills and expertise to create a classroom community that empowers children to learn. Students are subject to injustice if they are denied the opportunity to participate freely and equally within the classroom itself. *A just early learning environment is a place where equity is defined as children feeling safe, included, and equally valued.* In order to enact this understanding, teachers must be intentional in creating opportunities for students to engage in social community involvement and cooperation. In the literature, we saw different approaches toward reaching this goal. Carroll (2008) discussed the use of peer mentoring for breaking up cliques so that students would interact with all the students in their class. Johnson (2009) described the use of circle time, and Tenorio (1997) and Blackburn (1999) described class projects that illuminated the hurtful nature of excluding students from participating fully in the classroom.

In looking at the classroom environment, the central component to creating a socially just environment seems to focus largely on the sense of community present within the classroom. When students feel comfortable with one another and their teachers, they have a better opportunity to express their own ideas and respectfully respond to opinions that differ from their own. Some teachers consider this aspect of learning the foundation for educating socially minded citizens. In order to achieve that open environment, though, teachers must focus on fostering community between the students, which can be done in any number of ways. In the studies that we examined, teachers commonly employed the use of "circle time" as a means to promote social justice environments. During this part of the day, students can express their difficulties either with the class or with other students, and as a community the entire class can work toward either solving the problem or addressing a new task or project. This exercise demonstrates the importance of being able to peaceably solve disputes with others, and gives students a platform from which to cultivate this skill. It introduces the idea that all voices have the value to be heard and considered equally—a central tenet of more adult considerations of social justice. When students are uncomfortable within their learning environment, they are less likely to celebrate academic success; rather than concentrating on the material at hand, they are more likely to focus on more immediate problems of bullying, intimidation, or blatant discrimination.

By reorganizing the classroom structure and creating a more supportive environment, educators can alleviate imbalances related to the respect and recognition between students and instructors (Hytten & Bettez, 2011), as well as increase the amount of love, care, and solidarity shared among students (Hytten & Bettez, 2011). Furthermore, these practices create the opportunity for students to learn to peaceably handle conflict and to recognize when one person or another was not given an equal chance to participate, with the hope that such opportunities will minimize any discrimination or discomfort within the classroom itself.

Literacy for Social Justice Messages

Early childhood teachers are often expert storytellers and most all of them use some part of a large group time to read aloud stories. Teachers can be thoughtful about the literature they choose, and use stories to address the social dynamics at play within the classroom. As students discuss the treatment of the characters to each other, they may relate the fictional characters to their own experiences within the classroom. These conversations may engage students in critical thinking about fairness, equality, and the treatment of others. Building their empathy, and moral reasoning through fictional relationships, they may begin to relate their newly articulated understandings to the importance of the social dynamics at play within their own classroom. Technology today allows the teacher to be one click away from a list of children's literature that focuses on relationships and addresses fairness and morals.

Teachers may address emotional aspects of social justice by helping students become aware of both their feelings and how the expressions of their emotions influence others. Building on the idea of teaching students to peacefully handle conflict, students also need to understand that their emotions can disrupt peaceful classroom atmospheres. Within classrooms, one of the facets of social justice lies in the feelings of safety and inclusion that each student has within the room. If one students' anger or demeanor is directed at another student particularly, or even a group of students, it creates inequalities within that room, and prevents other students from celebrating the same degree of inclusion as the others. Bullying has increasingly been recognized as a root cause for discomfort in a classroom, and a primary concern for issues of inequality. In an attempt to counteract this phenomenon, anti-bullying curriculum helps students focus on refining their own emotional knowledge. By learning how to recognize their emotions and then, most importantly, how to manage them, teachers can help students create a sense of safety and inclusion throughout the classroom, thereby creating a more equitable and just classroom.

Second Step (Committee for Children, 2011) is one example of a preschool anti-bullying curriculum. This curriculum defines inequalities through an emotional standpoint, looking specifically at how different situations within a preschool classroom are subject to emotional intimidations caused by bullying. Its content and purpose of addressing and adjusting classroom inequalities, its connection and immediate relevance to the children's lives, and its emphasis on emotional development work together to help teach children about (a) how to recognize their emotions, and (b) how to properly channel those feelings in a way that will not negatively influence those around them. The curriculum attempts to address multiple areas of development, organizing its units around building "[skills] for learning, empathy, emotion management, and friendship skills and problem solving" (p. 6) skills, all of which contribute to creating more equitable environments within the classrooms themselves, and thereby providing the opportunity for a more socially just classroom.

The curriculum uses "brain builders" to foster the cognitive development of the children, songs to help teach children about their emotions and how to recognize them, and family letters and home links so that parents can be connected to their children's learning. Together, these activities aspire to teach children how to appropriately channel their emotions, with the hope of preventing problem behavior within the classroom and consequently "[promoting] success in school and life" (p. 6). With both the awareness of how emotions influence others and the instruction on how to self-regulate those emotions, children may work towards becoming agents of change within their preschool classroom.

Second Step addresses the emotional development of children with the hope that teachers and caregivers can work together to teach children how to interact peaceably with one another, creating a more comfortable and inclusive classroom environment. Although it does not address bullying specifically, teaching children about their emotions will hopefully transfer to areas such as bullying, as well as any other situations in which children might treat each other unfairly.

Second Step curriculum connects directly with children's lives, which makes it immediately relevant to use in the classroom. Topics include "welcoming" peers (p. 55), "identifying anger" (p. 63), and "caring and helping" (p. 66), all of which children can understand because they are scenarios that happen at home and in classrooms. Each topic includes a lesson that helps explain the personal connection, a story that demonstrates how one child's behavior can negatively influence those around them, and an opportunity for play, which enables children to practice appropriate responses in negative situations. These three components work concomitantly to help children recognize and appropriately address their learning community.

Second Step teaches children to channel their emotions correctly, rather than unleashing them negatively on other persons. Safe, secure children are required for establishing a just early childhood environment. But modeling the just environment isn't enough to teach social justice—it's a start. To teach children to look at the world through a critical lens, they must have opportunities for critical thinking and problem solving. These skills are often taught through project-based learning. In a comprehensive review of the literature on project-based learning, Thomas (2000) concludes, "There is ample evidence that PBL is an effective method for teaching students complex processes and procedures such as planning, communicating, problem solving, and decision making," (p. 35). An effective way to implement project-based learning in an early childhood environment is to use the Project Approach as described by Katz and Chard, (2000).

The Project Approach

The Project Approach, historically modeled after Dewey's work (1916), emphasizes hands-on experiences for students to pursue answers to their own questions. Katz and Chard (2000) articulated the Project Approach in three phases. In Phase 1 teachers assess what students already know and understand by asking students to share their experiences about the topic they are beginning to study. Students are encouraged to express their current levels of understandings through representations including drawings, models, and mathematical data displays such as graphs, timelines and charts. Rather than asking young students what they already know about a topic, teachers focus on students' memories and experiences they have had related to the topic. For example, if students are about to start the project investigation on the topic of water, students may write or dictate memory stories about water—such as the bathtub overflowing, their basement flooding, or the water turning into ice on their driveways. In Phase 1 students are encouraged to compare the similarities and differences in their experiences, and from those discussions, learn about their topic from other students, and value the differences as well as the similarities of their experiences. These comparisons provide opportunities for children to listen about the experiences of others and gain an appreciation for what others may know and understand about the topic. Discussions also result in more students' questions as they begin to see that different experiences may conflict with what they think they understand.

In Phase 2, students and teachers categorize experiences and questions to form study groups. These study groups provide opportunities for children to choose the questions that most entice them to pursue. For teachers, these study groups provide a structure for inquiry and relate to the big ideas and essential understandings that they feel are important for all children to understand about the topic. In Phase 2 children learn research skills, including how to collect, analyze, and display data. Young children may collect data through observation, questionnaires, interviews of experts, field studies, and secondary sources such as books or documents. Students share the findings of their research with others in Phase 3 when a culminating event is planned. In most cases parents are the audience for the culminating event. However, depending on the project, other classes, or community members may be the target for revealing the findings. Implementing projects often challenges teachers to facilitate inquiry. Teachers need to be flexible and enable students to take project investigations in directions of their interest, and not necessarily in directions that are planned in advance. However, the quality of a project depends on the depth of investigation and the significance of the big ideas and essential understandings explored. For a detailed calendar of how teachers might facilitate investigations, see Appendix A. For readers to see examples of projects, we suggest visiting the following websites http://www.projectapproach.org/ (sponsored by the Authors Sylvia Chard and Lilian Katz), and University Primary School in Champaign, IL (http://education.illinois.edu/ups/projects/) where project investigations are fully articulated in phases, and are tied to the Illinois Learning Standards.

The first author also has written about teachers implementing the project approach and with others has described several different interdisciplinary projects (Burns, Chi, & Hertzog, 2008; Hertzog, Klein & Katz, 1999; Hertzog, 2005; Hertzog, 2007). However, none of the above mentioned projects, although they were topics worthy of investigation, engaged children in social justice curriculum or instruction. One project on water lent itself to examining service learning (Chun, Hertzog, Gaffney, & Dymond, 2012) when the children wanted to help victims of the Tsunami. So, although project based learning in early childhood environments has been described as one of the most conducive approaches to teach students critical inquiry, the social activism aspect of social justice, and the immediate relevance of these issues and power structures on students' everyday lives, are less frequently described in the literature of young students undertaking such projects.

One example that we found on the Internet was the organization called iEARN Collaboration Center (https://media.iearn.org/projects/hunger) where educators from around the world post their projects. *Finding Solutions to Hunger* (retrieved 7/9/12 at https://media.iearn.org/projects/hunge) seems to be an exemplary project that engages students in the critical pedagogy necessary for students to explore social justice. A summary of that project reads, "Participants will research and discuss the root causes of hunger and poverty in the world and take meaningful actions to help create a more just and sustainable world." This project has students beginning with an exploration of their own food consumption, and then comparing their food consumption to those of others around the world. They then explore causes of hunger and complete the project by taking action in their own community. A related site shares a K-2 project entitled, "Finding Solutions to Hunger," (retrieved 7/9/12 at http://us.iearn.org/projects/curriculum-integration-toolkit/integration-plans/plan/finding-solutions-hunger-0). A project that engages children in finding the root cause of the social inequity is an opportunity to involve them directly in conversations about justice and to see themselves as informed citizens and agents of change.

INCLUSIVITY AND DIVERSITY

An early childhood environment that incorporates social justice in its philosophy must embrace principles of inclusion and values of diversity. Labeling children in any form supports divisive and exclusive pedagogies, and predisposes teachers to mindsets and expectations that may set up children for lower or higher achievement. How then, is it even possible for a school like the Roeper School that identifies and labels children gifted to also support the teaching of social justice? We believe the answer to this question lies in the ways in which gifted behaviors are perceived and talent development is nurtured and encouraged in that early childhood environment. Young children come to the classroom with a diversity of experiences that mostly relate to their home lives. *Valuing these diverse experiences as the starting point for nurturing potential is the foundation for social justice in early childhood education.*

SUMMARY

In this chapter we reviewed the complexity in defining and implementing a social justice curriculum in an early childhood environment. We described places where social justice can be explored, addressed, and enacted inclusive activities such as storytelling, read-alouds, anti-bullying curriculum and project based learning. We suggested that young students *can learn* to question privilege, power, and equity as equality relates to access to resources, respect and recognition, and power relationships as evidenced in the following vignette:

> A group of four students played beneath a playground slide making a home and family. The oldest child selected the mother role for herself and the other three decided to be her children. Together they combined flowers, grass, and sticks to make 'lollipops.' In the choosing of their roles and jobs, the older student, A, started to use her more powerful position within the group to control the game and the younger students responded to the power of her authority without question.
>
> C: My lollipop sugar is in my paw. I'm a kitty ...
>
> H: And I'm a big sister kitty. I look after you.
>
> C: No mamma looks after me.
>
> H: Well, sometimes I look after them.
>
> A: (the mom) Momma is bringing cookies.
>
> C: Lets go collect lollipop sugar.
>
> A: No I'll tell you what we'll do, follow me.

In finding roles and purposes in dramatic play, students establish their position in the group. When students lack voice and choice in this process, more powerful individuals or forces in their environment define their identity and purpose. As seen in this example, students with less social capital have less influence on decisions that affect them. This dynamic reflects macro social tendencies toward injustice and marginalization. Those with the greatest social capital are, in this case, older and more able to use language to change the story to benefit their position while the youngest with the least social capital have fewer influences on the choices that affect them. Would social justice education empower these younger students to question the primacy of the older student's knowledge and have a more equal role, rather than learn that one day it will be their turn to direct the lollipop factory? When students learn social and cultural tools through more capable peers they learn as well to imitate the ways that social capital is gained and used.

Childhood is a process of unfolding awareness. As children become more dexterously aware of the social environment they begin to make connections with other children. With greater social awareness and connection, children begin to group and sort themselves, often based on their own recognition of similarities and differences between them. Even in these early relationships, power is operative. For children, power is often established by age, and may be a proxy for both access and ability. An essential question regarding social justice education is, "What awareness of the power in those relationships could best help students negotiate healthy social and emotional development?" Social justice education engages students in examinations not only of their similarities, differences, and connections with others, but also, the power dynamics that underlie those relationships. Perhaps the strongest argument for the use of social justice education in early childhood classrooms is that because children are already able to recognize, be influenced by, and wield power in their early social relationships, they should be purposefully guided to use that power in just ways while they are young.

Early childhood educators have an opportunity to create socially just classrooms and introduce their students not only to ways in which fairness and equity issues touch their everyday lives, but also to open their hearts and minds to examine fully the root of injustice and inequality. Imagine our world in the future if we started teaching four year olds to be agents for social justice now.

Social justice is clearly at the heart of the Roeper School in that its founders began with the intent of developing citizens who would not easily be subjugated by unexamined influences dominant within society. The Roepers prioritized well-rounded education. To achieve that end, they implemented inquiry based learning to integrate an "emphasis on justice, equity, and altruism" (Ambrose, this volume, p. 288), promoted democratic approaches to education, emphasized an appreciation of diversity, and nurtured positive dispositions to learn (Ambrose, this volume). Stories posted on the school's website from alumni attest that a democratic education prevailed. Alumni wrote about their choices, and the guidance they had to become individuals and make contributions to society. Are they more attuned to social justice in the world? Have they become agents of change based on the educational paths they took? The Roeper School holds promise for future research in the area of social justice education and may be a source of answers for whether the ways in which students experience social justice in early childhood education impact their future perspectives of social justice.

ACKNOWLEDGEMENTS

I am often amazed at how much of my life happens serendipitously—and so is the case for my interest and engagement into the realm of social justice. My journey to Seattle has enabled me to embark on research projects and conversations with my graduate students and co-authors Megan Ryan and Nick Gillon. Our weekly conversations and unpacking of the literature on social justice has stirred my thinking of new priorities for early childhood learning environments. Already influenced by the pre-primary schools of Reggio Emilia, Italy where the sense of community in early learning is prioritized higher than individual achievement, I believe it is not enough for the teacher to be the creator of that community. Students must become their own agents of change, no matter how young, or how disempowered they feel to affect their community. I am indebted to my students for sharing their insights and challenging me to reprioritize the components of a high quality early childhood learning environment.

—Nancy Hertzog

REFERENCES

Ambrose, D. (2013). The Roeper School in the 21st century: Trends, issues, challenges, and opportunities. *The Roeper School: A model for holistic development of high ability.* Rotterdam, Netherlands: Sense.

Aronowitz, S., & Giroux, H. (1986). *Education under siege: The conservative, liberal, and radical debate over schooling.* New York, NY: Routledge.

Au, W. (2012). *Critical curriculum studies: Education, consciousness, and the politics of knowing.* New York, NY: Routledge.

Ayers, W., Quinn, T., & Stovall, D. (2009). *Handbook of social justice in education.* New York, NY: Routledge.

Blackburn, M. (1999). Studying privilege in a middle school gifted class. In J. Allen (Ed.), *Class actions: Teaching for social justice in elementary and middle school* (pp. 72–83). New York, NY: Teachers College Press.

Burns, Terry J. (2004). Making politics primary. Exploring critical curriculum in early childhood education. *Language Arts, 82,* 56–66.

Chun, E. J., Hertzog, N. B., Gaffney, J. S., & Dymond, S. K. (2012). When service learning meets the project approach: Incorporating service learning in an early childhood program. *Journal of Early Childhood Research.* First published on March 27, 2012 as doi:10.1177/1476718X1143019. Retrieved July 9, 2012 at http://ecr.sagepub.com/content/early/2012/03/21/1476718X11430199.full.pdf+html.

Dewey, J. (1916/1966). *Democracy and education.* New York, NY: Free Press.

Dewhurst, M. (2011). Where is the action? Three lenses to analyze social justice art education. *Equity & Excellence In Education, 44,* 364–378.

Dover, A. (2010, January 1). Teaching for social justice with standards-based secondary English language arts curriculum. ProQuest LLC http://gateway.proquest.com.offcampus.lib.washington.edu/openurl?url_ver=Z39.88-2004&rft_val_fmt=info:ofi/fmt:kev:mtx:dissertation&res_dat=xri:pqdiss&rft_dat=xri:pqdiss:3397695

Finding solutions to hunger, (retrieved July 9, 2012 at http://us.iearn.org/projects/curriculum-integration-toolkit/integration-plans/plan/finding-solutions-hunger-0).

Flavell, J. H. (2000). Development of children's knowledge about the mental world. *Monographs of the Society for Research in Child Development, 24*(1), 15–23.

Hankins, K. (1999). Silencing the lambs. In J. Allen (Ed.), *Class actions: Teaching for social justice in elementary and middle school* (pp. 61–71). New York, NY: Teachers College Press.

Harris, P. L. (1989). *Pride, shame, and guilt. Children and emotion: The development of psychological understanding* (pp. 81–105). Malden, MA: Basil Blackwell.

Hartlep, N. D. (2010). A critical analysis of the common elements of a high school social justice curriculum: Quantitative research vs. qualitative research. Proceedings from AERA 2010: The *American Educational Research Association* (AERA) Annual Meeting. Denver, CO.

Hertzog, N. B. (2005). Equity and access: Creating general education classrooms responsive to potential. *Journal for the Education of the Gifted, 29,* 213–257.

Hertzog, N. B. (2007). Transporting pedagogy: Implementing the project approach in two first-grade classrooms. *Journal of Academic Achievement, 18,* 530–564.

Hertzog, N. B, Klein, M. M., & Katz, L. G., (1999). Hypothesizing and theorizing: Challenge in an early childhood classroom. *Gifted International, 14,* 38–49.

Hytten, K., & Bettez, S. C. (2011). Understanding education for social justice. *Educational Foundations, 25*(1–2), 7–24.

Jaramillo, N. (2010). Social justice for human development. *Teacher Education and Practice, 23*, 492–494.

Johnson, E., Oppenheim, R., & Suh, Y. (2009). Would that be social justice? A conceptual constellation of social justice curriculum in action. *New Educator, 5*, 293–310.

Katz, L. G., & Chard, S. (2000). *Engaging children's minds: The project approach* (2nd ed.). Norwood, NJ: Ablex.

Klein, M., & Hertzog, N. B. (2001). *Step-by-step planning calendar for project work*. Unpublished Document, University of Illinois: Champaign-Urbana. Retrieved from http://education.illinois.edu/ups/curriculum2003/fire/genactivities.html

Michalove, B. (1999). Circling in: Examining prejudice in history and in ourselves. In J. Allen (Ed.), *Class actions: Teaching for social justice in elementary and middle school* (pp. 21–33) New York, NY: Teachers College Press.

Miller, G. R. (2010). Beyond a story well told: Using oral histories for social justice curriculum. *Action in Teacher Education, 32*(3), 55–65

Murphy, J. (1999). *The quest for a center: Notes on the state of the profession of educational leadership*. Available from http://www.eric.ed.gov.offcampus.lib.washington.edu/contentdelivery/servlet/ERICServlet?accno=ED433620

Paley, V. G. (1990). *The boy who would be a helicopter*. Boston, MA: First Harvard University Press.

Paley, V. G. (1992). *You can't say you can't play*. Boston, MA: First Harvard University Press.

Peterson, B. (1997). Teaching for social justice: One teachers' journey. In B. Bigelow, L. Christensen, S. Karp, B. Miner, & B. Peterson (Eds.), *Rethinking our classrooms: teaching for equity and justice* (pp. 30–39). Montgomery, AL: Rethinking Schools.

Piaget, J. (1969). *The psychology of the child*. New York, NY: Basic Books.

Picower, B. (2011). Resisting compliance: Learning to teach for social justice in a neoliberal context. *Teachers College Record, 113*, 1105–1134.

Rozas, L., & Miller, J. (2009). Discourses for social justice education: The web of racism and the web of resistance. *Journal of Ethnic & Cultural Diversity in Social Work, 18*(1–2), 24–39.

Second Step early learning program (2011). *Committee for children*. (www.secondstep.org)

Taylor, T. (1999). Addressing social justice in class meetings. *Class actions: Teaching for social justice in elementary and middle school* (pp. 34–43). New York, NY: Teachers College Press.

Tenorio, R., (1997). Race and respect among young children. In B. Bigelow, L. Christensen, S. Karp, B. Miner & B. Peterson (Eds.), *Rethinking our classrooms: Teaching for equity and justice* (pp. 24–28). Montgomery, AL: Rethinking Schools.

Thomas, J. W. (2000). *A review of research on project-based learning*. San Rafael, CA: Autodesk Foundation. Retrieved July 2, 2012 from http://www.bobpearlman.org/BestPractices/PBL_Research.pdf.

Vygotsky L. (1978). *Mind in society. The development of higher psychological processes*. Cambridge, MA: Harvard University Press.

Williams, K .C., & Cooney, M. H. (2006). Young children and social justice. *Young Children, 61*(2), 75–82.

Zacher, J. C. (2007). Talking about difference and defining social relations with labels. *Language Arts, 85*, 115–124.

Zeichner, K. (2003). The adequacies and inadequacies of three current strategies to recruit, prepare, and retain the best teachers for all students. *Teachers College Record, 105*, 490–519.

APPENDIX A

Step by Step Planning Calendar for Project Work

Phase 1

1	2	3	4	5
Opening Event	Brainstorm Ideas	Categorize Ideas	Label Categories	Share Personal Stories
Share a personal story, read a book, share a class experience to begin discussion of project topic with children.	Children list ideas from life experiences that relate to topic as the teacher writes. Begin a topic web.	Revisit with children to form categories of similar ideas. Share project topic with parents.	Children debate best name of categories. Children develop their topic web into categories.	Group Meeting: Share students' personal experiences with the project topic.

Phase 2

6	7	8	9	10
Illustrate Stories	Share Stories	Collect Data	Articulate Questions	Group Planning
Children draw, write, dictate, or dramatize to represent and share their prior experiences.	Children share their representations of stories, noting similarities or differences.	Develop surveys to find out what classmates already think they know and understand about the topic.	The teacher and the children voice their "wonderings" about the topic. Children dictate questions that they would like to answer about the topic.	In discussion, children think about what to do, where to go, who to ask to find answers to their questions.

11	12	13	14	15
Make Predictions	Engage in Field Work*	Debrief	Create Representations	Share
Before doing field work (site visits, experiments, observations, etc.) children predict (draw or dictate) what they might see or collect during field work.	Children collect data to answer questions. This may take weeks!	Children share experiences and compare findings with predictions.	Children represent their findings using a variety of means such as drawings, writings, constructions, paintings, and/or math and science organizers.	Progress on representations is shared with classmates offering suggestions.

16 Plans for Visiting Expert Children decide interview questions. Teacher charts predictions of the answers.	17 Expert Visitor Children ask questions and make drawings of answers or any artifacts.	18 Debriefing Children compare expects answers to their predictions.	19 Representations Sharing representations continues. Encourage a variety of mediums including, dramatic play, music, plays, & invented games.	20 Continue Investigation Additional days may be needed to continue to investigate. Additional experts, field-site visits and/or same site may be revisited.

Phase 3

21 Articulate What Children Have Learned Group Discussion: What have they learned about the topic.	22 Brainstorm Second Topic Web Children list ideas of "what they now know" about the topic. Begin to develop Topic Web II.	23 Categorize Ideas Children form categories of similar findings, understandings, and ideas.	24 Label Categories Children debate and name the categories. Children complete their Topic Web II.	25 Plan for Sharing Plan the culminating event and make invitations for the chosen audience.
26 Project Highlights Each child prepares to share the story of the learning achieved by the class by using posters, reports, plays, museum format, explanations, songs, and/ or videos, etc. They may choose to work individually, in a small group or prepare a whole class presentation.	27 Imaginative Activity Children may engage in more expressive activities using their new understanding in poetry, stories, pretend drawings, etc. Progress on their display is shared with classmates.	28 Display Children contribute to the class display. Work from all the phases is displayed to show the children's growth in understanding.	29 Culmination Parents, and other students visit to view the displays and hear children share what they have learned about the project.	30 Evaluation Children, parents and teachers reflect on the project.

(Klein & Hertzog, 2001)

COLLEEN SHELTON

A VIEW FROM THE PRESCHOOL CLASSROOM

The Child's Role in Creating a Socially Just Community

For me (and I think the Roeper philosophy supports this), teaching and incorporating any kind of social justice into the classroom is fundamental and ongoing. While we certainly do plenty of specific engaging around diversity, inclusion, and what is fair, it is the everyday moments that provide the best teachable moments. This is especially the case for young children, like the three- and four-year-olds in my Stage I classroom!

So, in answer to a key question—was it fair to close the play area because of an altercation?—the answer is absolutely no. Punitive consequences without discussion have no place in a classroom that talks about justice. Temporarily pulling all the children away to talk about the situation, yes, but not just closing it down. To teach justice, you must treat the children with justice, which means including the children in problem solving. For it is through these conversations that the children will lead you to an understanding of what has caused the upset.

As we move through the day, conflicts arise continually—some big, some small. My willingness to stop what I am doing to immediately pull together all the students involved lets them know, first of all, that this is important; and second, that everyone involved is part of the situation and will be part of the solution.

We find a quiet place to talk without distractions, which is why everyone on the second floor often finds the stairs blocked by us. As we begin the conversation, all children are reminded they will have a chance to talk, but may not interrupt others. Finding a solution, closure, or resolution will not occur unless everyone who was part of the problem is part of the solution. The kids all get a chance to have their say, hear what others are saying, argue their point, and hopefully accept responsibility for their behaviors. It is messy, time-consuming, and not always successful, but beginning this on the very first day sets up the framework and process. As with everything at Roeper, it is the process that is most important.

Conversations need to include everyone involved as there is always that kid who is the most tricky, the one who is often in the middle of almost every upset. Social justice—real justice—cannot be attained or modeled if adults assume that one child is always the instigator. As you work through the conversation, you might discover they were not. These are the amazing moments as that child (often the pot-stirrer) discovers he is being listened to and believed. Also, finding out why someone hit/

pushed/name-called/shut someone out of a play is important. What is the backstory? Has the child who seems to be getting the rough end of the deal been driving the other child crazy all morning? When I hear "You can't play with us!" this is a sign it is time to have a conversation not just about what was said, but why. Are the other kids just shutting someone out, or is there a reason? Perhaps the one being excluded did something earlier and now others are reacting. It is imperative to know what the kids are thinking and why they are reacting before adults can be of any help. The kids and adults need *all* the background.

I understand the need to teach anti-bullying and to share information about diversity in independent units, but these lessons must be interwoven into the culture and life of the classroom beginning on the very first day of school. For young children, it is always about experiences. If these ideas are not a part of conversations and activities each day, the students will not benefit from them. They have to be ongoing, constant, and consistent.

Understanding that young children are egocentric (and *can* begin to relate to others' feelings but still may not), it takes lots of time, repetition, understanding, and tears before the light begins to go on. It is also very important for kids to know that once an upset has been discussed and hopefully resolved, everyone moves forward. Don't back a child into a corner, and always allow her or him to save face. Each day/hour/minute/second is a clean slate. (I'm beginning to understand better why I am so tired all the time!) There must be respect towards these young children—and love. When I am talking with a child about an upset, I begin by telling them I love them. The discussion—from me—continues by letting the child know I won't let anyone hurt or upset them and I can't let them hurt or upset another.

As a teacher, am I successful with all of this all the time? Only in my dreams! But like the kids—perhaps because of the kids—adults need to own when they have made a mistake or handled something badly. Not only does acknowledging mistakes build bridges and trust with your students, it lets them know that no one needs to be perfect—a particularly important emotional lesson for gifted children.

What I found missing from this discussion was the inclusion of students, no matter how young- as part of the problem-solving/justice/equity process. Many great points and suggestions have been made, but they are primarily coming from the adults. Yes, the teachers and adults are responsible for setting the tone from the first day that this is a safe, inclusive, fair environment, but this is better achieved by treating the children justly than by any particular justice curriculum.

A just resolution has to include everyone, but for everyone to become involved, they have to feel safe about participating. The children need to feel equal; they need to feel certain they will be heard; and they have to know that honestly acknowledging their part in the upset won't jeopardize their being accepted. I find that kids can usually deal with the outcome as long as they were able to contribute. Gifted children in particular often have something they *need* to say, and need to be able to say it.

I've been teaching full-time at Roeper for almost thirty years, and spent my first years at the school in the 1970s, which gave me access to the wisdom of Annemarie

Roeper and her equally wise early colleagues, Hattie Wyatt and Sally Booth. They were my patient teachers in the idea that deep and profound respect—respect rooted in careful listening and honest responses—and a real affection for the diverse, intense humanity of children are the foundations of a socially just classroom and community.

SUSAN K. JOHNSEN

STANDARDS AND BALANCED ASSESSMENTS

Relationships to the Roeper School's Philosophy and Practices

To do things the way they were done in the past will not help our youngsters face our changing times. The ability to recognize, choose, and invent options, the ability to decide to learn how to learn—all this will better equip our youngsters for the future.
George Alexander Roeper (from a 1972 talk, "Open Education, Open Program, and Commitment")

As can be seen in the quote above, George Roeper, who along with his wife Annemarie founded the Roeper School, was not afraid of new perspectives or new ideas; he was committed to students' learning, to their understanding of new ideas and to their mastery of techniques. How does their deep commitment to humanistic education resonate with today's national focus on standards-based education? Do learner outcomes that are embedded within the Roeper School's philosophy and mission statements relate to the national standards movement and programming standards in gifted education? How do their development and personalized approaches to educating the whole child relate to today's emphasis on high-stakes testing? How are gifted and talented students able to show their deep understanding and their mastery of techniques?

This chapter investigates these important questions by examining today's standards and assessment movements, relating the critical dimensions of these movements to the Roeper School's philosophy and practices, and providing some direction for the Roeper School's future leadership in creating balanced assessment systems for schools with similar philosophical foundations.

STANDARDS

Since the 1980s, educators and policymakers have advanced standards as a means for improving curriculum, teacher preparation, and programming for students (National Commission on Excellence in Education, 1983; National Education Goals Panel, 1991). In the area of curriculum, the Goals 2000 America Education Act initially funded the development of national standards in the core subjects of math, English, science, social studies, and the arts. Since the 1990s, professional and related organizations have been involved in specifying the knowledge and skills within each of the content domains (e.g., International Reading Association/ National Council for Teachers of English, 1996; National Committee for Standards in the Arts, 1994; National Council for the Social Studies, 2010; National Council of Teachers of Mathematics, 2000; National Governors Association/Council for Chief State School Officers, 2010; National Research Council, 1996). These content standards have incorporated higher-order and more complex thinking skills, which recently have been elaborated and redefined as 21st-Century Skills (Partnership for 21st Century Skills, 2009). The key elements within these skills include learning and innovation skills (e.g., critical thinking, communication, collaboration, creativity), life and career skills, and information, media, and technology skills. The European Parliament and the Council of 2006 have also highlighted these learning-to-learn skills as key competencies for lifelong learning.

Following along with the national and international standards movement, gifted educators have developed standards in their field, primarily in the areas of teacher preparation and gifted education programs. The National Association for Gifted Children (NAGC) and The Association for Gifted/Council for Exceptional Children (CEC-TAG) collaborated in developing a set of initial standards for educators who are seeking their first certificate in gifted education (NAGC/CEC-TAG, 2006). The National Council for Accreditation of Teacher Education (NCATE) uses these standards for accrediting teacher preparation programs in gifted education. The teacher preparation standards were also used as the foundation for the development of the *Pre-K-Grade 12 Gifted Programming Standards* (NAGC Programming Standards; NAGC, 2010). These standards focus on the importance of developing each student's individual gifts and talents and identify specific student outcomes in each of six NAGC Programming Standards areas: Learning and Development, Assessment, Curriculum Planning and Instruction, Learning Environments, Programming, and Professional Development. These outcomes provide the foundation for examining the effectiveness of programming for gifted students.

THE RELATIONSHIP OF STANDARDS TO THE ROEPER SCHOOL'S PHILOSOPHY

The Roeper School was established well before the standards movements, but its founders were prescient in developing its philosophy around today's standards. For example, these student outcomes are embedded within its philosophy and practice statements (Roeper Board of Trustees, 2010):

- Students are committed to justice and human rights.
- Students respect and value individual differences and recognize the inherent dignity of every human being.
- Students define ethical and moral issues.
- Students are aware of complexities, take risks, and see themselves as valuable links in the chain of interdependence.
- Students learn to react in a flexible, clear-minded, intelligent manner.
- Students assume responsibility for their own learning and become independent thinkers, decision makers, and problem solvers.

- Students find their own voices and pursue their passions.
- Students become self-motivated.

As you will note in Table 1, these derived student outcomes from the Roeper School's philosophy statements are closely aligned to the 21st-Century Skills (2009) and the NAGC Programming Standards (2010). With the exception of technology and media, most of the 21st-Century Skills are addressed within the philosophy statement. Within the NAGC Programming Standards, the Roeper School places

Table 1. Relationship of the Roeper School's student outcomes to standards.

The Roeper School's Student Outcomes (2009)	Partnership for 21st Century Skills (2009)	NAGC Programming Student Outcomes (2010)
Committed to justice and human rights.	Social and Cross-Cultural Skills	Standard 1.2: Learning and Development—Self Understanding Standard 4.4: Learning Environments—Social Competence
Respect and value individual differences; recognize inherent dignity of every human being.	Communication and Collaboration	Standard 1.3: Learning and Development—Self Understanding Standard 3.5: Curriculum Planning and Instruction—Culturally Relevant Curriculum
Define ethical and moral issues.	Civic Literacy	Standard 4.3: Learning Environments Leadership
Aware of complexities, take risks, and see themselves as valuable links in a chain of interdependence.	Collaboration	Standard 3.5: Curriculum Planning and Instruction—Culturally Relevant Curriculum
React flexibly, clear-mindedly, and intelligently.	Flexibility and Adaptability	Standard 1.7: Learning and Development—Cognitive and Affective Growth
Assume responsibility and become independent thinkers, decision makers, and problem solvers.	Creativity and Critical Thinking	Standard 3.4: Curriculum Planning and Instruction—Instructional Strategies
Find and pursue passions.	Creativity and Innovation	Standard 3.3: Curriculum Planning and Instruction—Talent Development
Become self-motivated.	Initiative and Self-Direction	Standard 1.1: Learning and Development—Self Understanding. Standard 4.1: Learning Environments—Personal Competence

a heavy emphasis on the areas of Learning and Development (Standard 1) and Learning Environments (Standard 4), which fits its philosophy that stresses the importance of developing each student's self-understanding, awareness of needs, social responsibility, multicultural competence, interpersonal communication skills, and cognitive and affective growth.

ACCOUNTABILITY AND AUTHENTIC ASSESSMENT

The standards movement was also accompanied by demands for accountability and new forms of assessment that would address the content standards' emphasis on higher-order and more complex thinking skills (National Council on Educational Standards and Testing, 1992). In place of the traditional multiple-choice, matching, and fill-in-the-blank item formats, researchers recommended that more performance items and alternative assessments be developed that required complex, multistep tasks that focused on big ideas or concepts (Baker, 1998; Herman, Aschbacher, & Winters, 1992; Moon, Brighton, & Callahan, 2005; Wiggins, 1998). These assessments usually take the form of projects, demonstrations, essays, experiments, debates, simulations, presentations and other problem-based activities. They are significant because they affect both teachers' and students' judgments of what are important to learn and to teach (Crooks, 1988; Resnick & Resnick, 1992).

The nontraditional assessments that have been developed do appear to have a greater likelihood of assessing the knowledge, skills, and dispositions of the new content standards. They have engaged students in real-world tasks and problem solving, (Cheek, 1993; Gordon & Bonilla-Boman, 1996) and differentiated the products and performances of gifted and talented students (VanTassel-Baska, Bass, Reis, Poland, & Avery, 1998; VanTassel-Baska, Zuo, Avery, & Little, 2002). In their meta-analysis, Dochy, Segers, Van den Bossche, and Gijbels (2003) found that one form of authentic assessment, problem-based learning, had statistically and practically significant positive effects on the students' knowledge application. Effective assessments had problems that (a) occurred in authentic environments, (b) were novel to the students, (c) required students to transfer previously acquired knowledge and skills, (d) required students to analyze the influences of contextual factors on problem analysis, (e) required students to argue for their ideas on the basis of various relevant perspectives, and (f) integrated knowledge across domains (Baxter & Shavelson, 1994; Birenbaum & Dochy, 1996; Segers, 1997; Segers et al., 1999; Shavelson, Gao, & Baxter, 1996).

The Roeper School has incorporated a variety of alternative assessments that allow students to identify their interests and to select from a broad range of electives. For example, students may take calculus in the sixth grade or participate in self-developed electives, competitions, and/or school and community activities (e.g., Debate, Dungeons and Dragons, Forensics, Gay/Straight Alliance, Michigan Mathematics Prize Competition, Model United Nations, Sierra Club, Student Government) (Roeper School Home Page, 2010). In fact, the Roeper School is well known in the Detroit metro area for having a highly sophisticated upper school play at the high school and a middle school musical that are produced every year in its own theater. The students' theatrical skills are developed during the Summer Stock Theater when interested students are able to work with professional theater instructors who teach core training sessions in acting, singing and dancing and customize their sessions based on formative assessments of each student's needs from the beginner to the more experienced actor.

At the upper school, students may elect to develop an independent senior project. The senior project is totally student-directed but has a faculty advisor and an outside mentor. In a recent year, 17 of 51 Roeper seniors did a senior project (Murray, 2010). The projects ranged from the arts (e.g., creating dances, music, plays) to literary publications (e.g., children's book, novels, research) to technology (e.g., a 3-D Chatroom) to community action (e. g., creating a nonprofit to help the homeless, implementing a student-led peer mediation panel). Common threads throughout many of the projects show the influence of the Roeper culture and student outcomes that emphasize justice, diversity, and ethical and moral issues. For example, one student developed a collage, which reported 7- to 9-year-old children's perspectives about cultural and ethnic diversity. Another wrote an essay on the Irish "Troubles"; another wrote an original musical play of three teenagers discussing four famous African American entertainers; and another wrote a novel about a woman's journey after being diagnosed with cancer. Faculty and mentors conduct ongoing, informal assessments throughout the life of the project; and they are presented to an audience at an annual George A. Roeper Festival of Senior Projects.

These curricular and extracurricular choices at the lower, middle, and upper schools address those student outcomes focusing on flexibility, decision making, self-motivation, and pursuing passions (see Table 1). Students are allowed the freedom to choose electives, develop extracurricular courses, and pursue their interests through project and experiential-based learning. On the Roeper School Facebook page, one former Roeper student described the effects of his Roeper education:

> . . . the independence Roeper offers its students is one of the best things it does with regards to preparing for college and going out into the 'real' world. When I arrived at college, I was already used to the concepts of making my own schedules, having large amounts of free time to manage, and that the responsibility for my grades rests on myself alone. Roeper's individualized, personalized environment allowed me to grow in these areas, and the skill sets I gained have stuck with me and have scaled well, even to a place as large as U of M.

BALANCED ASSESSMENT SYSTEMS

With the advent of the Race-to-the-Top Assessment Program, researchers are now writing about next-generation assessment systems that include not only more authentic assessments but multiple forms of assessment—formative, summative, and interim (Darling-Hammond & Pecheone, 2010; Stiggins, 2006, 2008). Formative assessment generally occurs continuously in the classroom and is used to adjust curriculum and instructional strategies to improve student learning (e.g., questioning, exit tickets, learning activities, observations, anecdotal records, behavior charts, discussions, conferences, feedback, student reflections). Interim assessments occur at set points in time such as the end of a unit of study, a series of lessons or project activities, or a grading period to determine adjustments that might be needed in the curriculum (e.g., reading inventories, established rubrics for class products and performances, curriculum-based unit tests, school benchmark assessments). Summative assessments are usually used in evaluating the overall effects of specific interventions, the curriculum, programs, or other school goals (e.g., end of course exams, AP exams, norm-referenced tests). These systems are supposed to be (a) comprehensive because they address all of the important standards and student outcomes, (b) coherent because they link assessment to classroom curriculum and instruction and (c) continuous because they are able to monitor learning progress over time (Pellegrino, Chudowsky, & Glaser, 2001).

Formative/Interim Assessments

While some attention has focused on the use of balanced assessment systems in comparing student performance across schools or nations (Darling-Hammond & Pecheone, 2010; Schmidt, Wang, & McKnight, 2005), most researchers have emphasized the importance of the quality and characteristics of formative and interim assessments—not as instruments per se but as part of a process that informs the practice of teaching and learning (Heritage, 2010). Using the National Board Certification process, Sato, Wei, and Darling-Hammond (2008) developed an analytical framework, identifying six dimensions that captured the teachers' actions and decisions when using formative assessments in the classroom (p. 673). Other researchers' work has supported these dimensions as important to the formative assessment process:

1. Views and uses of assessment (Does the teacher view assessments as providing information for student learning and for instructional decision-making?). Shepard (2009) emphasized that it is the teacher's view and use of the instrument, rather than the instrument itself that warrants the claim of formative assessment (Shepard, 2009). If the teacher uses the assessment for grading only and not for instructional purposes, then the assessment is no longer formative, but summative. The teachers' views toward assessments also affect their students' views. When assessments are used for norm-referenced comparisons, they can reduce students' intrinsic motivation, their self perceptions of competence, their development of learning strategies, and increase their evaluation anxiety (Crooks, 1988).

2. Range, quality, and coherence of assessment methods (Does the teacher use a variety of quality assessment methods that are consistent with learning goals and further student learning?). A variety of data appear to be important in determining students' strengths and weaknesses (e.g., qualitative and quantitative aspects of performance) (What Works U.S. Department of Education, 2009). The range of assessment methods needs to align with the standards in the domain, the cognitive level of the standard, and the range and structure of the knowledge and skills addressed (Martone & Sireci, 2009; Royer, Cisero, & Carlo, 1993). The range might include measures of knowledge acquisition, depth of problem representation, mental models, efficiency of procedures, metacognitive skills, and automaticity of performance (Anderson, 1982). Moreover, the quality of the assessment needs to engage the student in learning (Hamilton, 1994).
3. Clarity and appropriateness of goals and expectations for learning (Are the learning goals and success criteria clearly articulated, conceptually important, and developmentally appropriate for the students?). To be developmentally appropriate, the selection of the assessments needs to be based on the learner's prior knowledge (Dochy, Segers, & Buehl, 1999). The assessments also must have known criteria that are challenging but attainable and are understood by both the teacher and the student (Crooks, 1988; Moon, Brighton, Callahan, & Robinson, 2005). These assessments provide multiple ways for students to demonstrate that they have met the criteria and use rubrics and other scoring procedures that focus on the essence of the tasks and evaluate what's important (Crooks, 1988; Moon, Brighton, Callahan, & Robinson, 2005).
4. *Opportunities for self-assessment (Are there quality opportunities for student self-assessment that the teacher guides?).* To assess one's own learning, students must understand the goal, hold a similar conception of quality as the teacher's, compare their actual level of performance with the standard, and engage in learning that helps them achieve the standard (Sadler, 1989). Teachers, in turn, need to scaffold and assist students in developing the skills to make judgments about their learning in relationship to the standard and in developing a repertoire of learning strategies that will help them make sense of what they are learning and organize new knowledge (National Research Council, 2000; Shepard, 1991; Vygotsky, 1978; Wertsch, 1985). As the learner progresses and competence grows, the teacher is able to reduce the scaffolding so that the learner becomes more independent in the process of self-assessment. This form of student analysis combined with feedback from teachers leads to statistically significant gains in student achievement (Phillips, Hamlett, Fuchs, & Fuchs, 1993). In addition, self-assessment is key to moving a novice learner to an expert level within a domain of study. Experts have not only extensive stores of knowledge that are well organized but they know through self-assessment what they need to practice to develop their expertise (Donovan & Bransford, 2005; Ericsson, 1993).
5. Modifications to teaching based on assessment information (Does the teacher consider the student's prior knowledge and demonstrate flexibility and

responsiveness to the student's needs and interests in making future instructional decisions?). Modifications that are made during the learning process are sometimes described as dynamic assessments where the teacher focuses on the interaction between the student and the task, providing assistance as needed to understand the student's strengths and weaknesses (Swanson & Lussier, 2001). Forms of dynamic assessment include identifying learning potential (e.g., Budoff, 1987), testing the limits (Carlson & Wiedl, 1979), mediated assessment (Feuerstein, 1980), and assisted learning and transfer (Bransford, Delclos, Vye, Burns, & Hasselbring, 1987; Campione, Brown, Ferrara, Jones, & Steinberg, 1985). If the dynamic assessment is to examine abilities and discover potential, the tasks must be novel, problem-based, and require complex strategies (Geary & Brown, 1991; Kurtz & Weinert, 1989; Scruggs & Mastropieri, 1985). On the other hand, if the assessment is used to assist the learner, then the teacher may modify the format, provide more examples, provide information on successful strategies, or offer increasingly more direct hints or prompts (Bransford, Delclos, Vye, Burns, & Hasselbring, 1987). Researchers have reported that dynamic assessment procedures and other progress assessment procedures improve students' performance substantially (Dochy, Segers, & Buehl, 1999; Swanson & Lussier, 2001).

6. Quality and appropriateness of feedback to students (Is the teacher's feedback specific to the task and tailored to students' needs? Does it prompt students to take further action?). Feedback is defined as information communicated to the learner that is intended to modify his or her thinking or behavior to improve learning (Schute, 2008). Feedback works at four levels: task level (e.g., how well tasks are understood and performed), process level (e.g., the main processes needed to understand and perform the tasks); self-regulation level (e.g., metacognitive skills such as self-monitoring, directing, and regulating of actions), and the self level (e.g., personal evaluations that affect the learner such as self-efficacy, self-competence) (Hattie & Timperley, 2007). Quality feedback that enhances learning is timely and frequent, specific, well-formatted, and constructive (Black, Harrison, Lee, Marshall, & Wiliam, 2003; Black & William, 1998; Brunner, Fasca, Heinze, Honey, Light, Mandinach et al., 2005, Clymer & William, 2007; Schunk & Swartz, 1992; Schute, 2008; Shepard, 1995). It needs to focus feedback on the task, not the learner, regarding errors as a source of learning (Dweck, 1999). In this way, the student develops a learning orientation and is more likely to formulate and achieve her or his own learning goals (Dweck, 1999; Gijbels, Dochy, Bossche, Segers, 2005). For high achieving students, delayed feedback, verification of their responses, and hints or prompts appear to be most effective (Hattie & Timperley, 2007). Tools that help students learn from feedback are templates for listing strengths and weaknesses and areas to focus on (Stiggins, 2007), lists of questions for students to respond to (Phillips et al., 1993), worksheets to facilitate reflection (Stiggins, 2007), graphs that track students over time (Clymer & Wiliam, 2007), and grids on which students can record baseline and interim scores to track gains over time in specific dimensions (Lane, Marquardt, Meyer, & Murray, 1997).

Examples of Formative and Interim Assessments

A variety of formative and interim assessments that emphasize more complex thinking skills have been described in the research literature, some specifically developed to address the needs of gifted and talented students. This section focuses on these formative assessments that are most often used in gifted education—products, performances, and portfolios.

Products. Products have been used in gifted education to assess students' creativity and understandings of more sophisticated, complex concepts and principles (Renzulli & Callahan, 2008). Researchers have designed rubrics to provide guidance to teachers and students in assessing products (Johnsen & Johnson, 2007; Reis, 1981; Schack, 1994). These rubrics focus on the content and process as well as the product itself, and may be holistic or specific to a particular product. For example, a holistic rubric might include these types of questions: Did the student address the questions or solve the problem (content)? Did the student use a novel approach in gathering her information (process)? Does the product present the information in a creative way (content and product)? Did the student's self-assessment correspond to the audience or her peers' assessments (process)? More specific rubrics are developed by delineating the specific characteristics or dimensions of a particular product (e.g., WebPage—purpose, title, information, layout, design, navigation) and describing the highest level of quality on each dimension (Callahan, 2002). The teacher communicates this information to the students so that they have opportunities for self-monitoring and self-assessment. Other questions used in developing rubrics may be found in reading Arter and McTighe (2001), Johnsen and Johnson (2007), and Lewin and Shoemaker (1998).

While products are sometimes used as an interim or summative assessment of student outcomes (e.g., Does the product demonstrate what the student has learned in this unit or in this course?), they also may be used to identify the next step in a learning progression, which might include both content knowledge and/or process skills. For example, assume that a gifted student is interested in "bees." His first study might focus on organizing knowledge that describes bees' characteristics, habitats, social order, life cycle, and benefits. He might gather this knowledge from books, the Internet, and interviews with beekeepers. His products would then reflect this level of knowledge (e.g., charts, diagrams, photos). However, in interacting with his teacher and the beekeepers and in his own self-assessments, his next study might focus on questions that examine the environmental factors that influence the maintenance of healthy European honeybees. In this case, he might need to learn field research techniques so that he could gather this information from systematic observations of honeybee hives. Products from this study might not only contain simple diagrams but data in the form of graphs that he collects from bee habitats in his community and a written report of his findings. This example shows how independent studies can build on one another and contribute to more sophisticated products. The products themselves might also be used formatively to help the student in improving the process (e.g., writing skills, data analysis) or the product (e.g., clarity, creative aspects).

Performances. Performance tasks require students to demonstrate their knowledge and skills in authentic contexts (Wiggins, 1993). Performance-based assessments may include oral discussions, debates, presentations, role plays, contributions in a group setting, problem solving in mathematics, scientific experimentation, simulations, dramatizations, and so on. In designing performance tasks for gifted and talented students, VanTassel-Baska (2008) used these five criteria: an emphasis on thinking and problem solving, off-level tasks that are challenging, open-ended formats to encourage creative responses, use of manipulatives for difficult problems, and opportunities for self reflection. Similar to product assessments, rubrics have been designed to assess the processes involved in the performance task (Airasian, 2001; Arter & McTighe, 2001; Johnsen & Johnson, 2007; Oosterhof, 2008; Wiggins, 1993). In developing performance criteria, Airasian (2001) suggests that teachers, professionals, and/or their students perform the task first and then list the important aspects of the performance. Next, they need to express the performance criteria in terms of observable behaviors and limit the performance criteria to those that can be observed during the student's performance. The final step is for teachers to arrange the performance criteria in the order in which they are likely to be observed. Feedback can be provided to a student using a checklist, narrative reports, or a rubric that displays varying degrees of proficiency.

An example of a performance-based assessment in the performing arts area is *The Talent Assessment Process in Dance, Music, and Theater* (Oreck, Owen, & Baum, 2003). Oreck et al. (2003) created this assessment to provide an authentic arts experience that allowed artistic behaviors to emerge. In the assessment situation, open-ended tasks were performed in groups, requiring students to work together, watch, listen, and respond to each other. They provided time for physical and mental preparation and warm-up and an atmosphere where students felt comfortable to take risks, communicate their feelings and ideas, and were fully engaged. Using this assessment approach, they were able to identify students' strengths and interests and predict their success in rigorous arts instruction.

Performance assessments can be augmented by product assessments (Atkin, Black, & Coffey, 2001). For example, in science experiments students are provided with apparatus and are expected to design and conduct an investigation and communicate their findings in a journal. Observations of students conducting the experiments along with the resulting products such as data sheets, graphs, and analysis can be used to determine the students' proficiency and the need for more instruction. The strengths of performance assessments are their ability to capture knowledge and skills in contexts that are authentic to the learner and to the domain.

Portfolios. Portfolios are purposeful and systematic collections of student work that provide a sample of a student's abilities, progress, and accomplishments in a domain

(Arter & McTighe, 2001). Portfolios share these characteristics: have a specific purpose; are aligned with standards, curriculum, instruction, and other assessments; show growth over time; use multiple sources and contexts; represent the student's performance in one or more domains; engage the students in their own learning through self-assessment and reflection; and guide teaching and learning (Johnsen, 2008). Portfolios may include baseline samples, journals or logs, observations, projects, artwork, writing, photos of products, CDs or DVDs of performances, professional reviews, and students' reflections.

In establishing a portfolio, the teacher and/or student need to identify its purpose. Will the portfolio evaluate a student's progress throughout a semester or school year? Will it contain products or performances that match a set of predetermined standards? Will it showcase exemplary work? Will it relate to a single learner outcome or goal? Next, the teacher and/or student need to identify the contents of the portfolio (Hadaway & Marek-Schroer, 1992; Hanson & Gilkerson, 1999). What specific items will be included? Third, decisions need to be made about the selection of the portfolio items (Duffey, Jones, & Thomas, 1999). Who will select them? Can they be in various stages of completion? Will the items be assessed formatively or summatively? How will the students reflect about their work? Fourth, identify what items will be assessed (Damiani, 2004). Will the process of creating the item be assessed (e.g., How did the student develop the product or performance? In what ways did the student collaborate with others?)? Will only the final product or performance be assessed (e.g., How significant is the product? How creative was it? How did it relate to the student outcome?)? Next, a scoring system such as a checklist, rubric, or rating scale needs to be developed (Arter & McTighe, 2001). Similar to the other alternative assessments, these may be focused on specific tasks or they may be more holistic. The scores, however, need to provide information about the important attributes of the portfolio and provide guidance to the student for continued growth. Along with the student, a committee that shares well-trained perspectives might also be involved in reviewing the portfolio (Royer, Cisero, & Carlo, 1993). This involvement would be particularly important for students who are more advanced in their studies or in highly technical fields. Next, a method needs to be identified for managing the portfolios (Fogarty, Burke, & Belgrad, 1996; Paulson, Paulson, & Meyer, 1991). How will they be stored? Will they be stored electronically? Will they be dated and described? Finally, throughout the process, students need to be involved in self-assessment and reflections (Hill, 2004). To assist with this involvement, the teacher will want to create regularly scheduled conferences and to provide written, constructive feedback.

Portfolios have been used for formative assessment in documenting progress in music, the visual arts, and imaginative writing (Gardner, Wolf, & Gitomer, 2006); in literacy and numeracy and exploratory reading projects from kindergarten through the fourth grade (Hill, 2000); in a physical education program at the elementary level (Melograno, 1994); in conferences with the teacher, students, their peers, parents and other professional in the school (Paulson & Paulson, 1996); and in an International

Baccalaureate program as a measure of arts learning (Stites & Malin, 2008). In the last example, students select their own entries that promote their independence, autonomy, and exploration. Using sample student artwork as benchmarks, the portfolio provides students and their teachers with a common understanding of what student work looks like at different achievement levels and encourages debate. The strengths of portfolio assessments are the opportunities that students and their teachers have in assessing each student's progress and in developing curricula and instructional plans.

Formative and Interim Assessments at the Roeper School

Given the Roeper School's emphasis on personalized education for the whole child (e.g., academic, moral, creative, emotional, physical, and social development), formative and interim assessments are used to address the School's learning outcomes. For example, at the lower school level, students are not placed in grades but in "stages" so that teachers are more likely to focus on an individual student's progress rather than their movement through a "graded" curricular sequence. Typical student groupings are kept together for two years with the same teachers so that teachers have opportunities to formatively assess students and accelerate the pace or the conceptual depth of curriculum. Interim assessments and conferences with students and their parents are scheduled two to four times per year. These assessments are primarily narrative reports that focus on a student's strengths and weaknesses.

Assessments at the middle and upper school allow students to accelerate, to identify their interests, and to select from a broad range of electives. Most of the Roeper School's assessments tend to be formative and more anecdotal in nature. This approach is more in line with the Roeper philosophy that focuses on learning rather than passing tests.

Within a balanced assessment system, the Roeper School's emphasis on formative and interim assessments places it in a unique leadership position in examining the effects of an education that is not based on high-stakes testing. It is strategically situated to examine these questions related to the previously described dimensions of formative assessment:

1. How do teachers and students view assessment within the Roeper culture—a personalized environment that focuses on development of the whole child?
2. What formative assessment data at each of the Roeper schools are particularly important in identifying students' strengths and weaknesses? Which of these assessments are most engaging to the students?
3. What assessment criteria are used with students in determining their readiness for advancement within a curricular or extracurricular area or to the next stage or school level?
4. How do assessment criteria assess the important aspects of learning at the Roeper School (e.g., commit to justice and human rights, respect individual differences, recognize interdependence, define ethical and moral issues, pursue passions)?

5. How do teachers and/or students develop and communicate their expectations for learning at the lower, middle, and upper schools?
6. Based on prior knowledge, mastery, and/or level of expertise, how do teachers and/or students modify learning expectations?
7. What teacher approaches in providing feedback enable students to accurately assess themselves, to assume responsibility for their own learning, and to develop their expertise within a domain?

Any activity undertaken by a student at the Roeper School will provide an opportunity to address these questions related to the dimensions of formative assessment. To ensure their validity, formative assessments might be complemented by interim or summative assessments. The student senior project is an excellent example of an interim or even summative assessment. The 2010 student projects clearly show many of the processes and content that are valued at the Roeper School—diversity, creative production, decision-making, independence, equity and justice, and pursuit of passions. Other summative or interim assessments might be considered for those students who did not participate or who did not complete a senior project.

Regardless of what form of assessment occurs, faculty at the Roeper School will want to keep in mind validity and reliability issues to make decisions about future actions and to authenticate their practices and achievements. Reliability addresses consistency within and across people and settings (e.g., Do teachers view the same performances and products similarly? Does performance in the classroom generalize to other contexts such as the community?). Validity addresses the degree to which the assessments do what they are supposed to do (e.g., Do they assess the Roeper School's learning outcomes? Do they predict performance outside the Roeper School?). Atkins, Black, and Coffey (2001) provide some excellent questions for applying validity and reliability concerns to classroom teaching (p. 71):

1. What is the teacher interested in assessing? Does this assessment capture that?
2. Is the assessment aligned with the curriculum? Have the students had an opportunity to learn the knowledge and skills?
3. Based on the results of the assessment, what can be said about the student's understandings? Are those claims legitimate?
4. Are the consequences and actions that result from the student's performance important to learning or justifiable?
5. Are there assumptions or inferences about other knowledge, skills, or abilities that are being made from the assessment that are not directly assessed?
6. Are there other factors that may be influencing the performance on the assessment?
7. Are the criteria being used consistently and fairly across students' products and performances?
8. What are the unintended consequences associated with the assessment?

In summary, the Roeper School has an assessment system that emphasizes formative and interim assessments. Some of its other assessments such as the senior project might be used summatively to examine the effects of its overall curriculum and program.

CONCLUSIONS

The Roeper School's philosophy has created a clear mission and vision for what the school hopes to accomplish. This mission has established a solid foundation for creating a learning community that is focused on the whole child. Embedded within its mission statement are clearly delineated student outcomes. These outcomes are timeless. They relate to the goals of the Roeper School when it was first created in 1941 and to today's gifted education learning outcomes and national and international standards that incorporate 21st-Century Learning Skills.

Formative and interim assessments, which are emphasized by researchers as improving classroom practices and student learning, are commonly used at all levels of the Roeper School. Given their frequent use of more informal assessments, the Roeper School could provide a leadership role in examining the specific qualities that inform their teaching practices and the learning of students with gifts and talents. They might describe in more detail the types of formative assessments that are used, their validity and reliability, and how they might lead to high quality, advanced senior projects and other summative-type assessments. The information that is gleaned from this type of research could inform not only their practices but also other schools that are focused on developing each student's gifts and talents.

REFERENCES

Airasian, P. W. (2001). *Classroom assessment: Concepts and applications* (4th ed.). Boston, MA: McGraw-Hill.

Anderson, J. R. (1982). Acquisition of cognitive skill. *Psychological Review, 89*, 369–406.

Arter, J., & McTighe, J. (2001). *Scoring rubrics in the classroom: Using performance criteria for assessing and improving student performance*. Thousand Oaks, CA: Corwin.

Atkin, J. M., Black, P., & Coffey, J. (Eds.) (2001). *Classroom assessment and the national science education standards. Committee on Classroom Assessment and the National Science Education Standards.* Washington, DC: The National Academies Press.

Baker, E. L. (1998). *Model-based performance assessment*. CSE Technical Report 465. Los Angeles, CA: Center for the Study of Evaluation, National Center for Research on Evaluation, Standards, and Student Testing, Graduate School of Education and Information Studies, University of California, Los Angeles.

Baxter, G. P., & Shavelson, R. J. (1994). Science performance assessments: Benchmarks and surrogates. *International Journal of Educational Research 21*, 279–299.

Birenbaum, M., & Dochy, F. (Eds.) (1996). *Alternatives in assessment of achievements, learning processes and prior knowledge*. Boston, MA: Kluwer Academic.

Black, P. J., & Wiliam, D. (1998). Inside the black box: Raising standards through classroom assessment. *Phi Delta Kappan, 80*, 139–148.

Black, P., Harrison, C., Lee, C., Marshall, B., & Wiliam, D. (2003). *Assessment for learning: Putting it into practice*. Maidenhead, UK: Open University Press.

Bransford, J. C., Delclos, J. R., Vye, N. J., Burns, M., & Hasselbring, T. S. (1987). State of the art and future directions. In C. S. Lidz (Ed.), *Dynamic assessment: An interactional approach to evaluating learning potential* (pp. 479–496). New York, NY: Guilford Press.

Brunner, C., Fasca, C., Heinze, J., Honey, M., Light, D., Mandinach, E., et al. (2005). Linking data and learning: The grow network study. *Journal of Education for Students Placed At Risk, 10*, 241–267.

Budoff, M. (1987). Measures for assessing learning potential. In C. S. Lidz (Ed.), *Dynamic testing* (pp. 173–195). New York, NY: Guilford Press.

Callahan, C. M. (2002). The ABCs of creating a performance assessment task and scoring rubric. *Gifted Education Communicator, 33*(2), 12–15.

Campione, J. S., Brown, A. L., Ferrara, R. A., Jones, R. S., & Steinberg, E. (1985). Breakdowns in the flexible use of information: Intelligence-related differences in transfer following equivalent learning performance. *Intelligence, 9*, 297–315.

Carlson, J. S., & Wiedl, K. H. (1979). Toward a differential testing approach: Testing the limits employing the Raven Matrices. *Intelligence, 3*, 323–344.

Cheek, D. W. (1993). Plain talk about alternative assessment. *Middle School Journal, 25*(2), 6–10.

Clymer, J. B., & Wiliam, D. (2007). Improving the way we grade science. *Educational Leadership, 64*(4), 36–42.

Crooks, T. J. (1988). The impact of classroom evaluation practices on students. *Review of Educational Research, 58*, 438–481.

Damiani, V. B. (2004). *Portfolio assessment in the classroom.* Bethesda, MD: National Association of School Psychologists.

Darling-Hammond, L., & Pecheone, R. (2010). *Developing an internationally comparable balanced assessment system that supports high-quality learning.* Princeton, NJ: Educational Testing Services.

Dochy, F., Segers, M., & Buehl, M. M. (1999). The relation between assessment practices and outcomes of studies: the case of research on prior knowledge. *Review of Educational Research, 69*, 145–186.

Dochy, F., Segers, M., Van den Bossche, P., & Gijbels, D. (2003). Effects of problem-based learning: A meta-analysis. *Learning and Instruction, 13*, 533–568.

Donovan, M. S., & Bransford, J. D. (2005). Introduction. In M. S. Donovan & J. D. Bransford (Eds.), *How students learn: History, mathematics, and science in the classroom* (pp. 1–28). Washington, DC: National Academic Press.

Duffy, M. L., Jones, J., & Thomas, S. W. (1999). Using portfolios to foster independent thinking. *Intervention in School and Clinic, 35*, 34–38.

Dweck, C. S. (1999). *Self-theories: Their role in motivation, personality and development.* Philadelphia, PA: Psychology Press.

Ericsson, K. A. (1993). The role of deliberate practice in the acquisition of expert performance. *Psychological Review, 100*, 363–406.

European Parliament and the Council of 2006 (2006). *Key competencies for lifelong learning.* Retrieved from http://www.europarl.europa.eu/oeil/file.jsp?id=5289042

Feuerstein, R. (1980). *Instrumental enrichment: An intervention program for cognitive modifiability.* Baltimore, MD: University Park Press.

Fogarty, R., Burke, K., & Belgrad, S. (1996). The portfolio connection: Real-world examples. In R. Fogarty (Ed.), *Student portfolios: A collection of articles* (pp. 89–100). Palatine, IL: IRI/Skylight Training and Publishing.

Gardner, H., Wolf, D. P., & Gitomer, D. (2006). *Arts PROPEL.* Retrieved from http://pzweb.harvard.edu/research/PROPEL.htm

Geary, D. C., & Brown, S. C. (1991). Cognitive addition: Strategy choice and speed-of-processing difference in gifted, normal, and mathematically disabled children. *Developmental Psychology, 27*, 398–406.

Gijbels, D., Dochy, F., Van den Bossche, P., & Segers, M. (2005). Effects of problem-based learning: A meta-analysis from the angle of assessment. *Review of Educational Research, 75*, 27–61.

Gordon, E. W., & Bonilla-Bowman, C. (1996). Can performance-based assessment contribute to the achievement of educational equity? In J. B. Baron & D. P. Wolf (Eds.), *Performance-based student achievement: Challenges and possibilities* (pp. 32–51). Chicago, IL: National Society for the Study of Education.

Hadaway, N., & Marek-Shroer, M. F. (1992). Multidimensional assessment of the gifted minority student. *Roeper Review, 15*, 73–78.

Hamilton, L. S. (1994, April). *An investigation of students' affective responses to alternative assessment formats*. Paper presented at the Annual Meeting of the National Council on Measurement in Education. New Orleans, LA.
Hanson, M. F., & Gilkerson, D. (1999). Portfolio assessment: More than ABCs and 123s. *Early Childhood Education Journal, 27*, 81–86.
Hattie, J., & Timperley, H. (2007). The power of feedback. *Review of Educational Research, 77*, 81–12.
Heritage, M. (2010, September). *Formative assessment and next-generation assessment systems: Are we losing an opportunity?* Washington, DC: Council of Chief State School Officers.
Herman, J. L., Aschbacher, P. R., & Winters, L. (1992). *A practical guide to alternative assessment*. Alexandria, VA: Association of Supervision and Curriculum Development.
Hill, C. (2000). The progress profile: Constructivist assessment in early childhood education. In A. L. Costa (Ed.), *Teaching for intelligence II* (pp. 211–230). Chicago, IL: Skylight.
Hill, C. (2004). Failing to meet the standards: The English Language Arts Test for fourth graders in New York state. *Teachers College Record, 106*, 1086–1123.
International Reading Association/National Council of Teachers of English (1996). *Standards for the English language arts*. Retrieved from http://www.ncte.org/library/NCTEFiles/Resources/Books/Sample/StandardsDoc.pdf
Johnsen, S. K. (2008). Portfolio assessment of gifted students. In J. L. VanTassel-Baska (Ed.), *Alternative assessments with gifted and talented students* (pp. 227–257). Waco, TX: Prufrock Press.
Johnsen, S. K., & Johnson, K. (2007). *Independent Study Program*, (2nd ed.). Waco, TX: Prufrock Press.
Kurtz, B. E., & Weinert, F. E. (1989). Metacognition, memory performance, and causal attributions in gifted and average children. *Journal of Experimental Child Psychology, 48*, 45–61.
Lane, C., Marquardt, J., Meyer, M. A., & Murray, W. (1997). *Addressing the lack of motivation in the middle school setting*. Chicago, IL: St. Xavier University, Master's action research project.
Lewin, L., & Shoemaker, B. J. (1998). *Great performances: Creating classroom-based assessment tasks*. Alexandria, VA: Association for Supervision and Curriculum Development.
Martone, A., & Sireci, S. G. (2009). Evaluating alignment between curriculum, assessment, and instruction. *Review of Educational Research, 79*, 1332–1361.
Melograno, V. J. (1994). Portfolio assessment: Documenting authentic student learning. *Journal of Physical Education, Recreation, and Dance, 65*(8), 50–55, 58–61.
Moon, T. R., Brighton, C. M., Callahan, C. M., & Robinson, A. (2005). Development of authentic assessments for the middle school classroom. *The Journal of Secondary Gifted Education, 16*, 119–133.
Murray, D. D. (2010, June). *With video: High school seniors in Birmingham dedicate themselves to various projects*. Oakland County, MI: The Oakland Press. Retrieved from www.theoaklandpress.com/articles/2010/06/01/life/doc4c05db9451d63237943483.txt?viewmode=fullstory
National Association for Gifted Children (2010, November). *NAGC Pre-K-Grade 12 gifted programming standards: A blueprint for quality gifted education programs*. Washington, DC: Author.
National Association for Gifted Children/Council for Exceptional Children (2006). *Initial knowledge and skill standards for gifted education*. Retrieved from http://www.cectag.org
National Committee for Standards in the Arts (1994). *National standards for arts education*. Reston, VA: The National Association for Music Education.
National Commission on Excellence in Education (1983). *A nation at risk: The imperative for educational reform*. Washington, DC: U. S. Department of Education.
National Council for the Social Studies (2010). *National curriculum standards for social studies: A framework for teaching, learning, and assessment*. Silver Spring, MD: Author.
National Council of Teachers of Mathematics (2000). *Principles and standards for school mathematics*. Reston, VA: Author.
National Education Goals Panel (1994). *The 1994 national education goals report: Building a nation of learners*. Washington, DC: Author.
National Council on Educational Standards and Testing (1992). *Raising standards for American education: A report to Congress, the Secretary of Education, the National Education Goals Panel, and the American people*. Washington, DC: U.S. Government Printing Office.
National Governors Association for Best Practices/Council of Chief State School Officers (2010). *Common core state standards*. Retrieved from http://www.corestandards.org/

National Research Council (1996). *National science education standards*. Washington, DC: National Academy Press. Retrieved from http://www.nap.edu/openbook.php?record_id=4962

National Research Council (2000). *How people learn: Brain, mind, experience, and school*. Washington, DC: National Academies Press.

Oreck, B. A., Owen, S. V., & Baum, S. M. (2003). Validity, reliability, and equity issues in an observational talent assessment process in the performing arts. *Journal for the Education of the Gifted, 27,* 62–94.

Oosterhof, A. (2008). *Developing and using classroom assessments* (4th ed.). Upper Saddle River, NJ: Prentice-Hall.

Partnership for 21st Century Skills (2009). *Framework for 21st Century Learning*. Retrieved from http://www.p21.org/documents/P21_Framework_Definitions.pdf

Paulson, F. L., & Paulson, P. R. (1996). Assessing portfolios using the constructivist paradigm. In R. Fogarty (Ed.), *Student portfolios: A collection of articles* (pp. 27–45). Palatine, IL: IRI/Skylight Training and Publishing.

Paulson, F. L., Paulson, P. R., & Meyer, C. A. (1991). What makes a portfolio a portfolio? *Educational Leadership, 48*(5), 60–63.

Pellegrino, J. W., Chudowsky, N., Glaser, R. (Eds.). (2001). *Knowing what students know: The science and design of educational assessment*. Washington, DC: National Academies Press.

Phillips, N. B., Hamlett, C. L., Fuchs, L. S., & Fuchs, D. (1993). Combining classwide curriculum-based measurement and peer tutoring to help general educators provide adaptive education. *Learning Disabilities Research & Practice, 8,* 148–156.

Reis, S. M. (1981). *An analysis of the productivity of gifted students participating in programs using the revolving door identification model*. (Unpublished doctoral dissertation). University of Connecticut, Storrs.

Renzulli, J. S., & Callahan, C. M. (2008). Product assessment. In J. L. VanTassel-Baska (Ed.), *Alternative assessments with gifted and talented students* (pp. 259–283). Waco, TX: Prufrock Press.

Resnick, L. B., & Resnick, D. (1992). Assessing the thinking curriculum: New tools for education reform. In B. R. Gifford & M. C. O'Connor (Eds.), *Changing assessments: Alternative views of aptitude, achievement and instruction* (pp. 301–328). Boston, MA: Kluwer Academic.

Roeper Board of Trustees (2010). *Philosophy*. Retrieved from http://www.roeper.org/TheRoeperSchool/aboutUs/philosophy.aspx

Roeper School Calendar 2010/2011 (2010). Retrieved from http://community.rceper.org/webadditions/RoeperCenPhotos.pdf

Roeper School Home Page (2010). The Roeper School. Retrieved from http://www.roeper.org/

Royer, J. M., Cisero, C. A., & Carlo, M. S. (1993). Techniques and procedures for assessing cognitive skills. *Review of Educational Research, 63,* 201–243.

Sadler, D. R. (1989). Formative assessment and the design of instructional systems. *Instructional Science, 18,* 119–140.

Sato, M., Wei, R. C., & Darling-Hammond, L. (2008). Improving teachers' assessment practices through professional development: The case of National Board Certification. *American Educational Research Journal, 45,* 669–700.

Segers, M. (1997). An alternative for assessing problem-solving skills: The overall test. *Studies in Educational Evaluation, 23,* 373–398.

Segers, M., Dochy, F., & DeCorte, E. (1999). Assessment practices and students' knowledge profiles in a problem–based curriculum. *Learning Environments Research: An International Journal, 2,* 191–213.

Schack, G. D. (1994). Authentic assessment procedures for secondary students' original research. *Journal of Secondary Gifted Education, 6,* 38–43.

Schmidt, W. H., Wang, H. C., & McKnight, C. (2005). Curriculum coherence: An examination of U. S. mathematics and science content standards from an international perspective. *Journal of Curriculum Studies, 37,* 525–559.

Schunk, D. H., & Swartz, C. W. (1992, April). *Goals and feedback during writing strategy instruction with gifted students*. Paper presented at the annual meeting of the American Educational Research Association, San Francisco, CA.

Scruggs, T., & Mastropieri, M. (1985). Spontaneous verbal elaborations in gifted and nongifted youths. *Journal for the Education of the Gifted, 9,* 1–10.

Shute, V. J. (2008). Focus on formative feedback. *Review of Educational Research, 78*, 153–189.
Shavelson, R. J., Gao, X., & Baxter, G. P. (1996). On the content validity of performance assessments: Centrality of domain specification. In M. Birenbaum & F. Dochy (Eds.), *Alternatives in assessment of achievements, learning processes and prior learning* (pp. 131–143). Boston, MA: Kluwer Academic Press.
Shepard, L. A. (1991, November). Will national tests improve student learning? *The Phi Delta Kappan, 73*, 232–238. Retrieved from http://www.jstor.org/stable/20404601.
Shepard, L. A. (1995). Using assessment to improve learning. *Educational Leadership, 52*(5), 38–43.
Shepard, L. A. (2009). Commentary: Evaluating the validity of formative and interim assessment. *Educational Measurement: Issues and Practice, 28*(3) 32–37.
Stiggins, R. J. (2006). *Balanced assessment systems: Redefining excellence in assessment.* Princeton, NJ: Educational Testing Service.
Stiggins, R. (2007). Assessment through the student's eyes. *Educational Leadership, 64*(8), 22–26.
Stiggins, R. J. (2008). *Assessment manifesto: A call for the development of balanced assessment systems.* Portland, OR: ETS Assessment Training Institute.
Stites, R., & Malin, H. (2008). *An unfinished canvas. A review of large-scale assessment in K-12 arts education.* Menlo Park, CA: SRI International.
Swanson, H. L., & Lussier, C. M. (2001). A selective synthesis of the experimental literature on dynamic assessment. *Review of Educational Research, 71*, 321–363.
VanTassel-Baska, J. (2008). Using performance-based assessment to document authentic learning. In J. L. VanTassel-Baska (Ed.), *Alternative assessments with gifted and talented students* (pp. 285–308). Waco, TX: Prufrock Press.
VanTassel-Baska, J., Bass, G., Reis, R., Poland, D., & Avery, L. (1998). A national pilot study of science curriculum effectiveness for high-ability students. *Gifted Child Quarterly, 42*, 25–36.
VanTassel-Baska, J., Zuo, L., Avery, L. D., & Little, C. A. (2002). Curriculum study of gifted-student learning in the language arts. *Gifted Child Quarterly, 46*, 30–44.
Vygotsky, L. S. (1978). *Mind and society: The development of higher mental processes.* Cambridge, MA: Harvard University Press.
Wertsch, J. V. (1985). *Vygotsky and the social formation of mind.* Cambridge, MA: Harvard University Press.
What Works U. S. Department of Education (2009). *Using student achievement data to support instructional decision making.* Institute of Education Sciences National Center for Education Evaluation and Regional Assistance. ES Practice Guide. NCEE 2009–4067. Washington DC: Author.
Wiggins, G. P. (1993). *Assessing student performances: Exploring the purpose and limits of tests.* San Francisco, CA: Jossey-Bass.
Wiggins, G. P. (1998). *Educative assessment: Designing assessments to inform and improve student performance.* New York, NY: Jossey-Bass.

PATRICK O'CONNOR

COLLEGE COUNSELING AND THE GIFTED STUDENT

> "These children are like plants that need stakes to grow against, with gentle ties where necessary to support their natural growth, instead of being rigidly espaliered to a stone wall in artificial designs someone else devised."
> —Stephanie Tolan

Thirty years may have passed since Stephanie Tolan's quote first appeared in *Guiding the Gifted Child*, but her observation succinctly describes the challenges students, parents, teachers and counselors face today when working together in the college selection process. With more students going to college than ever before, admission rates at many American colleges are at an all-time low, limiting access to many of these colleges for all students, including the gifted. When this increase is combined with frequent calls to make the American workforce more competitive in the global economy, it is easy to understand why some gifted children may feel pressured to make the "right" college decision as defined by external forces, especially if students are undecided about their academic or vocational plans.

An effective college counseling curriculum will embrace these challenges by demystifying the college admissions process and personalizing college choices for all students. This approach to college advising is a natural extension of the philosophy practiced at the Roeper School, where students of all ages explore diverse curriculum using a full range of critical thinking skills and personal reflection activities. By utilizing their intellectual and affective intuitions, gifted students can embrace the college selection process with an outlook that leaves them receptive to a wide array of postsecondary opportunities, an eagerness to explore these possibilities, and an excitement in choosing their next educational experience that will make for a smooth transition between life after high school and early adulthood—a transition that increases the likelihood every student will lead a healthy, strong, productive life.

THE NEED TO DEMYSTIFY THE COLLEGE ADMISSIONS PROCESS

Patricia McDonough (2008) identifies three phases of the college selection process: *predisposition*, when students shape general career and educational goals; *search*, when students explore colleges to discover the options that will best meet their needs, and *choice*, when students apply to colleges and make a decision based on the offers of admission they receive.

Of these three phases, the choice phase receives nearly all of the attention of the media. As a result, it is the main focus of gifted students and their families. Every fall, myriad stories blanket newsstands and Web sites about the keys of writing effective college essays and the do's and don'ts of visiting college campuses. Come spring, these same media sources devote vast space to coverage of the low percentage of students admitted to highly selective colleges, the anxiety of being placed on a college's waitlist (where admission is dependent on an already admitted student choosing not to attend that college), and the frustration of students not being able to attend their first-choice college due to lack of funds.

This cultural emphasis on the choice phase of today's college applicants has a profound impact on the predisposition phase of tomorrow's college applicants. Several studies suggest that gifted students are keenly aware of the world around them, and the practical experience of any teacher of the gifted affirms that the parents of gifted students are often equally aware of world events, if not more so. While media coverage is designed to record the complexities of the current environment of college admissions (see, for example, Caldwell, 2012), it is not unreasonable for younger gifted students and their families to use this coverage to make an intuitive leap about the world of college admissions they will face in a few short years. That leap will often lead them to wonder, "If college admissions is complicated and competitive now, how much more difficult will it be when it's time for me (or my child) to get into college?"

The impact of this choice-heavy coverage of the college selection process on younger students and their families could be minimized by the reassuring college counseling expertise of elementary and middle school counselors, but these counselors are in short supply. As a White House report indicates, (United States Executive Office of the President, 2011), recent cuts in education funding have led to higher cuts in support personnel than in classroom teachers, and school districts often maintain a full complement of high school counselors by reducing or eliminating counselors in K-8 schools. Combined with a lack of graduate-school training in college counseling as outlined in a report by Public Agenda (2010), elementary and middle school counselors are often unavailable or unprepared to ease the college anxieties of students and parents, leaving families to build a predisposition towards college that is biased by fear and uncertainty; a bias that increases every year the percentage of college-bound seniors grows (National Center for Education Statistics, 2012).

Students and families at Roeper tend to be swayed less by these concerns, in large part because of the value the school places on critical thinking at all levels of instruction. Making the most of a gifted student's desire to get past the "what" of an idea to explore the "why" behind it, Roeper fosters a curiosity in students that is manifested in everything from the exploration of an animal's habitat to the underlying assumptions of a best-selling author. In nurturing the ability for students to evaluate the components of an idea in every curriculum, Roeper's approach to teaching and learning prepares students for the college selection process with a depth and skill set that is realized by few other students, all without ever discussing college selection per se until it is included in the upper school curriculum.

THE NEED TO PERSONALIZE THE COLLEGE SELECTION PROCESS

Another unintended consequence of society's emphasis of the search phase of college counseling is an overreliance on simplistic and generalized college advice. While many books and Web sites offer sound college counsel that is practical and effective when thoughtfully applied to a student's individual circumstances, parents and students often look for relief from what they perceive to be the mystery of choosing a college by seeking a source that is easy to understand immediately and is apparently universal in its recommendations.

This explains part of the popularity of college rankings, the lists of colleges that prioritize the value of a college based on a certain set of criteria established by the publishers of the list. Touted with names that often include phrases like "Best Colleges," "Best Value," and "Happiest Colleges," these rankings are viewed by many families as an endless fountain of knowledge in what appears to be the otherwise dry and desolate terrain of college knowledge. Almost every college counselor can relate a story of meeting with a family to discuss college options that begins with the parents pulling out a copy of the most recent college rankings and saying, "Let's start with this."

This same easy access and uniformity of application can be found in Web sites that offer students and parents in the choice phase the opportunity to share their observations of the college selection process. Some of these remarks are based on actual experiences ("The dean of admissions talked about what they look for in a good college essay"), while others are simply reflections of individual or small group behavior ("My older son wrote about renewable energy and was admitted", and "Everyone seems to be writing about the upcoming election, so stay away from that topic").

Overreliance on these two sources in any phase of the college selection process can limit or misdirect any student's college choices. Students and parents read too much and too little into college rankings; some families build a child's entire college list by deciding to apply only to the top-ranked 6 or 8 colleges, while other families see a yawning chasm of excellence between the fourteenth and fifteenth-ranked colleges, when the distinction between the two colleges could be due to something as small as the difference in the number of applicants who are denied admission by the two colleges. Along the same lines, parents and students may use the advice of a chat room as the sole basis of deciding which colleges to apply to (because the chat rooms say every other student has decided to apply there), or what essay topic to write about (because everyone else is writing about something else, and a different topic will inherently give the student a "leg up" in the admissions process).

Dependence on these generic resources for specific college decisions in the choice phase closes the circle of misinformation that can surround all three phases of the college selection process. Parents of young children glean information about the challenges older students are facing in applying to college, and wonder if their own children will face these same challenges. This uncertainty remains with parents and students throughout the predisposition phase and is reinforced with the coverage of every graduating class. Once the student is old enough to enter the search and application phases, families looking for information—any information—about the college choice process lean on resources that are easy to access and to understand. This reliance increases the perceived value of these sources by all members of society, including families with younger children, whose predisposition phase now begins with an even greater air of uncertainty and concern.

The impact of the absence of a more meaningful approach to the college selection process cannot be underestimated. One college admissions officer tells the story of talking to a 17 year-old junior at a college fair. The junior began the conversation by saying, "Ever since I was young, I had two college goals: Attend your University, and get a degree in criminal justice." In relating this conversation to a group of high school counselors, the admissions officer said, "At that very moment, I was trying to figure out how to tell that student he couldn't achieve both of those goals at the same time, since our college doesn't offer a degree in criminal justice."

Another example shows that parents are not immune to these leaps of faith. A researcher told about a focus group of parents he convened to discuss the value of college. To begin the discussion, he had displayed diploma covers from different colleges on a nearby table; he then asked the parents to identify a "good" college from the diploma covers. One parent immediately selected the diploma cover from the Massachusetts Institute of Technology. When asked why MIT was a good college, the parent responded that students could get a good job with an MIT degree, just like the two hosts of a popular talk radio show about car repair, who had both graduated from MIT.

These two anecdotes are supported by research completed by Public Agenda (2010), which shows a majority of high school students felt they were largely left on their own to navigate the college application process. While some students received college help from their teachers, a high number of respondents felt they would have made different, and better, college choices with additional support.

This surface approach to college investigation is nicely rebuffed by Roeper's approach to learning in general, where students are encouraged to do anything but take a conclusion at face value. The earliest levels of Roeper's program encourage students to reflect on events in a personal way, including an activity where Stage I students are asked to express what Martin Luther King means to them, and Stage III students in a science class on inventing assess the impact their assumptions had on the outcome of their work. Combined with the support of an experienced, well-trained college counselor, students apply these same strongly developed skills to the college selection process, as well as a keen understanding of the strengths and limitations of external resources used in the investigation of any endeavor.

REVERSING THE TREND FOR GIFTED STUDENTS

Gifted students and their parents aren't always immune to the cycle of confusion and misinformation surrounding the college selection process. At the same time, they often possess the skills and dispositions necessary to look beneath the surface of society's college mania and develop a more reflective, personalized approach to choosing a college.

The best way to build an effective college counseling curriculum for a gifted student begins by putting the child at the center of the college selection process, an approach used in every curriculum and activity offered at Roeper. A good first step is to create a description of who the child is; how the child views the world, what the child thinks about, what the child worries about, what the child likes to do, what the child doesn't like to do, and the child's plans for the future. This can be done by asking students these questions and writing down their answers—or, better yet, having students develop their own answers through writing, poetry, pictures, or any other creative process. Parents, teachers, and others who know the student well (including peers) can provide answers to the same questions.

The next step is to get a sense of the student's history; where has the student lived and with whom, has childhood been influenced by any remarkable events, and how has the child interacted with learning and schools. There is often a tendency to rely on resources other than the student when creating a record of their past; while objectivity may be in short supply when asking students under 17 about their lives it is vital to understand their perceptions of life and the events that they feel shaped their lives, since these perceptions shape students' self-views and can shape their college expectations. This reflection tends to be especially rich with Roeper students, who are invited to engage in self-reflection and evaluation of every class they complete, starting at Stage I; when it comes to creating a strong understanding of self, there is no better teacher than experience.

It is also important to get a full view of the student's interaction with learning. Many gifted students engage in external learning opportunities they find far more satisfying than learning in the classroom, and the grades of gifted students rarely tell the entire story behind the student's learning experience in the classroom. It is best to speak directly to teachers, coaches, tutors, and others who have worked with the student; and it can be helpful to speak with teachers who may have had challenges working with the student, as well as those who have had success. With over 3600 colleges and universities to choose from in the United States, it is just as important to understand what environments won't work with a student as it is to understand places where a student has really clicked.

By understanding the student's identity and history, a series of experiences, discussions, and activities can be designed that will inform, engage, and inspire the gifted student in the college selection process with meaning and purpose. This is true regardless of the definition used to identify the gifted student:

- Gifted students who appear to meet the common assumptions of being highly skilled in many fields can understand how college can advance their understanding of several disciplines at the same time.
- Those students who show exceptional promise in one area can see how college gives them the opportunity to pursue the entire breadth and depth of the field they love.
- Gifted students who may have talents in some areas and need help with others can see how colleges are designed to offer individualized support that allows them to discover new concepts in the fields where they are strong and strengthen their understanding of key ideas in fields that challenge them.
- Students with talents in the arts, athletics, or interpersonal skills will have the opportunity to learn about specialized programs created to support the full development of their interests.
- Students who have found greater academic success in nontraditional learning settings can be introduced to colleges that offer opportunities to gain and assess knowledge that supports their desire to look at the world in a different way.
- Gifted students who haven't realized academic success in the classroom can be exposed to disciplines that may spark a previously unrealized interest.
- Students with exceptional abilities that haven't been identified by parents or the school can find affirmation or inspiration while being exposed to the research and individualized study options available at most colleges.

In sum, an effective college counseling curriculum introduces the concept of college as a natural but exciting next step in the student's deeper understanding of self, the world, and the interaction between self and the world. If it is well constructed, this curriculum will reach all students, including those who are not realizing success in their current school experience, and it can inspire all students to seek ways to get more meaning out of their current learning opportunities.

A QUALITY BASED APPROACH TO COLLEGE INQUIRY

Understanding the history, identity, and needs of the gifted student goes a long way toward developing the college counseling curriculum for that student to understand what college is and the promise college holds to helping the student lead a rich, fulfilled life. This is done by creating activities and experiences for students, and implementing in a way that takes full advantage of the qualities of gifted learners and the qualities of different colleges.

While definitions of giftedness vary widely, deep and critical thinking is an attribute affiliated with most of these definitions. The strong analytical thinker is able to evaluate the qualities of a good experiment; the gifted artist can discern the qualities of a successful composition or painting; the student highly talented in interpersonal skills knows when a conversation clicks; the successful athlete knows when a great play has been made. Not all gifted students may be able to articulate the qualities that make up a stellar example of the field they love, but they are able to recognize the presence of their qualities, even if they cannot assign names to them.

Because gifted students have an intuitive appreciation for deep thinking, it is essential to center all facets of the college counseling curriculum on interactions that allow them to use this skill as often as possible. This is the case in the predisposition phase, when a field trip to the science museum at a local college includes a short tour of the rest of the college ("What were the students in science class doing that was different than what the students in the history class were doing? Which one seemed more interesting to you, and why?"). It also applies to the search phase, when students are comparing colleges ("Both schools offer the major you're interested in. How did they feel different to you?"). It is also used in the choice phase ("My first choice college costs nearly twice what my second choice costs. Is the difference really worth it?").

A quality based approach to the college counseling curriculum offers several advantages to students and parents. First, it gives gifted students the opportunity to learn about college the same way they naturally learn, both in and out of the classroom. By using college exploration activities that encourage observation, discussion, comparison, reflection, and analysis, gifted students are able to see the same qualities in different colleges (and in colleges in general) that they find in math, science, art, sports, their favorite TV show, the frog they discover on their walk home from school, or the cloud formation they stare at for an hour. By applying the same thought processes and discerning the same qualities in colleges as they do in the rest of their lives, college will become a natural part of their lives, making it something to look forward to and prepare for with more confidence and less anxiety.

This quality-based approach to college awareness provides greater support to parents of gifted students as well. A significant part of any college counseling curriculum includes activities and services for the parents of college-bound students, and the service parents highly value includes counsel on how to approach the college selection process with their child—how to talk about it with their children, how to balance support with fostering a sense of autonomy in their children, and how to manage the logistics of college, including paying for college. By developing activities that give their children the opportunity to view college the same way they view the rest of their lives, schools are helping students create an important link between college and self. Just as important, they are showing parents that links exist very naturally in their children, a demonstration that can ease any anxieties the parents may have about their children's relationship to college.

This quality-based approach creates a common college bond between parent and student, which expands the number of successful college exploration activities the family can develop beyond the college counseling curriculum. Knowing their child is being exposed to the qualities of colleges in a meaningful way, parents become more discerning in their interpretation of media coverage of college admissions, and develop a better sense of what issues may affect their child, and which ones will not. This also helps parents create more meaningful college activities, such as enriching the trip back to a parent's alma mater with a tour of the campus before the football game, or having a greater purpose to visit a few colleges as part of a family vacation. Because the approach to understanding more about college is transparent to everyone, more college-learning activities can occur outside the school, enriching the college decision and strengthening the family's understanding of what the student is looking for in a college.

This approach is especially helpful when parents and students are tempted to include college rankings as part of the information used in the search and choice phases of the college selection process. Rather than take the rankings at face value, students and parents used to using critical thinking skills when considering a college are much more likely to look at a "Best Colleges" list and ask, "Best at what, based on what, and according to whom?" This questioning creates an opportunity for families and students to analyze the construction of the rankings and give the conclusions appropriate weight in the college admissions decision. It is not unusual to conclude the rankings are too abstract to offer any real help with their child's search and disregard them completely.

This approach is also helpful when parents and students face scrutiny from well-meaning family members or peers who need help understanding why a gifted child is attending a college that isn't as well known or is choosing to study at a college other than the one attended by most family members for generations. Basing a college choice on the fit between the student's needs and interests and the college's ability to meet those needs and interests leaves less room for doubt and more room for affirmation of the college choice by friends and family alike.

Because this quality-based approach to learning is inherent at Roeper, it should come as no surprise that Roeper students are able to approach the college selection process with a greater appreciation for differentiation. Finely-tuned critical-thinking skills, combined with years of learning at a school that recognizes itself as "a basic departure from the usual" (Roeper, 1981) fosters a sense of autonomy and independence that leads most Roeper students to a thorough examination of a wide array of college options, including those that may not be well known or understood by others. While many Roeper students go on to attend well-known colleges, including those consistently mentioned in the "best colleges" literature, the process each Roeper student uses in college selection is rich with analysis and self-understanding. The high quality of this process leads to an outcome that is rich in deliberation, and a commitment to making the most out of every learning experience available at the student's college of choice.

THE GIFTED CHILD AND THE CHOICE PHASE

A quality based approach to college exploration creates many avenues of investigation for gifted students to explore in both the predisposition and search phases, all with the common goal of having students create a transition plan from the high school years to college. This plan may be graduating from high school and beginning college studies the following fall, with a high school curriculum that includes appropriate internships, independent studies, and summer programs on college campuses; it could include replacing some high school courses with college-level classes taken before graduation; it may be based on a plan where the student begins attending college after the junior year of high school is complete, with or without a high school diploma; it may include plans to take a "gap" year after high school, where the student pursues volunteer service, work, or travel for a year before starting college; it could include postsecondary plans that lead the student into the military or vocational training; it may include leaving high school with no immediate plans. The first two phases of the college counseling curriculum are designed to give students a breadth of exposure to all postsecondary options that will reasonably ensure the student will make a smooth transition to life after high school.

The third phase—choice—includes a number of logistical variables that require specific skills that may not be possessed by all gifted students, and may require talents some gifted students may find in short supply. Unfortunately, without the successful completion of many of these logistics, the gifted student will be unable to make a reality of the college plans he or she has made.

The choice phase is where the activities of the college counseling curriculum narrow down to a required few (including test taking, essay writing, and application submission), but while the tasks themselves are limited, the approaches to the tasks are not. This is an important point to consider, since most of these tasks have to be completed in the junior and senior year in high school, a time when parents and students are most susceptible to the general fears surrounding applying to college. If the first two phases of the college counseling curriculum are well-designed, students and parents can be guided to the lessons learned through predisposition and search and lean on them as they team with the school counselor to build a strategy for negotiating the tasks affiliated with the choice phase.

Testing

Counselors remark that gifted students either love standardized tests, or they fear them. Gifted students with a keen sense of analysis, structure, and efficiency welcome the opportunity to test their wits against those of the test-makers. Gifted students who are creative thinkers are often easily befuddled by standardized tests, since they can make an argument why most every answer is right. Students whose gifts reside in areas beyond academics are loathe to expose themselves to one more test-taking experience to confirm what they already know about themselves. Perfectionistic gifted students are frustrated by the time limits on the exams that simply add more pressure to the experience on top of the pressure these students put on themselves.

One of the few benefits of the exhaustive media coverage of the college admissions process is a strong public awareness of the tests students are required to take to apply to many colleges. This awareness creates an early opportunity to discuss test readiness as a skill students can develop in a number of ways, the most effective being a thorough understanding of the material presented in the classroom. It also creates opportunities to discuss this skill as it relates to the student's academic and personal development, including discussion of which tests would best demonstrate the student's abilities, which test scores the student should (or must) submit to specific colleges, and which colleges require no standardized test scores from some or all of their applicants.

An early discussion of testing centered on the student's individual abilities and attitudes, combined with an early understanding of the testing requirements of each college that is of interest to the student, is the best way to help the gifted student develop a healthy attitude and skill set towards the role of testing in the college application process. This also gives the student the opportunity to develop strategies allowing them, as much as possible, to meet these requirements on their own terms.

Essay Writing

Nothing is more of a mystery in the college selection process than the anxiety surrounding the completion of application essays. Nearly all college-bound teenagers cherish the possibility of sharing their insights and opinions on nearly anything with nearly anyone willing to listen. However, when these same articulate, often highly opinionated students are asked to put these thoughts on paper for the benefit of their college to understand more about who they are, many often shrink at the very thought of doing so.

This fear of self-expression is particularly acute for three kinds of gifted students. Gifted students with perfectionistic tendencies will be perpetually frustrated by this exercise. Early on, they will come to your office and exclaim, "This isn't really about writing as much as it is about editing." They are completely correct in making this assertion. Colleges requiring essays want applicants to understand that the days of writing one draft of any academic paper are more or less over, and since more drafts leave perfectionistic students more opportunities to see what's wrong with their writing, these students quickly overthink the process.

Essays are also a challenge for gifted students whose talents lie outside of writing, or who may have trouble expressing thoughts in written form. For these students, the issue isn't about fine-tuning what they've written; it's about getting something written in the first place. This can be especially challenging if the essay prompt asks for reflection on a personal experience rather than on an academic endeavor. Many gifted students challenged by writing have developed successful strategies to construct strong academic papers, but these same approaches may not yield the same effective results when the student has to convey a personal experience in a more formal way.

College essays turn out to be a roadblock for gifted students who have done an excellent job of masking their uncertainties about going to college. While these students can "freeze" at any point in the choice phase (not signing up for required tests, not visiting any college campuses), the personal nature of many of the essay prompts somehow cues gifted students to realize that the next year of their life is likely to be radically different from anything else they've experienced. Adding to that is the realization that, while it will be different, they have no idea what that difference will look like at this point in time—and the clock just keeps ticking.

More often than not, all three of these reluctant gifted writers are supported by the same intervention. After asking the student for her or his perspective, the counselor asks the student, "Let's suppose this isn't an essay question. Let's say you were having a conversation with someone at the college—it may be the admissions officer, it may be a student, it may be a professor—you decide. If they asked you this question in a conversation, what would you say?"

In almost every case, the student will respond with an answer that will meet the requirements of a strong college essay. The perfectionistic writer will have mentally trimmed the essay to its perfectly edited essence, and the gifted student who doesn't see writing as a strength will now simply be typing something he or she already said, not writing something he or she needs to create. The answer of the student who is internalizing the reality of going to college creates a foundation for a series of follow-up questions, such as, "That answer really sounds authentic. Do you think other students at this college would respect your answer?" This can lead to a renewed discussion about what the student is looking for in a college, and the broader issue of why he or she wants to go to college in the first place.

There are many places in the college selection process where gifted students can overthink the matter at hand, but the application essay tends to be the place where this roadblock most occurs. Drawing the student away from the abstract nature of the question and focusing on self makes the task less formidable and more humane.

Application Submission

There are very few activities in the college selection process that can prepare a gifted student for meeting a college application deadline. With the exception of a few teachers who will take off significant points on assignments that are turned in late, young people have very little experience in meeting a "drop dead" due date that doesn't allow for exceptions, unusual circumstances, or a grace period of any kind.

The absence of experience with real deadlines is especially palpable with gifted students. Highly organized students who want to make sure they meet the deadline will complete the application the first day the application is available (often in early August) and submit it immediately. This can create two challenges: their high school won't send the required transcript until school opens in September, or the quality of their essays suffers greatly because they were written too early.

Between these two issues, the essays offer the greatest challenge. Gifted students who complete their applications early generally need to be reassured that their application will not be late, and it will be given full consideration when it is read.

Since colleges don't give greater consideration to applications submitted in August than they do to applications submitted in September, a reassuring note to the students gives them the opportunity to take satisfaction in knowing their part of the work is complete and their application will be given a complete review.

For these very same reasons, it is extremely difficult to tell an early applicant that the best thing she or he could possibly do for the application is wait before submitting it once it is complete, even though it is often to the student's advantage to hold on to the application. Students who submit early applications may complete more than one draft of the essay, but the desire to submit the application often limits her or his ability to review the essays with a more critical eye. This is especially true when a student completes essays in August for an application that is due in early January. The ensuing four months gives the student ample time to hone the overall tone of the essays and give a more comprehensive response to a question that asks why the student wants to go to college. That question can seem rather abstract before senior year starts. By December that answer should be on the tip of the student's tongue and at the forefront of her or his thought, and that readiness can make for a more compelling answer.

At the other end of the organizational spectrum, highly creative gifted students may have difficulty coordinating the many forms and essays required in a college application. Often, this has nothing to do with the information the form asks for or the prompt the essay offers. For some creative students, the task lies in creating some kind of order out of this aggregation of paper and submitting it in a timely fashion.

These students may be able to fall back on the organizational skills needed to turn in required final papers or research work. More often than not, these students will receive unrequested but welcome support from a parent or older sibling, who will align the steps needed to submit the material in a timely fashion. This may not make the college application process the exercise in autonomy it could be, but it could offer some organizational insights the student will take advantage of at a later date.

Roeper students draw on their finely-tuned skills of self-advocacy for help negotiating any of these three components of the college application process. Studying in a school that fosters an environment of mutual trust and support, Roeper students feel more confident and comfortable asking for more time on a standardized test; help smoothing out a college essay that isn't quite right, or asking for an extension on a class assignment in order to get a college application in on time. Roeper students have learned in an atmosphere that views school as a series of support structures, not an institution with rigid rules. This allows them to make the most of Roeper's resources without taking them for granted, an attitude Roeper students carry over with ease to their college experience.

Two final challenges await many gifted students in the latter stages of the choice phase. Many gifted students will experience a kind of "postpartum depression" in the months-long interval between the submission of their last college application and the receipt of their admissions decisions. Because so many gifted students are passionate learners, they have applied the same focus and energy to the college application process as they do in any learning experience; as a result, it is not uncommon for them to be anxious to hear "how they did," or some may simply miss the thrill of the application process.

Both of these responses are natural among gifted students. Students who genuinely miss applying to colleges should be congratulated for taking the process to heart, and reminded that the many skills they learned in completing college applications (research skills, interpersonal and personal communication skills, decision-making skills, time management) can be applied to all kinds of projects both in college and before. If students genuinely feel they have a "hole" in their lives that had been filled by applying to college, they should be encouraged to use these same skills in supporting senior year activities, or by reviewing their high school "bucket list" to see if there is any event they want to create or participate in before high school comes to a close. At Roeper, this hole is nicely met with the opportunity to complete a Senior Project, where the student assumes most of the responsibility for the development and implementation of an intense program of study. For other students, this pause in planning for "tomorrow" gives them the opportunity to reconnect with lifelong peers before graduation day launches them into new paths, paths that may separate students for the first time since they started school. The special atmosphere in the senior hallway at Roeper in the spring months is one that is nicely conveyed at the school's graduation exercises, but hard to describe; for many of the adults at the school, the camaraderie and maturity demonstrated by the seniors in their last few months at the school is a powerful affirmation of the school's success in bringing its mission to life.

Students eager to hear back from colleges require a different kind of counseling. The goal of the college selection process is for students to determine the next natural steps in their lives, and where they might be able to experience the best growth as a person after high school. If done well, the process gives students not just one college that will meet their needs, but several. This gives students the freedom to choose among several options late in their senior year, when the choice phase closes. Peer pressure, media coverage of college admissions, and the complexities of the college selection process can corrupt this goal, leaving students with a sense that success is based on where they "get in," not on the options they have to choose from once they have heard from every college.

The difference may seem subtle, but it is important. A student whose goal is to choose among several small liberal arts colleges where she can pursue the study of Art History is more likely to demonstrate balance and composure if one of her colleges rejects her application for admission. While some disappointment is understandable, the student's goal allows her to focus on the opportunities she's created for herself, and not on those she's been denied. This increases the likelihood she will make a smoother transition to college and make the most of the learning experiences her college affords her.

At the same time, a student whose goal is to get into a specific college has everything riding on the decision of one school, even though many of the factors behind that decision are well out of her control. Due to space limitations, a number of highly selective colleges are able to admit only six or seven percent of all students who apply for admission, even though nearly all applicants are highly qualified to attend the college. This reason alone significantly increases the chances the student will not be admitted to the college of her choice, even though she is a strong student whose personal qualities would greatly enhance any college she attends, let alone the world.

Advising this student in the final stages of the choice phase requires the right balance of support and clarity. By acknowledging the student's qualification for admission to her first-choice college, the counselor creates an opportunity to discuss the qualities of that college the student finds attractive. This allows the counselor and the student to affirm that many of these same qualities exist in the other colleges where the student applied, an exercise that brings the student back to a quality-based approach to college choice before her decisions arrive. Disappointment over a rejection from the student's first-choice school may still be strong, but this discussion gives the student the opportunity to see that the qualities of the college she will attend haven't changed because another college denied her admission; for that matter, neither have the personal qualities the student will take with her to college, and to the world beyond college.

LIFE AFTER COLLEGE COUNSELING: HOW DO THEY DO?

Hard data on the success of gifted students in college is hard to come by. Data on the college success of all students has only recently gained the attention of policymakers, and few, if any, colleges track gifted students as a subpopulation in their completion rates. Follow-up surveys from high schools rarely include gifted students as a subpopulation, and the response rate to these surveys is usually so low that extrapolation of the data to the entire population is impossible.

This absence of data suggests the best way to determine the success of a college counseling program is through a case study approach. This path is the best one to pursue with gifted students for a number of reasons, the most significant being the very individual plans and paths of the students making up the gifted population. A student with exceptional talent in an academic field may plow through the four-year curriculum of a highly selective college in three years, an accomplishment that policymakers would consider a college success. A student with exceptional gifts in sculpture who leaves college after two years of formal study to pursue a mentorship with a renowned artist would be considered a failure by this same bureaucratic system, even though this may be the most appropriate learning opportunity this student could take to advance her development as an artist and her growth as a person.

The challenges of assessing success in the college counseling process are highlighted by three case studies of highly gifted Roeper students, with some details modified to protect their identity. The first student was admitted to an accelerated dental program directly from high school. Five years later, and after experiencing some social challenges, she went on to complete the program and became a successful researcher of dental practices. A second highly gifted student graduated from high school with no intention of ever going to college. Nearly forty years later, the student was faithful to this pledge, having never gone to college, but experiencing great success as a dancer and businessperson.

A third student's story provides keen insights into the wisdom Roeper students typically demonstrate as they experience the changes in interests and priorities common to all students. This student attended a highly selective college immediately after graduating from high school. Two years later, the student ran into his college counselor at a social event where the student was playing guitar in a band performing at the function.

After catching up with questions about friends and family, the counselor asked the student how college was going, and the student responded by saying he had dropped out of college, at least for now. Another teacher from the school heard this response, and jokingly responded the student had clearly received bad college advice in high school; the student then responded by saying, "You know, given who I was when I was seventeen, I got the best advice I could have possibly hoped for." High school graduation surveys on the quality of college counseling may provide feedback from gifted students and their families immediately after their participation in the college selection process, providing important insights into procedural modifications the counselor can make to improve the delivery of college counseling services. At the same time, measuring the real success of the college counseling curriculum for gifted students, like measuring the effectiveness of any curriculum, is less a matter of the results of a test, the feedback of a survey, or even the completion of a postsecondary goal. Roeper's alumni publications are rich with testimonies of the difference Roeper's student-centered approach to learning has made in the lives of successful, creative people, and the impact they have had on the world as a result. This appreciation deepens as time passes, and is evidenced by the increasing number of Roeper alumni who enroll their children in the school.

The keen abilities and curiosity possessed by gifted students is usually more than enough for them to absorb the information and skills that make up a curriculum; as the Roeper philosophy points out, the true success of teaching the gifted can only be measured by the curriculum's ability to engage students in deeper reflection on themselves and the world around them. The multitudinous changes associated with going to college means a successful college counseling curriculum has to go well beyond the question of "getting in." Truly helping gifted students understand all that awaits them in life after high school requires an approach that equips the students with a vision and appreciation for qualities that serve them well in choosing a college, in making the most of college, and in embracing what George Roeper saw as their most important role—as citizens of the world.

REFERENCES

Caldwell, T. (2012, April 6). A first draft of 2012 admissions decisions at dozens of universities. *New York Times*. http://thechoice.blogs.nytimes.com/2012/04/16/college-admits-2012/

Johnson, J., & Rochkind, J. with Ott, A., & Dupont, S. (2010). *Can I get a little advice here? How an overstretched high school guidance system is undermining students' college aspirations*. Washington, DC: Public Agenda. Retrieved from http://www.publicagenda.org/files/can-i-get-a-little-advice-here.pdf

McDonough, P. M. (2008). Counseling and college counseling in America's schools. In National Association for College Admission Counseling, *Fundamentals of college admission counseling* (2nd. ed, pp. 2–19). Dubuque, IA: Kendall/Hunt.

Roeper, A., & Roeper, G. (1981). *The philosophy of Roeper City and Country School*. http://www.roeper.org/page.aspx?pid=1153

United States Executive Office of the President (2011). *Teacher jobs at risk*. National Economic Council, Domestic Policy Council, President's Council of Economic Advisers, Department of Education. Retrieved from: http://www.whitehouse.gov/sites/default/files/uploads/teacher_jobs_at_risk_report.pdf

National Center for Educational Statistics. *The condition of education 2012*. Retrieved from http://nces.ed.gov/programs/coe/

Webb, J. T., Meckstroth, E. A., & Tolan, S. S. (1982). Guiding the gifted child. *A practical source for parents and teachers*. Scottsdale, AZ: Great Potential Press.

CAROLYN M. CALLAHAN

NEXT STEPS FOR ROEPER SCHOOL

Evaluation and Research

Any program for gifted students is based on either assumed or overtly stated beliefs, philosophical tenets, and goals. In the case of the Roeper School, we have a case where these beliefs and philosophies and goals were clearly articulated by the school's founders and have driven programmatic and curricular decision-making throughout the school's history. However, like many other programs or services for gifted students, it is imperative that the beliefs, philosophies and goals that were the focus of the school's founders, must continue to be aligned with the emerging theory and research in the field of gifted education in order for the program to (a) remain defensible as an effective program, and (b) to be viable and attractive to its stakeholders. However, like many programs, the focus of administrators and teachers has been on the delivery of the highest conceivable quality services, leaving the task of evaluation of those services and the creation of a research program around investigating the impacts of the program on the "to do" list.

As a mature school and program, the Roeper School now faces the dual challenge and opportunity of evaluating the processes and outcomes of its programs and of making significant contributions to the literature of gifted education. While the purposes and procedures used to evaluate programs and to create a research literature are independent and unique, the evaluation process in a setting such as the Roeper School can provide the data and generate the hypotheses for research. The many purposes of evaluating gifted programs have been articulated elsewhere (e.g., Callahan & Caldwell, 1995). Among the most important purposes is to provide information for decision-making in order to improve the educational opportunities provided to gifted students. A second is to document the program—its essential components and impacts for others. These two evaluation purposes underlie the approach to evaluation described in this chapter. Extending the purpose of documentation to its next logical step is to provide hypotheses for research based on documented outcomes in the Roeper setting. Hence, the logical first step is to examine the evaluation process as it might be conceived to provide evidence of the ways in which Roeper has served gifted students.

DESCRIBING THE PROGRAM AS THE BASIS FOR EVALUATION

Nearly every model that drives program evaluation calls first for a description of the program in conjunction with the collection of input from key stakeholders about areas of concern to groups such as students, parents, teachers, administrators, etc. (Callahan & Caldwell, 1995; Frechtling, 2007; Renzulli, 1975; Yarbrough, Shula, Hopson, & Caruthers, 2011) These steps are critically important as they guide the identification of areas of evaluation that frame the scope of the evaluation and the refinement of those areas of concern into appropriate evaluation questions. Evaluation that does not reflect the input of key stakeholders is likely to be questioned, invalidated and/or ignored—hence wasting time, energy and money in its implementation.

Describing Roeper

Public documents provide one window into the school by describing agreed upon aspects of the program including philosophy and mission, definition of giftedness, identification processes and procedures, and program structures. For example, on the Roeper website we find statements about Roeper that clearly suggests the mission for the school:

> . . . we have been known for educating the whole child in an emotionally supportive, intellectually engaging environment. We work hard to empower children at every level, instilling the attitudes, values, and skills that will enable them to lead lives of meaning and substance. . . . The Roeper School offers a child-centred, personalized, challenging, active, empowering environment where all resources, staffing, and professional development are geared toward teaching gifted students. Roeper instills in its students a strong sense of self, personal and social awareness, respect for differences, need for community involvement, and a strong desire to make a difference in their world. (http://www.roeper.org/netcommunity/)

And we also find information about definition and identification.

> Roeper seeks candidates who are a match for our school. We find that gifted students who are curious about learning, internally motivated, self-directed, and have a high ability to think abstractly are most successful in our school environment. Admission to our school is based on a review of many factors, including a gifted IQ test result, strong prior academic performance, positive teacher report, a successful visit to our school, and the student's ability to enhance our school community. All admissions decisions are made by a committee of Roeper staff members who look for best-fit, gifted candidates. (http://www.roeper.org/netcommunity/)

The website also identifies other functions within the school. For example, the school publications range from *Mentoring Heights,* a newsletter for new Roeper families, to the *Roeper Review,* a professional journal distributed to an international audience of researchers and practitioners.

Collection of Other Key Data for Structuring an Evaluation

Further information from stakeholders can be derived from other sources. In many evaluations, such data can be derived from focus groups or survey. In the case of the Roeper School, the attributes of the school were articulated in a recent accreditation self-study. These attributes reflect the beliefs and goals of the founders and describe the presumed characteristics of the school, implied processes, and the implicit goals of the school.

The set of reputed characteristics that have implications for generation of evaluation questions include:

- The school is characterized as having an atmosphere of caring and respect with a balance between individual and community needs.
- The school achieves a balance between individual rights and responsibilities.
- The school honors diversity in points of view, ethnicity, socioeconomic status, and religion.
- The curriculum of the school is configured to attention to the whole child; integration of the cognitive, social, emotional, motivational, and physical aspects of the student.
- Special attention is given to the social and emotional development of students.
- The school climate is characterized by a collaborative, democratic approach to governance and innovation.
- A collaborative spirit exists among faculty, staff, and administration.
- Curriculum development and delivery of instruction are influenced by relationship-based partnerships among students and teachers.
- Families are engaged in the learning process.
- A low student-faculty ratio is central to quality programming.
- Learning opportunities are personalized and provide for creative exploration.
- The flexible curriculum adjusts for varying ability and skill levels while responding to students' interests. (e.g., independent study and online course offerings …).
- Faculty are given autonomy in curriculum design, to the extent possible.
- Arts have a prominent place in the curriculum.
- Science teaching is based on inquiry-based instruction with lab-based approaches to achieving scientific understanding.
- The framework for curriculum and instruction represents a balance between product and process emphases.

The outcomes suggested by the self-study report include the following:

- Students generally feel emotionally, physically, socially, and intellectually safe.
- Students develop a commitment to equity and justice, ethics and altruism; service to, and integration with, the community and the world.
- Students develop intrapersonal intelligence: learning their own strengths, weaknesses, and motivations and then use that self-knowledge to guide their future development.

- Students' individual interests act as driving forces for motivation and learning.
- Students develop the capacity for lifelong learning.

At the time of the self-study the school staff also identified challenges to the school. As these were identified as areas which were considered important to school development, an evaluation subsequent to the self-study would address the degree to which the school:

- capitalized on new developments in technology,
- strengthened and expanded its work on enhancing diversity, both in terms of recruiting diverse faculty and students and in terms of strengthening diversity in curricular offerings in some subject areas,
- strengthened provisions for students with learning differences,
- provided professional development in gifted education,
- developed diverse forms of assessment that engaged students and provided them with senses of ownership for their education,
- balanced faculty autonomy and student choice with the need for consistent academic excellence,
- expanded the community service aspect of programs to ensure that these are more widespread throughout the school,
- the arts had become more of a central focus in the curriculum,
- reduced undesirable competition among students over grades,
- decreased apathy in the student body,
- expanded curricular offerings in the sciences (e.g., earth science/environmental science).

Finally, the field of gifted education itself suggests that any program for gifted students will be best serving those students if it meets particular standards of quality. The 2010 *Pre-K-Grade 12 Gifted Programming Standards* of the National Association for Gifted Children provide a research-based framework to use in examining the quality of gifted programs. These standards are articulated in full at http://www.nagc.org/ProgrammingStandards.aspx. The Roeper School mission, vision, and goals and the areas of concern summarized above suggest a great concordance between the student outcomes and evidence-based practices articulated in the categories of Learning and Development, Assessment, Curriculum Planning and Instruction, Programming, Learning Environments, and Professional Development of the NAGC Standards. Further, the standards suggest several other areas of concern that should be considered by Roeper School in formulation of evaluation plans. In particular, the areas of student outcomes need further explication and attention. While outcomes described by public documents and the self-study include student goals in the realms of social and emotional development (e.g., students develop a commitment to equity and justice, ethics and altruism as well as service to, and integration with, the community and the world; students develop intrapersonal intelligence: learning their own strengths, weaknesses, and motivations and then use that self-knowledge to guide their future development; and students develop the capacity for lifelong learning), the more academic aspects of student outcomes are not given equal attention. A dominant theme in the NAGC standards reflects the goals that "Students with gifts and talents demonstrate advanced and complex learning."

USING THE DATA TO IDENTIFY FUNCTIONAL COMPONENTS OF THE PROGRAM, AREAS OF CONCERN AND EVALUATION QUESTIONS

The data provided by documentation and stakeholder input described above and supplemented by a review of the standards can be consolidated into components of the program: (a) identification, (b) curriculum planning and development, (including frameworks used in direct, traditional instruction in classrooms and the implicit curriculum of community involvement and service and the creation of an environment that enhances development of independence), (c) the actual instruction of students, (d) administration and management, (e) communication, and (f) professional development. Within each of the components the development of evaluation concerns stems from a general sense of the purpose of each component—for example, two concerns arise from consideration of the curriculum component:

- the degree to which the school environment has been structured to lead to the achievement of stated goals—both cognitive and affective, the degree to which the curriculum contributes "value-added" learning and development to the students who attend Roeper School (across all levels of initial aptitude and affective status), and
- the degree to which resources (including technology) are allocated effectively and efficiently to achieve relevant goals.

A concern that would emerge from the professional development component of the program would be:

- the degree to which teacher skills are continuously refined to contribute to the development of the curriculum and environment necessary to achieve the goals of the school.

Within each component specific evaluation questions would emerge as stakeholders refine their thinking around the more general terms that have been put forward and as the second stage of description emerges—the stage of defining the resources, activities and products that characterize the program offered to students.

The Next Steps in Description

There are two common errors in program evaluation. One is to examine only the program processes or activities and then draw conclusions about the program based only on the degree to which program staff are "doing the right thing" according to some predetermined criteria. Unfortunately, the appearances, and even, the actuality of doing the right thing may not lead to achieving the desired goals of a program. A second common error in evaluation is to examine outcomes only. When program evaluations fail to consider the resources and the activities that are part of every program component, the conclusions drawn about outcomes may not be interpretable. For example, it is possible to find that attendance at the Roeper School does, in fact, result in greater student social awareness. That is a positive finding, but if we cannot determine which activities of the program contribute to the awareness then there may be a great deal of wasted resources in teacher and student time and energy in various courses and activities when fewer resources might have achieved the same outcome. Or we may find that social awareness is not an outcome, but because we have not documented the resources and activities, we cannot determine what else should be done to bring about the desired change. Hence, the next step in the evaluation process is to look closely at each component to be sure that the evaluation plan encompasses the full scope of potential questions for eliciting critical data.

Delineating the Resources, Activities and Outcomes of Program Components

A full program description as the basis for developing an evaluation design would articulate the resources, activities and intended outcomes of each component of the program. Because of space limitations and the relative importance of curriculum development and instruction in the Roeper School and because these two aspects of the school have the greatest potential to offer substantive data leading to further research, those two components are developed as illustrations of the process. First, consider curriculum development.

Essentially curriculum development is the core process of determining what will be taught to students. Even when the curriculum development process is implicit rather than explicit, someone is deciding what to teach students. At Roeper, the process of curriculum development is both a large decision (what will be the sequence of courses and what will be the general content of those courses) and more "localized" course decisions (what will be the detailed syllabi of the courses). Curriculum in a school like Roeper is also extended beyond the traditional classroom to encompass all those activities that extend learning in other environments. To develop a plan to evaluate the process of curriculum development requires the delineation of the resources used in curriculum development, the processes or activities that are carried out to create the curriculum, and the intended outcomes of the curriculum development process. Table 1 provides an outline of the parameters that should be considered in evaluating the curriculum development process. Note that there is not a one-to-one linear correspondence across the chart. That is, many of the resources listed in the Resources or Inputs column can be used to carry out one of the activities in the Activity/Process column and it may take one or several activities in that column to achieve the goals or Output/Product listed in the last column.

Table 1. A sample input/process/output chart: Curriculum development.

Inputs/Resources	Activities/Processes	Outputs/Goals/Products
Teacher time	Develop a scope and sequence of courses in the disciplines	A curriculum framework and course curricula that are child-centred, personalized, challenging, and involve active learning.
Standards of professional associations in the disciplines	Identify all expected outcomes for each course in the scope and sequence	A curriculum framework and course curricula that incorporate learning opportunities that lead to a commitment to equity and justice, ethics and altruism; service to, and integration with, the community and the world
Common Core Standards	Develop a list of big ideas, themes, generalizations, and concepts to be taught in each course	A curriculum framework with a clear scope and sequence of learning outcomes supported by activities leading to those outcomes.
Goals of the Roeper School	Develop a list of skills to be taught in each course	A curriculum that integrates inquiry-based instruction
Data on student achievement levels	Develop pre-assessments to be used to differentiate activities and outcomes according to student readiness to learn, interests, learning style	A curriculum framework that provides opportunities for differentiation according to individual student readiness to learn, interests, and learning profiles
Budget information	Develop formative assessment tools and outcome measures to assess student progress within units/ classes and across the curriculum	A curriculum that includes pre-assessment, formative, and summative assessments
Resources in the community	Identify needed resources on hand that need to be purchased or rented	A curriculum and course curricula that include opportunities for students to develop intrapersonal intelligence: learning their own strengths, weaknesses, and motivations and then using that self-knowledge
References on quality curriculum design in general	Develop suggested activities to be taught within each unit in each course with appropriate suggestions for differentiation according to learner readiness, interests, and learning style	A curriculum framework and course curricula that represent academic excellence and challenge for gifted learners
References on quality curriculum for the gifted	Identify curriculum that will be taught outside the classroom	The framework for curriculum and instruction represents a balance between product and process emphases.

IDENTIFYING EVALUATION QUESTIONS

Generation of Questions

The evaluation questions that can be derived from the Output/Product column are direct and obvious. For example, from the Curriculum Development IPO chart these questions (among others) would emerge:

- To what degree do the curriculum framework and course outlines reflect child-centred, personalized, challenging, and involve active learning?
- To what degree does the curriculum framework offer a clear scope and sequence of learning outcomes supported by activities leading to those outcomes deemed characteristic of the Roeper School?
- To what degree do the curricular offerings incorporate inquiry-based learning? Appropriate technology?
- To what degree are there opportunities built into the curriculum for differentiation according to individual student readiness to learn, interests, and learning profiles?

Similarly, the Instruction IPO chart yields an obvious set of evaluation questions. Among those would be:

- To what degree have students developed a strong sense of self, personal and social awareness, respect for differences, need for community involvement, and a strong desire to make a difference in their world?
- To what degree is classroom instruction characterized by stakeholders as relationship-based partnerships among students and teachers?
- To what degree are classroom and other school environments characterized by stakeholders as collaborative and fostering a democratic approach to governance and innovation with minimal competition between and among students over grades?
- To what degree do students feel emotionally, physically, socially, and intellectually safe in all school environments?
- To what degree do students learn content, skills, and production skills at a level beyond that of the traditional curriculum offered in other school settings?

However, as mentioned before, to ask only the outcome questions is to deprive the School of valuable information needed to make quality decisions. To know that students did not "develop a strong sense of pride" without an evaluation of the content, process, procedures and fidelity of implementation will not help the decision-makers make appropriate adjustments that would lead to better outcomes in the future. In fact, in the absence of such information, they may make curricular, staffing or resource adjustments that lead to negative impacts.

So, some resource questions that should be asked might include:

- To what degree is the technology available in Roeper classrooms state-of-the-art allowing for maximizing the integration of the latest tools of technology into the classroom instruction? (Inputs and Resources)

- To what degree has staff development adequately prepared teachers and other staff to deliver the curriculum in ways that contribute to achieving the goals of the school? (Activities and Processes)
- To what degree is achievement and aptitude data incorporated into curriculum planning and instructional delivery? (Inputs/Resources and Activities/Processes)

As the reader can well imagine, the full range of questions that would be generated by six different charts of the nature of Tables 1 and 2 (one each for Identification, Curriculum Development, Instruction, Program Administration, Communication, and Professional Development) would be broad, far-ranging, and perhaps overwhelming. To make an evaluation plan conceivable, it is important to narrow down those questions into a set of questions that will generate data that will be helpful in decision-making, for after all is said and done, the most important function of program evaluation is to make decisions that will improve the program for students.

Narrowing the Scope of Questions

As the decision-makers consider which evaluation questions should form the basis for collecting data on the program inputs, processes, and outputs, the following three guiding principles can be used for that focusing process.

Core functional concerns of key stakeholders. The first guideline in choosing those evaluation questions that will be the focus of evaluation is to attend to questions that are of greatest importance to the key stakeholders. In the case of the Roeper School these would be the parents, the students, and the governing board. Then the key concerns of teachers and administrators would follow. To the degree that a question is of high importance to multiple groups its significance increases.

Central functional importance. The second criterion for ranking evaluation questions is the degree to which gathering data to address the evaluation questions provides evidence that key functions are operating as expected or key outcomes are being achieved. For example, if the learning environment at the Roeper School fails to reflect the overarching premises of its founders and to live up to the expectations of the founding principles of the school then little else matters in the development of curriculum or the integration of technology or the other aspects of programming.

Importance to outside constituencies. In the case of the Roeper School, this last guide takes on additional importance. As the earlier discussion suggested, the long term existence of the Roeper School with a unique set of goals and unique history sets the stage for the generation of data that can provide preliminary evidence to answer research questions and generate hypotheses around which further research programs could develop. For example, a full examination of the questions of effectiveness of the curriculum in developing independence, a community of caring, etc. can provide

Table 2. A sample input/process/output chart: Instruction.

Inputs/Resources	Activities/Processes	Outputs/Goals/Products
Teacher time	Professional development on curriculum implementation and instructional strategies	Students have developed a strong sense of self, personal and social awareness, respect for differences, need for community involvement, and a strong desire to make a difference in their world.
Student time	Delivery of courses to students using pre-assessment and formative assessments to modify curriculum and instruction as provided in curriculum	Classroom and other school environments are characterized by stakeholders as collaborative and fostering a democratic approach to governance and innovation. There is minimal competition between and among students over grades.
Curricular framework and course outlines	Assess student outcomes	Classroom instruction is characterized by stakeholders as relationship-based partnerships among students and teachers.
Materials and resources	Provide feedback to assist in curricular revision	Learning opportunities are personalized and provide for creative exploration and observations of instruction validate adjustments for varying ability and skill levels while responding to students' interests.

Resources	Strategy	Outcome
Administrative planning time, teacher time, student time, and travel funds	Provide learning opportunities outside of traditional classroom	Instruction which balances faculty autonomy and student choice with the need for consistent academic excellence
Teacher time and staff development resources	Create learning environments that allow for creative exploration; develop caring and respect; strike a balance between individual and community needs, achieve a balance between individual rights and responsibilities; honor diversity in points of view, ethnicity, socioeconomic status, and religion; integrate instruction across the cognitive, social, emotional, motivational, and physical aspects of the student; are characterized by a collaborative, democratic approach to governance and innovation; and involve family in the instructional program	Students generally feel emotionally, physically, socially, and intellectually safe in all school environments.
Teacher time, student time, specific curricular opportunities		Students develop a commitment to equity and justice, ethics and altruism; service to, and integration with, the community and the world
Teacher time, student time, innovative curriculum		Students are motivated to learn and have developed the capacity for lifelong learning.

data that will help inform the field of gifted education about ways to infuse such curricular ideas into the curriculum for all gifted students. Data reflecting the ways in which families contribute effectively and collaboratively to student development can inform the literature on parenting and suggest additional research questions.

Using these criteria as guides, the evaluation framework will evolve, but another important step must occur before data can be collected.

DEFINING TERMS: KEY REFLECTION QUESTIONS FOR ROEPER

Meaningful evaluation of the school program is dependent on clear understanding of the terms used to describe components of a program or the expected outcomes. Mission statements and goals are most often written in terms that are very nebulous and broad. Hence, they can have many meanings. Unless those who are seeking to develop tools to measure the construct can come to an agreement with the decision-makers on the exact meaning of the terms there is likely to be little agreement on the meaning of the data collected. Most evaluators also argue that unless these terms are well-defined it is unlikely a program can effectively structure itself to achieve stated goals. The Roeper School is not unique in this respect. A quick look at phrases from the intended outcomes or goals of the school reveals a list of terms that beg for further definition:

- Child-centred, personalized, challenging
- Active learning
- Equity and justice, ethics and altruism; service to, and integration with, the community and the world
- Inquiry-based instruction

To take the next step in quality program development or evaluation requires that staff specify in operational terms the meanings of these terms. It is not acceptable at this point in the program development or in program evaluation to say, "We'll know it when we see it." The staff must be able to come to agreement in answers to questions such as:

- Altruism as defined by…?
- What behaviors describe the outcomes called altruism?
- What does inquiry based instruction look like?
- What will a child-centred, personalized classroom look like?
- How does a child who has learned to be (or is learning to be) an independent learner differ from one who is not?
- What is a student doing who "has a strong desire to change the world?"

DEVELOPING A WORK PLAN

The creation of a plan for gathering data involves five steps:

1. Deciding what information is needed to answer each question (Data Requirements)
2. Determining where to get the information (Information Sources)

3. Settling on data collection strategies and choosing or constructing instruments (Instrumentation)
4. Developing a plan for analysing data (Information Analysis)
5. Drafting a plan for sharing findings (Reporting)

This stage of the evaluation process is a bit more complex as it involves carefully delineating the data that will be collected and the ways the data will be analysed and reported. There are many crucial decision points involved and the ways in which those decisions are made will determine the credibility of the findings, the usefulness of the data, and the generalizability of findings to the field of gifted education. To give one example, let's look at the question of the degree to which the desired outcome of whether or not the curriculum and instruction "instill a greater sense of altruism." If we wanted to both provide a valid answer to this question that would assist in making programmatic decisions and provide guidance to the field of gifted education we might proceed as follows:[1]

1. We would first determine that we need to gather data on changes in students over the course of their enrollment in the Roeper School and as a result of their participation in activities offered within and outside the classroom. Hence, we would see student data that measures student altruism and student participation data (year of enrollment, number of years of participation, classes attended, outside of class activities) as information requirements.
2. Our sources of information would be (a) scores on assessments of students' attitudes over time (ideally longitudinal data would be collected, but cross-sectional analysis could suffice until longitudinal data were available), (b) student records that include year of enrollment, number of years of participation, classes attended, and outside of class activities.
3. The collection of student data from records would require the development of a recording sheet. The collection of assessment data on student altruism would require that we search available instruments that would yield reliable and valid data on that construct *as it had been operationally defined.* There are many approaches to measuring altruism so the match between the way it has been defined by staff and the way it is defined by the authors of those assessments and validity evidence that the construct being measured matches the school's definition is critically important. There are also a wide variety of ways to measure altruism from simple checklists of attributes (VanDyne & Pine, 1998) or past behavior such as what the person has done in the community, or organizations to which the person belongs (Organ, 1990) to hypothetical scenarios (DeWall, Baumeister, Gaillot, & Maner, 2008). Examination of each approach and its appropriateness and match to the desired outcome (and the resources needed to administer and score the instrument) would be taken into consideration in the choice of instrument.
4. The absence of any reasonable control group or comparison group makes data analysis more dependent on using the students as comparisons to one another. For example, data analysis could be carried out by comparing students who have

been in the program differing numbers of years, classes taken, and activities participated in to see whether length of enrollment, enrollment in various classes, or outside activities have impacted development of altruism. One could not compare younger children to older children because there are developmental factors associated with development of this trait, which would bias the results.
5. Finally, the issue of who receives the results would be determined *not by the findings but by the usefulness of the data* in decision-making. If the data were carefully collected and analysed in the fashion noted above, the study could provide useful information to a field interested in how various curricular and instructional activities contribute to the development of altruism in gifted students.

THE RESEARCH PARADIGM

The very brief illustration of the development of an evaluation question is but one illustration of the ways in which the Roeper School has the potential of contributing to the literature in gifted education. The students at Roeper are a unique, but important sample of gifted students whose development and education have the potential for informing the field. In addition, the extensive curriculum development and instructional experimentation that has contributed to the current educational program should be documented in terms of impact and viability across other settings. Thus, evaluation and research could become a very feasible and effective tandem if the officials—administrative and governing—were to develop a plan to move Roeper forward in this direction in the coming years.

REFERENCES

Callahan, C. M., & Caldwell, M. S. (1995). *A practitioner's guide to evaluating programs for the gifted.* Washington, DC: National Association for Gifted Children.
DeWall, C. N., Baumeister, R. F., Gailliot, M. T., & Maner, J. K. (2008). Depletion makes the heart grow less helpful: Helping as a function of self-regulatory energy and genetic relatedness. *Personality and Social Psychology Bulletin, 34,* 1653–1662.
National Association for Gifted Children. (2010). *NAGC PreK-Grade 12 gifted program standards.* Retrieved from http://www.nagc.org/index.aspx?id=1863
Organ, D. W. (1990). The motivational basis of organizational citizenship behaviour. *Research in Organizational Behavior, 12,* 43–72.
Renzulli, J. S. (1975). *A guidebook for evaluating programs for the gifted and talented.* Ventura, CA: National/State Leadership Training Institute on the Gifted/Talented.
Van Dyne, L., & LePine, J. A. (1998). Helping and voice extra-role behaviors: Evidence of construct and predictive validity. *Academy of Management Journal, 41,* 108–119.
Yarbrough, D. B., Shulha, L. M., Hopson, R. K., & Curuthers, F. A. (2011). *The program evaluation standards: A guide for evaluators and evaluation users.* (3rd ed.). Thousand Oaks, CA: Sage.

PART IV

EMERGENT, DEMOCRATIC LEADERSHIP

DOROTHY SISK

DEVELOPING LEADERSHIP CAPACITY IN GIFTED STUDENTS FOR THE PRESENT AND THE FUTURE

In the 1970's there were very few public or private schools dedicated to serving gifted students, so when an invitation to visit the Roeper School came from George and Annemarie Roeper, I rearranged my schedule to accommodate a visit. At that time, I was director of the Office of Gifted and Talented in Washington D.C. and most interested in learning more about the school to share with other educators interested in developing schools for the gifted. And what a visit that was, being a house guest with the Roepers, sharing soft-boiled eggs served in elegant egg holders, home-made bread and jam, and then fully experiencing the Roeper School's ambience. I was struck by the contagious enthusiasm of the students and the low student-faculty ratio, but mostly by the schools' collaborative, democratic approach to governance and innovation. The collaborative spirit was evident including the faculty, staff, and students all engaged in the process of learning. I was fascinated by their focus on the development of student leadership in what Annemarie and George called relationship-based activities. They introduced me to one group of students who eagerly shared their poems and short stories, and it was obvious these students felt emotionally, physically, socially, and intellectually safe. They were exploring and taking risks without fear of being called "nerds" or "brains" in a derogatory manner. Personalized learning and creative exploration were a central focus of the faculty and the students.

Over the years, leadership continued to be a prime interest for me that evolved in the co-authoring of two books on leadership, one with Doris Shallcross, *Leadership: Making things happen* (1986) and *Leadership: A special type of giftedness* (1987) with Hilda Rosselli. A Leadership Skills and Behavior Scale was developed at the University of South Florida Center for Creativity, Innovation and Leadership (Sisk, 1987), as well as the Sisk Model for Developing Leadership Giftedness (Sisk & Rosselli, 1987). The model was adapted in 2010 and can be used to plan and develop leadership activities for children and youth. In this chapter, the focus will be on defining leadership as a type of giftedness, definitions of leadership, theories about leadership, characteristics of leadership in gifted children and youth, screening and identifying students gifted in leadership, current research on leadership development, new ways of thinking about leadership and the classroom of today with emphasis on being a global citizen, and an introduction of the Sisk Leadership Model with exemplary lessons. This chapter will present leadership through the lens of the Roeper School and its positive attributes. Over the years, working with Annemarie Roeper in the World Council for Gifted and Talented (WCGT) and more recently in the Global Awareness Network of the National Association for Gifted Children (NAGC) which she helped to initiate, I am consistently struck by Annemarie's continued insightful and inspired focus on the needs of gifted students for the present and the future, hence the title of this chapter.

Interest in identifying and nurturing leadership potential can be traced to the time of Aristotle and Plato. Aristotle in *Nicomachean Ethics* concluded that the role of the leader is to create an environment in which all members of an organization have the opportunity to realize their potential. He said the ethical role of the leader is to create the conditions under which followers can achieve their potential, rather than enhancing the power of the leader. Aristotle has been dead for nearly 2,400 years, but his ideas about leadership are still timely for today. One flaw in Aristotle's ideas about leadership; however, was his conviction that men were more suited to leadership than women.

Plato used an extended allegory in *The Republic* to illustrate "our nature in its education and want of education" (Watt, 1992, p. 514). He used the cave as an allegory to explain the world of the senses and the intelligible world with its effect on the philosopher. The allegory is about gaining knowledge and represents the beginning of Plato's argument that only philosophers should rule and lead. In the dialogue between Socrates and Glaucon, Plato wrote of prisoners chained to face a wall, and behind and above the prisoners, people carried objects along a road. Beyond the road there was a fire that cast shadows of people onto the wall in front of the prisoners, so these images were all the prisoners could see. If prisoners were freed and forced to turn around, they would see the people on the road and then the fire, and experience reality as it was, not as it seemed to be in the cave. Plato wrote about those who were not content with the bondage of the chains breaking free so that they might discover the cause of the dancing shadows, only to return and find deaf ears, as they tried to share their new knowledge. The allegory is related to Plato's Theory of Forms or Ideas as the highest and most fundamental kind of reality, and not the material world of change known to us through sensation. According to Plato, only knowledge of the Forms or Ideas constitutes real knowledge. Both Aristotle and Plato practiced the use of dialogue and engaged learners in building their own knowledge. Aristotle said virtue and wisdom will definitely elude leaders who fail to engage in ethical analysis of their actions (Watt, 1997). This last statement of Aristotle is reflected in the work of Sternberg (2005) in his WICS model of leadership.

LEADERSHIP AS A TYPE OF GIFTEDNESS

The first formal definition of giftedness was provided by the Marland report (1972) in which leadership was listed as one of six areas of giftedness. The most recent definition of giftedness established in the Jacob K. Javits Gifted and Talented Students Education Act (1988), defines gifted as:

> The term 'gifted and talented students' means children and youth who give evidence of high performance capability in such areas as intellectual, creative, artistic or leadership capacity, or in specific academic fields; and who require services or activities not ordinarily provided by the schools in order to develop such capabilities fully. (Public Law 100–297, Section 4103. Definitions)

Most of the states make use of the federal definition of gifted and talented students in state plans and state legislation; however, the majority of the programs focus on the intellectually gifted. This is most notable in states that have adopted the term "Advanced Academics" in lieu of Gifted Programs. Stephens & Karnes (2000) in their research found only 18 states included leadership as part of their state definition, and they said even though leadership has been included in the federal definition for over 39 years, it is the least served area or domain of giftedness. Yet, gifted students have the potential to function as leaders with their empathy and sensitivity to justice, honesty, fairness, and a sense of responsibility for making a difference. These characteristics of the gifted can accelerate their development of the necessary knowledge, skills, and cooperative attitude needed to function in and contribute interdependently with their school and community.

SELF-ACTUALIZATION AND INTERDEPENDENCE

The process of developing leadership potential can be an amazing journey in self-actualization, and through activities that enhance intrapersonal and interpersonal skills, and learning to relate to others in a spirit of interdependence, gifted students can develop their leadership potential. This process is embodied in the philosophy of the Roeper School in Birmingham, Michigan. In *Educating Children for Life: The Modern Learning Community*, Annemarie Roeper co-founder of the Roeper School with her husband George said:

> Humanity has made two promises to its children. The first is to prepare a world, which accepts them and provides them with opportunities to live, grow and create in safety. The other is to help them develop their whole beings to the fullest in every respect. Education is the vehicle through which we try to keep these promises. (Roeper, 1990, p. 3)

Definitions of Leadership

In the *Handbook of Leadership* Bass (1981) concluded after a review of leadership literature there were almost as many definitions of leadership as there were people trying to define the concept. More recently, Matthews (2004) reviewed publications on leadership education specifically for gifted and talented youth. He included articles from 1980–2004 and found common themes that characterize most of the definitions: 1) its social nature is usually expressed through relationships and the use of interpersonal influence; 2) developmental aspects which involved building general as well as task-specific skills; and 3) leadership's particular context including the organizational setting surrounding individuals and other external structural features that influence the ways in which individuals express their leadership abilities. Some representational definitions include:

- Leadership can be viewed as a relationship between those who are exerting influence and those who are being influenced (Hollander, 1964).
- Leadership is clearly a role that leads toward goal achievement, involves interaction and influence and usually achievement, and usually results in some form of changed structure or behavior of groups, organizations, or communities (Lassey & Fernandez, 1976).
- Leadership is the process of influencing the activities of an individual or a group in efforts toward goal achievement (Hersey & Blanchard, 1977).
- Leadership is an ability that may lead to a better job, to more security and self-confidence and to greater service to society as a whole (Richardson & Feldhusen, 1987).
- Leadership is the ability to influence the activities of an individual or group toward the achievement of a goal (Addison, 1984).
- Leadership is the avenue to the achievement of our personal and corporate goals (Calloway, 1985).
- Leaders fill a void or need in that there must be a group, which is willing, or more likely wants to be led (Lipper, 1985).
- Leadership is the process of persuasion or example by which an individual (or leadership team) includes a group to pursue objectives held by the leader or shared by the leaders and his or her followers (Gardner, 1990).
- Leadership is an interpersonal relation in which others comply because they want to, not because they have to (Hogan, Curphy, & Hogan, 1994).
- Leadership is the capability to guide others in the achievement of a common goal (Dobosz & Beaty, 1999).
- Leadership is the ability to create a vision for positive change, help focus resources on right solutions, inspire and motivate others, and provide opportunities for growth and learning (Martin, 2007).
- Leadership can be defined as one's ability to get others to willingly follow (Hakala, 2008).
- Leadership is the capacity of a system or a community to co-sense and co-create its future as it emerges (Scharmer, 2009).

These definitions differ as Matthews (2004) found in his review. The variety of leadership definitions points to the multitude of factors that affect leadership and the different perspectives from which to examine leadership as a construct (Karnes & Bean, 2000).

THEORIES OF LEADERSHIP

Trait Theory

The trait theory is the oldest theory of leadership. It often is referred to as the "Great Man" theory and can be traced to the early ideas of Aristotle who thought leaders were born, not made. Stogdill (1974), an internationally known leadership researcher, reviewed 124 studies of personal factors that could be associated with leadership. He found the personality trait theory could not be substantiated. Stogdill said leadership is an active process and not merely the possession of a combination of traits. He was convinced there was a working relationship between members of a group and the leader, and noted the leader earned status through active participation and demonstration of an ability to complete tasks. Stogdill identified five personal factors that appeared to interact with four situational factors. Personal factors include intellectual capacity, achievement, responsibility, participation, and status. Situational factors include mental level, status skills, needs and interests of followers, and objectives to be achieved. These personal and situational factors not only interact, but also are influenced by the work situation or leadership setting.

Leadership Style Theory

The second type of leadership theory to be examined is the Leadership Style theory. The classic work in this theory was conducted by Lewin, Lippit, and White in 1939. They identified three patterns of leadership: democratic, autocratic, and laissez-faire. Democratic leadership was described as situations that are fair and just, with everyone having an opportunity to offer ideas, opinions, and solutions. Autocratic was described as situations in which absolute obedience was called for by the leaders with little or no opportunity for adding ideas or showing any kind of dissent. Last, laissez-faire was described as situations in which the leader was non-involved, provided little or no leadership and confusion and chaos reigned. The work of Lewin et al. was extended by Tannenbaum, Weschler and Massarch (1961) who suggested leadership could be conceptualized on a continuum of leadership ranging from boss-centred leadership to subordinate-centred leadership.

McGregor (1960) provided another example of leadership style as a theory with his Theory X and Theory Y. This theory was congruent with the authoritarian vs. democratic leadership. Theory X viewed power coming from one's position and subordinates were considered unreliable. Theory Y viewed leadership as being given to the group and subordinates were considered self-directive and creative, if they were properly motivated. McGregor's theory viewed leadership as relational and was the forerunner of the third type of leadership which is situational.

Situational Leadership Theory

In this theory, individuals are perceived as having leadership manifested in specific situations. Hollander (1964) described leadership as a relationship between people exerting influence and those who are influenced. Hersey & Blanchard (1982) extended Hollander's ideas and introduced three components of situational leadership: task behavior, relationship behavior and effectiveness. Concern for task was described as productivity, and relationship behavior was described as concern for people. In addition, they introduced the concept of task-relevant maturity with two types of maturity, job maturity and psychological maturity. Job maturity was defined as competence, achievement motivation, and willingness to take on responsibility. Psychological maturity was defined as self-respect, self-confidence, and self-esteem. Hersey & Blanchard also suggested that the attitudes and behaviors of subordinates can provide cues to the leader on how to best interact with them.

With new employees or antagonistic or lethargic subordinates, the leader focuses on high task orientation "get the job done" and low relationship. As employees learn the job or change their attitude, the leader can then move to high task and high relationship. As they mature, the leader lessens the emphasis on task and invests more in relationships. Finally, as subordinates demonstrate full maturity, the leader lessens task concern and concern for relationships. A more recent situational model is one including a transformative component.

The Social Change Model of Leadership Development

The Social Change Model of Leadership Development (HERI, 1996) described leadership is a relational, transformative, process-oriented, learned and change-directed phenomenon (Wagner, 2006). The Social Change Model (SCM) is based on the principles of situational leadership as a purposeful, collaborative, values-based process resulting in positive social change. In the SCM, social responsibility and change for the common good are achieved through the development of eight core values targeted toward enhancing the level of self awareness of individuals and their ability to work with others. The individual core values include: consciousness of self, congruence, and commitment. The group core values include: collaboration, common purpose, and controversy with civility. The core value for society and community values is citizenship. The interaction between and across these seven core values facilitates social change for the common good, which is the eighth value. The SCM model has considerable applicability to leadership programs (Kezar, Carducci, & Contreras-McGavin, 2006); particularly, for gifted students with its focus on empowering individuals to address social change and socio-cultural issues. The SCM model is depicted in Figure 1.

Developing the seven C's of the SCM with gifted students entails attention to the following values and attributes.

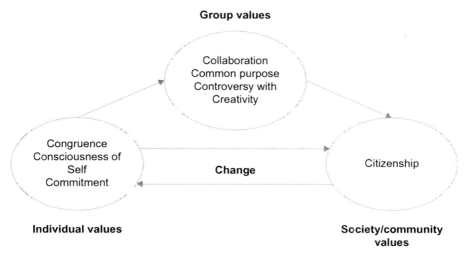

Figure 1. Social change model.

Individual Values

- Consciousness of self can be developed by encouraging gifted students to develop and to use their intrapersonal skills with activities and experiences to build awareness of their beliefs, values, attitudes, and emotions that motivate them to take action. As gifted students develop consciousness of self, they will become mindful and aware of their current emotional state and the "perceptual lens" they may be using. The Roeper School pays special attention to the social and emotional development of their students.
- *Congruence* can be encouraged and reinforced by engaging gifted students in reflecting in journals and discussing socio-cultural issues in small groups. They can reflect on their interpersonal actions and note if they are able to act in ways consistent with their values and beliefs. One activity to build congruence is providing time for gifted students to examine the biographies of leaders who were able to behave with consistency, genuineness, authenticity, and honesty toward others in the face of challenges and stress, and then to reflect on the thinking, feeling, and behaving of these leaders.
- *Commitment* development can be encouraged in gifted students by creating an environment to support their individual learning passions. As the students identify service projects in their schools or in their communities, they will develop a significant investment in the projects, and their energy for the projects will be reflected in increased intensity and perseverance. The Roeper School emphasizes equity and justice, ethics and altruism, service to, and integration with the community and the world.

Group values

- *Collaboration* can be experienced by gifted students as they work on group projects focusing on generating creative solutions and actions such as Future Problem Solving which calls for shared responsibility and group accountability. The power of the group process can be enhanced if the groups are dissimilar in ethnicity and skill level to encourage gifted students to realize the importance of different points of view and the power of diversity.
- *Common Purpose* is essential in the SCM and one initial activity for gifted students in a leadership program is to develop a shared vision and purpose for their group. As the students share aims and values, a common purpose can be realized.
- *Controversy with Civility* is an essential skill for gifted students. With their critical and dominant nature, they need to learn how to be able to listen to all points of view and to do so with civility. Gifted students need to be guided to recognize that differences in viewpoint often lead to creative outcomes. The Roeper School guides their students in learning their strengths, weaknesses, and motivations and then ways to use self-knowledge to guide their future development.

COMMUNITY VALUES

- *Citizenship* can be developed as gifted students engage in social-service projects and come to recognize that members of a community are interdependent. Individuals or groups from the community working in projects with responsibility for others can be invited to share their vision and active involvement with the students.

CHANGE

- *Change* is the essential goal of leadership development in the SCM model, and one goal for gifted students is to become part of positive social change. Gifted students want to make a difference and to make the world a better place for themselves and others, and the SCM model can be an essential tool in enabling them to develop their leadership.

ELIAS: A Theory U Inspired Model

Still another contemporary leadership model is field-based and transformational. Scharmer (2009) said the single-person-centric concept of leadership is outdated and real leadership takes place through collective, systemic and distributed action. Emerging Leaders Innovate Across Sectors (ELIAS) is a Theory U inspired model. Participants who work through the ELIAS program go through systems change beginning with stages that Scharmer calls *downloading* and *denial* in which there is a focus on the past; this is followed by *debate* in which the problem is viewed and blame is placed on others; then there is *dialogue* in which multiple perspectives are viewed including each person's part in creating the issue. This is followed by *connecting to source* in which there is an uncovering of common will and a shift from a "me" to "we" focus. This stage is followed by *envisioning* in which there is a crystallizing of the vision and intention; then *enacting* in which there is a prototyping of the "new" by linking head, heart, and hand; and finally *embodying* in which there is institutionalizing of the "new" in processes and practices. Throughout the ELIAS leadership experience there is an emphasis on open mind, open heart, and open will. These situational conceptual theories and frameworks can add considerable meaning and relevance to the development of viable leadership programs for gifted students.

Sternberg's WICS Model of Leadership

Sternberg (1999) said good leadership is in large part a decision-making process. Therefore, developing leadership will involve guiding future leaders, the gifted students in developing the skills to ask the kind of questions they need to ask, and the decision-making skills to make wise creative decisions. Sternberg and Lubart (1995) defined key creative decision-making skills as being able to redefine problems, analyse problems, sell solutions, realize the limitations of knowledge, take sensible, principled tasks and overcome obstacles. Successful leaders propel followers from where they are to where the leader wants them to go (Sternberg, 1999). In addition, the leader will be successful to the extent that followers reach the destination willingly, with maximum positive and minimum negative outcomes for the leader-follower system (Sternberg, Kaufman & Pretz, 2002). The WICS model of leadership is composed of four components: wisdom, intelligence, creativity, synthesized. Sternberg (2005) said we need creative skills to come up with functional ideas and to convince others of the values of the proposed ideas. Wisdom balances the effect of ideas on the individual, on others, and on institutions in both the short and long term.

Intelligence is not enough. Leaders can be creatively intelligent, analytically intelligent and practically intelligent without being wise (Sternberg, 2005). Wisdom is especially important in today's world as a result of advances in technology, including destructive technology. This mismatch between the development and the lack of development of wisdom places the world at enormous risk (Sternberg, 2005).

It is often difficult for gifted students to think wisely because they lack wise role models, and they may have perceived self interests in a "What's in it for me?" attitude or "What's in it for us?" which represent thinking in short-term rather than long-term effects. There also is a lack of dialogue and dialectical thinking that the ELIAS theory identified as components of leadership. Wisdom according to Sternberg (2005) involves the use of intelligence, creativity and experience toward a common good. The Roeper School has an atmosphere of caring and respect with a balance achieved between individual and community needs, and guidance of the students to balance individual rights and responsibilities.

WICS can provide a useful model for leadership development involving synthesizing wisdom, intelligence, and creativity. Sternberg stressed the importance of conceptualizing leadership as decision-making. Therefore, in working with gifted students it is important for educators to help the students develop and make use of their characteristics of sincerity, honesty, integrity, and compassion in making wise decisions. Service projects can build on these characteristics as gifted students engage in activities that provide experiences towards a common good. Programs such as the Future Problem Solving Program can help gifted students further develop their creative problem solving skills.

The Future Problem Solving Program (FPSP)

The Future Problem Solving Program (FPSP) focuses on the creative problem solving process and futuristic issues to develop the skills necessary to adapt to a changing world and shape the future (Future Problem Solving Program Coach's Handbook, 2001). The FPSP includes different components: Future Problem Solving (FPS), Community Problem Solving (CmPS), and Scenario Writing (SW).

The six-step problem solving model. Future problem solvers receive the Future Scene, then they work through it using a 6-step model, based on the Creative Problem Solving (CPS) process: (a) Understanding the Problem, which includes: (1) Identifying Challenges and (2) Selecting an Underlying Problem; (b) Generating Ideas including: (3) Producing Solution Ideas; and (c) Planning for Action, which includes: (4) Generating and Selecting Criteria, (5) Applying Criteria, and (6) Developing an Action Plan (FPSP, 2001, p.15).

The future problem solving program. The program: (a) provides students with unique opportunities to enhance awareness of everyday issues; (b) models effective processes that can be used throughout their lives; (c) incorporates the basic skills taught in the classroom by extending students' perceptions of the real world; (d) promotes responsible group membership; (e) encourages real-life problem solving experiences; (f) promotes continuous improvement through the evaluation process; and (g) offers authentic assessment in the product produced (FPSP, 2001, p. 11).

The creative problem solving process. The process: (a) helps students to improve analytical thinking skills; (b) aids students in increasing creative thinking abilities; (c) stimulates students' knowledge and interest in the future; (d) extends students' written and verbal communication skills; (e) encourages students to develop and improve research skills; (f) provides students with a problem-solving model to integrate into their lives; (g) guides students to become more self-directed and responsible; and (h) promotes responsible group membership for future problem solving and community problem solving (FPSP, 2001).

The Future Scene (pre-determined by the teacher) describes an ill-defined situation taking place 20 to 30 years into the future. Students are required to use the knowledge gained and project it into the future. Students are required to follow the problem solving steps identifying and selecting the problem. After generating 16 varied and unusual solutions, they are asked to come up with the five most appropriate criteria for judging the solutions. The last stage requires writing an action plan based on their highest scoring solution idea. The students are to complete the whole booklet within 2 hours.

Tools for generating options, enhancing convergent and divergent thinking include: Brainstorming, SCAMPER (Substitute, Combine, Adapt/Add/Alter, Minify/Magnify/Modify, Put to other uses, Eliminate or Elaborate, Reverse/Rearrange/Reduce), Morphological Matrix, Hot Spot and Paired Comparison Analysis (FPSP, 2001).

In addition, it is essential that educators encourage gifted students to be courageous, to tolerate ambiguity and, most important with the current emphasis on accountability in education, to provide time for them to be creative. The Roeper School meets this need with an emphasis on personalized learning and creative exploration. George and Annemarie developed the essence of their educational focus, which they described as an idealistic philosophy of life based upon self-actualization, interdependence, diversity and human rights (Roeper & Roeper, 1981 cited in Shane, 2009).

WHAT DOES IT TAKE TO BE AN EMERGING LEADER?

Emerging leaders become role models and inspire or motivate group members to persevere when actions or ideas are stalled, provide intellectual stimulation, and recognize matches between individual group members' traits and the tasks that need to be accomplished (Guastello, 1995). Leadership qualities are listed in the Scales for Rating the Behavioral Characteristics of Superior Students (SRBCSS) (Renzulli, Smith, Callahan, Hartman, & Westberg, 2002) :

- Responsible Behavior
- Follow-through on projects
- Respect and willing compliance of others
- Self-confidence
- Ability to organize
- Ability to cooperate
- Tendency to direct activities when involved with others.

These behavioral characteristics suggest gifted students demonstrating leadership characteristics can be problem solvers, facilitating and directing actions to identify solutions and to become emerging leaders (Davis & Rimm, 2004).

CHARACTERISTICS OF LEADERSHIP IN GIFTED YOUTH

Leadership as defined by Hakala (2008) is the ability to get others to willingly follow. He said leaders can be found and nurtured, and it is this role the Roeper School demonstrates by actively involving students in leadership activities by providing "choice" in the activities the students pursue. Hakala identified nine characteristics of leadership qualities: Integrity, dedication, magnanimity, humility, openness, creativity, fairness, assertiveness, and a sense of humour.

- *Integrity* involves the ability to integrate outward actions with inner values. Leaders with integrity can be trusted because they are the same on the outside with their actions, as they are on the inside with their values. Leaders with integrity do not veer from their values in stressful situations; consequently, followers always know where they stand.
- *Dedication* is demonstrated by leaders who do whatever is necessary to get a task completed. By setting an example, the leader can inspire group members to stay with a task until it is completed, and the group can see that they have been able to achieve a great product.
- *Magnanimity* is when the leader shares the spotlight and makes sure every group member is recognized for her or his part in the project.
- *Humility* is evidenced as the leader recognizes all group members and is humble. Hakala (2008) pointed to Gandhi as a role model for humility with his "follower-centric" leadership role.
- *Openness* is demonstrated as the leader listens to others, and accepts new ideas. It also involves suspending judgment which encourages group members or followers to feel comfortable in sharing new ideas.
- *Creativity* is defined as being able to think outside of the box and to reward the ingenuity and originality of group members. Encouraging the group to use What if? statements can spark followers to think differently and come up with new ideas.
- *Fairness* is essential for a leader and taking time to check for accuracy and precision in the facts and before moving along with a solution or action. It also means treating all group members fairly; it involves decreasing impulsivity and avoiding leaping to conclusions.
- *Assertiveness* involves being able to clearly state the goal, the expectations, and the time-line so all of the group members are on the same page. Assertiveness is not the same as aggressive behavior; it is being able to clearly state expectations, so there are no misunderstandings.
- *Sense of Humour* is a leadership characteristic that can relieve stress or tension and even redirect hostility. Hakala (2008) said humour builds camaraderie and bonding in the group.

These leadership characteristics listed by Hakala are similar to the twelve intellectual indicators identified by Costa (2000), and the 16 habits of mind (Costa & Kallick, 2004). In his ideas about transformative education, Costa championed teaching for intelligence. The Costa intellectual indicators included: Persistence, decreasing impulsivity, listening to others, flexibility in thinking, metacognition, checking for accuracy/precision, questioning, drawing on past knowledge, precision of language and thought, using all senses, ingenuity, originality, creativity and wonderment, enjoyment, and curiosity.

SCREENING AND IDENTIFYING STUDENTS GIFTED IN LEADERSHIP

Over the last 40 years a number of instruments were developed to screen and to identify leadership in elementary and secondary students; however, the number of instruments with reliability and validity are limited. Most of the instruments can provide information about leadership characteristics and behaviors, and this information can be used in planning and developing leadership programs, as well as for measuring the impact of leadership programs on the participating students. Most of the available instruments are self rating, but teachers and parents can rate the students to provide additional information concerning the leadership of students being considered for leadership programs. Friedman, Jenkins-Friedman, and Van Dyke (1984) conducted a study to ascertain whether self, peer, or teacher nomination was more effective in identifying students with leadership ability. They found students who self-nominated either singly or in combination with other types of nomination scored more highly on leadership than students nominated by their peers or teachers or both.

When students are involved in leadership activities in schools that encourage active involvement and independent research, it is important that the identification of leadership be an ongoing process since the students with leadership potential may be able to qualify as they experience leadership activities. Methods available to identify leadership potential include: parent, teacher, and self-rating checklists or nomination forms, socio-metric assessment, observations of group tasks in leadership activities, and commercially prepared screening and identification instruments (Bean & Karnes, 2001). A selected number of instruments are listed that can be useful in identifying students with potential in leadership.

One instrument widely used in local school programs is the Rating the Behavioral Characteristics of Superior Students Scale (SRBCSS), originally developed in 1976 and revised in 2002, that lists seven leadership characteristics. The original scale had four rating areas: learning, motivation, creativity, and leadership. Leadership Characteristics (Part 4) was validated by Hartman (1969) who compared the ratings of teachers and peers. He found correlations were high for teachers and students in grades 4, 5 and 6. Additional studies conducted found the Leadership Characteristics Part 4 assessed many behavioral characteristics found in the research on leadership. Burke, Harworth and Ware (1982) used a factor-analytical structure of the SRBCSS and concluded the behavioral characteristics were descriptive of leadership expectations in a school setting. The SRBCSS manual contains information on construct validity, alpha reliability and inter-rater reliability, as well as detailed information on how to develop local norms.

Another self-rating scale is the Roets Rating Scale for Leadership (Roets, 1986). The scale can be administered to students in grades 5–12. Twenty-six items are listed and students respond on a Likert 5 point scale of Almost Always, Quite

Often, Sometimes, Not Very Often, and Never. The Roets Scale was field tested with 1,057 students in both public and private schools. Validity was established by administering two other measures of leadership with correlations of $r = .71$ and $.77$. An investigation of reliability of the Roets Scale with the SRBCSS leadership scale yielded a correlation of $r = .55$.

The Eby Gifted Behavior Index was developed by Eby (1989) and contains six checklists to identify the behavioral processes of elementary and secondary gifted students in a number of talent areas, verbal, math, science, problem solving, musical, visual, spiritual and social leadership including: active interaction with the environment, reflectiveness, perceptiveness, persistence, goal orientation, originality, self-evaluation, independence, and effective communication of ideas. A 5 point Likert scale is used and validity and reliability studies on the social/leadership checklist are included in the manual.

The Khatena-Morse Multitalent Perception Inventory was developed by Khatena & Morse (1994) to measure artistry, musical, creative imagination, initiative, and leadership. Form A contains four leadership items, and form B contains six items in leadership. The Inventory has a technical manual that includes standardization data and information on the validity and reliability of the test.

The Gifted and Talented Evaluation Scale (GATES) was developed to evaluate giftedness as defined in the federal definition of gifted education and includes items to measure intellectual ability, academic skills, creativity, leadership, and artistic talent. There are ten items in the leadership section. Teachers, parents and others can rate the students on the GATES. It has been field tested with 1,000 gifted and talented students. Studies of test-retest reliability and internal consistency yielded 90 coefficients (Gilliam et al., 1996)

The Leadership Skills and Behavior Scale was developed by Sisk (1987). The scale is based on the definition of leaders as creative problem solvers and consists of items for gifted students to self-rate on eight skills including: Decision-making, problem-solving, group dynamics, communicating, organizing, implementing, planning, and discerning opportunities. In addition, there are two items focusing on motivation and positive self-concept. Students respond to the questions using a rating scale of 1–5 with Never, Seldom, Sometimes, Often, and Always. Validity and reliability are not provided, but the Leadership Skills and Behavior Scale has been used as a pre-post test measure for a number of three week residential leadership programs for academically gifted students, and the mean score differences on the pre-post tests of leadership were significant at the .05 level (Sisk, 2010).

CURRENT RESEARCH ON LEADERSHIP DEVELOPMENT

Authentic Assessment of Leadership in Problem-Solving Groups

During a spring problem/solving conference for middle and high school students, Jolly & Kettler (2004) engaged students in the creative problem-solving process.

Students were given a common "mess," according to the creative problem-solving process requiring an ill-defined problem or issue, then they formed a problem statement and developed a solution. Working in small groups, the students presented solutions to one another using a number of creative methods. Observers reported a recognized leader emerged in each of the small groups. Jolly & Kettler (2004) concluded group members were able to agree on a leader, and they identified four specific leadership behaviors: (a) keeping the group focused, (b) offering acceptable compromises, (c) being respected and listened to by the groups, and (d) the group agreed with them. This study would suggest that leaders can be identified during observation of students engaged in problem-solving activities.

Using Visual Learning to Enhance the Leadership of Gifted Students

Karnes & Zimmerman (2001) introduced characteristics of leaders to gifted students including: desire to be challenged, ability to solve problems creatively, ability to reason critically, ability to see new relationships, facility of verbal expression, flexibility in thought and action, ability to tolerate ambiguity, and ability to motivate others. The gifted students were asked to reflect on these characteristics of leaders and then to take photographs of students demonstrating some of the characteristics, as well as photographs of symbols of leadership such as buildings, statues, monuments, and memorials. Other activities included interviewing leaders in the community, shadowing a specific person for a day and capturing the day with photographs, and staging a great leader party to share their visual representations.

Emotional Intelligence, Moral Judgment, and Leadership of Academically Gifted Students

Lee and Olszewski-Kubilius (2006) addressed three research questions: Is there a relationship between academic, emotional, moral, and leadership ability? Do gifted adolescents differ from their age or grade normative sample, or by gender in these abilities? and, Are there differences in these abilities between students who attend leadership programs as opposed to academic acceleration programs? Three psychological scales were used that measured adaptability, emotional intelligence, stress management, impulse control, moral judgment, and leadership. The findings indicated academically gifted students have greater leadership potential than other students; however, gifted students did not have a significant difference in strength in emotional intelligence when compared to heterogeneous groups of adolescents. Gifted male students showed a high level of adaptability in problem-solving and flexibility, while gifted females showed higher interpersonal abilities. An overall weakness was found in stress management, tolerance, and ability to control impulses among both the male and female gifted students. Lee & Olszewski (2006) suggested further investigation needs to be conducted concerning the relationship between a low level of emotional control and high academic giftedness. They concluded advanced cognitive reasoning abilities provide gifted students with higher moral and leadership development potential, but special programs are needed to optimize the development of these attributes.

Building Leadership Skills in Middle School Girls through Interscholastic Athletics

Membership on an athletic team is one avenue to acquire, assess, refine, and demonstrate leadership skills that are developmentally appropriate for middle school students. Hart (2002) found in a sample of 108 girls in middle school that girls on the soccer team held more leadership positions in school organizations and attained more leadership positions within the student council compared to non-athletic girls. Hart concluded that for the middle school female athletes, confidence and empowerment are acquired through competitive sports and school leadership. The mastery of time management, setting priorities, and multitasking were listed as early stepping stones to leadership. The athlete's competitive spirit steered many of the team members to compete for student leadership positions such as team captain or to seek election to the student government.

Leadership Skills of Gifted Students at the Secondary Level in a Rural Setting

Gifted students in grades 9–12 in a rural school district volunteered to participate in a year-long program (Team Lead). Eleven students were administered the Leadership Skills Inventory (LSI) (Karnes & Chauvin, 2000) as a pre-assessment of their leadership skills. The LSI yields scores in nine categories of leadership: fundamentals, written communication, speech communication, character-building, decision-making, group dynamics, problem-solving, personal skills, and planning. The students in Team Lead participated in a book club, leadership activities, and the ropes training course. Milligan (2004) reported that when the LSI was administered as a post-test assessment, the gifted students increased their leadership in all nine categories.

Trends in Creative Leadership Research and Implementations for Education

The Center for Creative Leadership (CCL) is a global provider of executive professional development education that seeks to unlock individual and organizational potential through a focus on creative leadership. CCL helps individuals worldwide to develop creative leadership, and in 2007, researchers at CCIL asked 247 senior executives around the globe about leadership trends in business. One trend most often mentioned was a shift from an autocratic style to one that is more participative. The executives predicted future success would depend on the ability of the leader to be collaborative and to focus on the team rather than on the individual. Another trend was for leaders to make more effective use of technology as a communication and virtual tool, as well as a management tool. Empathy was listed as a fundamental construct of leadership, since authentic leaders need to have empathy to be aware of others and to be more person-focused. Past CCL research reports such as the Changing Nature of Leadership, Leadership Gap, and Leadership Across Differences stressed that leaders in a global world need to collaborate with others, cross organizational and cultural boundaries, and that there is a need for creative shared direction, alignment and commitment between groups with very different histories, perspectives, values, and cultures.

Leadership Intervention Needs to be Cross Generational

In September of 2009 the World Bank held a round table meeting to discuss leadership development. They began the meeting by acknowledging we live in a world of massive institutional failure, a world that represents current and emerging generations of leaders with unprecedented challenges. They discussed the need to co-sense problems and co-create solutions, emphasizing open mind, open heart, and open will. The group agreed leadership intervention must be cross generational and put youth and emerging leaders into the driver's seat of change. According to the World Bank Report (Scharmer, 2009), at present, more than 50 percent of the global population is under the age of 25. These young people are the real stakeholders of the future in their countries. The necessity of identifying the gifted in this global population of youth and developing their global understanding and leadership is becoming imperative.

New Ways of Thinking about the Nature of Leadership and Leadership Development

Increasingly, leadership and leadership development are viewed as collaborative, social and relational (Day, 2001). As a result, leadership in the future will be understood as a collaborative capacity of all members of an organization or community to accomplish critical tasks such as setting direction, creating alignment, and gaining commitment. The Theory U-based model of Scharmer (2009) identified levels of responses to change including: (a) Reacting; (b) Redesigning; (c) Reframing; and (d) Regenerating. In this model, at the micro level, listening is identified as an essential individual skill, and conversing is identified as a group skill involving debate, dialogue, and collective creativity.

NEW WAYS OF THINKING ABOUT THE CLASSROOM OF TODAY

One challenge leaders face today is to perform effectively in an environment of uncertainty and ambiguity and to reconcile the diversity of interests, needs and demands of multiple stakeholders in a global economy. Schraa-Liu & Trompenars

(2006) said research studies identify competence in reconciling dilemmas as the most discriminating feature to differentiate successful and less successful leaders. They stated that reconciling outer dilemmas starts with the inner world of leaders involving self-discipline and self-mastery. They suggested one way to promote positive change in individuals is to use experiential learning such as simulations. Svobod and Whalen (2005) listed four characteristic of experiential learning: (a) It is based on actions; (b) It gives the chance to receive feedback on the actions and to explore the results, (c) It helps to change the mental frames that prevent the participants from achieving the results they want, and (d) It builds links between the learning process and real-world challenges. Simulation provides opportunities to practice in a consequence-free environment with immediate feedback to address strengthening knowledge and understanding of one's inner world to enable the outer world to be addressed. Senge (2003) said in an increasingly interdependent world, system thinking must become an educational priority. He stressed that business leaders, as well as teachers and other professionals count on both wisdom of the past and their own experiences to create more inclusive ways of living and working globally in the present and in the future. Passig (2004) agreed with Senge (2003) and said learning about the past is not enough; we should exploit and be able to develop an understanding of future possibilities and options. In order to survive in a fast–changing world, people need to make active use of their imagination to create images progressing beyond traditional paradigms, in order to discover, explore, invent and investigate new images in the present.

Passig (2004) described a state of mind he called Future Time Span (FTS) which characterized thinkers in ancient times. Future time span is a reflective awareness, that conceives the duration of time and events that take place in it, for increasingly greater ranges of time, and which is able to concretize the long-range implications of the things that might occur over that time. This is an awareness that can motivate the ability to change behavior in the present, in light of the conceptualization of the future. One strength of the Roeper School is the faculty autonomy in curriculum design and the use of inquiry-based and lab-based approaches that provide opportunities for students to discover, explore, invent and investigate.

Thomas Friedman (2005) in *The world is flat: A brief history of the twenty-first century* said globalization has leveled the playing field of many countries. He described the world as becoming increasingly "flatter" or "connected," and emphasized the old ways of doing things politically and socially will no longer be effective. He said classrooms of today need to engage students in gaining new kinds of knowledge, skills, and dispositions to enable them to function successfully in an increasingly interconnected global society. Friedman pointed out that digital technologies offer many ways to foster global awareness in the classroom. By infusing global education and technology in teaching and learning, teachers can develop gifted students' understanding of the interrelationships of peoples worldwide; thereby, helping to prepare them to participate meaningfully as global citizens.

WHAT IS A GLOBAL CITIZEN?

In an article entitled *Becoming International,* Singh *(2003)* identified ten characteristics of an international citizen. This list can serve as a guide for gifted students and their teachers in establishing goals, planning and developing lessons of inquiry to address global issues, and in assessing individual student and group performance. International citizens are:

- *Inquirers.* They have natural curiosity. They have acquired the skills necessary to conduct purposeful constructive research. They actively enjoy learning.
- *Thinkers.* They exercise initiative in applying thinking skills critically and creatively to solve complex problems.
- *Communicators.* They receive and express ideas and information confidently in more than one language including the language of mathematical symbols.
- *Risk-Takers.* They approach unfamiliar situations without anxiety and have confidence and independence of spirit.
- *Knowledgeable.* They have explored globally relevant and important themes.
- *Principled.* They have a sound grasp of the principles of moral reasoning. They have integrity, honesty, and a sense of fairness and justice.
- *Caring.* They show sensitivity toward the needs and feelings of others. They have a sense of personal commitment to action and service.
- *Open-minded.* They respect the views, values, and traditions of others.
- *Well-balanced.* They understand the importance of physical and mental balance and personal well-being.
- *Reflective.* They give thoughtful considerations in their own learning and analyse their personal strengths and weaknesses in a constructive manner. (Singh, 2003)

As gifted students are provided services and activities to become more aware and sensitive to the experiences of others, they can become international and global citizens. The Roeper School gives attention to the whole child, integrating the cognitive, social, emotional, motivational and physical aspects of the students, which serves to develop many of the characteristics identified by Singh (2003).

A MODEL FOR DEVELOPING LEADERSHIP

The original Sisk Model for Developing Leadership was published in *Leadership: A special type of giftedness* (Sisk & Rosselli, 1987) and adapted in 2010 to respond to the need for gifted students to develop global leadership. The current model differs with the addition of several Characteristics of Leadership: open-minded, caring, risk-taking, responsibility for making a difference, honest, sensitivity to justice, and reflective. Selected Teaching Strategies added include: Project-based learning, issues-based learning, teaming, debate, dialogue and collective creativity. The Teaching/Learning Models are the same, except for the addition of the Gardner (1983) Multiple Intelligences Model. The Selected Key Concepts or big ideas now include: Leadership and the use of power and several of the issues Eriksson (2009) identified as concerns of gifted students: global warming, animal extinction, terrorism, depletion of natural resources, pollution, and endangered cultures, as well as other areas the students may choose to address in their studies. The 2010 Sisk Model for Leadership is depicted in Table 1.

Table 1. Sisk model for development of leadership giftedness.

Characteristics of Leadership Giftedness	Selected Teaching Strategies	Selected Teaching/ Learning Models	Selected Key Concepts
Positive Self Concept	Self Awareness Activities	Bloom Taxonomy	Leadership and Community Structure
Open Minded		Gardner's MI Model	
Verbal Skills	Futures Study	Guilford Structure of Intellect	
Questioning Attitude	Bibliotherapy		Leadership and the Use of Power
Reflective	Higher Level Questioning	Herrmann Whole Brain* Teaching Learning Model	Multicultural Roots
Sensitive/Empathetic			
Tolerance of Ambiguity	Group Dynamics		Global Warming
	Collective Creativity	Renzulli Triad	Animal Extinction
Sensitivity to Injustice	Inquiry	Taylor Multiple Talents Model	Need for Managing Global Information
Honest	Dialogue		
Independent	Debate	Williams Model	Terrorism
Persistent	Creative Problem Solving		Need for Celebration and Creative Expression
Sociable			
Risk-Taker	Visualization		
Decision Making Skills	Teaming		Depletion of Natural Resources
	Simulation		
Serious Minded	Project-based Learning		Pollution
Critical			Endangered Cultures
Enthusiastic	Journal Writing		Impact of Technologies on Communities
Flexibility in Thought and Action	Issues-based learning		
	Media Therapy		
Need for Achievement			
High Energy Level			
Wide Range of Interests			
Curiosity			
Dominant			
Responsibility for Making a Difference			

SISK MODEL FOR DEVELOPING LEADERSHIP GIFTEDNESS

Students gifted in leadership demonstrate many unique characteristics and these characteristics are listed in Column 1 of the model. These characteristics cause gifted students to behave in certain ways, and the resultant behaviors can be "clues" for planning and implementing services and activities to further develop the leadership of gifted students. In addition, many teaching strategies complement these leadership characteristics, and these teaching strategies are listed in Column 2, including: project-based learning, issues-based learning, debate, teaming, dialogue and collective creativity. Teaching and learning models that can be used to plan a variety of levels of thinking and activities are listed in Column 3. These models include: Bloom, Gardner, Guilford, Herrmann®, Renzulli, Taylor, and Williams. Key concepts or big ideas are listed in Column 4 of the model.

Teaching and Learning Models

A brief description of the Teaching and Learning Models is included as a preface to the exemplary leadership lessons based on each of the models.

1. *Taxonomy of Educational Objectives* (Bloom 1956) includes structured cognitive processes through the use of a hierarchy of classes of thinking (knowledge, comprehension, application, analysis, synthesis and evaluation).
2. *Structure of the Intellect* (Guilford, 1967) is a factor analytic model of cognitive functioning including 120 different thinking abilities, resulting from a combination of operations (cognition, memory, convergent production, divergent production, and evaluation). Content includes figural, symbolic, semantic, and behavioral. Products include units, classes, relations, systems, transformations, and implications.
3. *Taylor's Multiple Talents* (1967) is a teaching model to develop creative thinking consisting of skill components of academic, predicting and forecasting, communicating, productive thinking, planning, decision making, discerning opportunities, implementing, and human relations.
4. *Renzulli Enrichment Triad* (1977). The triad is based on the interaction of three types of enrichment activities: Type I (General Exploratory), Type II (Group training), and Type III (Individual and small group investigation of real problems).
5. *Herrmann Whole Brain® Teaching/Learning Model* (1999) is a model with four brain quadrants metaphorically representing four different learning styles, the upper right and left and the lower right and left. Respectively, broad categories of facts, open-minded, feelings and controlled behavior depict the four quadrants with four descriptors for each quadrant.
6. *Williams' Plank* (1970) is a model developed to stimulate creativity consisting of three dimensions: dimension 1 is subject matter, dimension 2 is teaching strategies, and dimension 3 consists of pupil behaviors.

7. *Multiple Intelligences (MI)* (Gardner, 1983) The MI model lists abilities to solve problems or make products using eight intelligences: linguistic, logical-mathematical, spatial, musical, bodily-kinesthetic, interpersonal, intrapersonalabilities. Later, Gardner (2010) added the naturalist and has considered adding the existential intelligence.

EXEMPLARY GLOBAL LEADERSHIP LESSONS

The Sisk Leadership Model is a planning instrument to assist teachers in designing lessons to develop leadership. First, the teacher selects characteristics from column 1 to be addressed in the lesson; then strategies are selected to be implemented from column 2; then a teaching/learning model is selected on which to base the lesson from column 3; and last from column 4 the key concepts or big ideas that will be a focus for the lesson are selected. Seven individual lessons illustrate how to use the selected leadership characteristics, strategies and key concepts with each of the seven teaching learning models. The following lesson planning template can be used to guide the lesson-planning process:

- *Characteristics:* list the specific characteristics of gifted students to be addressed in the lesson.
- *Strategies:* identify the teaching strategies to be used in the lesson.
- Model: identify the teaching/learning model to be used in organizing the lesson.
- *Key concept:* list the big ideas or key concepts upon which the lesson will focus.
- *Levels:* identify the levels or level of education that the lesson will address— primary, intermediate, or high school.
- *Content areas:* identify the content areas that the lesson will use as a focus.
- *Boundary breaker:* identify the open-ended question that will serve as an opening engagement activity.
- *Activities:* list the activities that the students will experience in the lesson.
- *Extenders:* identify activities to be used as independent work for students, or as a further extension of the lesson.

The first lesson is *Imagineland*, which focuses on an examination of leadership and begins with an activity calling for introspection of individual leadership. The lesson is based on the Guilford (1967) Structure of the Intellect Model.

Imagineland

Characteristics: Independent, Enthusiastic, Responsibility for making a difference, Serious minded

Strategies: Issues-based Learning, Simulation

Model: Guilford Structure of the Intellect

Key Concept: Depletion of Natural Resources

Level: High School

Content Areas: Science, Social Studies

Boundary Breaker: If you had absolute power in a developing country, what one problem would you address? (Evaluation)

Activities:

1. Imagineland is an imaginary country representing the world's least developed countries (LDCs). In small groups of five, examine the informational data sheet with key statistical data to build background information about Imagineland. (Cognition)
2. Discuss in full group the fact that processes leading to overuse of natural resources differ within the country of Imagineland. Consider Joachim von Braun's theory that conflict over natural resources may increase and significantly endanger development efforts in contexts where increased competition over natural resources can spill over to political spheres and lead to political violence. (Convergent Production, Divergent Production, Evaluation)
3. In your small groups of five decide who will work on researching similar LDCs that present high potential areas, medium potential areas, low potential areas and urban areas. (Evaluation)
4. In full group share the findings of your small groups. What were the most critical socioeconomic and ecological processes you discovered? What were the most seriously affected resources? (Evaluation, Memory)
5. Discuss the impact of rural-urban migration and industrial development and its effects on water resources and the growing urban population's need for energy in Imagineland. (Convergent Production and Divergent Production)
6. Read and discuss excerpts from Poverty and conservation: Lanscapes, people and power (Fisher, Maginnis, Jackson, and Barrow, 2005). (Convergent Production, Divergent Production and Evaluation)
7. In small groups discuss two projected major global changes over the next twenty years and their effect on Imagineland (genetically modified crops and vaccination of AIDS/HIV). (Convergent Production, Divergent Production and Evaluation)
8. In full group compare your findings and projections with eight experts who worked in a similar simulation with Imagineland. Compare and contrast your findings and their implications for the United States and the LCDs you researched. (Evaluation, Convergent Production and Divergent Production)

Extenders:

1. Read the report *Trends Until 2025* (Inforesources) and compare their research with that of the experts. (Cognition and Evaluation)
2. Research the "polluter pays principle" and its effect on the natural resources; particularly, on the environmental quality and the health situation in cities and downstream areas. (Cognition)

The next lesson is based on the Taylor (1967) Multiple Talents Model, which provides gifted students opportunities to examine their concerns about animal extinction.

Will Killing an Endangered Rhino Save the Species?

Characteristics: high energy level, flexibility in thought and action, curiosity, responsibility for making a difference

Strategies: simulation, role playing, creative problem solving, group dynamics

Model: Taylor's Multiple Talents (Totem Poles)

Key Concept: animal extinction

Levels: intermediate and high school

Content Areas: social studies, science

Boundary Breaker: What is one animal that you think is on the endangered species list?

Activities: In this activity, work in teams of four or five to examine legalized hunting as a means to save endangered species. Research the position of the International Fund for Animal Welfare, the Endangered Wildlife Trust, the World Wildlife Fund and CITES. Each group member will become conversant with one of the organizations' stands on legalized hunting and one group member will role play a spokesperson from each of the four organizations in a round table discussion.

1. Research the four agencies with considerable investment in the issue of legalized hunting. Become conversant with their positions and decide which of the four agencies' point of view has the most promise to help save endangered species. (Academic, Decision-Making)
2. Read the report of burstadt@bloomberg.net for background information on the killing of #65, a black rhino for $150,000, and note the role of John Hume in creating a market for shooting and harvesting animals on the endangered species list. (Academic)
3. In small groups, discuss the fact that in 1968 there were 1,800 white rhino and today there are 19,400 and investigate if this was a result of legalized hunting. (Productive Thinking, Communication)
4. In a round table discussion role play representatives of the Fund for Animal Welfare, the Endangered Wildlife Trust, the World Wildlife Fund and CITES (each small group will identify a spokesperson for each group) and one student will role play John Hume who is an advocate for legalized hunting. Note the group dynamics as the representatives and John Hume interact. What were the major points? Did delivery have anything to do with your opinion? (Communication, Human Relations, Discerning Opportunities)

5. Invite an environmental biologist to the Round Table and ask him or her to share his or her point of view on legalized hunting. Engage in Q & A with the quest speaker. (Communication, Implementing)

Extenders:

1. Write a letter to the editor of your local paper about legalized hunting? (Communication, Implementing)
2. Research if there is legalized hunting of endangered species in your state? (Academic)
3. Predict how legalized hunting will affect the Endangered Species Act of 1988 and predict if it will it be changed? (Predicting)

Images of Terrorism

Characteristics: sensitivity to injustice, questioning attitude, decision-making skills, serious minded

Strategies: issues-based learning, higher level questioning

Model: Renzulli Enrichment Triad

Key Concept: terrorism

Levels: intermediate and high school

Content Areas: social studies, language arts

Boundary Breaker: When you think of terrorist groups, what individual or group comes to mind?

Activity:

1. Using the internet of your school, home, public or university library, identify known terrorist organizations or terrorist groups. (Level One)
2. From your investigation, share with your class the names of the various organizations or groups that you were able to identify. What new information did you learn about terrorism? What are the motives of terrorists? Can the world answer the threat of terrorists? What skills do you need to develop to be able to understand terrorism? (Level Two)
3. As a class, design an information sheet with resources that can be tapped such as Homeland Security Blogs, and the report by the Center for Defense Information (CDI) on global response, terrorist organizations, targets and Homeland Defense that can be shared with others (teachers, parents, and professionals). Create a section of a class bulletin board for current developments or items of interest related to terrorism. Encourage your class to place questions in an envelope on the bulletin board for further student research on terrorist actions and appoint a team to find the answers. (Level Three)

Extenders:
1. Conduct an essay contest in your class with the information that has been collected and select representative essays to share with your school newspaper.
2. Research the Peace Operation Training Institute that studies peace and humanitarian relief. What courses do they have available?

The next lesson is based on the Williams' (1970) Plank model. The lesson *Endangered Cultures* provides gifted students opportunities to practice and to further develop their decision-making skills as they focus on this current issue from the perspective of two videos by Wade Davis and Phil Borges on endangered cultures.

Endangered Cultures

Characteristics: sensitive, flexible in thought and action, verbal skills, wide range of interests

Strategies: creative writing and reading, research, higher level questioning and thinking

Model: Williams Plank

- Intended Pupil Behaviors: Dimension 3
  - flexible thinking
  - elaborative thinking and complexity
- Content Areas: Dimension 1
  - social studies and language arts
- Teacher Behavior: Dimension 2
  - evaluate situations
  - skills of search
  - creative writing skills
  - creative reading skills
  - creative visualization skills

Key Concept: endangered cultures

Levels: intermediate and high school

Boundary Breaker: If you could ask a leader from the past for advice regarding the current global issue of endangered species, who would you ask?

Activities:

1. Watch the video of Phil Borges and Wade Davis on endangered cultures in Tibet and compare and contrast the two points of view. (Evaluate Situations)
2. In small groups of four, discuss the importance of 6,000 languages being spoken on Earth right now, and that 3,000 of these languages are not spoken by children. (Evaluate Situations)

3. Research and evaluate the work of Paredisec—a Cross Institutional Project supporting work on endangered cultures. (Skills of Search, Evaluate Situations)
4. Read *An Endangered Culture Under the Lens* by Manasi Singh (One World South) and write a What, So What and Now What response paper. (Evaluate Situations, Creative Writing Skills)
5. Research the conflict of mining bauxite and the impact on Dongria Kondh, an ancient indigenous community in the hills of Eastern India. The people have a symbolic relationship with the forests. The forest provides food and shelter, and their lifestyle and religion protect the forest. What are the issues involved? (Evaluate Situations, Creative Reading Skills)
6. Create a montage` of endangered cultures that can be shared with other classes to illustrate the lives of the indigenous cultures and their peoples. (Creative Visualization Skills)

Extenders:

1. Select one indigenous culture and write an essay on the importance of maintaining their culture. (Evaluate Situations, Creative Writing Skills)
2. Research the effect of climate change on native cultures and write a persuasive essay summarizing your views. (Evaluate Situations, Creative Writing Skills)

The next lesson is based on the Multiple Intelligences Model (MI) of Gardner (1983) and will involve the students in using higher-level questioning skills.

Managing Communication Overload

Characteristics: independent, verbal skills, curious, questioning attitude

Strategies: higher-level thinking/questioning, issues-based education, role-playing

Model: Multiple Intelligences Model (MI)

Key Concept: need to manage global information

Levels: intermediate and high school.

Content Areas: math/history/music/art/dance

Boundary Breaker: What is one communication device that you use daily? (Intrapersonal)

Activities:

1. Make a list of all the information sources you and your family use on a daily basis.

Discuss the statement: Do youth raised on media take new applications for granted, viewing them as just another "cool tool"? Reflect on your response and then share your view with the class (Linguistic, Intrapersonal, and Interpersonal)

2. In small groups of four students, compare and contrast the Internet and magazines. Reflect on the statement: "We surf the Internet and we swim in magazines." Factor in this information blog in your discussion: During the 12 years of Google, magazine readership actually increased 11%. A new medium doesn't necessarily displace an existing one. Journal your response and share your response with the entire group. (Linguistic, Intrapersonal/Interpersonal)
3. Research the new voice analysis software and its implication for global information management, as well as individual applications in medicine. Select a spokesperson and share your findings with the whole group of students. (Linguistic, Interpersonal)
4. In your small group, construct a timeline of inventions in communication over the last 20 years. Select another 20-year period, and compare and contrast the inventions in communication. Create a montage of your findings. (Linguistic, Logical/Mathematical, Spatial)
5. "Death by Powerpoint"—You have many assignments that require powerpoints. In your small group, create a survey that can be given to at least 10 individuals and ask the question: What do you find most irritating about powerpoint? Check your findings with those of a national survey that found: Speaker reading the slides 60%; Text too small to read 51%; Text too wordy 48%; Poor slide colour choices 37%; Moving text or graphics 25%; Irritating sounds 22%; and Complex charts 22%. Graph your findings to share with the class. (Linguistic, Logical/Mathematical, Spatial)
6. Research the symptoms of communication overload and identify ways of coping with communication overload in your small group. Create a rap, a musical or dance response to what you have found. (Linguistic, Musical /Spatial, Interpersonal)
7. Researchers at Kings College in London University found that communication overload causes a professional's IQ to drop 10 percentage points. Create a short skit to demonstrate and role play the effects of "continuous partial attention" and being bombarded by multiple information streams. (Linguistic, Interpersonal)
8. Discuss the excessive use of communication devices and the effect on an individual's need to develop an inner self. When can one find the "downtime" to be quiet and reflective? (Existential)

The next lesson is based on the Herrmann Whole Brain® Teaching/ Learning Design Model called *Global Leadership* in which the students discuss leadership in its broad spectrum including pressures leaders face and strategies they use to overcome problems.

Global Leadership

Characteristics: questioning attitude, independent, need for achievement

Strategies: higher-level thinking/ questioning

Model: Herrmann Whole Brain® Teaching/Learning Model

Key Concept: leadership and community structure

Levels: intermediate and high school

Content Areas: language arts, drama

Boundary Breaker: If you were describing yourself to someone, what one adjective would you use?

Activity: Identify five leaders in today's global society, and discuss some of the surrounding pressures they need to address? (A: Upper-Left) Which pressures do you feel are the strongest? Are any of these pressures ones you have experienced? (C: Lower-Right)

1. What do you think is meant by the following statement: (All four quadrants: A, B, C, D)

"Even at its worst, leadership which is frequently demanding, chaotic, frustrating, tiring, and, unappreciated is never boring. For most leaders, this escape from boredom is an ultimate fix." (David Campbell, 1985) Do you agree with this statement? (Cerebral: Lower Right-Feelings).

1. Research techniques or strategies that could be used to reduce stress in your often demanding and sometimes chaotic schedule? Which of these techniques could you use later in life when stress begins to build up? (Cerebral Lower Left-Controlled)
2. During a college lecture on negotiation; Richard Hughes, a financial expert identified the following principles:
   a. Do your research and be better informed than individuals with whom you are dealing.
   b. Recognize that most people have egos and give them acceptable reasons for switching to your viewpoint.
   c. Try to understand what is important to the other individual by role-playing their point of view. In what ways could you apply these principles to situations in your life? (Cerebral Lower Left-Controlled)
3. Using the Internet, locate newspapers from at least two countries, and identify five examples of people in leadership positions dealing with problems. Determine whether you think their actions were successful in defusing the problem. (Cerebral Left-Facts)
4. Examine the list of leadership roles identified by Henry Mintzberg (1994) in his research on Chief Executive Officers:
- Interpersonal Roles
   ◦ Leader
   ◦ Liaison
   ◦ Figurehead
- Informational Roles
   ◦ Monitor

- ○ Disseminator
- ○ Spokesperson
- Decision Roles
  - ○ Entrepreneur
  - ○ Resource Allocator
  - ○ Disturbance Handler
  - ○ Negotiator

Circle the ones you feel best describe your roles in student leadership. Do you think some of the roles are more important than others? (Cerebral Lower Right-Feelings) Describe a situation in your own future that might require a combination of these roles. (Cerebral Left – Facts and Cerebral Lower Left-Controlled)

1. Create a leader for the future who could deal with global issues. (Cerebral Right-Open Minded) and list probable causes of stress for your leader, as well as stress relievers he/ she could use.
   a. name of leader
   b. causes of stress
   c. stress relievers

Extenders:

- Select a method of stress reduction, which is new to you and explore it in depth. (Cerebral Right-Open Minded)
- Try using the method you selected for several days and report on the results to your classmates. (Cerebral Lower Left-Controlled)

LEADERSHIP: A SKILL THAT CAN BE TAUGHT

In many instances the seven exemplary lessons focus on a specific process students can apply in all of their studies. These processes include situations that require group decision-making skills, based on limited data, predicting activities using intuition, or problem-solving skills that introduce a range of creative thinking. The emphasis on group activities helps build a sense of community. According to Annemarie Roeper (1990), the learning community is the context that provides a safe harbor for the child to explore his or her place in the world. These types of activities provide opportunities for students to practice leadership skills sorely needed for success in the 21st century. Once students build their leadership skills, they can then be encouraged to seek other opportunities in the community to apply these skills. In all of the exemplary lessons, there is a need for sharing responses and results and this process is crucial. The types of engaging questions teachers ask after an activity can help students personally process elements dealing with group relationships and how to deal with different points of view during the activities. All of the lessons include extenders designed for students who demonstrate an avid interest in the topic. It has been my experience that once students begin recognizing their leadership skills, they frequently show greater motivation in engaging and challenging activities that further develop their intellectual gifts.

Concluding Thoughts

Research on the theories of leadership have evolved to include situational social change models based on the principles of situational leadership as a purposeful, collaborative, values-based process resulting in positive change. The Social Change Model (SCM) is demonstrated in the Roeper School in its daily collaborative interaction between faculty, students and staff. This type of leadership is a relational, transformative, process-oriented, learned, and change-directed phenomenon. The SCM model is particularly applicable for gifted students as it empowers individuals to address social change and socio-cultural issues. Gifted students want to make a difference and the Leadership Skills and Behavior Model (Sisk, 2010) can serve as a model to develop engaging curriculum in social science, earth science and environmental science, building on the Roeper School emphasis on independent study and online research and course offerings. This type of curriculum development can provide opportunities for the Roeper School students to become more aware of geopolitical tensions and environmental issues at the national and global level with the goal of working toward all nations living together peacefully and productively. Gifted students need skills of global awareness and global understanding to function in an increasingly interconnected global society. As Don Ambrose said later in this volume, "the Roeper School has a long and storied history…with its primary emphasis always on individual self-discovery and ethical navigation in the world" (p. 294). As Annemarie stressed "We are concerned with the whole impact of life on the young person and the impact the person will have on society. We are concerned with the development of 'self' and the interdependence of all 'selves'" (Roeper, 1990, p.15). The Roeper School will continue to be on the forefront of the 21st century with emphasis on global education and developing global citizens.

REFERENCES

Addison, L. (1984). *Investigation of the leadership abilities of intellectually gifted students*. Unpublished dissertation. Tampa, FL: University of South Florida.
Burke, J., Haworth, C., & Ware, W. (1982). Scale for rating behavioral characteristics of superior students: An investigation of factor structure, *Journal of Special Education, 16*, 477–485.
Bass, B. (1981). *Stogdill's handbook of leadership: A survey of theory and research*. New York, NY: Free Press.
Bean, S., & Karnes, F. A. (2001). Developing the leadership potential of gifted students, In F. A. Karnes & S. M. Bean (Eds.), *Methods and materials for teaching the gifted* (pp. 559–536). Waco, Tx: Prufrock Press.
Bloom, B. (1956). *Taxonomy of educational objectives: The classification of educational goals. Handbook I: Cognitive domain*. New York, NY: David McKay.
Burke, J., Harworth, C., & Wave, W. (1982), Scale for rating behavioral characteristics of superior students: An investigation of factor structure. *Journal of special Education, 16,* 477–485.

Calloway, W. (1985). The promises and paradoxes of leadership. *Directors and Boards, 9,* 12–16.
Costa, A. (2000). Teaching for intelligence. *Transforming Education, 18,* 22–30.
Costa, A., & Kallick, B. (2009). *Leading with habits of mind: 16 Essential Characteristics for success,* Alexandria, VA: ASCD.
Davis, G., & Rimm, S, (2004). *Education of the gifted and talented.* Boston, MA: Allyn & Bacon.
Day, D. (2001). Leadership Development: A review in context. *Leadership Quarterly, 11,* 581–613.
Dobosz, R., & Beaty, L. (1999). The relationship between athletic participation and high school students' leadership ability. *Adolescence, 34,* 215–220.
Eby, J. (1989). *Eby gifted behavior index (Administration Manual).* East Aurora, NY: D.O.K.
Eriksson, G.(2009). *Redefining giftedness in a contemporary African context.* Paper presented at the 18th World Conference for Gifted and Talented, Vancouver, Canada.
Friedman, P., Jenkins-Friedman, R., & Van Dyke, M. (1984). Identifying the leadership gifted: Self, peer or teacher nomination? *Roeper Review, 7,* 91–94.
Friedman, T. (2005). *The world is flat: A brief history of the 21st century.* New York, NY: Farrar, Strauss and Giroux.
Future Problem Solving Program. (2001). *Future problem solving program coach's handbook* (p. 15). Lexington, KY: Author.
Gardner, H. (1983). *Frames of mind.* New York, NY: Basic Books.
Gardner, H. (1990). *On leadership.* New York, NY: Free Press.
Gardner, H., & Scherner, M. (1999). The understanding pathway: A conversation with Howard Gardner. *Educational Leadership, 57*(3) 12–16.
Gardner, H. (2000). *Intelligence reframed: Multiple intelligences for the 21st century.* New York, NY: Basic Books.
Gillian, J., Carpenter, B., & Christensen, J. (1996). *Gifted and talented evaluation scales.* Austin, TX: Pro-Ed.
Guastello, S. (1995). Facilitating style, individual innovation, and emergent leadership in problem solving groups. *Journal of Creative Behavior, 29,* 225–239.
Guilford, J. P. (1967). *The nature of human intelligence.* New York, NY: McGraw Hill.
Guilford, J. P. (1981). *Way beyond IQ.* Buffalo, NY: Creative Education Foundation.
Hakala, D. (2008). The top 10 leadership qualities. *HR World.* Retrieved from www.HRworld.com
Hart, L., Mahan, G., Creney, C., & Homefield, C. (2003). *Building leadership skills in middle school girls through interscholastic activities.* ERIC Counseling and student services Clearinghouse
Hart, L. (2002). *Middle School-aged female interscholastic soccer players and their academic achievements, leadership position attachments and extracurricular club/group participation.* Unpublished Master's Thesis, Kean Univ., Union, NJ.
Hartman, R. K. (1969). *Teachers' identification of student learners.* Unpublished paper, University of Connecticut, Storrs.
Higher Education Research Institute [HERI]. (1996). *A social change model of leadership development: Guidebook version III,* College Park MD: National Clearinghouse of Leadership Programs.
Herrman, N. (1999). *The creative brain.* Lake Lure, NC: Brain Books.
Hersey, P., & Blanchard, K. (1982). Leadership style: Attitudes and behaviors. *Training and Development Journal, 36,* 50–52.
Hogan, R., Curphy, G., & Hogan, J. (1994). What do we know about personality: Leadership and effectiveness? *American Psychologist, 49,* 493–504.
Hollander, E. (1964). *Leaders, groups and influence.* New York, NY: Oxford University Press.
Jacob K. Javits Gifted & Talented Students Education Act. (1988). P. L. 100–297. Title IV, Part B, Sec. 1101.
Jolly, J., & Kettler, T. (2004). Authentic assessment of leadership in problem-solving groups. *Gifted Child Today, 27*(1), 32–39.
Karnes, F. A., & Chauvin, J. C. (1985). *Leadership skills inventory.* Scottsdale, AZ: Gifted Psychology Press.
Karnes, F. A., & Chauvin, J. C (2000). *Leadership development program.* Scottsdale, AZ: Gifted Psychology Press.

Karnes, F., & Zimmerman, M. (2001). Employing visual learning to enhance the leadership of the gifted. *Gifted Child Today*, *24*(1), 56–61.

Karnes, F., & Bean, S. (2009). Developing the leadership potential of gifted students. In F. Karnes & S. Bean (Eds.), *Methods & Materials for Teaching the Gifted* (pp. 593–628). Waco, TX: Prufrock Press.

Kezar, A., Carducci, R., & Contreras-McGavin, M. (2006). Rethinking the "L" word in higher education: The revolution in research on leadership. *ASHE Higher Education Report*, Vol. 31, #6. San Francisco, CA: Jossey-Bass.

Khatena, J., & Morse, D. (1994). *Khatena-Morse multitalent perception inventory*. Bensonville, IL: Scholastic Testing Service.

Lassey, W., & Fernandez, R. (1976). Dimensions of leadership. *Leadership and Social Change* (pp. 10–15). La Jolla, CA: University Associates.

Lee, S., & Olszewski-Kubilius, P (2006). The emotional intelligence, moral judgment, and leadership of academically gifted adolescents. *Journal for the Education of the Gifted*, *30*, 29–67.

Lewin, K., Lippit, R., & White, R. (1939). Patterns of aggressive behavior in experimentally created social climates. *Journal of Social Psychology, 10*, 271–299.

Lipper, A. (1985). *Leadership: Making things happen*. Buffalo, NY: Bearly.

Marland, S. P. (1972). *Education of the gifted and talented: Report to the Congress of the United States by the U.S. Commissioner of Education and background papers submitted to the U.S. Office of Education*, 2 vols. Washington, DC: U. S. Government Printing office (Government documents, Y4.L 11/2: G36).

Martin, A. (2007). *The changing nature of leadership*. Greensboro, NC: Center for Creative Leadership.

Matthews, M. (2004). Leadership education for gifted and talented youth: A review of the literature. *Journal for the Education of the Gifted. 28*, 77–113.

McGregor, D. (1960). *The human side of enterprise*. New York, NY: McGraw-Hill.

Milligan, J. (2004). Leadership skills of gifted students in a rural setting: Promising programs for leadership development [Electronic version]. *Rural Special Education Quarterly*. Retrieved September 12, 2010, from http://findarticles.com/p/articles/mi_qa4052/is_200401/ai_n9369127.

Mintzberg, H. (1994, January-February). The fall and rise of strategic planning. *Harvard Business Review*, 107–114.

Passig, D. (2004). Future time span as cognitive skill in future studies. *Futures Research Quarterly, 19*, 27–47.

Renzulli, J. (1977). *The enrichment of triad model: A guide for defensible programs for the gifted and talented*. Mansfield Center, CT: Creative Learning Press.

Renzulli, J., Smith, L., Callahan, C., Hartman, R., & Westberg, K. (2002). *Scales for rating the behavioral characteristics of superior students-Revised edition*. Mansfield Center, CT: Creative Learning Press.

Richardson, W., & Feldhusen, J. (1987). *Leadership education: Developing skills for youth*. Monrop, NY: Trillium Press.

Roeper A., & Roeper, G. (1981). *Roeper philosophy*. Unpublished Manuscript.

Roeper, A. (1990). *Educating children for life: The Modern learning community*. Minneapolis, MN: Free Spirit Publishing.

Roets, L. (1986). *Roets rating scale for leadership*. Des Moines, IA: Leadership Publishers.

Scharmer, O. (2009). *Ten Propositions on transforming the current leadership development paradigm*. Amherst, MA: Massachusetts Institute of Technology.

Schraa-Liu, T., & Tropenaars, F. (2006). Toward responsible leadership through reconciling dilemmas. In T. Maak & N. M. Pless (Eds.), *Responsible leadership* (pp. 138–14). Arlington, Oxon: Routledge.

Senge, P. M. (2003). Creating desired futures in a global economy. *Reflections, 5*, 1–12.

Shane, M. (2009). Annemarie Roeper: Nearly a century with giftedness. In S. Daniels & M. Piechowski (Eds.), *Living with intensity* (pp. 185–202). Scottsdale AZ: Great Potential Press.

Singh, N. (2003). How global is the curriculum? *Educational Leadership, 60*(2), 38–41.

Sisk, D. (1985). *Sisk model for developing leadership*. Tampa, FL: Center for Creativity, Innovation and Leadership, University of South Florida.

Sisk, D., & Shallcross, D. J. (1986*). Leadership: Making things happen*. Buffalo, NY: Bearly.

Sisk, D. (1987). Leadership skills and behavior scale. In *Leadership: A special type of giftedness*. Monroe, NY: Trillium Press.

Sisk, D., & Rosselli, H. (1987). *Leadership; A special type of giftedness.* Monroe, NY Trillium Press.
Sisk, D. (2010). *Texas Governor's School Final Report.* Texas Higher Education Coordinating Board, Austin, Texas.
Stephens, K., & Karnes, F. (2000). State definitions of the gifted and talented revisited. *Exceptional Children, 66,* 219–238.
Sternberg, R. J., & Lubart, T. I. (1995). *Defying the crowd: Cultivating creativity in a culture of conformity.* New York, NY: The Free Press.
Sternberg, R. J. (1999), *Wisdom, intelligence, and creativity synthesized.* Cambridge, MA: Cambridge University Press.
Sternberg, R. J., Kaufman, J. C., & Pretz J. E. (2002). *The creativity conundrum: A propulsion model of kinds of creative contributions.* New York, NY: Psychology Press.
Sternberg, R. J. (2005). A model of educational leadership: Wisdom, intelligence, and creativity synthesized. *International Journal of Leadership in Education: Theory & Practice. 8,* 347–364.
Stephens, K., & Karnes, F. (2000). State definitions of the gifted and talented revisited. *Exceptional Children, 66,* 219–238.
Stogdill, P. (1974). *A handbook of leadership: A survey of theory and research.* New York, NY: Free Press.
Svoboda, S., & Whalen, J. (2005). Using experiential simulation to teach sustainability. *Greener Management International, 48,* 57–65.
Tannenbaum, R., Weschler, I., & Massarch, F. (1961). *Leadership and organization: A behavioral science approach.* New York, NY: McGraw-Hill.
Taylor, C. (1978). How many types of giftedness can your program tolerate? *Journal of Creative Behavior, 12,* 39–51.
Watt, S. (1997). *Introduction: The theory of forms (Book 5–7) Plato's Republic,* London, England: Wordsworth Edition.
Wagner, W. (2006). The social change model of leadership: A brief overview. *Concepts & Connections, 15*(1), 9.
Williams, F. (1970). *Classroom for encouraging thinking and feeling.* Buffalo, NY: D.O.K.

LISA BAKER

EMERGING LEADERS

Believing in Children and Building Leadership Capacity Over Time

The primary purpose of The Roeper School, as stated in our mission, is to develop "independent thinkers who are constructive and caring" and to be a place that "not only prepares, but also allows, each child to make meaningful decisions and solve important problems." Teachers are expected to "embrace the value of authentic relationships with students and treat them as intellectual partners." Our school philosophy aligns with Aristotelian belief in the "ethical leader" as well as in Martin Buber's focus on the critical importance of relationship. Hollander (1964) described leadership as a "relationship between those who are exerting influence and those who are being influenced" (p. 1). Although George and Annemarie Roeper retired in the early 1980s, we continue to live by the ideals that the Roepers shared with Dr. Dorothy Sisk when she visited in the 1970s: ideals that empower The Roeper School to be a place where leadership is fostered and allowed to flourish.

In observing Roeper students, it can be difficult to tell where the "leader" exists because students often shift between exerting influence and being influenced. Most are comfortable in either role, and uncommon leaders often emerge. We are interested in developing leadership skill and potential in all students rather than limiting such attention to the nominative leaders such as the Class President, Student Government officers, or team captains. We recognize that leadership is not a single act exerted on an unsuspecting follower. Rather, leadership requires a deep understanding of cooperation, a respect for interdependence, a belief in our ability to influence our own destinies, and the ability to take responsibility for our own actions.

Building these skills takes years of practice, trial and error, discussion, direction, and coaching. It also requires that our institution remain open to the needs of individual students and that we stay attuned to their specific goals and priorities. We must honor them in word and in deed. Werner Roennecke, Class of 2011 and Roeper student for 13 years, says, "I think that the Roeper experience and world view isn't something that can be attained in one year or two years. I feel like it's been a gradual shaping." Werner is a reserved and unassuming young man who might be overlooked as a potential leader. Yet he proposed a unique Senior Project—to spend a year studying in Argentina. Werner worried that he had grown too comfortable and wanted to force himself to live in a different country, master a new language, and confront some of his own fears. Convincing the adults around him was no simple task. Werner had to clarify his own rationale regarding the plan he had for his senior year and articulate why his needs were different from that of the rest of the class. Ultimately, he was successful, and after six months in Argentina he reflected, "This has helped me find my determination for sure, my drive. It's brought me to realize there is no mountain too high to climb…it's made me much more comfortable talking to new people." Leaders must challenge assumptions, know themselves deeply, and be willing to navigate uncharted territories. Werner's leadership skills emerged over time—he is an uncommon leader.

Many institutions wait until adolescence to begin leadership-training programs. The Roeper School begins to build leadership capacity from the start of their school careers. Each day, students develop a sense of individual and collective responsibility. Lower School teachers employ some form of "leader for the day" procedure in the classroom. The "leader for the day" might lead morning meetings, facilitate discussions, explain and model homeroom traditions, or share stories. Even the most shy and reserved child is given this chance to stand in front of his or her peers—and comes to understand it as an opportunity as well as a responsibility.

The multi-aged groupings in our Lower School homerooms provide the opportunity for students to practice leadership skills with their peers. Amber Webb, Stage I (ages 3–5) teacher, points out, "Second year students demonstrate procedures and routines . . . the following year, the younger students remember how 'cool' it was to have the big kids help them, and they can't wait to do the same." The experience of alternating between being the "first year" student being acclimated and welcomed by their more experienced peers and the "second year" student who is expected to show additional responsibility and to be a guide for their new classmates provides the groundwork for leadership development. As one seven-year-old "second year" student said on the first day of school, "This is going to be a tough year. I can't just look after myself. Now I have to look out for the first years too. I may be tired when I get home."

This sense of care taking and responsibility for others is continued in the Middle and Upper School. For example, students often tutor one another in structured environments such as the Resource Room or Math Support, but these alliances can be seen in informal settings as well: in the Student Life Center, students debrief assignments in the midst of debating issues of the day, trading insights on the music they have just discovered, and planning the evening's activities. The value of this collaboration to the students who need academic help is somewhat obvious, but the benefit to the tutors is equally rich: they gain an increased capacity for dexterous and creative thinking as well as sensitivity to the needs of their peers. Math teacher Christina Miceli observes:

> The Upper School students [tutors] practice listening first and then acting… they have to assess the needs of the group and act accordingly. When their explanation doesn't make sense they must try a different approach. . . . They practice being assertive without talking down to younger students. They

demonstrate openness because the sixth graders will often have a new approach to a problem that could counter how the Upper School student has always done it. Finally, they are excellent motivators and always find ways to encourage the students with whom they are working.

The importance of interdependence, compassion, and empathy as components of leadership cannot be overstated. Roeper students understand themselves as a part of the whole. Colleen Shelton, Stage I teacher (ages 3–5), points out that students are encouraged to "find their voice from day one." Teachers help them to learn to "speak up to others, especially if they are upset or feel 'wronged.'" Students are constantly encouraged to ask questions and to advocate for themselves. They understand their strengths and can quickly articulate the strengths of their peers. Even those in elected leadership roles such as Student Board Member or Class President rely on their classmates for support and assistance. When teachers ask students to take the lead or make a presentation, students will often suggest that one of their classmates is better suited for the job—and they are often right. These students are not shirking responsibility or afraid to step forward, rather they understand who is most skilled and are confident enough in themselves and value the benefit to the community more than the "spotlight" they might experience individually. A "winner take all" mentality is not a part of the culture at Roeper. Cathy Wilmers, Stage III (grades 2–3), points out:

> Our aim is to support each child in working through their own understanding of who they are and what qualities they possess. . . . We do not limit our definition of leadership. Some children lead through example (for example, sitting calmly in a meeting), while others lead by keeping a reasonable pace as they lead morning meeting. Others may be tuned into classmates' feelings and check in with them if they are needing a little TLC.

Our definitions of *leader* and *leadership skills* are broad, as we expect that our students will be asked to play many roles in their lives. We also expect that students will need to continue to practice these skills as they move into adolescence and early adulthood. Most students are comfortable working alone—the more difficult, less controlled challenge, involves working together. Teachers create projects that are novel and require students to recognize that leadership is a collaborative effort. In Eighth Grade Health, for example, students engage in a mock job application process in which they must come to consensus about who to hire for their "department." The class works to have individual voices heard while building consensus. Through each experience, students build their own capacity, and on occasion, teachers witness a moment of transformation, or at least the beginning of it. Colleen Potocki, Middle School English teacher, recounts the reaction of one of her seventh-grade students during their extensive film festival project:

> Max uttered one of my favorite film festival work-in-progress lines. His film group suffered much initial group dysfunction but rallied to a beautiful close when they became comfortable depending on each other. Max said, 'Hey, did

you know Ryan is a genius?' Ryan was sitting in the room with us. Skilled at editing, both boys realized their need and respect for the other. They had redefined what is needed for leading a project to conclusion: shared leadership and collaboration.

Working as a part of a team can be challenging and often frustrating. Gifted students often like to prove their individual intellectual prowess, and many relish the chance to engage in verbal banter that ends by defeating their challenger. Working in groups allows these students to practice a skill set that is required in the world beyond school in a world that needs gifted minds to work collaboratively and to find solutions to large-scale problems.

Collaborative learning is one element of an educational program that encourages students to become flexible and adroit in approaching challenges. However, a singularly social approach to learning would be limited to developing that sharp intellect, just as simply providing a caring and nurturing environment would be insufficient in supporting emerging leaders. The Roeper School is a school for gifted students. The depth of their understanding, the quality of their thinking, and the intensity of their experiences with intellectual work cannot be ignored. These students must be challenged and provided the opportunity to solve real-world problems or they will disengage no matter how strong our process or caring our environment.

Emma Kirby, Class of 2012, reflects:

> Empathy and leadership are not simply boxes waiting to be checked. They are not skills that are gained through the completion of some precious Roeper experience. . . . These qualities are not fostered by treating high school as an audition for college. . . . The goal of a school founded on humanist principles is to foster traits such as compassion, but it is not something that is done with a pithy and approachable speech. It is something that is accomplished through strenuous intellectual labor and intelligence.

Annemarie Roeper believed that Adolf Hitler was likely a gifted child who was not provided with appropriate emotional support and guidance. Although this could be interpreted as hyperbole, Hitler's misguided intellectual power was a part of George and Annemarie's 1957 decision to shift the focus of their school to educating gifted students. They wanted to help the gifted understand interdependence, and they challenged teachers to help students avoid the "perceived self interests…which represents thinking in short term rather than long term effects" that Dr. Sisk points out. The Roeper School is not a specialized leadership training school. Rather it is a school where teachers believe in the capacity of all students to share leadership. In describing his experience of leadership on the Model United Nations team, Joey LoCascio, Class of 2011, points out,

> Leadership derives itself from mutual respect, not from titles or the abilities of a leader to force his will on someone he leads. The result is a collaboration

that is enjoyable and frictionless. Our minds function better in the intellectual stimulation of MUN when we are not hampered by the hierarchy of an overly-rigid leadership apparatus.

Roeper teachers endeavor to set this example of collaboration coupled with intellectual rigor; they foster an environment where students develop their leadership skills gradually while strengthening their individual abilities.

Werner Roenneke has said that Roeper allows students to build their own personal rocket ships piece by piece, so that by the time they graduate, they are ready to take off on their own journey. If the Center for Creative Leadership, described by Dorothy Sisk in this volume, is correct in their prediction that leadership success in the future will be collaborative and focused on a "team rather than an individual" then Roeper graduates are poised for success because they practice it every day.

REFERENCE

Hollander, E. P. (1964). *Leaders, groups, and influence*. New York, NY: Oxford University Press.

EMERY PENCE

LEADERSHIP AT THE ROEPER SCHOOL

My intention in this chapter is to discuss what kind of leader best creates an optimal learning environment for gifted students facing the crazy, challenging 21st-century and best does so in accordance to the Roeper philosophy. The discussion here is based on my years serving as a formal and informal leader at Roeper, from reading the words of George and Annemarie Roeper, and from conducting focus-group discussions with groups of Roeper leaders. Below is a list of these leaders and their roles in our school and community:

- Peter Roeper: Former student and son of George and Annemarie Roeper.
- Mary Windram: Retired teacher after 29 years of making the Roeper philosophy work in the Lower School, and parent of an alumna.
- Doug Winkworth: Parent of an alumnus. Former chair of the Board of Trustees.
- Dick Halsey: Former Roeper teacher and administrator in the 1960s and 1970s. Later became Headmaster of Kingsbury School and Executive Director of the Association of Independent Michigan Schools.
- Randall Dunn: Father of two former students and, at the time of the discussion, Headmaster of Roeper. Presently Head of the Latin School of Chicago.
- Denita Banks-Sims: Mother of two alumni and Development Office Head for many years.
- Patrick O'Connor: Alumnus, former Roeper math teacher and college counselor, and parent of two alumni.
- Steve Milbeck: Father of two alumni and Chair of the Board of Trustees as of this writing.
- Mary Ellen Gurewitz: Mother of an alumnus and former Chair of the Board of Trustees.
- Marcia Ruff: Mother of an alumna and current School Historian.
- Belal Ezzedine: Alumnus who is currently an attorney after attending the University of Michigan and the University of Virginia Law School.
- Lori Lutz: Alumna, mother of two alumnae, and former Chair of the Board of Trustees.

To read a transcript of their discussion around Roeper leadership please go to <http://www.roeper.org/leadership-video?> or email me at emery.pence@roeper.org. The transcripts are quite enlightening.

I dedicate this chapter to David Feldman, the new headmaster of Roeper. Hopefully, it will help him as he leads our school and community forward. Thanks to School Historian Marcia Ruff, my partner-in-thought and proofreading wordsmith who always keeps me on my intellectual toes.

Before delving into the specifics of leadership at the Roeper School, it's important to frame the discussion with some pertinent comments generated by the school's founders, George and Annemarie Roeper (from the 1981 Roeper philosophy):

> Within this structure not only the role of the members of the community but also that of the leadership (board of trustees, administrators) becomes differently defined. The trustees are the guardians of the philosophy, the administrators its chief implementers. This also requires a different type of skills and attitude on the part of leadership. For this leadership is not based on the authority vested in the power on the top of the hierarchy, but rather on the confidence in the expertise and goodwill of the leaders. It requires skills to establish open communication and respect in the constituency, as well as their legitimate participation in decision making. Only those who are affected by a decision experience its consequences and therefore should participate in reaching it in some form, and to the extent they are able. It included the obligation to be continually aware of the rights of each individual and maintain a balance between all of those individual rights. It requires leadership which sees the members of the community as models for the children and sees the living environment and the overall atmosphere as a part of the education program for the child. It includes a commitment to mutual responsibility and therefore a realistic system of mutual accountability and evaluation. Such a philosophy can only function if it is expressed in the attitudes and feelings of the members of the community. These can only grow and develop if the government structure represents the philosophy. It includes a commitment to a pluralistic society, which means the constituency, the leadership and the staff represent all racial, religious and economic groups. It means careful working toward a goal, which diminishes economic restrictions as far as realistically possible.

Traditional views of leadership with an emphasis on top-down decision making are wholly inappropriate and potentially disastrous in the education of gifted students, whom we want to be the leaders and problem solvers in the rapidly changing world with its huge challenges. We need leaders who are inspirers, communicators, consensus-builders, visionaries, empowerers, and culture-creators.

Effective leadership at Roeper has to take three elements into consideration: the characteristics of gifted children, the nature of the world for which we are preparing them, and the attributes that George and Annemarie believed were necessary to achieve the outcome they sought—confident, compassionate, self-aware gifted adults who are dedicated to working for justice and a better world.

Let's start with characteristics of the gifted as we commonly think of that term at the school. I recognize that "giftedness" is a contested construct but the descriptions

I provide below represent elements of an operational definition for much of the work we do. (Note that much of what I am going to put forward would be of use in creating empowered, confident citizens, gifted or otherwise, of a global society.) I am loathe to generalize about giftedness or anything else as I'm an educator who works with the people and circumstances as they are; reification is my enemy. When I start to generalize about giftedness, a student will gently remind me, "Emery, you have known me since I was six. Don't call me gifted; my name is *Ian,* or at least it will be until next week when I might change it to *Josh."* But as long as we keep reminding ourselves not to take our operational definitions as gospel, we can use them to remind ourselves that many of our students do share some common characteristics.

So, here goes. *Gifted kids are idealistic, have high standards of right and wrong, and worry a lot about justice.* Just because they don't always live up to their own high standards doesn't negate these high standards; it just means they will be upset about their shortcomings. They can be our society's resource—our moral leaders and creators of a more just society. Or, they can be disillusioned, cynical and/or depressed people whose vision and idealism are wasted or perverted.

Could Hitler, a dreaming, brilliant young boy, have been saved by going to Roeper, circa 1900? We won't know for sure until I get the time machine in the basement functioning, but even if the answer is "no," maybe education that offers what we do could help develop others who could help offset the damage of the Hitlers and others so emotionally wounded.

Back to overgeneralizing. *Gifted people have minds that make quick connections and delve deeper into matters than do the minds of most people.* Ideas and thinking mean a lot to them. Their intellectual and emotional intensity runs deep; they are passionate and feel things intensely. Their self-identity can be based on their ideas and what they belief and think. So, sometimes when faced with opposing ideas, it threatens their sense of who they are. Open-mindedness and compromise can seem like self-betrayal. Disagreement can sometimes mean to a gifted child that the other person is stupid or, perhaps, just doesn't understand the idea so why not express it louder? Intense, opinionated people are not always the most likely candidates for collaboration or for being invited to a lot of parties. To deal with this kind of intensity and the resulting chance of being hurt by social exclusion, gifted individuals sometimes retreat into their shells. This is not always bad but can be lonely and isn't the best avenue for enabling their wonderful ideas to benefit society.

Next, we are educating our gifted students to survive and hopefully thrive in an increasingly complex world. What is the world going to be like when they graduate? What skills and qualities will they need to be successful in it? Already the world is fast-paced and rapidly changing. Old answers can't keep up. Too much information is like a wind that blows out the flame rather than nourishing it. We are coming into both real and virtual contact with people from around the world. I think of my granddaughter, who at 3 ½ is on the computer, has friends and relatives of different ethnicities, religions, and backgrounds; enjoys sushi; and loves Johnny Cash. Contrast that to me as a 5th grader in 1960 who had never had Mexican food, let alone raw fish, went to school with all Protestants (actually, all Baptists) and loved Johnny Cash. Back then most dads I knew worked for General Motors for 30 years and then retired. Those days are gone, and more exciting, challenging ones have replaced them.

So, what do we have to do to get kids ready for such a free-for-all world of environmental threats, economic uncertainty, and change, change, change? First and foremost, people can't be afraid, or at least not paralyzed. Needing to look for opportunity in the challenges and to embrace life instead of hunkering down, individuals facing the "undiscovered country" (Hamlet was referring to death with this phrase, but I like to think of it as referring to the journey to the future) will need to be confident if they are to be self-fulfilled and to work for a better world.

Similarly, students need to have hope and to feel empowered. They need to be active, not passive. For those who quickly detect the shortcomings of all possible solutions, it becomes imperative that they learn what they can do and learn to accept that insisting on a perfect solution is a trap, not a way forward.

Besides factoring in the general characteristics of the gifted, as operationally defined here, and what we need to do to help kids get ready for an already-arrived crazy world, we also need to describe the Roeper philosophy if we are to discuss what a Roeper leader should be and do.

The Roeper philosophy can be summed up as an approach to education and life oriented towards helping individuals create and/or find their authentic selves in a communal context—to become healthy, self-actualized human beings working together to make a better world. This type of person would be more likely not to follow (or be) a Hitler. Our school was founded by German refugees to prevent holocausts.

From this emphasis on the individual and the community, we then develop "roots and shoots." These are the characteristics of an education and community that both support healthy individuals and community ("roots"), and are also the results of them ("shoots").

The Roeper philosophy considers a number of characteristics as critical to making this journey possible:

- *Respect* is an overused term but it is the best one-word summary for treating others as equal and independent human beings, not as abstractions or objects to be manipulated. We discover our own humanity and individuality through recognizing the humanity and individuality of others and helping others find theirs.
- *Authentic relationships,* which are derived from, as well as built on, respect. Especially important are *healthy relationships between adults and students,* for kids need to trust themselves and their environment in order to accept challenges and take risks. This is a lot more likely when they have a teacher, coach, or custodian to talk to and have as backup in times of adversity. An alumnus I talked to this summer recounted how when he "came out" as gay in the late 1990s as a

Roeper student, he had four teachers who helped him deal with it. It is telling that he referred to them as "friends" rather than teachers.
- *Safety,* emotional and physical, is necessary for folks to explore, try things, make mistakes, change, reach out to others, and do whatever else is needed for growth.
- Empowerment comes when people have the skills, knowledge, and confidence to feel like they are in charge of their own education and own lives. The *conditions to build a sense of empowerment* are derived from experiences, both positive and negative, and from reflecting on those experiences. Self-esteem and empowerment are not given but earned by being an active creator rather than a passive recipient.
- *Collaboration* is needed because individuals require others to respect and facilitate their journeys of growth. And, to build a better world, we will need to band together to utilize our passions and strengths. We are social animals and unless we plan on living on desert islands talking with volleyballs, we will need to have experience working with others, having conflicts and learning from them, and reveling in coming together. Skills and practice in being an involved member of a democratic learning community is great practice for being an involved member of a democratic society.
- Self-knowledge and the ability to manage one's education and to grow are critical outcomes. They can only be obtained by being given *opportunities to reflect and define oneself.* To go beyond being an object to be manipulated, be it by political leaders, advertisers, or that mean girl in the cafeteria, requires a lot of safe opportunities to ponder and contemplate and plan the next course of action.
- *Freedom* is an absolute necessity if one is to practice taking responsibility for one's self. Messy and fraught with conflict as it is, it's important to give kids appropriate space and opportunity to take charge in the "lab class" that makes all the Roeper experience real and relevant. We adults may want to avoid hassle for ourselves and pain for our students, but the students won't grow unless they face real challenges with real consequences. We shouldn't (and can't anyway) always protect them from themselves. After they stumble, we have to dust them off and let them go again. In addition, the presence of a democratic structure helps them learn how to be responsible not just for themselves, but also for their community.

Some people have been mystified by the Roeper philosophy as I have just described it. They think it sounds too dreamy and general to be of much use in running a school and community. How can it be applied on a day-to-day basis?

If you think of the central tenets and the "roots and shoots" as commonly held values and reference points embraced by the entire community, then we need a way to make them concrete and relevant to the day-to-day experience. How can the abstract and general Roeper philosophy guide us in making decisions? What could serve as the functional link between the Philosophy and making it real in a community?

Individuals and groups have to, with the Philosophy always in mind, continuously come together to create a new reality and new community. The Philosophy is something we not only *have* but *do.* The lessons of the past and the tenets of belief combine with the realities of the present to help create a new school and new community on a daily basis.

We sometimes say that our only non-negotiable is that we have to negotiate. Obviously, there isn't the time and energy to talk everything out to every last person's satisfaction on every last issue and you can't revisit every decision every day. According to folks at Roeper in the early 1970s, such as former administrator Dick Halsey, we lost some top-notch teachers and administrators who were burnt-out from having to talk everything to death. A more realistic approach is to foster the belief that every opportunity, every decision, even every disaster is a talkable moment that strengthens both the individual and the community—while knowing and accepting that not every opportunity will be usable. Our default position and first alternative is, as it says in the Book of Isaiah, "Come, let us reason together."

The limits of time and energy and the need to move forward will always pull us away from a crazy insistence on perfection. Doug Winkworth, former Board of Trustees Head, remembers the time when a very elderly Annemarie and a very hobbled Doug were using the Birmingham campus elevator and she noticed that it required a code for operation. She asked him if the students all had the code. Doug said the elevator was for the use of those who needed it and, so, no, only some people had the code. Annemarie questioned how people could be taught to handle responsibility if they didn't have the chance to talk about it and the freedom to handle it or not. Doug thought to himself, "Doesn't this lady ever relax?" We need Annemaries and uppity seventh graders with a copy of the Roeper philosophy to keep reminding us why we do what we do. But we need to be able to agree on how to pick and choose which discussions to have and how often to revisit them.

Buddhists believe that we should apply three criteria to judge whether work (or any activity) is meaningful and should be undertaken. They are in order of ascending importance:

3. Does the action get the immediate job done?
2. Does the action build community?
1. Does the action help individuals learn and grow?

I believe we focus too much on No. 3 in our haste to be efficient and to mark off the job as done.

PUTTING IT ALL TOGETHER

So, what does all this about giftedness, the future, and the Roeper philosophy mean for what a leader in our school and community must be able to be and do? A Roeper leader must realize that it not about him or her—it is about a community of individuals who are travelling down a road both individually and together. You can't control the educational outcomes if education truly belongs to the student. Empowering means empowering and serving others, not gaining power for yourself. As former student Peter Roeper said, "Roeper leaders shouldn't be too impressed with their own power. My parents didn't set the school up on a 'power-based' approach. They worked towards shared decision-making." Doug Winkworth added that at Roeper it usually isn't a matter of assumed power over the community but authority granted by the community.

It helps a Roeper leader keep his or her eyes on the prize to remember why he or she is in the position—to help people and the community get stronger and to grow. When I was guiding my 6-year-old daughter from behind as she was learning to ride a bike and then she wobbled away from me on her own, I was both sad that she didn't need me as much but proud that she didn't need me as much. My job was to help her become a strong, separate human being. Beware of the educational leader who needs to be the star, power centre, or decider in order to fulfill a need to be needed. Better she or he be a "leader-servant," committed to building others up so they can be stronger and do more.

I can hear a reader out there saying, "But doesn't somebody need to make decisions?" Of course, but do you really think that the biggest problem is that smart, strong leaders aren't making decisions? Smart, strong leaders can sometimes make decisions to make it easy for themselves: increase enrollment or avoid conflict? The trick is learning how to make decisions efficiently that also build strong individuals and strong community.

A Roeper leader can best work towards our goals by helping create the atmosphere and milieu in which people grow and develop and help others grow and develop. A farmer preps the soil, waters the crops, and manages the weeds, but the plants themselves do the growing. Traditionally, we have thought of a leader as only a decider—the one where the buck stops. There are times, of course, with emergencies or with the total breakdown of consensus that a leader will have to be primarily a decision maker. But that is usually because there has been a failure of vision, preparation, and organization that finally necessitated such directive action.

The leader needs to be an inspirer—one who models the ability to listen, compromise, take risks, apologize, work hard, and generally be an adult. He or she constantly reminds people what our beliefs and principles are, why they are important, and how they pertain to the situation at hand. Sometimes, the leader believes in folks when they don't believe in themselves.

Keeping an open mind, the leader talks to people, seeks information, and shares that information and generally elevates the conversation. To do this, a *consensus builder* leader needs to be intellectually curious, humble, and emotionally secure. The leader realizes that the collective judgment of the community, if properly harvested, can offer much wisdom, and that people who are consulted before a decision is made are more likely to be on board when that decision is implemented. We go forward together if leaders realize that mobilizing the community to pull together is a lot more effective than pushing it towards something they don't agree to or understand.

At a leadership seminar I was asked to visualize a pictorial metaphor to represent what I did as a leader. After flirting with the images of throwing my body into the gears of a giant machine to lubricate it or frantically twirling plates on rods on the Ed Sullivan Show, I settled on the more comforting (and hopefully, more accurate) metaphor of a telephone linesman who strings wires to connect people. One of our jobs is to build a synergy of folks working together. Just as the linesman doesn't have to listen in to every phone conversation, a leader can connect people and then let them work things out without the need to micromanage. Of course, a little maintenance of the connection here and there is always necessary.

Being a leader requires being a communicator who can sum up and convey the sense of the community, the mission of the institution, the realities of the situation, and the dreams of all. He or she needs to invent new and better ways to get the message out while also facilitating the communication of others. Obviously, a person with great communicative abilities has power for good or bad. A leader who truly respects others and who is grounded in our Philosophy will not manipulate, lie to, or mislead no matter how powerful his or her skills of communication, for to do so would be disrespectful and humanity-denying.

In addition to the attributes and behaviors listed earlier, what's required for such leadership? Most important is someone with an emotionally secure and psychologically strong personality who isn't threatened by the empowerment of others, by disagreement, or by the messiness of people growing. Dick Halsey, former Roeper administrator, pointed out that George and Annemarie taught our community respect and openness by modeling it every day and in every way. Even though they did some radical things, such as integrating our school before other schools, they were such friendly and warm people who minimized conflicts and disarmed potential enemies.

Roeper leaders as well as our community must always be growing. As veteran Roeper teacher Mary Windram observed, "A Roeper person, especially one in a leadership person, must constantly be reflecting and learning about one's self as well as learning from others."

Also crucial is a sense of integrity, for without it, the community will not trust and follow the leader. Any person or group of people foolish enough to think that our community will not see that "the Emperor has no clothes" if they cut ethical corners, will soon learn that trust lost is trust difficult to recover. Denita Banks, Roeper's Head of Development, noted that a Roeper leader needs to be a person of integrity who shows consistency of character to all people in all situations.

This person has to deeply understand our core values and beliefs and be able to keep them in everybody's consciousness as we work towards making our school and community more aligned with them. Patience, trust in the Roeper philosophy and process, and the ability to think long-term, combined with a sense of humour, are prerequisites for anybody trying to survive the day while working towards the creation of the conditions for a vibrant, strong community of learners in the year 2030.

Current and Future Challenges for Roeper Leadership

School historian Marcia Ruff pointed out that both George and Annemarie are gone and many of those who knew them personally have (or will, shortly) also be leaving Roeper. How do we make sure that the nuanced, complex, hard-to-reduce-to-a-bumper-sticker Roeper philosophy is passed on to be lived by future generations?

How can Roeper leaders (or anybody else) plan for a future that is so unknown, complex, and evolving? I understand that the future has always and will always be unknown, but the rapidity of change and the chaos of the 21st century make it hard for anyone to even have a clue what it might become. Programming students like robots will not work in the face of uncertainty, but helping folks become nimble, creative, and confident just might.

Roeper is bucking some current trends in education. The chimeras of standardized testing and technology worship are just two examples of bandwagons that Roeper is being pushed to join. We need to take a close look at what testing and technology are offering and see if any of it gets us closer to our goals and cores. Roeper shouldn't be provincial and insular, nor should it be faddish.

Societal influences on our school are knocking louder and louder on our doors. How can we deal with some of the more negative influences affecting our kids, their families, and our school? How can we keep the school diverse in all ways and still be financially sustainable? How can we keep Roeper affordable?

Are there dangers or difficulties in pursuing a Roeper kind of leadership? Since so much of the leadership rests on the need for a strong individual who is constantly balancing, talking, listening, deciding, inspiring, connecting—an artist of leadership rather than a manager—it could lead to burn-out or to overreliance on a single personality. I won't go as far as paraphrasing the Buddhists to say, "If you see George Roeper on the road, kill him," meaning that no one holds all the truth and don't create idols. Exalting one person upon high can be avoided if authority and decision-making power are spread around. There needs to be a strong, conscious attempt to create new leadership, well versed in the concepts and practices of modern leadership theory. The leader should be looking to discover and empower new leaders, be they students, parents, staff, or Board members. The best leader would be the one who works himself or herself out of a job, or at least one who is not at the centre of all attention. Former Headmaster Randall Dunn never sensed that a success or failure at Roeper was ever one person's accomplishment or failure; it was always a collaborative effort.

Student Saul Hansell back in the 1980s wrote, "Roeper should be a place where no one is too small to contribute or too big to listen." In a school that belongs to everybody and where the philosophy says that everyone has the responsibility to take care of the community, you are inevitably going to have a tension between those principles and getting things done, between cutting off discussion when needed and having everybody feel satisfied that they had enough opportunity to participate in the decision making. Such tension, if not handled correctly, can lead to charges of the Philosophy not being honoured and of the leader(s) drifting towards autocracy. The leader has to be clear about the decision-making process to be used and has to be transparent with information. At times, trust and goodwill built up in less stressful times will have to be spent.

In an institution with the core values of flexibility and personalization and with an emphasis on people working things out rather than relying on "rules and regs," there can be the danger of perceived favoritism and abuse. When one rule applies to everybody, no exceptions, it may not serve individuals or the community well, but at least no one can easily claim special treatment. It's clean and easy. At Roeper, to counter the perceptions (or even realities) of different rules for different folks or "he who pushes hardest gets his way," there has to be transparency in information sharing and decision making. The leader has to earn the trust of the community and to constantly ask himself or herself why he or she is deciding in a certain way. If the leader's relationships with people are healthy and authentic, distrust and suspicion of favoritism shouldn't be a problem, especially if he or she can articulate to the community the rationale behind the decision.

FINAL THOUGHTS

Is this path of leadership easy? Frankly no, and be wary of anybody whose main goal is to make it so. It can help knowing that you have the trust, goodwill, and respect of the community. But there is no escaping that it is emotionally draining, physically exhausting, time-consuming, and damned messy, which is why many organizations fall back on top-down management, eliminating conflict instead of using it for growth, and making rules and pronouncements instead of involving the community in creating those rules. No one is immune to the lure of shortcutting and opting for the convenience of just getting the job done. Because of the expectations of others, market forces (or perceived market forces), and our own feelings of responsibility, we sometimes neglect to create teachable moments for individuals and the community. Anyone can falter.

At the Roeper Middle School and Upper School, we have a policy that students can post anything on the outside of their lockers as long as they agree that if anybody objects, there will be a conversation between the locker owner and the objector. A lawyer would say we have no "prior restraint." I can't think of a time that talking it out didn't solve the problem, but I do remember the evening I was dead tired, trying to get out of there to go home and not feeling particularly Roeperian, and I encountered a locker with a rather disgusting cartoon about diarrhea. Worried about what parents and prospective students might think, exhausted, I... I... I... ripped it down and threw it away. One last thing, a good Roeper leader must be able to accept is that he or she is capable of falling short, can always do better next time, and needs to go home earlier every now and then.

ALEXANDRA DICKINSON

LEADERSHIP AT THE ROEPER SCHOOL THROUGH THE EYES OF AN INSIDER

AUTHORITY—OR A LACK THEREOF

When I think back on my 15 years as a Roeper student, I do not remember any authority figures. That's not to say that there were not plenty of people who made decisions. In fact, I remember very few decisions that were made in my time at the school that did not feature a consensus of multiple voices. There were board members, administrators, teachers, student leaders—any number of individuals who spoke on behalf of the decisions—but to me, they never felt like authority. Of course, this does not mean that I ever disrespected the ability of these individuals to lead—it means Roeper has something different.

Authority as it exists outside of Roeper is often defined by a "buck stops here" mentality. At work you will have a supervisor and oftentimes whatever he or she says goes. In the government, we cede our own individual voice in favor of someone else who takes the lead and represents us all. These authority figures are integral to the functioning of many structures and indeed, any community needs people who are empowered to make and act on decisions. The only real factors that change throughout the decision-making process have to do with who feels like they contributed and who actually was able to contribute to the final outcome.

The word authority has an interesting history. The etymology of the word says that as early as the 13th century people were using *autorite* to refer to a "book or quotation that settles an argument." This textual reference struck me. In many ways, the Roeper philosophy fits the etymological definition of authority; it's found in books and fragments of documents and quotations—and yet the word "authority" feels so far from the Roeper ideal. But at times we treated the text as an authority. I can remember many occasions where my fellow students, empowered by the school's structure, attempted to find passages of the philosophy that backed their own opinion.

It's only now as an adult that I realize it never mattered if we had found "the perfect quote" from George and Annemarie to back up our stance. What mattered instead was that we had the power to look for it. Roeper was never about having one person who settled an argument; it was about having a conversation to reach a consensus that settled an argument.

It is that conversation—that very unique and very integral conversation—that I explore a little more here. There are a lot of components that go into being a leader at Roeper, but fundamentally, when we look at what distinguishes leadership at Roeper from leadership anywhere else, we are talking about leadership by conversation.

That distinction between Roeper and the rest of the world troubles me in some ways. People have a tendency to think about Roeper as something completely separate from the rest of the world, a cocoon of support, if you will. This mindset is repeatedly reflected in one common question that most Roeper community members are familiar with: *Does the school prepare you for the real world?*

I have always found that question to be somewhat bizarre and loaded with assumption. To myself, I think, "Of course—I'm alive and in the 21st century, right?" But in truth, I think the reason that it takes me by surprise so often is because of something different and important. I believe that the way leadership, power, and authority are addressed at the school uniquely prepares each and every student for success in navigating the challenges of the 21st century.

Let's return to this idea of leadership by conversation. There are any number of elements and conditions that go into creating a space conducive to learning amongst a group of gifted people. Empowerment, a sense of justice, respect, and emotional awareness are all prominent among these factors. But none of these things are particularly unique to Roeper. In fact, any successful workplace could incorporate similar qualities. So what is the element that really sets Roeper students apart in their ability to navigate the 21st century? Conversation.

There is not a single moment where I remember a traditional authority figure at Roeper, because there was not a single important moment in my tenure at the school where there was not a conversation that surrounded the decision being made. There were times when I may have felt there was not enough conversation, but there was always the opportunity for more. To be a leader at Roeper is to know how to lead through listening and to know how to structure a conversation. To highlight this point, I bring up a few important examples that illustrate these principles.

Fort Quincy

In the first year of Stage IV[1], my homeroom only had six girls in it, including me. I hardly remember gender division being a huge factor in any element of my tenure at Roeper, but in this particular instance it led to a very easy playground grouping. The Lower School campus backs right up to a large property, and our classroom was right by the fence. The fence was partially obscured by shrubbery, which lent itself nicely to fort building. As our group of intrepid girls formed, we opted to claim a particular area adjacent to the fence. We cleared out the dead brush, divided the territory equally among us, and named the whole place Fort Quincy after the neighbor's dog.

The group of six girls spent every chance we could over in Fort Quincy. We created games, brought art projects, read, knitted—did anything we could over in that space. In the first year, on a few occasions, there were some playground conversations about others taking over our space, but we never felt a need to open it up to others. It was a space uniquely our own. As our first year of Stage IV ended and we returned for our second year, our homeroom grew and the original six girls were no longer the only girls there.

In the first week of school we resumed our normal grouping of six inhabiting our space in Fort Quincy, but it was not long before we began to attract the attention of the other girls in our homeroom. After an incident in which one of the newer girls felt as though she was being excluded, a homeroom teacher intervened. At the end of one lunch period she brought all six of the original Fort Quincy girls and all of the ones who had voiced a feeling of exclusion in for a lunchtime conversation to discuss exclusion.

At no point in time during this conversation was there an accusatory tone that would put the original six girls on the defensive. We began by talking about what exclusion meant and the teacher asked if what we were doing was exclusion. This facilitated conversation allowed us all to examine our behavior and realize that our informal policy was not a fair one. At no point in the conversation were we treated as anything less than thinking, feeling individuals. The teacher led us to conclude that our actions were unjust and to change our ways through conversation. Each of us felt as though this was the right decision, and each of us felt as though we owned a piece of this decision. From that day forward, no girls or boys were denied access to Fort Quincy.

Columbine

It was not until after the school day was over on April 20, 1999, that most of my peers and I learned of the tragedies across the country at Columbine High School. That evening the news was inescapable and the prospect of returning to school was suddenly fraught with unthinkable concerns. Very few people felt unsafe—it was more the sudden recognition of our vulnerability as human beings. Vulnerability is a difficult emotion to navigate, especially in a community of emotionally aware individuals—but vulnerability is also one of the few emotions that typically challenge and define leadership.

For many of us, the day after Columbine marked a transformation. Having spent years at the school cultivating our sense of global citizenship, these events marked a singular moment where the realities of violence changed our perception of the rest of the world. There was nothing anyone could say that was going to make what happened go away. But there was the distinct opportunity and need for something to happen in our community.

Leadership is often most apparent in a time of crisis, and for the Roeper community this moment was no different. Recognizing the need to address what had happened up front, the following day the administration juggled classes and activities and the normal school day was put on hold to accommodate for a rare all-school assembly in the gym. To give you a sense of what this meant, an all-school assembly featured a gathering of more than three hundred 11- to 18-year-olds, in addition to teachers and other staff, in a fairly small space.

No one in that room could escape the sense of a hunger for safety and community, and the opportunity for conversation gave us exactly what we needed. We spent hours allowing everyone who wanted to say something, to say something. Slowly but surely throughout the process we shared this conversation, which allowed us to address reality and reaffirm our safety in our community.

This example demonstrates a remarkable instance of the school's administration using their power to determine our schedule and pave the way for an important conversation. This was not an instance of an administrator standing up and facilitating the conversation as much as it was an instance of school leadership reading the situation correctly and empowering students. On that day we experienced the leadership of conversation—and the ability of a community to help heal and grow in the face of reality.

Changing Heads

While leadership is often most present in times of crisis, it is also prevalent in moments of change. My senior year at Roeper marked the last year of Ken Seward as Head and meant that the school was to embark on the process of selecting a new Head. At that time, I was one of two student representatives to the Board of Trustees, which had bottom-line responsibility for the selection. The selection process at this juncture involved in-depth interviews with potential candidates and assemblies and opportunities for student conversations and questions.

At the beginning of the process I had the opportunity to speak to Annemarie Roeper. As with many conversations with Annemarie, I went in with an idea of what I wanted to talk about and left with at least 20 more things that I wanted to talk about. I had intended to talk to her about how to share the philosophy with an incoming Head, but instead she was interested in hearing my thoughts about how I was going to represent the students in this crucial moment. After spending some time outlining what I felt my role in the process was, Annemarie pointed out that I had not talked about what the role of the rest of the student body was in the process. She was right and I re-evaluated my role.

In that moment I recognized that in my capacity as a leader, my most important job was to listen. For weeks surrounding the Head selection process, I spent my free time at school listening to my fellow students and assessing what the student body felt were the most important characteristics of our next leader. I took notes and spent time considering the decision at hand.

Finally, the night for the board meeting came. As all of the board members assembled, I remember distinctly being treated as an equal. At no point in time did any of the adult members of the board indicate that I had no right to be there. The meeting went on later than normal and was emotionally charged. Everyone felt as though they represented an important segment of the community and the schools' operations, and everyone wanted to be heard. The other student representative and I felt passionately that we represented the will of the students, and when the conversation began to focus on the administrative elements of this process, we began to feel as though the rest of the Board was missing the point. As soon as this positioning became clear, there was a break in the proceedings and we were given the floor once again. After expressing our opinions and feelings I noticed a change in the room. Everyone suddenly realized that it was not about who they were representing or what operation they were responsible for; instead, we were all responsible for the same thing—the community.

While viewpoints and perspectives evolved and changed throughout the meeting, the whole process was dominated by conversation. The Chair of the Board was responsible for managing the meeting and our expectations. Leadership in this moment was not an easy process. And the greatest challenge to leadership by conversation became clear in this moment. A leader at Roeper needs to know how to sense what the topic of conversation should be and needs to coordinate processes to enable the emergence of an equal and fair sharing of voices. Handling this is easier said than done, but it is in everyone's best efforts to make it happen so that the real success of the community is unlocked.

THE LEADERSHIP OF CONVERSATION IN THE REAL WORLD

The notion of the real world is still something that I have difficulty defining. In so many ways Roeper is different. It's a better example of a community. It's a better example of respecting human dignity. It's a better example of what the world can be. But in no way is Roeper separate from the rest of the world. To be a leader within these settings requires one to encourage respect across generations, to allow every individual to be empowered, to identify processes for efficient decision-making, and to put conversation above all else—but to be a good leader anywhere else in the world means to embody these exact same qualities.

I have had the opportunity to immerse myself in many different work atmospheres since leaving Roeper and in countless other group settings throughout the years since graduating from the school. Not everyone works the way a Roeper student works. Not everyone immediately appreciates the value of conversation or what it can do for leadership. But everyone knows what authority is and what it feels like. By growing up in an environment of listening, sharing, justice, and commitment to making something better, I've been able to bring something important to every leader I've encountered and every leadership opportunity I've had.

Life is not always as easy now as it was when I was surrounded by a community of like-minded thinkers. But any time I am in a room where decisions are being made, I find myself listening and evaluating. I think about the sense of justice that I found within myself on the playground in Stage IV. I remember the vulnerability of tragedy and the tremendous power that conversation can have to overcome it. I value myself as an equal to my leaders today because, even without having the final say, I realize our shared humanity. All of these values that I hold dear to me I can trace back to the fundamental strength of leadership by conversation that I learned from my time at Roeper.

Due to the leaders I worked with in the Roeper community, today I understand authority to be a reflection of the guiding principles that define a community. It was not about quoting the text of the philosophy; it was always about living it. The leaders who created the best space for me and our fellow students, and the ones who taught me what a good community was all about were the ones who were able to coalesce the guiding principles of the philosophy into the conversation or our daily lives. I do not remember any authority figures in my time at Roeper, but I absolutely remember the community of leaders who made that place what it was.

NOTE

[1] In the Roeper Lower School there are no traditional Grade groupings (i.e. third grade, forth grade). Instead, students are divided into Stages—Stage I (Preschool), Stage II (K-1), Stage III (2–3), and Stage IV (4–5). Each stage incorporates two traditional grades and so student will spend two years in one grade.

DAVID H. FELDMAN

PROCESS AND VOICE

The Roeper philosophy calls upon us to foster "a willingness to allow the child to participate in the shaping of his/her own destiny and to consciously prepare him/her for it."

—George and Annemarie Roeper

As I sat at my desk reading and re-reading those words, I tried to consider how our School, or any school, could live this concept in the 21st century. I've spent nearly 30 years teaching in independent schools; I've seen mission statements, philosophies, mottos, and value statements. The challenge with each of these pieces of writing is: How does the school actually live what it says it does? Congruence is truly the difference between a successful school, and the ideas of an educator on paper.

Arriving at The Roeper School as the new Head of School in the summer of 2012, I have watched an incredibly dedicated group of teachers work closely with parents and students to help develop the voice of each student. This is done in a deliberate and thoughtful way that is empowering, and from my perspective, uniquely Roeper.

From a child's days in preschool when he/she enters Stage I, he/she is given the opportunity to make choices and to help direct his/her learning. Teachers listen closely to children, watch their interactions and play, and then work cooperatively with children to create emergent curriculum. Throughout their years in Lower School, students have options in the selection of special area classes; there is a personalization to the learning that yields a feeling of empowerment. Nowhere was this empowerment and development of voice more evident to me than in the work that went into the Upper School's theatrical production of *Rent*.

As a candidate for the Head of School position, I was invited to see the Upper School production. It was a great opportunity to meet parents, talk to faculty and students, and to support the School's arts program. I had a chance to see how the School did what it said it did—a real test of living this philosophy that so many people wanted to make sure that I understood.

When I learned the students were performing *Rent* I was surprised. I had seen *Rent* on Broadway, watched the movie adaptation, and knew the material to be incredibly provocative with themes that were mature and highly sensitive. I was filled with questions: How could a high school theater group make this work? Why *Rent*? How would the audience react? Isn't the Birmingham campus a 6th grade through 12th grade group? Was this a developmentally appropriate selection? I anxiously settled in for the performance, and waited to see if my questions and concerns would be answered.

My introduction to the School production began with a reading of the playbill. Contained in the overview was a statement by student cast members inviting feedback from the viewers on the content and delivery of the production. The students shared that they had collaboratively gone through the script line by line and reviewed the language and content of the material. They made conscious artistic choices regarding whether to edit lines.

Before the first act, a second group of students came on stage and shared with the audience the process they had undertaken in preparation for the performance. Students shared their service-learning work in Detroit with the homeless population, an area AIDS clinic, and a shelter working with people battling substance abuse. Working with the director, the cast had taken on discussions about homosexual relationships, homelessness, and addiction—mature themes that were central to the play. The students providing the introduction concluded their talk by asking audience members to donate to support the clinic and shelter with which they had worked. The lights dimmed, and the Upper School students presented a version of *Rent* with little censoring of language, and a deep respect for the content they were sharing.

I have to admit that while I was surprised by the content, I was incredibly impressed by the process. One can certainly make the argument that adolescents seek to stretch boundaries and often intend to shock. I can say with honesty that they achieved both goals with great aplomb; however, for me the lesson was not about content. Rather, the lesson I gleaned, and ultimately my decision to join the community, was based on the high degree of trust adults placed in students to work through difficult material. No one said *Rent* was too mature, too sophisticated, or too adult. Instead, students were empowered to make choices, and, most importantly, accept ownership for their decisions.

The final line in the playbill was from the students. It invited audience members with thoughts, concerns, or complaints to send a note—and it listed the e-mail addresses of the student leaders. The invitation to engage in dialogue was made. The students knew they were being provocative, and they wanted to engage the community in important conversations. They had learned a series of incredible life lessons, and they wanted to share them with anyone who would take the time to engage. With power comes responsibility, and indeed the decision-making power we give to our students each day comes with immense responsibility. Yet, is there anything more powerful than active and engaged learners?

Research, review, reflection, and conversation all went into the decision-making process. Students set a goal that stretched them in directions that most adults wouldn't think them capable to journey—and yet they did. When we create an environment that allows children to participate in the shaping of their own destinies, and support them by facilitating, mentoring, and coaching, they can do amazing things.

George Roeper wrote, "To do things the way they were done in the past will not help youngsters face our changing times. The ability to recognize, choose, and invent options, the ability to decide, to learn how to learn—all this will better equip our youngsters for the future." The Roeper School philosophy is a living, breathing document because of this future-focused belief of empowering and including students in decision-making. It is what has shaped the School for generations, and it is what brought me to its doors last fall.

DOUGLAS WINKWORTH

OBSERVATIONS ON GOVERNANCE AT THE ROEPER SCHOOL

Although I've played a variety of roles during my 40-year association with The Roeper School, it's from my perspective as a former Chair of the Board of Trustees that I'm writing here. In this capacity, I'll try to confine myself to the broad view of board governance.

The day-to-day experience of the School takes place in both a physical and emotional environment. As a Board, our job is not to manage the daily experience the School, but to care for the environment. Literally, to "keep the lights on"; to provide and maintain the physical environment that is the stage for the Roeper experience.

More importantly, we are also responsible to "keep the lights on" of our philosophy, child-centred approach, academic excellence, and professional best practices through our Head of School and outstanding faculty, administrators, and staff.

Given the challenges presented by our educational model, great dedication and commitment is required of our Trustees to see to it that the daily reality of the Roeper experience serves our community well.

But what more are we asked to do? We don't teach, although there are Trustee positions reserved specifically for faculty; nor are we students, although students are elected Trustees as well. It is important to note that the Roepers envisioned the Board as separate in function, but not in behavior, from the rest of our community. Specifically, they charged the Board of Trustees to be "guardians of the philosophy," making it clear that Trustees are to demonstrate the same fidelity to the Roeper philosophy as any other part of our community.

From the beginning of my decades-plus Board service, Annemarie Roeper challenged me to see the Board function in a manner fully consistent with their philosophy. The Roepers understood that a board was a potential weak link in terms of living the philosophy as they envisioned. It was a highly responsible body that functions largely out of view; but nevertheless, it affects the entire life of the School. It also has a diverse membership that is often less fluent in the application of our philosophical foundations than other parts of the community.

It was a genuine challenge to understand the core of the philosophy and interpret its impact on school governance and my own management style. This has proven to be an ongoing process, and I reflect on it to this day. The journey took me to a place where Board practices and perspective on the School are built on four indispensible characteristics. Specifically:

1. The Roeper School is first and always focused on the importance of its desire and ability to know each individual child as essential to understanding how to educate that child.
2. Every individual is worthy of respect as a matter of right. From this core principle many of our values and practices are derived. In terms of governance, we are led to a commitment to pursue consensus in decision-making. While the pursuit of consensus may be difficult at times, it bears witness to the respect given every community member.
3. The nature and use of power within the School community so as to maximize consensus.
4. The nature and use of time within the School community so as to maximize consensus.

To governance, the significance of the individual child creates essential context. The desire (read this as "the will") and ability to know each child is an institutional mandate, non-negotiable and essential to success. Frankly, many see our commitment to it as fundamentally inefficient. It leads to practices that create serious financial and functional challenges; but we choose this path as critical to the quality of our desired outcomes.

For example, at its core, knowing anyone requires time shared. There is a direct correlation between the quantity and quality of one-on-one interaction with someone and our knowledge of, and feeling for, that person. Hence, low student-teacher ratios. Hence, the expectation that faculty are to be available to students beyond the usual school hours, and so on, and so on.

Then, once gained, or at least begun, knowledge of a child leads administration and faculty to identify ways to meet the particular needs of that child. This is not an efficient process. Even when resources can be found readily within our community, there are often scheduling accommodations, unique teacher interactions and preparation, special classes and self-studies, and always the need for the will and energy to take the extra time and effort to "make it happen" for that child.

This scenario is amplified even more when required/desired assets to meet a particular child's passion and gifts are outside our normal resource base. Meeting the needs of individual children requires the effort of many individuals; and you can readily imagine the efforts required to satisfy a host of unique requirements for an entire student body. A school is thousands of daily interactions. Every unique accommodation will affect untold numbers of those interactions.

From a governance and management perspective, you can quickly understand the pressure on administration and faculty to find time to consider and act on the unique needs of students. Here I want to mention "line/action" and "staff/preparation" functions and the conflicts that arise for "line" people when they need time for "staff" function. This is the very definition of Roeper teachers and administrators; but it's too long a discussion for here.

The *"...we need low student-teacher ratios, because we need the quality of interactions necessary to know our students, and thereby, to know how best to evolve their unique education plan..."* approach is not the easiest way to build a financially secure model. In fact, many education industry experts will tell you that it's suicide. Well, it may not be suicide, but it can certainly be torture. For governance, there is constant temptation on the business side of our brain to tinker with the equation.

The less obvious, but nevertheless critical, challenge is what I refer to as the "institutional scale" of commitment required. Truly, each of our teachers and administrators know these daily challenges. It is tiring and often stressful; but there is another player: institutional will.

If the environment and practices of the institution are not supportive of individual accommodation, then no matter how hard teachers work, we will ultimately fail. The institution must be *deliberately* willing to accept constant change, when its natural inclination is to have regularity and order.

This is where governance and, particularly, administrators find themselves straddling the line. It's a hard one. For most people, it's difficult to make sense of this larger scale of the issue; but the fact is, our individual practitioners function within an environment that either supports or hinders what they are attempting to do. That environment is at institutional scale, and it's our responsibility.

The School's governance needs to internalize this mandate—the significance of the individual child—and its fundamental tension. If we are going to function effectively and creatively in The Roeper School's best interests, our governance needs to understand that we choose to "do it the hard way."

Understanding and accepting who we are helps us move beyond the nearly constant temptation to revisit our commitment to "do it the hard way." It permits us to get on with the extremely difficult task of dealing creatively with our self-inflicted challenges.

Knowing "who we are" keeps our goals before us and improves our ability to govern in the best interests of the School. To some, this may seem obvious, but I cannot emphasize too strongly the need to reinforce this understanding within a group whose membership is so diverse and changing. This understanding empowers not only our approach to problem solving, but also our philosophical fidelity in the Board's uses of power and time around decision-making.

Exercise of power within the School community is a matter that receives constant attention. The principal reason for this is that our philosophy asserts our respect and value for each individual. We demonstrate this with a commitment to effectively share power as equals by pursuing consensus, thereby empowering each member of the community to participate in decision processes.

Of course, in the legal sense, the administration and, ultimately, the Board is accountable. There are laws after all. *(Note that The Roeper School owns itself and has a self-perpetuating Board. There are no shareholders—only stakeholders.)*

However, this legal reality is not, as a matter of daily practice, treated as an excuse for the Roeper Board to exercise unilateral power in decision-making. This is a fairly subtle point and it is taken very seriously by the Board. In the last analysis, Trustees do have fiduciary responsibility, so we cannot have others making decisions for us; but the Board willingly, as a matter of philosophical conviction, opens its processes to include broader debate on matters of interest to other constituencies. Our philosophical commitment is that each process seek consensus to the maximum extent feasible.

A further example of respect demonstrated through power sharing is expressed in the relationship of the Board to its student Trustees. For decisions that under law must be made by a vote of members of legal age, it has become the Board's practice to record the vote in accordance with the law, but to also record the votes of student Trustees in the published minutes. In all matters, their voice is heard and recorded.

What must be apparent from this brief mention of self-imposed transparency and open participation is that additional time (beyond what the Board might have expended itself) is required to move through the entire decision-making process. This is true, not only of the Board, but also the administration and for any activities that affect the broader school community.

This brings us to my fourth characteristic about the nature and use of time in the Roeper community. A couple of years ago, during the search for an interim head of school, I told the search committee that one of the essential qualities necessary to lead this community was patience. A little over a year later, this view was endorsed by Phil Deeley (our fine interim head) in his farewell speech to Board members, saying that in his year at the helm he learned that patience was the leadership skill in greatest demand at Roeper.

For effective governance, patience is critical. The parents and volunteers who serve on our Board are characteristically diverse in skills, backgrounds, and motivations. They bring their "real-world" experiences and leadership skills with them—including their value for, and perceptions of, time.

So naturally, the first thing we do with new Board members is ask them to buy into a philosophically altered model that asks them to work their usual magic in a somewhat unusual way. This is not always an easy or successful process.

The first instinct of many new Trustees is to assume that any inconvenience presented by the philosophy of the school can be easily set aside when the grown-ups are talking real-world issues. I suspect that as you read this book, you may perceive as inefficient many of our everyday practices such as deliberative process and full community access to decision-making.

This perceived inefficiency actually translates for some as "wasting time" and they often find it irritating. After all, "leaders don't waste time, they save time," or at least use it for things that are essential to the question.

I have seen the struggle of many new Trustees who have so much to give us, but who just can't get past the value decision: "Is time valuable because it is (1) a scarce resource, or (2) a resource to be invested to improve outcomes"? Or, more crudely stated, "I see the answer and I have the power. Why not make the decision now and move on?"

Successful leaders in the Roeper community have learned the value of invested-time and the return-on-investment of genuine "buy-in" and consensus support for timely implementation. We are most effective when we do not view the time taken for decisions as separate from time taken for their implementation.

The hierarchical, real-world experiences of many of our governance volunteers is challenged by our alternative world philosophy and approach. But, this is really the point. The Roeper School seeks to be an alternative real world. We strive to show that our approach is no less rigorous or fiscally demanding; and we remain legally accountable in the so-called real world.

We accept the challenge of our philosophy to pursue a preferred future reality. We do not accept any assertion that we are somehow not "real world." In fact, it is our conviction that the reality of our world is that we do more, not less, in making our way. After all, it is a mandate of the Roeper philosophy to "make a difference."

PART V

LOOKING FORWARD: A MOST UNUSUAL, THOUGHT-PROVOKING, TIME-TRANSCENDENT SCHOOL

DON AMBROSE

THE ROEPER SCHOOL IN THE 21ST CENTURY

Trends, Issues, Challenges, and Opportunities

Like most academics who navigate in the fields of gifted education and creative studies I have known about the Roeper School for a long time. In years past this school was lodged away in the corner of my mind where other special schools for the gifted were categorized. Only in the last eight years have I come to know the institution well. As editor of the *Roeper Review*, the refereed, academic journal affiliated with the Roeper Institute, I have visited the Roeper School periodically because they have hosted our editorial advisory board meetings on a number of occasions. While there, the students, teachers, and school administrators always kindly invite us to visit and observe their operations. At this point, I have interacted with all of the administrators and most Roeper Institute board members, most of the faculty, and many of the students, as well as some of their parents.

When Tracy Cross, the editor of the journal before me, was helping with the editorial transition he made the comment, "You're going to love this school." Seldom is Tracy wrong about anything so it wasn't a surprise when I came away from every visit to the school impressed and energized. A proponent of creative, student-centered learning, I saw so much in the school that aligned with the best ways in which bright young people learn.

Recently, my wide-ranging, interdisciplinary scholarly pursuits have added to my appreciation of the school. Always on the lookout for research and theory that can be imported from diverse academic disciplines to generate insights about creative intelligence, I gradually built a large, interdisciplinary knowledge base and much of it provides useful perspectives on 21st-century trends, issues, and problems.

For example, one of my books (Ambrose, 2009a) drew 87 theories and research findings from 29 different academic disciplines and fields and then employed the process of creative association to produce new insights about creative intelligence, which is operationally defined in the project as any blend of high-level creativity, intelligence, talent, or giftedness. Here are a few examples of creative-association connections generated in the project:

- Discoveries from political science, history, primatology, and philosophy revealed some of the reasons for ethnic conflict in today's international trouble spots (Chirot & McCauley, 2006; de Waal, 2006, 2009; Koonz, 2003; Scott, 2007).

- Research findings in economics, law, and political philosophy showed the shortcomings of the rational-actor model in the social sciences, especially in economics (Beckert, 2002; Dan-Cohen, 2002; Konow & Earley, 2007; Monroe, 1996). This model tends to generate shortsighted, egocentric thought and action that can lead individuals and groups down counterproductive paths in the turbulent 21st-century environment.
- Scholarship in organizational management showed how the strategic-planning process tends to be long on fine-grained analysis but short on creative thinking (Mintzberg, 1994), which is absolutely necessary for successful entrepreneurship and ethical organizational initiatives in a threat-filled, globalized world.

Mulling over these and many other interdisciplinary insights while simultaneously contemplating what I was seeing at the Roeper School switched on a mental light bulb, dimly flickering at first but then glowing brighter as each new construct was added to the mix. The final result, when the bulb shed sufficient light, was this investigation of the ways in which the Roeper School aligns with the demands of the 21st century.

In the analysis to come, I begin with a depiction of the ways in which the Roeper School functions. This portrayal is derived from a synthesis of insights based on my multiple visits and interactions with the school, as well as analyses of its strategic plan and accreditation report. After that, I generate an overview of 21st-century trends, issues, and demands that young people will face when they graduate from school. Derived from diverse, interdisciplinary sources, this overview provides the basis for a subsequent outline and description of the knowledge, skills, and dispositions young people will require for success in today's world. Finally, I use this list of knowledge, skills, and dispositions to carry out an analysis of the fit between the education provided by the Roeper School and the demands of the 21st century.

THE NATURE OF THE SCHOOL

The Roeper School has a long and storied history, which is dealt with in more detail elsewhere in this book. Its primary emphases always have been on individual self-discovery and ethical navigation in the world. A central intent of the school's founders, George and Annemarie Roeper, was to create an educational environment that would prepare young people to recognize and resist the ascendance of reprehensible, totalitarian governance systems such as the one they experienced in Nazi Germany. While working diligently to address this core purpose, the school also does much more. The following attributes of the Roeper School guide the thoughts and actions of its students, teachers, and administrators.

An Emphasis on the Whole Child

While shortsighted, misguided policymakers are energetically pushing the nation's schools backward toward a confining, fragmented curriculum addressing a narrow set of easily measurable knowledge and skills in a few basic subject areas (Apple, 2007; Berliner, 2012; Bracey, 2004; Kumashiro, 2012; Meier & Wood, 2004; Nichols & Berliner, 2007; Ravitch, 2010; Zhao, 2009, 2012), the Roeper School attends to the multiple dimensions of the individual. Academic subject areas certainly are addressed, usually in great depth; however, the school also emphasizes other aspects of intellectual growth, especially the development of creative and critical thinking. It also encourages intrapersonal self-discovery by honoring the emotional and intuitive facets of cognition. Engaging emotion, intuition, and deep-level creative and critical intellectual functioning encourages the individual to light the wick of intrinsic motivation, which catalyzes the exploration of phenomena due to keen personal interest instead of reacting to reward and punishment (extrinsic motivation). The school also emphasizes development of the aesthetic, artistic, and physical aspects of the individual. Overall, the emphasis on the whole child has the potential to make a young person well rounded and much more aware of his or her interests, strengths, and weaknesses.

Differentiated, Personalized, Inquiry-Based, Interest-Based, Creative Exploration

One of the hallmarks of an effective education for the gifted is the ability of educators to adapt instruction to the differing abilities and interests of the student (Tomlinson, 1999; Tomlinson & Brighton, 2003). In many schools this takes the form of adjusting assignments here and there to make them a little easier for struggling learners or a little more complex for the gifted. Since its founding the Roeper School has positioned a personalized education at the core of its mission; consequently, its professionals are finely attuned to the need for differentiation of instruction. Much of the differentiation occurs through an emphasis on children's discovery of interests and the encouragement to pursue those interests wherever they may lead. The curriculum at the school is flexible enough to allow such interest-based side trips, which can lead students to discover intriguing phenomena as well as their own aspirations. Students have the opportunity to discover who they really are through engagement in problem-based learning, pursuit of keenly interesting ideas, and mastery of intriguing, complex phenomena. Moreover, this pursuit takes creative forms. It can follow the suggestions of teachers, the interesting questions of peers, or the happy coincidence of creative mind explosions generated by the collision of two or more remotely associated ideas.

Democratic Ethos

An atmosphere of bottom-up, participatory democracy prevails throughout the school. For example, students are represented on important decision-making committees, which are populated solely by adult representatives in virtually all other institutions. While teachers do manage and guide the students in their classrooms, the flavor of adult influence throughout the school is inclusive and nonhierarchical. The intent is to push as much decision-making power as possible into the hands of students so they will respond by taking responsibility for their own actions and for the overall evolution of the institution for which they feel ownership. This democratic approach creates a productive integration of individuals within a community. Overall, students generally appreciate and strive to maintain the resultant atmosphere of caring and respect while balancing individual rights with responsibility.

Emphases on Justice, Equity, and Altruism

Consistent with this democratic ethos, children and adults at the school aim to maintain a respectful, egalitarian tenor that ensures fair and just treatment for all. Moreover, they apply this mindset both to their study of events and phenomena in their classrooms, and into the larger world. More than most young people, the students in this school pay attention to injustice and inequity, and often take steps to provide service to those in need.

Honoring and Embracing Diversity

The members of this school enrich their democratic and altruistic values with a healthy respect for various forms of diversity—diversity of viewpoints, ethnicity, spiritual belief, and socioeconomic background, to name a few important ingredients. But respect for diversity doesn't stop here. Students, teachers, and administrators seem to recognize that diverse backgrounds and viewpoints can enrich problem solving and decision making when all voices are heard. Consequently, the intellectual environment of the school resembles a mosaic of rich and diverse, separate but vibrantly interacting parts instead of a melting pot in which diverse ingredients are boiled down into a homogenous whole.

Focus on the Future

A primary aim of the school is to prepare children for the future. If students discover their interests, develop their aspirations and talents, gain deep, intrapersonal insights, and become keenly aware of problems and opportunities in the larger world, they will have earned the opportunity to become lifelong learners. Such an opportunity will enable them to direct their lives proactively instead of reactively sleepwalking through life. This focus on the future also applies to the school as an institution. The school seems to have a strong, flexible core set of beliefs and values that enables it to endure the tempests of change over time while reinventing itself periodically without losing its identity.

These key attributes provide the school and it's students with an important set of tools for use in the world beyond the walls of the institution. The early 21st century represents a fascinating and daunting environment for students and their school to explore.

TRENDS, ISSUES, CHALLENGES, AND OPPORTUNITIES IN THE 21ST CENTURY

My interdisciplinary search for research findings and theories that can generate new thinking about the nature and nuances of creative intelligence has turned up a variety of insights and perspectives relevant to understanding of the chaotic, threatening, and opportunity filled 21st-century socioeconomic and cultural context. A comprehensive treatment of all the relevant discoveries would be far too lengthy for this chapter; however, those that follow provide a useful basis for the analyses in subsequent sections. The discoveries in this subsection emerge from the following academic fields and disciplines: climatology, complexity theory, creative studies, critical theory, cultural anthropology, economics, geophysics, history, legal theory, management theory, microbiology, paleontology, philosophy, the history and philosophy of science, political science, primatology, psychology, sociology, and theoretical physics.

Innovation-Driven, Rapidly Evolving, Knowledge Economy

Modern nations and regions that used to rely on industrial production now are well along in a transition to knowledge-based economies, which generate information services and scientific and technological innovation (see Peters, 2010; Rooney, Hearn, & Ninan, 2008). These economies are driven by innovations in digital technologies, bioinformatics, knowledge management, and other forms of creative, intellectual development. Transition to a knowledge economy entails significant socioeconomic disruption as industrial sectors of national and regional economies decline and corporations outsource work to third-world nations to capitalize on cheap labor and other lower production costs.

Unpredictable Technological Determinism and Integration

Economic transactions in the knowledge economy are becoming seamless and more transnational because they are facilitated and streamlined by global information networks (Xu, 2009). This makes them less predictable than they were in the old, industrial economy. Even less predictable are the innovations emerging from the more creative, cutting-edge knowledge industries. For example, biotechnology promises to generate new crops, medical applications, and even new hybrid species through genetic engineering, so much so that the 21st-century is being called the age of biology in contrast with the 20th century, which was the age of physics (see Beckwith, 2002; Carlson, 2010). Materials science is on the cusp of generating entirely new products, from new transportation systems to new buildings. Nanotechnology, the science of manipulating material at the microlevel, could revolutionize industrial production and medicine (David & Thompson, 2008). Cognition enhancement is another area of enterprise ready to expand exponentially (Caplan, 2003). Simple, mild cognition enhancers such as coffee and prescription drugs have been around for some time; however, pharmaceutical developments are making it possible that cognitive processes will be enhanced in the near future to the point where those with access to the new products will be capable of super cognition. All of these developments in information- and biological technology bring with them great promise and serious ethical concerns about fairness (who will benefit and who will not) and unintended consequences.

Flexible, Fluid, Networked Organizations

The more successful organizations in today's knowledge economy are deviating from the pyramid-shaped, top-down hierarchical, excessively bureaucratic structures of the industrial era (see DiMaggio, 2001; Espinosa, Harnden, & Walker, 2007; Powell, 2001). They are transforming into flatter, less-hierarchical organizational systems with fewer layers of management. Decision making and work processes occur within lattice-like, highly interactive information networks through which employees meet with one another spontaneously to solve problems or to take advantage of opportunities and then the groups disband when no longer needed. The constitution of these groups usually is unpredictable because who is to be involved depends on what the problem entails. Such organizational structures facilitate innovation and generate creative opportunity at the cost of some security and predictability.

Shifting and Conflicting World Views and Values Frameworks

Populations within nations and regions always have clustered together around sets of values, which usually derive from unique cultural, ethnic, and religious perspectives on the world. In the past, identity groups with differing values could stick to themselves much of the time, occasionally coming into conflict with outside groups. In today's highly networked, globalized environment, which features instantaneous, international electronic communication and frequent international travel, identity groups are in much more frequent contact. Results of this trend include the current tendency for Western culture to overrun and "westernize" cultures in other parts of the world. Other cultures react by embracing elements of Western culture but also clinging more firmly to their own value systems, thereby simultaneously and paradoxically becoming more global and parochial (Rosenau, 2003).

While this dynamic tension between localization and globalization has been occurring worldwide, massive shifts from modern to postmodern values also have been taking place. Employing the World Values Surveys, which cover over 60 societies representing 75% of the world's population, Inglehart and colleagues (Inglehart, 1997, 2000; Inglehart & Welzel, 2005) showed that the populations of most nations are shifting along two continua, from survival to well-being concerns, and from preferences for traditional authority to secular-rational authority.

Those in underdeveloped nations tend to be bound up in survival concerns (e.g., striving to acquire the basic necessities of life) and align themselves with the authority of traditional, mostly religious values. Modernization of a society generates sufficient material security to encourage a shift from reliance on traditional authority to alignment with rational-legal values, which frame decision making and settle disputes on the basis of bureaucratic norms and legal frameworks. As developed nations become even more affluent and secure they shift away from the materialistic focus of modern values frameworks to emphasize postmodern, quality-of-life concerns because additional material acquisition has diminishing returns. Postmodern values emphasize the benefits of creative self-expression, appreciation for diversity, and aesthetic and humanistic considerations.

Most affluent nations are well along in the transition from modern to postmodern values although the United States represents a special case. While subgroups in the United States are at the forefront of the values shift to postmodern values, large segments of the population are retaining the emphasis on traditional, mostly religious, authority.

Unprecedented Human Impact on the World

The rapid advancement of industrialization and population growth throughout the past two centuries has generated significant environmental damage. While environmental activism and laws in various nations have suppressed the damage to some extent, the destruction persists and promises to become ever more devastating in the years to come. Recently, attention has been turning to the long-term impact of climate change (Archer, 2009; Flannery, 2006). Extinction of species, desertification of regions, and severe climatic events are on the rise. If climate change is not expeditiously and sufficiently addressed, the long-term prospects include mass migrations of climate refugees when their homelands no longer can sustain life adequately, flooding of coastal regions, the spread of epidemics, the collapse of ecosystems, unprecedented resource shortages, and frequent, vicious wars.

In addition to climate change, extractive resource industries (e.g., coal, petroleum) encouraged by zealous government deregulation in large regions of the world are setting the stage for more enormous environmental disasters along the lines of the 2010 BP oil spill in the Gulf of Mexico. Scientists and some policymakers are striving to address these issues but so far their efforts have not kept pace with the problems (Park, Conca, & Finger, 2008).

The Prevalence and Persistence of Macroproblems

The growing human impact on the environment combined with the rapid pace of technological innovation and electronic networking in today's globalized world create optimal conditions for the emergence of macroproblems (Ambrose, 2009a; Hunter, 1991). A macroproblem is transdisciplinary because its solution requires the expertise of creative and critical thinkers from multiple disciplines. It is international because it doesn't respect national boundaries. It is long term because it takes decades or even centuries to create and likely will take many years to solve. Examples of macroproblems include the aforementioned issue of climate change; exploitative socioeconomic systems that generate and sustain gross inequality; and the troubling erosion of democracy, which is caused by colonization and manipulation of the governance process by powerful corporate interests and their lobbyists in many nations worldwide (Hacker & Pierson, 2005; Wolin, 2008).

Another pressing macroproblem is the seeming inability of humankind to break free of its own dogmatic insularity when it comes to identity frameworks. Gewirth (1998) argued that universalist morality, as opposed to particularist morality, is essential for ethical behavior and self-fulfillment. People who are guided by universalist morality may show some favoritism toward their own particular identity group (e.g., ethnicity, religious group, nationality) but insider-outsider distinctions fall away when an "outsider" is in dire circumstances and needs help.

For example, Monroe (1996, 2004) discovered that those who rescue others in great danger do not make identity group distinctions when they engage in rescuing behavior, even at the cost of their own safety. At a fundamental level they simply see outsiders as part of the same macro-identity group—the human race. In contrast, particularists may be kind and generous toward others as long as they share their identity group affiliation; however, they can be dismissive, callous, or even cruel to outsiders, up to and including engaging in genocide. Until humanity recognizes the moral failings of particularist-universalist identity distinctions and works to overcome particularism, the turbulent 21st century world will be plagued with periodic outbreaks of dangerous identity group conflict.

The Emergence of Macro-Opportunities

While the intricately networked, unpredictable, 21st-century globalized world presents us with macroproblems, it also makes room for macro-opportunities that could transform billions of lives for the better. It is difficult to discern all the possible macro-opportunities that could emerge but the following represent a sampling of some that have come to the fore in the new millennium.

Agile niche innovation and quick discovery of niche markets. Highly specialized or avant-garde individuals or groups always have faced great difficulty finding and capitalizing on market niches for their unusual skills or products; however, this is becoming much easier in the 21st century. Exponentially expanding electronic social networks are helping those with something unusual to sell find interested audiences. Zhao (2009) employed an interesting garage sale-eBay analogy to illustrate the marketing promise of the new electronic networking platforms. Those who have tacky pieces of used merchandise to sell at garage sales have trouble selling them because those who are able to drive or walk the short distance to such a sale usually already have similar junk. However, selling these items on an electronic network can expand the customer base almost without limit, making it much more likely that the seller will come in contact with others who actually want or need the merchandise. The same phenomenon can occur with the marketing of one's unusual, arcane talents. In view of this, it is becoming much easier to make and market something very different, or to *be* very different and to market unusual skills.

Cognitive diversity and motley coalitions. Page (2007), a complexity theorist-economist-political scientist, synthesized much interdisciplinary research and theory on complex, collaborative problem solving in private sector and governmental organizations. Cognitive diversity exists if a group encompasses diverse perspectives or interpretations, diverse heuristics, and diverse predictive models. Diverse perspectives or interpretations correspond to varied ways of philosophically viewing, representing, categorizing, or framing problems or issues. Diverse heuristics imply varied methods of problem solving. Diverse predictive models represent varied ways of inferring cause and effect (e.g., diverse theoretical perspectives).

Page analyzed discoveries about the problem-solving capacities of groups engaged in various endeavors ranging from the work of interdisciplinary teams, to the dynamics of organizations, markets, and democratic processes at the national level. His summary of findings indicated that cognitive diversity is at least as important as intelligence for dealing with complex, multidimensional issues. A cognitively diverse team, undistinguished in terms of measured intelligence, is likely to be as effective as, or even superior to, a team of gifted but like-minded people who share a single perspective or problem-solving approach. Of course a team combining intellectual power with cognitive diversity will be stronger yet. These insights apply only to the study and solution of complex problems. Cognitive diversity can be ineffective or even counterproductive when dealing with simple problems requiring algorithmic approaches.

The macroproblems mentioned earlier certainly are complex so the diligent and artful work of cognitively diverse teams will be required for their solution. Fortunately, the expanding, efficient electronic networks of the 21st century are making it easier for cognitively diverse teams to coalesce around problems, even very large, nettlesome, daunting ones.

Anthropologists have discovered the effectiveness of *motley coalitions* that arise for the purpose of solving difficult problems. A motley coalition is a loose or tight alliance of people who normally would not interact but join together to fight for a common cause. For example, Tsing (2004) discussed the remarkable formation and effectiveness of motley coalitions fighting to save Indonesian rainforests, which were being destroyed by rapacious, exploitative, extractive industries. These coalitions included democratic reformers, activists supporting the rights of indigenous peoples, cosmetic-industry entrepreneurs, and union organizers. Members of the coalitions came from far-flung regions of the world and likely would have found reasons to oppose one another under other conditions; however, the rainforest issue gave them a common problem of interest to which they collectively applied their diverse skills and perspectives. While the problem of rainforest devastation still exists, they did have an impact.

Without 21st-century social networking it would be very unlikely that these groups could form, pull together their diverse abilities, and generate high-potential, creative strategies for solution. Those who can combine cognitive diversity with the formation of motley coalitions can capitalize on one of the 21st century's most promising macro-opportunities.

KNOWLEDGE, SKILLS, AND DISPOSITIONS REQUIRED FOR SUCCESSFUL NAVIGATION IN A COMPLEX 21ST-CENTURY ENVIRONMENT

The unprecedented, complex, 21st-century socioeconomic and cultural global context will demand much from those currently graduating from our schools. Ideally, these graduates will be armed with an impressive array of abilities. The following is a description of the knowledge, skills, and dispositions that should give our young people the best chances to survive, thrive, and exert positive impact in today's world.

Knowledge and Skills

For many years, the general public, policymakers, and even academics assumed that the essential knowledge and skills required of high school graduates and even college graduates were rather simple to define and promote. The new millennium, however, has created a context that will demand much more than ever before in terms of what young people must know and be able to do.

The three Rs and academic content knowledge. The abilities to read, write, and compute formed the core of a 20th-century education and they remain important today. Mastering the knowledge base in the various subject areas also remains important. In essence, one must be capable of effective information processing and creation in an information-drenched era. However, the 3Rs and academic content knowledge are necessary but no longer sufficient for an effective education.

Multimodal literacy. Most of the learning of the three Rs entails logical, verbal-symbolic information processing but the 21st century also requires facility with other thought modalities. Young people today must be able to process more than linguistic and computational information. For example, they also must be technologically literate and be able to process and create in the visual thought modality. Much of the thinking and creating they do takes place through information-technology systems and those systems increasingly rely on visualization of complex concepts (Sibbet, 2008; Spaltera & van Dam, 2008).

A simple thought experiment illustrates this point. Imagine yourself transported back in a time machine to a computer lab in the late 1970s. In front of you is a small computer monitor with a black screen and a horizontal row of amber or green symbols, which had to be typed in perfect sequence for the program to operate. A logical, linear-sequential, verbal-symbolic student navigated well in that environment but an imaginative, visual thinker such as a little Albert Einstein would have experienced considerable boredom, difficulty, and frustration.

Now your time machine moves forward into the late 1980s and you confront another generation of information-technology devices. These computer monitors are a few inches larger and feature color as well as some rudimentary images (e.g., garbage-cans icons). Most of the information processing still is logical and verbal-symbolic text based; however, there is a little more room for the imaginative, visual thinker.

Finally, your time machine takes you to a top-end computer lab in the present day. Here, the monitors are huge, filled with confusing, elaborate, three-dimensional moving graphics. While verbal-symbolic processing still is important, the most sophisticated problem solvers now rely heavily on three-dimensional graphic representations, which sophisticated programs have created from thousands of pages of symbolic data. The problem solver must be able to process highly complex visual graphics. Visual thinkers now are at a premium and students must become proficient with visual-technological literacy.

Creative, divergent thinking. In a world fraught with seemingly impenetrable macroproblems, today's young people must learn to employ creative, divergent thinking artfully. Divergent thinking entails beginning with a focal point such as an intriguing question or a distillation of a complex problem and then branching out in all directions to generate many different responses, ideas, and possibilities (Baer, 1993; Guilford, 1968; Runco, 1991, 1999, 2004; Sawyer, 2012; Torrance, 1995). The "what if" question is a particularly helpful prompt for generating divergent thinking in problem solving situations. For example, a cognitively diverse team of experts from multiple disciplines working together on the issue of climate change could come up with hundreds of different ideas about how to grapple with this macroproblem. Many of the ideas would be banal or ridiculous but some could be promising starting points for an eventual solution.

Nuanced, critical thinking. Grappling with complex macroproblems also requires acute critical thinking that goes beyond binary logic, which can lock thinkers into either-or, black-and-white choices (Nicolescu, 1996). Nuanced judgment entails sensitive perception of shades of gray between polarized positions and nuance is required for understanding the complicated issues, values, and biases typically embedded within macroproblems (Resnick, 1987).

Critical thinking is a highly complex area of study in and of itself, encompassing but going beyond the large number of logical fallacies dealt with by philosophers and other critical thinking experts (see Bassham, Irwin, Nardone, & Wallace, 2002; Elder & Paul, 2012; Lee, 2002; Moore & Parker, 2009; Paul & Elder, 2002, 2009; Teays, 2006). While young people can benefit from study of logical fallacies they also can benefit from distillations of critical thinking developed by educational scholars such as Marzano (2000) and Resnick (1987). Examples of useful questions derived from their frameworks and applied to some of the macroproblems and macro-opportunities previously discussed in this chapter include the following: What criteria would you use to assess the effectiveness of BPs response to the 2010 oil spill in the Gulf of Mexico? How might you modify, refine, or replace your initial hypotheses about the causes of poverty in central-African nations now that you have read about the late-20th century policies of the International Monetary Fund and the World Bank?

Interpersonal acumen. While dispositions certainly come into play in the exercise of this ability, it is categorized here under knowledge and skills because it seems to be primarily skill-based. Those with strong interpersonal ability are able to work well with others by cooperating and leading artfully and by exercising exquisite sensitivity to the feelings, moods, and motivations of followers, leaders, and other colleagues (Gardner, 1983, 2006). Interpersonal acumen always has been important for success; however, the ever-tighter integration of the world, the more frequent interactions between potentially conflicting groups, and the need for collaboration to solve macroproblems and capitalize on macro-opportunities seems to magnify the importance of this ability in the 21st century.

Connective, interdisciplinary thinking. In earlier ages it was possible for great thinkers to become Renaissance scholars—polymaths capable of navigating in multiple disciplines and areas of technical expertise. Leonardo da Vinci was the classic example of this ability because he excelled in the visual arts, the sciences, and inventive engineering (Bramly, 1991).

When knowledge grew exponentially in later centuries it became much more difficult to perform well in multiple disciplines so scientists and scholars became specialists, and then, later, hyper-specialists prevailed to the point where academic disciplines and professional fields became a cluster of discrete, nearly impenetrable information silos.

Now, the persistent pressure of transdisciplinary, international macroproblems requires much more interdisciplinary thinking. Twenty-first-century scholars and policymakers must develop at least some proficiency with interdisciplinary thought, or at least with transdisciplinary collaboration (Ambrose, 2009a). Fortunately, there have been a few late 20th/early 21st-century Renaissance scholars who demonstrated the ability to synthesize important constructs drawn from multiple disciplines. An excellent example comes from the eminent cultural anthropologist Clifford Geertz (2000) who wrestled with large-scale academic problems by employing insights from his own discipline as well as cognitive science, psychology, philosophy, history, and political theory.

A helpful first step in enabling this kind of interdisciplinary synthesis is to bring together important theories and research findings from multiple disciplines in a common forum so they can be combined through processes of creative association. This can be done through the mind of a single synthesizer (e.g., Ambrose, 2009a), or through the collective minds of multidisciplinary collaborators (see Ambrose & Cross, 2009; Ambrose & Sternberg, 2012; Ambrose, Sternberg, & Sriraman, 2012).

Panoramic scanning and WICS. When contemplating the massive scale, broad scope, and extended timelines that must be considered when grappling with a macroproblem or macro-opportunity our minds must expand outward, backward, and forward to encompass these enormous conceptual dimensions. If today's young people are to have a chance when contending with current and future macroproblems and to avoid turning macro-opportunities into macroproblems, they must develop panoramic-thinking abilities and deep wisdom. Unfortunately, the Western culture in which they grow up works against panoramic scanning and wisdom by encouraging short-term thinking. For example, although some corporate leaders might want to think in the very long term, the structure and dynamics of the corporate world require them to plan on the basis of quarterly reports. Similarly, politicians must ensure that their initiatives show results within their two-year, four-year, or six-year terms so they can be reelected. Anything beyond those time windows becomes peripheral regardless of importance.

Panoramic scanning enables broad, interdisciplinary and/or international perception of contributing factors to a problem and long-range vision of implications (Ambrose, 1996). Sternberg's (2005, 2009) conception of wisdom, intelligence, and creativity synthesized (WICS) is helpful for addressing macroproblems because it encourages thinkers to generate wise problem solutions by generating creative ideas and then using incisive, analytical intelligence to evaluate the quality of those ideas, which are in turn assessed for their positive and negative impact on all stakeholders; hence, the wisdom.

For example, a team of scientists and policymakers capable of panoramic scanning and WICS who are intent on exploring the macro-opportunity of genetic engineering for enhanced crop production would contemplate a number of very broad issues as well as their own thought processes before getting too far into the topic itself. They would scan the issue broadly to see what disciplinary perspectives should be incorporated to generate comprehensive thinking on the topic. After bringing in a few other experts they had initially forgotten to include, they think creatively about some genetic-engineering possibilities and then employ their analytic intelligence to think critically about some problems and implications their proposals might generate. Once they have some promising ideas that might be worth pushing forward they think about all the possible stakeholders: the potential beneficiaries, those who would lose livelihoods or suffer health problems as a result of the innovations, and more. Finally, they would contemplate the very long-range. How might the innovations positively or negatively affect the ecosystem in decades or centuries to come?

Dispositions

While skills and knowledge are important for success in any environment, an individual's dispositions also are essential. Dispositions include the attitudes, values, and appreciations that provide a core basis for a person's behavior in interactions with others and in problem-solving situations.

Intrapersonal discovery. Individuals with strong intrapersonal propensities tend to be highly intuitive and introspective. They are sensitive to their own motivations and feelings, and this provides them with deep self-understanding (Gardner, 1983, 2006). Consequently, they are able to assess their own strengths and weaknesses as well as the ways in which they typically react in diverse situations.

In centuries past, young people often didn't have to be very introspective, at least when it came to some important dimensions of their lives. For example, in the medieval era most simply aligned their behavior with the strictures of tradition and followed the work path of their parents to engage in apprenticeships that prepared them for a highly predictable lifelong career.

It isn't certain what knowledge, skills, and dispositions are required for success with specific tasks and complex careers in the highly confusing, ever-evolving 21st-century environment. Many of today's problems are ill-defined, even those much smaller than the macroproblems under discussion in this chapter. Career options are not clear-cut and they transform quickly.

Young people who lack self-awareness and intuitive sensitivity are even more adrift in such an environment so intrapersonal discovery is becoming increasingly important. In the growing complexity and unpredictability of the 21st century, they must be highly attuned to their own motivations, aptitudes, and intuitive insights so they can find their way in a turbulent world. While intuition can lead one astray it also can provide valuable insights that are inaccessible to conscious reason (Myers, 2002; Policastro, 1999). Those who remain sensitive to their intuitive, intrapersonal illuminations and then critically assess and refine them will be more likely to find personal and professional success by discovering their talents, interests, and sense of purpose while contributing to the betterment of the world.

Appreciation for cognitive diversity. Consistent with the earlier discussion of motley coalitions and the value of cognitive diversity in the formation and function of those coalitions, attitudes favorable to cognitive diversity in the makeup of problem-solving groups will be valuable in the 21st century. Young people will function better in a complex world if they understand that groups attempting to solve complex problems are more effective if they are made up of people who represent differing philosophical and theoretical perspectives, differing sets of values, and differing sets of problem-solving heuristics. Instead of seeing others from differing disciplines, nations, ethnicities, or religions as misguided or even innately malevolent, they will be able to appreciate the unique perspectives of these outsiders who can enrich problem-solving efforts by injecting ideas otherwise unavailable to homogenous teams.

Aesthetic appreciation. The complex uncertainty of the 21st century environment makes necessary yet another disposition that enables individuals to deal effectively with nuance. According to Bennett (2001), a leading political theorist, ethical decision-making must be guided by a blend of moral codes, provided by one's culture, and a cultivated aesthetic sensibility about what is right because neither moral codes nor aesthetic impressions are sufficient on their own. Moral codes from a culture can encourage one to follow outdated, oppressive guidelines. Stoning women for adultery is an extreme example of this. Aesthetic impressions also can be flawed because they can be based on the whims or mistaken assumptions of the individual. But the blending of moral codes and aesthetic sensibility is more likely to render a just outcome in ethical decision-making. In a complex world fraught by inter-group conflict, young people need to refine their aesthetic sensibilities so they can achieve this more accurate, albeit still imperfect, ethical judgment.

Another form of aesthetic appreciation is relevant here. The exploratory phases of the scientific-research process often are driven strongly by the aesthetic sensitivity of the scientist (see Holton, 1996; Weschler, 1988). The greatest scientists aesthetically sense that they are onto something important when they see hints of beauty in the phenomena they are playing with, or in theories they are constructing. Just as a glowing ember can burst into flame, their aesthetic sensitivity can burst into euphoria when they come closer to the truth of their discoveries. The rapidly growing knowledge base in the sciences today coupled with the growing capacity presented by technological innovation should make more room for aesthetically driven scientific discovery. Researchers with a finely honed sense of aesthetics and an appreciation for the beauty of discovery will be well positioned to succeed in the natural sciences, and likely in other fields and disciplines.

Altruism and empathy. When the world's population wasn't so large, open spaces were more available, resources were relatively plentiful, and weaponry wasn't as devastating, the human race could get away with its propensity for dividing up into parochial identity groups that misunderstood, distrusted, or even hated one another. It also could get away with allowing the self-absorbed and conscience-free to engage in self-aggrandizing, hyper-materialistic power grabbing and resource hoarding.

Today's world makes it potentially much more damaging to cluster together in parochial, particularist identity groups and to engage in extremely self-centered behavior. Consequently, today's youth must understand the distinction between egoistic individualism and the relational self (see Martin, 1997; Monroe, 1996,

2004). Egoistic individuals tend to satisfy their own needs, even their own frivolous wants, before thinking about the desperate needs of others, if they think about them at all. In contrast, relational altruists tend to consider both their own needs and those of others because their empathic capacities are stronger. We also need more universalists and fewer particularists when it comes to the moral-ethical dimensions of human thought and action (see Gewirth, 1998, and the earlier discussions of universalism and particularism).

The eminent primatologist Frans de Waal (2006, 2009) bolsters the importance of empathy and altruism, which have great benefits for individual and group survival in threatening environments. According to de Waal, the dominance of Social Darwinism (a deceptive pseudo-theory) in sociocultural thinking has caused us to overemphasize ruthless competition and to undervalue collaboration and empathy. While ruthlessness and competition do exist in nature they are counterbalanced by the survival benefits provided when individuals empathize with one another and cooperate in teams. Moreover, even if the animal world truly was red in tooth and claw, dominated by ruthless, competitive aggression, which it is not overall, there is no good reason why humanity should not aspire to rise above such behavior.

HOW THE ROEPER SCHOOL FITS THE DEMANDS OF THE 21ST CENTURY

After having engaged in the foregoing analyses of the nature and dynamics of the Roeper School; the trends, issues, challenges, and opportunities embedded in the 21st century environment; and the knowledge, skills, and dispositions required by that environment; we can think about the ways in which the Roeper School might align with the demands of the 21st century. The following analyses address the likely extent of this alignment.

Emphasis on the Whole Child

Addressing the multiple dimensions of the child instead of just a few narrow, cognitive elements makes it far more likely that graduates of the school will be more well rounded than their peers from other institutions when it comes to facing the many different challenges of the 21st-century environment. For example, one of the most distinguishing attributes of the school; its emphases on the intrapersonal, emotional, intuitive, and aesthetic, inner dimensions of the child (see Kane, 2003); align very well with important 21st-century knowledge, skills, and dispositions. Intuitive, unconscious processing is an important element of creative, divergent thinking (Policastro, 1999) and it is vital for intrapersonal discovery of talents, interests, and one's purpose in life. It also contributes to aesthetic appreciation and altruistic sensitivity.

Moving beyond the inner world of the child, strengthening interpersonal and social capacities sets the stage for appreciation of cognitive diversity because the person who can interact well with others is more likely to develop and retain an open mind while interacting with people from differing identity groups. Stronger interpersonal ability also should facilitate connective, interdisciplinary thinking when building interdisciplinary knowledge requires interaction with experts from multiple disciplines.

Democratic, Individual-Community Integration

When the school develops a child's interpersonal capacities by creating extensive opportunities for participation in authentic, democratic processes it obviously attends to the need for interpersonal acumen in a tightly integrated, globalized world that requires more effective collaboration. Less obviously, participation in democratic processes exercises both creative, divergent thinking (required for solving difficult, shared problems) and nuanced, critical thinking (required for refinement of those creative ideas, and for dealing with the inevitable conflicts that arise in interpersonal dynamics). An individual who has been immersed in a participatory democratic environment has the opportunity to strengthen both interpersonal skills and higher-order thinking capacities.

Emphases on Justice, Equity, and Altruism

The participatory democratic atmosphere of the school engenders caring and respect for others as well as appreciation for individual rights and responsibilities. These aspects of the Roeper education align well with the school's admirable focus on justice for all, equality of opportunity, and kindness toward others. Children who live and breathe caring and respect throughout the school experience, and learn to balance their own individual rights with responsibilities, will be less likely to become self-aggrandizing, atomistic, egocentric individuals who deceive and ruthlessly exploit others in pursuit of vainglory. This makes it more likely that they will achieve the deep self-fulfillment that comes from the altruism of universalist morality instead of the shallow, short-term gratification of hyper-materialistic individualism or the misguided moral certitude of those confined by dogmatic, in-group-favoring particularist morality.

According to scholars of moral-ethical dynamics, reining in atomistic egoism and strengthening universalist morality is needed for the creation of a better world (see Ambrose, 2003, 2005, 2009b; Gewirth, 1998; Monroe, 1996, 2004). Preparing young people to contribute to the betterment of the world is at the core of the Roeper School's mission, and it seems ever more important as we move forward into a turbulent, threat-filled 21st century plagued by ethnic conflict and ruthless exploitation.

Honoring and Embracing Diversity

As with most things they do, the students, faculty, and administration of the school think more deeply than most about the nature and nuances of diversity. While recognizing and directly addressing the need for fairness in the treatment of those from diverse identity groups, they also take opportunities to capitalize on the benefits that can be gained from bringing divergent-thinking, cognitively diverse teams together for problem solving. Combining this penchant for honoring cognitive diversity with participatory democratic processes enables the school to prepare its young people for a world requiring divergent and critical thinking for solution of macroproblems.

The willingness and ability to embrace diversity also makes it more likely that the school's graduates will employ and appreciate the multiple literacies necessary for optimal success in an era requiring stronger technological abilities and visual-thinking capacities. For example, academia is full of brilliant but narrow-minded scholars who have little appreciation for the nonlinear, creative, visual thinking Albert Einstein and other great scientists used to generate visual-metaphorical interpretations of complex phenomena and achieve important breakthroughs (for overviews of these thought processes see (Feist, 2006; Holton, 1996; Miller, 1986, 1989, 1996, 2001; R. Root-Bernstein & M. Root-Bernstein, 2001; West, 1991). Capitalizing on macro-opportunities and solving macroproblems likely requires more than the traditionally favored linear-sequential, binary logical, verbal-symbolic thought processes favored by the traditional academic screening process. We need these thinkers but they should be augmented with nonlinear, highly imaginative visualizers to develop the conceptual leaps necessary for success in the 21st century.

Personalizing and Differentiating Inquiry-Based Instruction for Creative Discovery of Interests

Those worried that a school doing so much to develop the intrapersonal, intuitive, emotional, aesthetic, ethical, and altruistic dimensions of the individual will ignore the basic skills should set aside their fears. The blend of a personalized approach to learning and creative, problem-based learning processes generates interest-based, intrinsic motivation. Young people who become keenly interested in a phenomenon will pursue it doggedly and overcome barriers that might seem insurmountable to unmotivated peers. According to Cohen (1998), interest-based, intrinsic motivation encourages stronger learning of the basics. For example, children who recognize that they must read more ably to learn more about a topic of interest will seek or accept help more readily and will diligently refine these skills. In view of this, Roeper graduates should have no shortage of basic skills combined with their many other capacities when they confront the complexities of the 21st century environment.

In addition, an education that enables individuals to customize their learning to their own interests and abilities while engaging in creative, problem-based inquiry should enable graduates to find and thrive innovatively within the promising, specialized market niches of a networked, globalized environment. They should be well positioned to find personal success and self-fulfillment while also finding ways to contribute creative new products and services to the world. There certainly is plenty of room for creative, niche innovation. For example, Muhammad Yunus (2008), the Bangladeshi Nobel-Peace-Prize-winning economist and "banker to the poor" generated a highly innovative microcredit system for putting small amounts of capital in the hands of impoverished people, mostly women, who have no collateral. The system creates small-scale but very widespread entrepreneurship that lifts millions out of poverty. Roeper graduates are very well positioned to generate niche innovations like this in many different professional fields and walks of life.

Aiming Ahead

The tendency for a Roeper education to encourage young people to focus on the future and to incline themselves toward lifelong learning should help graduates of the school take on a helpful macro-mindset for navigation through a highly complex 21st-century world. Individuals too fearful of the future will cling excessively to habit and tradition because the familiarity of the past provides comfort in a tempestuous environment. In contrast, those who see themselves as exploratory complex-adaptive systems who perpetually seek knowledge and grow their minds will be well-equipped for capitalizing on emerging trends, adjusting during times of crisis, and maintaining a sense of direction in the midst of confusion. Just as a gyrocompass keeps an aircraft generally on course, a Roeper graduate's inner gyrocompass, comprised of intrapersonal awareness, keen interest, and intrinsic motivation, will keep her or him moving in a purposeful, general direction even when tumultuous environmental conditions make perception of a successful path through life seem unattainable to others.

This overview of the ways in which the Roeper School matches the complex, 21st-century environment isn't exhaustive. It shows some of the more obvious and beneficial connections but there likely are many more. This chapter should be considered a living, evolving analysis requiring ongoing additions and refinements. It would be most helpful if those additions and refinements came from stakeholders closest to the school (e.g., current and former students, teachers, administrators, parents, and board members) who use the portrayal of 21st-century demands; the knowledge, skills, and dispositions required for success in the new millennium; and the nature and dynamics of the Roeper School as catalysts for their thinking as they analyze their own experiences. The outline in table 1 can help these individuals or groups of stakeholders carry out their analyses because it provides a simplified juxtaposition of the attributes of the Roeper School with the capacities required in the new millennium. The numbers in brackets in the right-hand column indicate my suggestions for the most likely, fruitful connections between the school and the capacities for success, which are designated by number in the left-hand column.

Table 1. *Alignment of the Roeper School with the knowledge, skills, and dispositions required for success in the complex 21st-century environment.*

21ST-CENTURY KNOWLEDGE, SKILLS, & DISPOSITIONS	ATTRIBUTES OF THE ROEPER SCHOOL
Knowledge & Skills: 1. 3 R's 2. Multiple Literacies (multimodal: linguistic, visual, technological…) 3. Creative, Divergent Thinking 4. Nuanced, Critical Thinking 5. Interpersonal Acumen 6. Connective, Interdisciplinary Thinking 7. Panoramic Scanning/WICS *Dispositions:* 8. Intrapersonal Discovery (talents, interests, purpose) 9. Appreciation for Cognitive Diversity 10. Aesthetic Appreciation 11. Altruism	• Whole Child (intellectual, emotional/ intrapersonal/intuitive; interpersonal/social; motivational; physical; aesthetic/artistic dimensions) [2, 3, 4, 5, 6, 7, 8, 9, 10, 11] • Democratic Individual-Community Integration (caring/respect, rights/ responsibilities) [3, 4, 5, 6, 7, 9, 11] • Emphases on Justice/Equity/Altruism [3, 4, 5, 7 ,8, 9, 11] • Diversity (of viewpoints, ethnicity, socioeconomic status, religion…) [2, 3, 4, 5, 7, 9, 11] • Differentiated, Personalized, Inquiry-Based, Interest-Based, Creative Exploration [1, 2, 3, 4, 8, 10] • Focus on the Future (life-long learning for the individual; school is enduring but reinventing itself…strong, flexible core) [1, 2, 3, 4, 5, 6, 7, 8, 9, 10, 11]

Note. Numbers in brackets in the second column designate connections with 21st-century knowledge, skills, and dispositions.

CONCLUDING THOUGHTS

National educational initiatives for the past several decades have been pushing American schools to narrow and fragment the curriculum in service of accountability. The national policy, No Child Left Behind (NCLB), is possibly the most retrograde iteration of this movement (see Apple, 2007; Berliner, 2012; Bracey, 2004; Meier & Wood, 2004; Nichols & Berliner, 2007; Ravitch, 2010). Zhao (2009), a scholar who has studied both the Chinese and American educational systems in depth and detail, illustrated how China is lamenting its excessively mechanistic and shallow emphases on didactic instructional processes and easily measured outcomes, and is struggling vigorously to become more like the creative, student-centered elements of the American educational system. Ironically, American policymakers are doing the exact opposite, moving as quickly as possible in the wrong direction to replicate "rigorous," narrowly focused, superficially measurement-driven, foreign education systems such as the one the Chinese are trying to leave behind.

Regrettably, most policymakers and citizens have too shallow a grasp on what really counts in education so they go along with ill-conceived initiatives such as NCLB. Given these conditions, the nation and the world desperately need awareness of exemplary models of schools and school systems that generate the vibrant forms of student-centered learning necessary for success in a highly complex, ever-shifting, threat-filled, and opportunity-filled 21st-century environment. Fortunately, the Roeper School provides such an example. While no complex human organization is perfect, and the various stakeholders at the Roeper School recognize that they always will be able to find ways to improve, this school comes remarkably close to ideal alignment with the demands of the 21st century. Moreover, its students, teachers, administrators, and other stakeholders are passionate about the purposeful direction the school has followed historically, and continues to pursue. Policymakers and citizens within and beyond the United States would serve their children well if they set aside tired models of education and instead followed the lead of a group of children, teachers, and administrators who strive to blend deep, personal, self-discovery with a passion for improving the world.

REFERENCES

Ambrose, D. (1996). Panoramic scanning: Essential element of higher-order thought. *Roeper Review, 18*, 280–284.

Ambrose, D. (2003). Barriers to aspiration development and self-fulfillment: Interdisciplinary insights for talent discovery. *Gifted Child Quarterly, 47*, 282–294.

Ambrose, D. (2005). Aspiration growth, talent development, and self-fulfillment in a context of democratic erosion. *Roeper Review, 28*, 11–19.

Ambrose, D. (2009a). *Expanding visions of creative intelligence: An interdisciplinary exploration.* Cresskill, NJ: Hampton Press.

Ambrose, D. (2009b). Morality and high ability: Navigating a landscape of altruism and malevolence. In D. Ambrose & T. L. Cross (Eds.), *Morality, ethics, and gifted minds* (pp. 49–71). New York, NY: Springer Science.

Ambrose, D., & Cross, T. L. (Eds.). (2009). *Morality, ethics, and gifted minds.* New York, NY: Springer Science.

Ambrose, D., & Sternberg, R. J. (Eds.). (2012). *How dogmatic beliefs harm creativity and higher-level thinking.* New York, NY: Routledge.

Ambrose, D., Sternberg, R. J., & Sriraman, B. (Eds.). (2012). *Confronting dogmatism in gifted education.* New York, NY: Routledge.

Apple, M. W. (2007). Ideological success, educational failure? On the politics of no child left behind. *Journal of Teacher Education, 58*, 108–116.

Archer, D. (2009). *The long thaw: How humans are changing the next 100,000 years of earth's climate.* Princeton, NJ: Princeton University Press.

Baer, J. (1993). *Divergent thinking and creativity: A domain-specific approach.* Hillsdale, NJ: Lawrence Erlbaum Associates.

Bassham, G., Irwin, W., Nardone, H., & Wallace, J. M. (2002). *Critical thinking: A student's introduction.* Boston, MA: McGraw-Hill.

Beckert, J. (2002). *Beyond the market: The social foundations of economic efficiency.* Princeton, NJ: Princeton University Press.

Beckwith, J. (2002). *Making genes, making waves: A social activist in science.* Cambridge, MA: Harvard University Press.

Bennett, J. (2001). *The enchantment of modern life: Attachments, crossings, and ethics.* Princeton, NJ: Princeton University Press.

Berliner, D. C. (2012). Narrowing curriculum, assessments, and conceptions of what it means to be smart in the US schools: Creaticide by design. In D. Ambrose & R. J. Sternberg (Eds.), *How dogmatic beliefs harm creativity and higher-level thinking* (pp. 79–93). New York, NY: Routledge.

Bracey, G. W. (2004). *Setting the record straight: Responses to misconceptions about public education in the U. S.* Portsmouth, NH: Heinemann.

Bramly, S. (1991). *Leonardo: Discovering the life of Leonardo da Vinci.* New York, NY: HarperCollins.

Caplan, A. L. (2003). Is better best? *Scientific American, 289*(3), 104–105.

Carlson, R. H. (2010). *Biology is technology: The promise, peril, and new business of engineering life.* Cambridge, MA: Harvard University Press.

Chirot, D., & McCauley, C. (2006). *Why not kill them all? The logic and prevention of mass political murder.* Princeton, NJ: Princeton University Press.

Cohen, L. M. (1998). Facilitating the interest themes of young bright children. In J. F. Smutny (Ed.), *The young gifted child: Potential and promise, an anthology* (pp. 317–339). Cresskill, NJ: Hampton.

Dan-Cohen, M. (2002). *Harmful thoughts: Essays on law, self, and morality.* Princeton, NJ: Princeton University Press.

David, K., & Thompson, P. B. (Eds.) (2008). *What can nanotechnology learn from biotechnology? Social and ethical lessons for nanoscience from the debate over agrifood biotechnology and GMOs.* Burlington, MA: Academic Press.

de Waal, F. (2006). *Primates and philosophers: How morality evolved.* Princeton, NJ: Princeton University Press.

de Waal, F. (2009). *The age of empathy: Nature's lessons for a kinder society.* New York, NY: Random House.

DiMaggio, P. (2001). The futures of business organization and paradoxes of change. In P. DiMaggio (Ed.), *The Twenty-first century firm: Changing economic organization in international perspective* (pp. 210–243). Princeton, NJ: Princeton University Press.

Elder, L., & Paul, R. (2012). Dogmatism, creativity, and critical thought: The reality of human minds and the possibility of critical societies. In D. Ambrose & R. J. Sternberg (Eds.), *How dogmatic beliefs harm creativity and higher-level thinking* (pp. 37–39). New York, NY, Routledge.

Espinosa, A., Harnden, R., & Walker, J. (2007). Beyond hierarchy: A complexity management perspective. *Kybernetes, 36*(3/4), 333–347.

Feist, G. J. (2006). *The psychology of science and the origins of the scientific mind.* New Haven, CT: Yale University Press.

Flannery, T. (2006). *The weather makers: The history and future impact of climate change.* New York, NY: Atlantic Monthly Press.

Gardner, H. (1983). *Frames of mind: The theory of multiple intelligences.* New York, NY: Basic Books.

Gardner, H. (2006). *Multiple intelligences: New horizons.* New York, NY: Basic Books.

Geertz, C. (2000). *Available light: Anthropological reflections on philosophical topics.* Princeton, NJ: Princeton University Press.

Gewirth, A. (1998). *Self-fulfillment.* Princeton, NJ: Princeton University Press.

Guilford, J. P. (1968). *Inteligence, creativity, and their educational implications.* San Diego, CA: EDITS.

Hacker, J. S., & Pierson, P. (2005). *Off center: The Republican revolution and the erosion of American democracy.* New Haven, CT: Yale University Press.

Holton, G. (1996). On the art of scientific imagination. *Daedalus, 125*, 183–208.

Hunter, K. W. (1991, January-February). Big Messes: Problems that grow bigger and bigger. *The Futurist, 25*, 10–17.

Inglehart, R. (1997). *Modernization and postmodernization: Cultural, economic, and political change in 43 societies.* Princeton, NJ: Princeton University Press.

Inglehart, R. (2000). Globalization and postmodern values. *The Washington Quarterly, 23*, 215–228.

Inglehart, R., & Welzel, C. (2005). *Modernization, cultural change, and democracy: The human development sequence.* New York, NY: Cambridge University Press.

Kane, M. (2003). A conversation with Annemarie Roeper: A view from the self. *Roeper Review, 26*, 5–11.

Konow, J., & Earley, J. (2007). The hedonistic paradox: Is homo economicus happier? *Journal of Public Economics, 92*, 1–33.

Koonz, C. (2003). *The Nazi conscience*. Cambridge, MA: Harvard University Press.
Kumashiro, K. K. (2012). *Bad teacher! How blaming teachers distorts the bigger picture*. New York, NY. Teachers College Press.
Lee, S. P. (2002). *What is the argument: Critical thinking in the real world*. Boston, MA: McGraw-Hill.
Martin, G. T. (1997). Eschatological ethics and positive peace: Western contributions to the critique of the self-centered ego and its social manifestations. In L. Duhan-Kaplan & L. F. Bove (Eds.), *Philosophical perspectives on power and domination* (pp. 79–92). Amsterdam, The Netherlands: Rodopi.
Marzano, R. J. (2000). *Designing a new taxonomy of educational objectives*. Thousand Oaks, CA: Corwin Press.
Meier, D., & Wood, G. (Eds.) (2004). *Many children left behind: How the No Child Left Behind Act is damaging our children and our schools*. Boston, MA: Beacon Press.
Miller, A. I. (1986). *Imagery in scientific thought: Creating 20th-century physics*. Cambridge, MA: MIT Press.
Miller, A. I. (1989). Imagery and intuition in creative scientific thinking: Albert Einstein's invention of the special theory of relativity. In D. B. Wallace & H. E. Gruber (Eds.), *Creative people at work* (pp. 171–188). New York, NY: Oxford University Press.
Miller, A. I. (1996). *Insights of genius: Imagery and creativity in science and art*. New York, NY: Springer-Verlag.
Miller, A. I. (2001). *Einstein, Picasso: Space, time, and the beauty that causes havoc*. New York, NY: Basic Books.
Mintzberg, H. (1994). *The rise and fall of strategic planning*. New York, NY: Free Press.
Monroe, K. R. (1996). *The heart of altruism*. Princeton, NJ: Princeton University Press.
Monroe, K. R. (2004). *The hand of compassion: Portraits of moral choice during the Holocaust*. Princeton, NJ: Princeton University Press.
Moore, B. N., & Parker, R. (2009). *Critical thinking*. New York, NY: McGraw-Hill.
Myers, D. G. (2002). *Intuition: Its powers and perils*. New Haven, CT: Yale University Press.
Nichols, S. L., & Berliner, D. C. (2007). *Collateral damage: How high-stakes testing corrupts America's schools* Cambridge, MA: Harvard Education Press.
Nicolescu, B. (1996). Levels of complexity and levels of reality: Nature as trans-nature. In B. Pullman (Ed.), *The emergence of complexity in mathematics, physics, chemistry, and biology* (pp. 393–417). Vatican City: Pontifical Academy of Sciences.
Page, S. E. (2007). *The difference: How the power of diversity creates better groups, firms, schools, and societies*. Princeton, NJ: Princeton University Press.
Park, J., Conca, K., & Finger, M. (Eds.) (2008). *The crisis of global environmental governance: Towards a new political economy of sustainability*. London, England: Routledge.
Paul, R., & Elder, L. (2002). *Critical thinking: Tools for taking charge of your professional and personal life*. Upper Saddle River, NJ: Pearson.
Paul, R., & Elder, L. (2009). Critical thinking, creativity, ethical reasoning: A unity of opposites. In D. Ambrose & T. L. Cross (Eds.), *Morality, ethics, and gifted minds* (pp. 117–131). New York, NY: Springer Science.
Peters, M. A. (2010). Three forms of the knowledge economy: Learning, creativity and openness. *British Journal of Educational Studies, 58*, 67–88.
Policastro, E. (1999). Intuition. In M. A. Runco & S. R. Pritzker (Eds.), *Encyclopedia of creativity* (Vol. 2, pp. 89–93). New York, NY: Academic Press.
Powell, W. W. (2001). The capitalist firm in the twenty-first century: Emerging patterns in western enterprise. In P. DiMaggio (Ed.), *The twenty-first-century firm: Changing economic organization in international perspective* (pp. 33–68). Princeton, NJ: Princeton University Press.
Ravitch, D. (2010). *The death and life of the great American school system: How testing and choice are undermining education*. New York, NY: Basic Books.
Resnick, L. B. (1987). *Education and learning to think*. Washington, DC: National Academy Press.
Rooney, D., Hearn, G., & Ninan, A. (Eds.) (2008). *Handbook on the knowledge economy*. Cheltenham, UK: Edward Elgar.

Root-Bernstein, R. S., & Root-Bernstein, M. (2001). *Sparks of genius: The thirteen thinking tools of the world's most creative people*. New York, NY: Houghton Mifflin Harcourt.
Rosenau, J. N. (2003). *Distant proximities: Dynamics beyond globalization*. Princeton, NJ: Princeton University Press.
Runco, M. A. (1991). *Divergent thinking*. Norwood, NJ: Ablex.
Runco, M. A. (1999). Divergent thinking. In M. A. Runco & S. R. Pritzker (Eds.), *Encyclopedia of creativity* (Vol. 1, pp. 577–582). New York, NY: Academic Press.
Runco, M. A. (2004). Creativity. *Annual review of Psychology, 55*, 657–687.
Sawyer, R. K. (2012). *Explaining creativity: The science of human innovation*. New York, NY, Oxford University Press.
Scott, J. W. (2007). *The politics of the veil*. Princeton, NJ: Princeton University Press.
Sibbet, D. (2008). Visual intelligence: Using the deep patterns of visual language to build cognitive skills. *Theory Into Practice, 47*, 118–127.
Spaltera, A. M., & van Dam, A. (2008). Digital visual literacy. *Theory Into Practice. 47*. 93–101.
Sternberg, R. J. (2005). WICS: A model of giftedness in leadership. *Roeper Review, 28,* 37–44.
Sternberg, R. J. (2009). The nature of creativity. In J. C. Kaufman & E. L. Grigorenko (Eds.), *The essential Sternberg: Essays on intelligence, psychology, and education* (pp. 103–118). New York, NY: Springer.
Teays, W. (2006). *Second thoughts: Critical thinking for a diverse society* (3rd ed.). New York, NY: McGraw-Hill.
Tomlinson, C. A. (1999). *The differentiated classroom*. Alexandria, VA: ASCD.
Tomlinson, C. A., & Brighton, C. (2003). Differentiating instruction in response to student readiness, interest, and learning profile in academically diverse classrooms: A review of literature. *Journal for the Education of the Gifted, 27,* 119–145.
Torrance, E. P. (1995). *Why fly: A philosophy of creativity*. Norwood, NJ: Ablex.
Tsing, A. L. (2004). *Friction: An enthography of global connection*. Princeton, NJ: Princeton University Press.
Weschler, J. (Ed.) (1988). *On aesthetics in science* (2nd ed.). Boston, MA: Birkhauser.
West, T. G. (1991). *In the mind's eye: Visual thinkers, gifted people with learning difficulties, computer images, and the ironies of creativity*. Buffalo, NY: Prometheus.
Wolin, S. (2008). *Democracy incorporated: Managed democracy and the specter of inverted totalitarianism*. Princeton, NJ: Princeton University Press.
Xu, Z. (2009). The enterprise organizational structure change strategy in Internet times. *International Business Research, 2,* 204–206.
Yunus, M. (2008). *Creating a world without poverty: Social business and the future of capitalism*. New York, NY: Punlic Affairs.
Zhao, Y. (2009). *Catching up or leading the way: American education in the age of globalization* Alexandria, VA: ASCD.
Zhao, Y. (2012). *World class learners: Educating creative and entrepreneurial students*. Thousand Oaks, CA, Corwin Press.

DANIEL FAICHNEY

THE ROEPER SCHOOL FROM 12 YEARS OUT

Reflections of a 2001 Graduate

In this response chapter I address the following key themes from Dr. Ambrose's chapter on the Roeper School within the context of 21st-century trends and issues:
   The Prevalence and Persistence of Macroproblems: "Examples of macroproblems include the aforementioned issue of climate change; exploitative socioeconomic systems that generate and sustain gross inequality; and the troubling erosion of democracy, which is caused by colonization and manipulation of the governance process by powerful corporate interests and their lobbyists in many nations worldwide (Hacker & Pierson, 2005; Wolin, 2008)" (Ambrose, this volume, p. —).

- *Emphases on Justice, Equity, and Altruism:* "Consistent with this democratic ethos, children and adults at the school aim to maintain a respectful, egalitarian tenor that ensures fair and just treatment for all. Moreover, they apply this mindset both to their study of events and phenomena in their classrooms, and into the larger world." (Ambrose, this volume, p. —).
- *An Emphasis on the Whole Child:* "Engaging emotion, intuition, and deep-level creative and critical intellectual functioning encourages the individual to light the wick of intrinsic motivation, which catalyzes the exploration of phenomena due to keen personal interest instead of reacting to reward and punishment (extrinsic motivation)." (Ambrose, this volume, p. —).
- *Appreciation for Cognitive Diversity:* "Now, the persistent pressure of transdisciplinary, international macroproblems requires much more interdisciplinary thinking." (Ambrose, this volume, p. —).

On the morning of September 11, 2001, I was awakened by the strange and unforgettable sound of many dorm room televisions, all tuned to the news, echoing against the walls of the University of Michigan's East Quadrangle. Since blogs and networking web sites had just started to take off, I might have turned to social media for breaking news from New York, Washington, and Pennsylvania. However, I preferred to seek out the company of an old friend. At Michigan's Residential College (R.C.), a destination for many Roeper graduates, it was easy to find one: Roeper students entered the R.C. in large numbers, attracted by its emphasis on creative scholarship and independent study. As telephones rang and students paced up and down the corridors, I walked to my friend's room and joined one of the many small groups who spent the day puzzling over the shocking events.

Roeper prepared us to explore important issues deeply and rationally, both in class and as citizens of the world. On September 11, we began our discussion with the question on everyone's mind: Who did it? It was easy enough to acknowledge that an organized group of individuals carried out the attacks, though on that Tuesday morning their identity remained unclear. We heard rumors that the attacks were connected to an international terrorist group, but knew little more. What did the attacks mean? In spite of the confusion, it was evident to us that the scenes of destruction in New York, Pennsylvania, and Washington would force us to develop a new paradigm: if Manhattan was "ground zero," what, if anything, separated the familiar and safe domestic world from *terra incognita*? There were some parallels with Pearl Harbor, but that attack was an act carried out by a state rather than a far-flung global network. September 11 was something different: a dark hour in an increasingly interconnected world, the emergent manifestation of a long-simmering bundle of religious, ethnic, economic, and political grievances.

In the days that followed, my Roeper friends and I focused on President Bush's famous question, *"Why do they hate us?"* It captured a sense of shock shared by many people and acquired an immediate resonance. My friends and I worried that it overlooked a larger and arguably more significant question: If, indeed, the attacks demonstrated that the boundaries between states and cultures have become more porous and vulnerable, what can individuals and states do to encourage peace and goodwill in the new borderlands?

Our questions grew more galling as more information about the attacks became available. It eventually became clear that the attacks were not carried out by a small and isolated group of radicals, but rather by a well-established international network. Economic inequality, political instability, and international conflict all seemed to encourage the hatred that fuelled terrorist recruiters and planners. The attackers were supplied and coordinated by a diffuse group of actors in locations both remote and nearby. To my friends and me, the events of September 11 represented our first direct encounter with a *macroproblem.* What were its moral dimensions—and how would our lives change as a result of its emergence? International terrorism invited us to ask many difficult questions, but suggested no easy answers. During that Tuesday's anxious hours, and in the months that followed, my R.C. friends relied on values and skills learned at Roeper in order to parse the problem and respond to it. Key among the issues brought to the fore by September 11 was the manner in which groups define and use the terms and concepts of *us* and *others.* Particularistic interpretations of these terms by one identity group can dehumanize others; such dehumanization may, in turn, serve to justify horrific acts. George and Annemarie Roeper learned this lesson in Nazi-occupied Europe, and upon their arrival in the United States made respect for the dignity and worth of all individuals a foundational, and indeed quite functional, element of their educational philosophy. In the wake of September 11, their humanistic approach seemed especially relevant.

Roeper students and parents frequently referred to the school as a safe haven, signifying by extension that it was a world unto itself. Many Roeper teachers encouraged divergent and creative thinking, facilitating a broader form of student- and teacher-led inquiry within core subjects and enabling the development of interdisciplinary courses. Photographic fieldwork and readings on nature drawn from Thoreau, Hemingway, and Terry Tempest Williams were combined in *Nature Literature and Photography*, a course that facilitated not only literary and artistic inquiry, but also the development—on my part, at least—of a spiritual communion with nature. *Constitutional Law*, another course, used in-class debates and case briefs to provide a survey of U.S. constitutional jurisprudence from *Marbury v. Madison* (1803) to *Casey v. Planned Parenthood* (1992), culminating in the student-led delivery of oral arguments on a controversial case to a panel of practicing attorneys and judges in a real courtroom.

To the dismay of some stakeholders and the delight of others, Roeper employed a variety of participatory decision-making processes. These included student-faculty working groups, school-wide assemblies, and a tolerance for a robust and active Student Government. In many areas, these processes supplanted the (possibly more expedient) exercise of legitimate power, creating an atmosphere that was at once contentious and deeply respectful of differences. Social justice values, particularly those of equity, inclusion, and altruism, provided a basis for Roeper's participatory community and served as the pillars of Roeper's humanistic approach to education. This approach is very much alive in the school's emphasis on fairness, attention to the least powerful voices as well as the most powerful ones, and openness to dissenting views within the school community.

During my time at Roeper, 1996 to 2001, critics of the school suggested that it was out of touch with the "real world." Indeed, many excellent schools employ a narrower approach to creativity, make do with a less participatory approach to decision-making, and embrace a competitive paradigm for learning and community life. In some ways, these educational models are more congruent with the broader social context: our competitive culture rewards those individuals and institutions that outperform others in objective performance measurement domains such as standardized tests and placement in elite organizations and academic institutions. While many Roeper graduates eventually enter academic programs and industries with some competitive and hierarchical characteristics—and, indeed, succeed in them—they do so with unique experiences and skill sets rooted in their Roeper experience, including a foundation in ethical philosophy and action, openness to new perspectives and experiences, and a willingness to explore the deeper underpinnings of multidimensional issues and problems. In my experience, the characteristics that made Roeper a world unto itself also played a key role in preparing my graduating class, and many others, for engaged and active citizenship in their workplaces and communities.

Such preparation, while certainly useful in college classrooms, has also proven valuable to me in the face of historical turning points such as September 11 and in the series of personal and career decisions I have made since graduating in 2001. I organized food drives and attended local nature preserve meetings as a Roeper upper school student; in so doing, I developed a strong interest in community development and advocacy work. Since then, I have been a lifelong volunteer and current professional practitioner in fields related to causes about which I feel passionate: economic opportunity and social justice, community development, and urban planning. This work has taken many forms; and in each, I have felt echoes of my Roeper experience.

As an undergraduate, I wrote for the Michigan Daily Editorial Board, where I sought out opportunities to write about local government and urban issues, and wrote stridently. Later, I pursued opportunities to advocate on behalf of Ann Arbor's renters, and in favor of environmental sustainability. During that time, I spoke to the Ann Arbor City council in favor of approving new housing development for a series of unused land parcels in Downtown Ann Arbor. My position angered some meeting attendees who wanted to turn the parcels into a greenway. I supported the development of these parcels because I believed it would increase housing opportunities in the urban core, a more environmentally sustainable location than the outlying suburban areas where new housing development might otherwise go. The atmosphere at the council meeting—contentious, but mostly respectful—was reminiscent of Roeper's all-school assemblies. Although I was only 21 years old and a novice public speaker at the time, I had investigated both sides of the downtown development issue and hence was at least somewhat prepared, and certainly motivated, to take a stand in the public debate. I had participated in many debates and discussions at Roeper assemblies and on Roeper's Student Government, and felt comfortable doing so in the "real world" of city council meetings, among my very real neighbours, as a part of a public discussion of an important issue.

In hindsight, I would change some things if I could live through my undergraduate years all over again: I would speak and write more carefully and spend more time exploring the issues with advisors, friends, and opponents. I might focus more on direct service and incremental change, as I have done for the past five years in Chicago's nonprofit workforce development sector. However, in spite of my occasional missteps, I left Roeper with an urge to participate in public life and with the preparation necessary to do so. As a new Roeper graduate, I was ready to assess the benefits and drawbacks of issues, and felt comfortable considering the ethical and moral ramifications of opposing views. In the downtown development case, I initially supported the greenway: new parks are, after all, nice to have. In considering the potential impacts of pushing development away from the city core, I reconsidered. Although I might construct my arguments differently today, I believe that Roeper prepared me to be an active citizen, and I am grateful for that preparation.

With nearly twelve years separating Fall 2001 from this writing, it may seem strange that I chose to focus on September 11—an event that occurred only three months after my graduation—as the initial subject of my reflection on Roeper. My life and career have, since that time, been defined not by international work but by engagement with issues at the local level. Although September 11 inspired some Roeper graduates and many others to work or serve abroad, it confirmed, for me, that local conditions, whether they are economic, political, environmental, or social in nature, are fundamentally linked to conditions throughout the world. Suffering and resentment in one community might ripple outward and affect thousands or millions of others on distant continents. On the other hand, a local organization, program, or set of best practices that benefits and transforms one community might also have the same effect upon another.

The Roeper School is, I believe, an ideal example of a beneficial and transformative institution. Its embrace of creative thinking, its participatory approach to decision-making, and its focus on social justice and equity made it a safe haven, in the best sense, for me and for other students. From its campus in suburban Detroit, Roeper's value is evident in the meaningful lives of its alumni, whose careers and present geographic locations are as diverse as they are, and also in the enduring resonance of its educational model, which would have a transformative impact in any place where people need an education encouraging creativity, mutual respect, and compassion— that is to say, anywhere. As emergent macroproblems and crises pose new challenges across the globe, Roeper offers hope and promise: hope that innovative solutions are not out of reach, and promise that education can play an important role in bringing these solutions to light. I am proud to be a member of the school's extended family and hope that my life and work represent a fulfillment of its promise, and always will.

CONTRIBUTORS

Don Ambrose is professor of graduate education at Rider University in Lawrenceville, New Jersey, editor of the *Roeper Review*, and past chair of the Conceptual Foundations Division of the National Association for Gifted Children. He serves on the editorial boards of five international, refereed journals and for three book series. Don has initiated and led numerous interdisciplinary scholarly projects involving eminent researchers and theorists from gifted education, general education, creative studies, cognitive science, ethical philosophy, psychology, political science, economics, law, history, sociology, theoretical physics, and critical thinking. Most of his scholarship entails theoretical syntheses and philosophical analyses based on a wide-ranging, interdisciplinary search for theories, philosophical perspectives, and research findings that challenge, refine, and expand thinking about the development of creative intelligence. Some of his books include *How Dogmatic Beliefs Harm Creativity and Higher-Level Thinking* (Routledge; with Robert J. Sternberg); *Confronting Dogmatism in Gifted Education* (Routledge; with Robert J. Sternberg and Bharath Sriraman); *Expanding Visions of Creative Intelligence: An Interdisciplinary Exploration* (Hampton Press); *Morality, Ethics, and Gifted Minds* (Springer Science; with Tracy L. Cross); *Creative Intelligence: Toward Theoretic Integration* (Hampton Press; with LeoNora M. Cohen and Abraham J. Tannenbaum); *Imagitronics* (Zephyr Press); *The Roeper School: A Model for Holistic Development of High Ability* (in press with Sense; with Bharath Sriraman & Tracy L. Cross); and *A Critique of Creativity and Complexity: Deconstructing Clichés* (in press with Sense; with Bharath Sriraman & Kathleen Pierce). Venues for some of his recent and forthcoming keynote presentations include Dubai, United Arab Emirates; Istanbul, Turkey; Ulm, Germany; Winnipeg, Canada; Jerusalem, Israel; Paris, France; Kraków, Poland; and Nairobi, Kenya.

Lisa Baker is the Upper School Director at The Roeper School in Birmingham, Michigan. She holds a Master of Science in Counseling from Johns Hopkins University. She began her work in education in Montgomery County (Maryland) Public Schools where she served as a middle and high school teacher, department chair, counselor, and staff development specialist. In recent years, she has been engaged in the development of student-directed, project-based learning for high school students as well as creating authentic work for students in service learning and social justice. Lisa has presented at various conferences including Creating Leadership Teams Focused on Instruction at the National Staff Development Council annual meeting.

CONTRIBUTORS

Denita Banks-Sims has served as the Director of Development and Publications for The Roeper School for twenty-five years. She is the proud parent of two Roeper alumni and cherishes the profound impact George and Annemarie Roeper have had in her life. Prior to this appointment, she was the Public Relations Director for the Rochester Philharmonic Orchestra and the Director of Corporate and Foundation Relations for the University of Rochester. Her early career was spent in broadcast journalism as a producer and community affairs director.

Dylan Bennett is a senior at The Roeper School, where he has been a student since 2007. Over the years, he has taken advantage of opportunities in which he believed he could thrive, make a contribution to the community at large, and engage other members of the greater Roeper community to better our society. The city of Detroit is Dylan's true passion, and he has sought out ways to make a contribution to its future. During the summer of 2012, he was an intern at Detroit's Eastern Market and also with Detroit City Council President Charles Pugh, where he learned much about the city's relationship with both the public and private sectors. In the summer of 2013, he worked at D:hive, Detroit's official welcome center, connecting new residents with jobs, leisure activities, and a place to call home. He believes every individual has an obligation to better his or her surrounding community, and he is striving to do that with the city of Detroit.

Carolyn M. Callahan, Commonwealth Professor of Education at the University of Virginia, developed the program in gifted education at the University and is the founder of the Saturday and Summer Enrichment Program. She has been the principal investigator on projects of the National Research Center on the Gifted and Talented for more than 20 years and principal investigator on four Javits grants. Dr. Callahan has published more than 200 refereed articles and 50 book chapters across a broad range of topics including the areas of identification of gifted students, program evaluation, gifted females, the development of performance assessments, and curricular and programming options for highly able students. She has been recognized as Outstanding Professor of the Commonwealth of Virginia and Distinguished Scholar of the National Association for Gifted Children. She has served as President of the National Association for Gifted Children and is past editor of *Gifted Child Quarterly* and the *Journal for the Education of the Gifted*.

Tracy L. Cross holds an endowed chair, Jody and Layton Smith Professor of Psychology and Gifted Education, and is the Executive Director of the Center for Gifted Education at The College of William and Mary. Previously he served Ball State University as the George and Frances Ball Distinguished Professor of Psychology and Gifted Studies, the founder and Executive Director of both the Center for Gifted Studies and Talent Development and the Institute for Research on the Psychology of Gifted Students. He has published more than 150 articles, book chapters, and columns; made more than 200 presentations at conferences; and published four books. He has previously edited four journals in the field of gifted studies (*Gifted Child Quarterly, Roeper Review, The Journal of Secondary Gifted Education, Research Briefs*) and is the current editor of the *Journal for the Education of the Gifted.* He received the Distinguished Service Award from The Association for the Gifted (TAG) and the National Association for Gifted Children (NAGC), the Early Leader and Early Scholar Awards from NAGC, and in 2009 was given the Lifetime Achievement Award from the MENSA Education and Research Foundation. In 2004, he was named the Outstanding Researcher for Ball State University. In addition to an active scholarly agenda, for 9 years, Dr. Cross served as the Executive Director of the Indiana Academy for Science, Mathematics, and Humanities, a residential high school for intellectually gifted adolescents. He has served as director of two state gifted associations (Wyoming Association for Gifted Education and Indiana Association for the Gifted). He also served as president of TAG and on the Board and Executive Committee of NAGC and is currently the NAGC president.

David Yun Dai is an associate professor of Educational Psychology and Methodology at University at Albany, State University of New York, and a Zijiang Lecture Professor of Education and Psychology at East China Normal University. He received his doctoral degree in psychology from Purdue University, and worked as a post-doctoral fellow at the National Research Center on the Gifted and Talented, University of Connecticut. Dr. Dai was the recipient of the Early Scholar Award in 2006 conferred by the National Association for Gifted Children, and a Fulbright Scholar to China during 2008-2009. He currently serves on the editorial boards of *Gifted Child Quarterly, Journal for the Education of the Gifted,* and *Roeper Review.* He has published 7 authored or edited books and over 80 journal articles, book chapters, encyclopedia entries, and book reviews in general psychology, educational psychology, and gifted education. His research interests include foundational issues in gifted education, talent development, creativity, intelligence and intellectual development, learning and teaching.

Alexandra M. Dickinson is a Roeper School alumna from the class of 2004. Currently, she lives in Washington, D.C., and works as a social media consultant and account director at Beekeeper Group. Her work experience includes time as a production assistant at C-SPAN and she has a deep passion for education and history.

Dan Faichney is a Roeper School alumnus (2001). Currently, he is a law student at Northwestern University specializing in civil litigation and dispute resolution. Before law school, he served as a Program Director at Jane Addams Resource Corporation, a nonprofit organization that provides workforce development and financial support services that enable people and families to transition out of poverty. In his spare time, he enjoys long-distance cycling and improvisational theater.

CONTRIBUTORS

David H. Feldman is the Head of School at The Roeper School. He received his bachelors in English and education from the University of Wisconsin and his Doctor of Jurisprudence from the John Marshall Law School in Chicago, Illinois. David has served as the Head of Middle School at the University of Chicago Laboratory Schools, Headmaster of the Foote School in New Haven, Connecticut, and Head of School at the Greta Berman Arbetter Kazoo School in Kalamazoo, Michigan. David has been a lecturer at Northeastern Illinois University and Western Michigan University on Progressive Education, and an adjunct faculty member at the Graham School of Continuing Education at the University of Chicago. He is the recipient of the National Association of Independent Schools' E. E. Ford Foundation Fellowship for Educational Leadership and has spent over twenty-five years as a teacher, administrator and leader in independent school education. In his work as a teacher and administrator, David has worked with students in pre-school through graduate school. He has written about, spoken to, and taught parents, faculty and community members about child development and the particular developmental needs of early adolescents.

Nick Gillon is a community college humanities professor, doctoral student, and course instructor in the Early Childhood and Family Studies department at the University of Washington in Seattle. He is an experienced early childhood educator and school administrator committed to improving practice and expanding access to high quality early childhood education. He believes that the best teaching results from informed practice, authentic engagement, and critical reflection, and that the best learning results from adequate challenge and attentive support in an environment that recognizes and respects each student. He is currently conducting doctoral research on early childhood teacher education programs in community colleges and developing teacher education courses for the National Center on Quality Teaching and Learning.

Nancy B. Hertzog is currently a Professor of Educational Psychology in the College of Education and the Director of the Robinson Center for Young Scholars at the University of Washington. Prior to her appointment there, she was on the faculty at the University of Illinois at Urbana-Champaign in the Department of Special Education and the Director of University Primary School. Her research focuses on curricular approaches and teaching strategies designed to differentiate instruction and challenge children with diverse abilities. Specifically, she has studied teachers' implementation of the Project Approach in classrooms with both high-achieving and low-achieving children. She has over 25 years of service in various leadership positions for the National Association for Gifted Children, including being the Chair of the Early Childhood Division and Co-Chair of the Education Commission. At the state level she served on the board of the Illinois Association for Gifted Children, and has been the president of the East Central Illinois Association for the Education of Young Children. Dr. Hertzog has written web-based curricular guides that have won national recognition from the National Association for Gifted Children. She has published two books on early childhood education and numerous articles in the *Journal of Curriculum Studies*, *Gifted Child Quarterly*, *Journal for the Education of the Gifted*, *Journal of Advanced Academics*, *Roeper Review*, *Teaching Exceptional Children*, *Early Childhood Research and Practice*, *Journal of Research in Childhood Education*, and *Young Exceptional Children*.

Susan K Johnsen, PhD, is professor in the Department of Educational Psychology at Baylor University where she directs the PhD program and programs related to gifted and talented education. She is the author of tests used in identifying gifted students and over 200 publications including books related to the national teacher preparation standards in gifted education, identification of gifted students, implementing Response to Intervention with gifted students, and adapting the Common Core State Standards with gifted and advanced students in mathematics. She is editor-in-chief of *Gifted Child Today*. She serves on the Board of Examiners of the National Council for Accreditation of Teacher Education, is a reviewer and auditor of programs in gifted education, and is chair of the Knowledge and Skills Subcommittee of the Council for Exceptional Children and co-chair of the National Association for Gifted Children (NAGC) Professional Standards Committee. She is past president of The Association for the Gifted (TAG) and past president of the Texas Association for Gifted and Talented (TAGT). She has received awards for her work in the field of education, including NAGC's President's Award, TAG's Leadership Award, Texas Association for Gifted/Talented Students (TAGT) President's Award, and Baylor University's Investigator Award, Teaching Award, and Contributions to the Academic Community.

Michele Kane is Associate Professor in the Department of Special Education and the Coordinator of the Master of Arts in Gifted Education Program at Northeastern Illinois University in Chicago. She holds advanced degrees in Counseling & Guidance and Educational Administration. Michele is an active member of state and national gifted organizations and is Past President of the Illinois Association for Gifted Children and Past Chair of the Global Awareness Network of the National Association for Gifted Children. An inveterate storyteller, Michele found a home in narrative research and enjoys sharing the tales from parents of gifted learners and other gifted adults. Her passion for good storytelling is evident as she recounted the life history and legacy of Annemarie Roeper for her doctoral dissertation.

Wendy Mayer teaches science in the Roeper Middle School. Her academic background includes a Bachelors Degree in Psychology and a Masters in Education, both from Wayne State University, Michigan. Her interests include development of creative and engaging methods for teaching and a way to bridge academic disciplines using thematic projects. Work experience includes 10 years of teaching at The Roeper School and two years of teaching in the Detroit Public Schools.

CONTRIBUTORS

Susannah Nichols teaches English in the Roeper Upper School. After graduating from the University of Michigan with a BA summa cum laude in English, Susannah completed a tour with Teach for America in Detroit and worked for several non-profits before coming to Roeper. She has also worked as a freelance sportswriter since college, covering hockey and lacrosse in a variety of print and online publications. She has served as a faculty representative to the Board of Trustees and currently serves as the English department coordinator, coaches volleyball, and helped launch the Roeper Service Corps, an initiative devoted to providing students with the resources needed to pursue their interests in service learning and social justice. Her professional passions include the cultivation of an authentic voice in one's writing, a humanities-based approach to the study of literature, and leadership development in students. She has presented at the Progressive Educator's Network conference on the topic of student-directed staffing as a tool for academic empowerment.

Patrick O'Connor attended Roeper for seven years and has served in many roles at the school, including director of college counseling. A past president of the National Association for College Admission Counseling, Patrick is currently Associate Dean of College Counseling at Cranbrook Kingswood School, and is on the Political Science Faculty at Oakland Community College. He has written two college guidebooks and teaches a course in college counseling to school counselors.

Emery Pence has been a member of the Roeper community in many capacities for thirty years. As Teacher, Middle School Director, Roeper philosophy Dude, Head of Alumni Relations, parent of two alumni, spouse of one who has been at Roeper even longer than he, and someone connected to all things Roeper, he wants to thank George, Annemarie and all the others who have created a school and community where people can grow and become all they can be for the benefit of all.

Annemarie Bondy Roeper (1918–2012) was born in Vienna and educated in progressive schools founded by her parents, Max and Gertrud Bondy. Forced out of Germany because of the family's Jewish heritage, Annemarie was studying medicine at the University of Vienna and preparing to study child psychoanalysis with Sigmund and Anna Freud when she was forced to flee again in 1938 when the Nazis invaded Austria. Once in the U.S., she married George Roeper in 1939 and the two founded a school in Detroit in 1941 with an educational vision that encompassed a profound respect for the individual with freedom of growth and learning within a secure community. Annemarie's interests centred on the social and emotional development of children, particularly in the early years. She was President of the Metropolitan Detroit Preschool Association and worked with federal and local government on the Head Start program. In 1968, she consulted with Joan Ganz Cooney on the development of Sesame Street. She taught at Oakland University, co-founded the *Roeper Review* with George in 1978, and received an honorary doctorate from Eastern Michigan University in 1978. After retiring from

Roeper School in 1980, Annemarie continued an active career as a writer, speaker and consultant in gifted education. She developed the Annemarie Roeper Method of Qualitative Assessment to provide a more holistic understanding of a child's abilities and personality. In 1989, Annemarie received the inaugural President's Award from the National Association for Gifted Children for a lifetime of distinguished service. Over her career, she published more than 100 articles and chapters, three scholarly books, four children's books and two memoirs.

George Roeper (1910–1992) was born in Hamburg, Germany and attended Marienau, a boarding school founded by progressive educators, Max and Gertrud Bondy. There he met their daughter Annemarie, whom he married in 1939. After graduating from Marienau in 1930, he studied economics at the Universities of Munich and Cologne, earning the equivalent of a masters degree. George's defense of his doctoral dissertation at the University of Greifswald was interrupted when he had to flee Germany in 1938 because of political persecution by the Nazis. He taught in Switzerland and New Jersey and was Headmaster of Windsor Mountain School in Lenox, MA, before founding a school with Annemarie in Detroit in 1941. George's interest in giftedness led to the school becoming in 1956 the second elementary school in the country devoted exclusively to gifted children. George was also active in the Comparative Education Society in the 1950s and '60s, visiting schools in Europe, Russia, Africa, and Asia and contributing to Society publications. In 1978, he and Annemarie founded the Roeper Review, a peer-reviewed professional journal of gifted studies. Head of Roeper School until he retired in 1979, George was also a Research Associate Professor in the Department of Special Education at Eastern Michigan University, teaching courses on gifted education. As an educator, he was interested in creativity and the sources of motivation to learn among the gifted, as well as the ways education can further social justice. He was awarded an honorary doctorate from Eastern Michigan University in 1978. After retiring, George was active with human rights and nuclear non-proliferation organizations.

Annemarie Bondy Roeper (1918–2012) was born in Vienna and educated in progressive schools founded by her parents, Max and Gertrud Bondy. Forced out of Germany because of the family's Jewish heritage, Annemarie was studying medicine at the University of Vienna and preparing to study child psychoanalysis with Sigmund and Anna Freud when she was forced to flee again in 1938 when the Nazis invaded Austria. Once in the U.S., she married George Roeper in 1939 and the two founded a school in Detroit in 1941 with an educational vision that encompassed a profound respect for the individual accompanied by freedom in growth and learning within a secure community. Annemarie's interests centered on the social and emotional development of children, particularly in the early years. She was President of the Metropolitan Detroit Preschool Association and worked with federal and local government on the development of Head Start. In 1968, she consulted with Joan Ganz Cooney on the creation of Sesame Street. She taught at Oakland

CONTRIBUTORS

University, co-founded the Roeper Review with George in 1978, and received an honorary doctorate from Eastern Michigan University in 1978. After retiring from Roeper School in 1980, Annemarie continued an active career as a writer, speaker and consultant in gifted education. She developed the Annemarie Roeper Method of Qualitative Assessment to provide a more holistic understanding of a child's abilities and personality. In 1989, Annemarie received the inaugural President's Award from the National Association for Gifted Children for a lifetime of distinguished service. Over her career, she published more than 100 articles and chapters, three scholarly books, four children's books, and two memoirs.

Marcia Ruff is School Historian at The Roeper School. She has been on the staff for 12 years, writing for internal publications and marketing until five years ago, when she began researching the school's history. She spent many hours talking with Annemarie Roeper and has interviewed faculty and students of the school dating back to 1941. She is helping to organize the school's archives to make George and Annemarie's groundbreaking educational thought more accessible and to integrate the school's history into the daily life of the school. Marcia has a Masters degree in Journalism from New York University and worked for many years as a magazine journalist.

Megan Ryan is a California native who earned her BA in History from Pepperdine University and recently graduated from the University of Washington with her MEd in Educational Psychology. Her research interests focus on the social and emotional aspects of learning, highly capable learners, social justice education, and early childhood education. Previously, she published a paper, "Sir John Gardner Wilkinson: The Preservation and Pillage of Ancient Egypt," in Pepperdine's *Global Tides* journal, and presented several papers at undergraduate history conferences. Her masters thesis, "The Gift of Giftedness? A Closer Look at How Labeling Influences Social and Academic Self-Concept in Highly Capable Learners" questions the impact and use of intelligence labels. Currently, Megan lives in Seattle, enjoys exploring the city and the greater Seattle area, and hopes to work in curriculum and program development.

Colleen Shelton is a Head Teacher at The Roeper School in Stage I teaching children ages two and a half through young fives. Colleen has a Master of Education in Early Childhood with a ZA Endorsement from the University of Detroit-Mercy. She began at Roeper as a co-op student while in high school and is still there after some thirty-plus years. Colleen is very fortunate to have worked with both Annemarie and George Roeper and tries to approach all she does each day with students and families with the lessons she learned from them. Colleen has had a number of positions while at Roeper, but the past twenty years have been spent with the youngest students, who are her first love and passion. She believes in play-based, hands-on experiences following the passions and interests of her students, as well as creating a welcoming community that includes not only her students but also their families. Colleen feels that at the end of the day students need to be covered in fun--dirt, paint, whatever--to consider the day a success. Colleen speaks at the Michigan Association for Young Children conference every year and with parent groups and college classes. Both of her children are Roeper graduates.

Dorothy A. Sisk holds an endowed chair in education of gifted students at Lamar University in Beaumont, Texas. Dr. Sisk is an international consultant focusing on leadership and creativity development. She was a professor at the University of South Florida, coordinating programs for training teachers of the gifted, and the former director of the U.S. Office of Gifted and Talented in Washington, DC. She currently directs the C.W. Conn Gifted Child Center at Lamar University, and teaches the courses for endorsement in gifted education. She received the Distinguished Leaders Award from the Creative Education Foundation (CEF) in 1989, the Distinguished Service Award from the National Association for Gifted Children (NAGC) in 1983 and 1994, the Creative Lifetime Award from CEF in 1994, and was selected for the Hall of Fame Award of CEF in 2005. Dr. Sisk served as one of the founders and first president of the American Creativity Association, and president of The Association for Gifted and Talented (TAG), the Florida Association for Gifted, and the World Council for Gifted and Talented Children (WCGTC), where she was executive administrator, and editor of *Gifted International* from 1980-1990. She has conducted training sessions throughout the United States and internationally. Dr. Sisk is author of *Creative Teaching of the Gifted, and Making Great Kids Greater;* coauthor with Doris Shallcross of *Leadership: Making Things Happen, The Growing Person,* and *Intuition: An Inner Way of Knowing;* coauthor with E. Paul Torrance of *Gifted Children in the Regular Classroom and Spiritual Intelligence: Developing Higher Level Consciousness;* and coauthor with Susan Israel and Cathy Block of *Collaborative Literacy: Using Gifted Strategies to Enrich Learning for Every Student.* In addition, she has contributed numerous articles and chapters in books on gifted education.

Bharath Sriraman is Professor of Mathematics at The University of Montana and on the Faculty and Advisory Board of Central/SW Asian Studies, where he occasionally offers courses on Indo-Iranian studies/languages. He holds degrees from Alaska (BS in mathematics, University of Alaska- Fairbanks) and Northern Illinois (MS & PhD in mathematics, minor in mathematics education). He maintains active interests in mathematics education, philosophy, history of mathematics, gifted education and creativity. He has published 300+ journal articles, commentaries, book chapters, edited books and reviews in his areas of interest and presented 200+ papers at international conferences, symposia, and invited colloquiua. Bharath is the founding editor of *The Mathematics Enthusiast,* the founding Co-Series Editor of *Advances in Mathematics Education* (Springer Science), and four other book series including *Advances in Creativity and Giftedness* (Sense Publishers). He serves on the editorial panel of a dozen or so journals, including *Roeper Review, Gifted Child Quarterly,* and *High Ability Studies.* Bharath is more or less fluent in 7–9 languages (English, German, Farsi, Hindi, Tamil, Urdu, Kannada, basic French and Danish) and travels/holds active ties with researchers all over the world. He received the 2002 NAGC Outstanding Brief of the Year Award, was nominated for the 2006, 2007 NAGC Early Career Scholar Award, named the 2007 Outstanding Early Scholar by the School Science and Mathematics Association, and in 2009, Northern Illinois University named him as one of 50 "Golden alumni" in the last 50 years for his significant contributions to research in mathematics education, gifted education, and interdisciplinary research at the intersection of mathematics-science-arts.

Joyce VanTassel-Baska is the Jody and Layton Smith Professor Emerita of Education and founding director of the Center for Gifted Education at The College of William and Mary in Virginia where she developed a graduate program and a research and development center in gifted education. She also initiated and directed the Center for Talent Development at Northwestern University. Prior to her work in higher education, Dr. VanTassel-Baska served as the state director of gifted programs for Illinois, and as a teacher, coordinator, and regional and state director of programs in Illinois and Ohio. She has worked as a consultant on gifted education in all 50 states and for key national groups in the USA and throughout the world. She is past president of various organizations including The Association for the Gifted of the Council for Exceptional Children and the National Association for Gifted Children (NAGC). She has published 28 books and over 550 refereed journal articles, book chapters, and scholarly reports. Recent books include, *Content-based Curriculum for Gifted Learners* (2011) (with Catherine Little), *Patterns and Profiles of Low Income Learners* (2010), *Social and Emotional Curriculum for Gifted and Talented Students (*with Tracy L. Cross and Rick Olenchak) (2009), and *Alternative Assessment With Gifted Students* (2008). She also served as the editor of *Gifted and Talented International.* Dr. VanTassel-Baska has received numerous awards for her work, including the NAGC Early Leader Award, Distinguished Service Award, and Distinguished Scholar Award; the State Council of Higher Education in Virginia Outstanding Faculty Award; the Phi Beta Kappa faculty award; the President's Award of the World Council on Gifted and Talented Education; the Distinguished Service Award of CEC-TAG; induction as an American Educational Research Association (AERA) Fellow in 2010; and the Mensa Lifetime Achievement. Honors also include selection as a Fulbright Scholar to New Zealand and as a visiting scholar to Cambridge University. Her major research interests are on the talent-development process and effective curricular interventions with the gifted. She has served as principal investigator on 62 grants and contracts totaling over $15 million, including eight from the United States Department of Education (USDOE).

Cathy Wilmers has taught at the Roeper Lower School for more than twenty years. Both of her children went through Roeper and are the people they are today as a result of their experiences and relationships at the school. She has a Bachelor of Applied Science from the University of Guelph, Canada, and has a Master of Education with an Early Childhood endorsement from Wayne State University, Michigan. Cathy had the opportunity to work with Annemarie Roeper while taking a class on gifted children through Oakland University. Annemarie's gift of encouraging questioning, truly understanding children and their internal life and motivations, and her deep thoughtfulness transformed Cathy's approach to understanding children. Being in a homeroom of gifted, inquisitive, complex, and sensitive children is constantly challenging, and each day is a new venture requiring innovative directions, wonderings, and constant questioning. Creating a strong sense of community within homerooms has always been a passion. The highest compliment is when adults in our community ask to join our Morning Meeting (led by children) to get their day started off right. When not teaching, preparing to teach, or processing children, Cathy enjoys spending summers in Canada at her cottage, reading and soaking up Lake Huron with its many changing facets and possibilities.

Doug Winkworth is a former Chair of The Roeper School Board of Trustees. His association with the School began in 1977 with the enrollment of son, Rob, in Stage I. Doug has served on the Board since 1991, concluding his 11th year as Board Chair in 2006. He presently serves as an honorary trustee with a lifetime appointment. Doug holds degrees in Architectural Design and a masters in urban economics from the University of Detroit. He has extensive experience with strategic planning for a variety of companies and not-for-profits; and has actively participated in all of the School's strategic planning efforts beginning with the first such plan in the early 1990's. Doug and his wife Mary Beth own Festivities Studio, a graphic design firm in Birmingham, Michigan. Both continue to be active at the School and maintain a keen interest in education issues and in advocating for the principles of the Roeper philosophy.

SUBJECT INDEX

Accountability, 11, 47, 178, 179, 232, 235, 266, 312
accreditation, self-study, 12, 15, 43, 79, 80, 176, 211, 294, 327
Adler, Mortimer, 134
Administration, 31, 37, 45, 119, 121, 211, 213, 217, 277, 278, 286–288, 310, 327
aesthetic appreciation, 307, 308, 312
altruism, 4, 16, 165, 211, 212, 215, 319, 220, 221, 222, 231, 296, 307, 308, 309, 312, 317, 319
alumni, alumna, alumnus, ix, 3, 4, 6–9, 13–16, 37, 108, 111–122, 165, 207, 265, 268, 321, 324, 325, 328, 332
anti-bullying, 154, 160, 164, 172
anti-Semitism, 76
application essays, for college admission, 202, 203
assembly, all-school, 277, 278
assessment, 10, 11, 12, 60, 131, 138, 140, 176, 178–187, 212, 221, 234, 329, 332
  authentic, 178–180, 234, 238
  dynamic, 182
  products, 184
  performances, 184, 324
  portfolios, 186
  rubrics, 138, 180, 181, 183, 184
assessments, 24, 138, 178, 181, 182, 185–187, 221, 324
  formative, 140, 179, 180, 183, 185–188, 215, 218
  interim, 180, 183, 186–188
  summative, 180, 183, 187, 215
The Association for Gifted/Council for Exceptional Children (CEC-TAG), 176, 327, 331, 332

athletic policy, no-cut, 104
authentic relationships, 7, 59, 259, 268
authority, 11, 47, 112, 116, 154, 164, 266, 271, 273, 275, 276, 279, 280, 298, 299
biology, the age of, 297
biotechnology, 297
Board of Trustees, ix, 14, 33, 37, 43, 47, 123–127, 176, 265, 266, 270, 278, 285, 328, 333
Bondy, Max and Gertrud, 23, 27, 39, 43, 111, 328, 329
Bullying, 159, 160, 161
cave, Plato's, 226
Center for Creative Leadership, 240, 263
Choice, 36, 61, 63, 65, 80, 93, 116, 118, 137, 164, 193–196, 199–201, 203–206, 212, 221, 236
circle time, 159
citizenship, active, 319
City and Country School, 28–30, 70–72, 77
climate change, 10, 15, 62, 145, 146, 148, 149, 251, 299, 300, 303, 317
cognition enhancement, 297
cognitive dissonance, 59
collaboration, 4, 7, 9, 14, 83, 114, 126, 156, 163, 176, 177, 230, 231, 232, 260, 262, 263, 267, 269, 304, 308, 309
Columbine tragedy, 14
community
compassion, 99, 100, 116, 234, 261, 262, 266, 321
competition, 5, 30, 37, 44, 46, 60, 67, 84, 90, 99, 107, 127, 178, 212, 216, 218, 247, 308

335

SUBJECT INDEX

conflict resolution, 9, 61, 108, 109
constancy, 3, 6, 7, 21–38, 50
constructivism, 133
continuous progress program, 32
cooperation, 22, 37, 45, 46, 48, 60, 61, 67, 156, 159, 259
Costa intellectual indicators, 236
Creative Problem Solving process, 234, 238, 239
creative thinking, 16, 136, 141, 234, 245, 254, 260, 294, 319, 321
critical engagement, 113
critical literacy, 157
critical thinking, 12, 71, 112, 114, 138, 153, 160, 161, 176, 177, 193, 194, 198, 200, 295, 303, 304, 309, 310, 312, 323
curriculum of the self, 35
debate, 83, 102, 108, 109, 113, 114, 116, 131, 147, 168, 169, 178, 184, 186, 232, 241, 243–245, 288, 319, 320
definition of giftedness, 13, 82, 83, 210, 226, 227
dehumanization, 318
desegregation, 70, 76
dialogue, 59, 115, 126, 226, 233, 241, 243–245, 282
differentiation, 10, 131–141, 200, 215, 216, 295
divergent thinking, 235, 303, 308–310, 312
diversity, 10, 16, 21, 61, 76, 94, 101, 153, 163, 165, 171, 172, 179, 187, 211, 212, 219, 232, 235, 241, 296, 299, 301, 302, 306, 309, 310, 312, 317
diversity, cognitive, 16, 301, 302, 306, 309, 310, 312, 317
early childhood, 11, 70, 153–165, 326, 327, 330, 333
education
  traditional, 23, 32, 33, 48, 99

progressive, 6, 21–41, 326, 328, 329
  non-graded, 32
egoistic individualism, 307, 308
emotional, 6, 8, 9, 16, 21, 30, 34, 35, 38, 46, 58, 59, 79, 80, 81, 83, 85, 100, 119, 128, 157, 158, 160, 161, 165, 172, 186, 211, 212, 231, 239, 243, 262, 267, 269, 276, 285, 295, 308, 310, 328–330, 332
  intelligence, 239, 240
  intensity, 59, 267
empathy, 34, 35, 59, 89, 112, 113, 160, 161, 227, 241, 261, 262, 307, 308
empowerment, 8, 9, 14, 107, 121, 240, 269, 272, 276, 281, 328
engaged learners, 226, 282
entrepreneurship, 294, 311
equality, 101, 157, 160, 164, 309
equity, 16, 153, 157, 159, 164, 165, 172, 187, 211, 212, 215, 219, 220, 231, 296, 309, 312, 317, 319, 321
flexible learning environment, 49
flow, 33, 55, 133
forensics, 22, 100, 105, 107, 108, 117, 147, 178
freedom, 9, 36, 46, 84, 85, 86, 99, 101, 102, 107, 108, 112, 116–118, 149, 179, 205, 269, 270, 328, 329
Freudian principles, 27
Future Problem Solving Program, 234, 235
Future Time Span, 242
Gifted and Talented Evaluation Scale (GATES), 238
Gifted Child Institute, 29, 40, 69–72, 77
Gifted Programming Standards, NAGC, 12, 124, 125, 138, 176, 177, 212, 213, 226, 325, 327, 331, 332

gifted, characteristics of the, 227, 266, 268
giftedness, definitions of, 13, 198
Goals 2000 America Education Act, 175
Guantánamo, 112, 113
Herrmann Whole Brain Teaching/Learning Model, 244, 245, 252
hierarchical institutions, 8, 101
high expectations, 8, 84, 88, 102, 149
higher-order thinking, 3, 7, 10, 132
Hitler, Adolf, 262, 267, 268
human rights, 21, 22, 38, 43, 44, 156, 176, 177, 186, 235, 329
humanism, 49, 116, 120
humanistic education, 175
impoverished students, 127
inclusion, 5, 101, 104, 153, 159, 160, 163, 171, 172, 319
Indiana Academy for Science, Mathematics and Humanities, 127, 325
Inequality, 11, 15, 155, 157, 160, 165, 300, 317, 318
Inequity, 154, 163, 296
Integrated Curriculum Model (ICM), 10, 131–141
Intellectual,
  humility, 7, 59
  rigor, 115, 263
interactionism, 133
interdependence, 6, 21–38, 44–46, 48, 50, 58, 176, 177, 186, 227, 235, 255, 259, 261, 262
interdisciplinary, 4, 5, 10, 15, 16, 126, 131, 134, 140, 145–151, 163, 293, 294, 297, 301, 304, 305, 309, 312, 313, 317, 319, 323, 332
international citizen, 243
interpersonal acumen, 3, 304, 309, 312
intrapersonal discovery, 10, 306, 308, 312
jurisprudence, U.S. constitutional, 319

justice, 11, 16, 43–45, 49, 57, 89, 111, 112, 123, 153–166, 171, 172, 176, 177, 179, 186, 187, 196, 212, 215, 220, 227, 231, 243, 266, 267, 276, 279, 296, 309, 317, 319–321, 323, 328–330
knowledge economy, 297, 298
leader,
  as consensus builder, 266, 271
  as communicator, 243, 266, 272
leadership,
  Aristotle's ideas about, 226, 229
  by conversation, 14, 276, 279, 280
  characteristics of, 225, 235–237, 239, 243–246
  definitions of, 225, 227, 261
  Emerging Leaders Innovate Across Sectors, 232, 233
  model of, 226, 230, 233
  Roets Rating Scale for, 237, 238
  Sisk Model for Developing, 225, 243, 245
  situational, 230, 255
  Skills and Behavior Scale, 225, 238
  social change model of, 230
  student, 225, 240, 254
  style theory of, 229
  trait theory of, 229
  WICS model of, 226, 233
learning,
  community, 23, 38, 58–66, 161, 188, 227, 254, 269
  styles, 34, 61, 121, 215, 245
literacy, visual-technological, 303, 312
macro-opportunities, 15, 300, 302, 304, 305, 310
macroproblems, 15, 299–301, 303–306, 310, 317, 318, 321
Marienau, school, 39, 111, 117, 329
materials science, 297
microcredit, 311
mistakes, acknowledging, 172

SUBJECT INDEX

moral judgment, 239
morality, 71, 300, 309, 323
   particularist, 300, 309
   universalist, 309
motivation, intrinsic, 3, 8, 11, 67, 91, 180, 295, 310, 311, 317
motley coalitions, 301, 302, 306
multi-aged groupings, 260
multiculturalism, 134
multimodal literacy, 302
multiple intelligences, 243, 246, 251
nanotechnology, 297
National Association for Gifted Children, 9, 12, 176, 212, 226, 323–327, 329–331
National Defense Education Act, 75
networked organizations, 298
niche, 80, 83, 90, 93, 300, 311
   innovation, 300, 311
   markets, 300, 311
Nicomachean Ethics, Aristotle, 226
open classroom, the, 29, 31–33, 35
opinions, anonymous, 46
Paedaeia proposal, 134
panoramic scanning, 305, 312
parenting, 84, 115, 220
participatory, 29, 31, 37, 295, 309, 310, 319, 321
   decision-making, 319
   democracy, 29, 31, 37, 295
   democracy model of administration, 31
Passow, A. Harry, 7, 8, 29, 30, 40, 69–72, 77, 124
patience, as a leadership skill, 272, 288
personality development, 30, 71
personalized education, 102, 186, 295
philosophy,
   of the school, 5–9, 13, 15, 19, 21–128, 227, 288
   guardians of, 15, 47, 266, 285
pluralistic society, 47, 266
prejudice, 29, 59, 101, 154

problem solving, 4, 62, 81, 138–140, 145, 146, 161, 171, 172, 178, 184, 232, 234, 235, 238–240, 244, 248, 254, 287, 296, 301, 303, 306, 307, 310
problem-based inquiry approach, 7, 58, 66, 67, 310
program evaluation, 10, 12, 210, 212–214, 217, 220, 324
programming standards, National Association for Gifted Children, 12, 176, 177, 212
project approach, the, 161–163, 326
Project Clarion, 136
project-based learning, 134, 161, 243–245, 323
race, 29, 84, 155, 158, 179, 300, 307
racial tensions, 29
Rating the Behavioral Characteristics of Superior Students Scale (SRBCSS) scale, 235, 237, 238
Renaissance scholars, 304
Renzulli Enrichment Triad, 244, 245, 249
Respect, 22, 23, 35, 45, 47, 48, 51, 53, 59, 76, 84, 99, 101, 102, 111, 114, 116, 118, 120, 134, 135, 140, 157, 160, 164, 172, 173, 176, 177, 186, 203, 210, 211, 216, 218–220, 227, 230, 233, 235, 243, 259, 262, 266, 268, 269, 272, 274, 276, 279, 282, 286–288, 296, 299, 309, 312, 318, 321, 328, 329
responsibility, 5, 6, 8, 27, 36, 37, 44–47, 67, 71, 92, 103, 117, 118, 149, 153, 171, 176–179, 187, 205, 227, 229, 230, 232, 243, 244, 246, 248, 259, 260, 261, 266, 269, 270, 273, 274, 278, 282, 287, 288, 296

Rickover, Admiral, 70, 71
Roeper Institute, 123, 124, 126, 127, 293
Roeper Legacy, the, 30
Roeper Review, 34, 37, 40, 79, 123–126, 210, 293, 313, 323, 325, 327–330, 332
Roeper, Annemarie, 21, 38, 39, 61, 76, 97, 108, 208, 257, 265
Roeper, George, 21, 39, 77, 208, 257
Safety, 6, 23, 58, 61, 100, 160, 227, 269, 278, 300
scaffolding, 133, 137, 141, 181
science camps, 150
second step curriculum, 161
self-actualization, 9, 21, 22, 24, 26, 35, 36, 86, 227, 228, 235
self-discipline, 84, 149, 242
self-efficacy, 89, 92, 182
self-knowledge, 80, 211, 212, 215, 232, 269
senior project, 179, 187, 188, 205, 259
September 11, 2001, 317–320
service learning, 7, 10, 14, 58, 62, 63, 64, 66, 67, 131, 163, 282, 323, 328
social,
  activism, 163
  capital, 164
  Darwinism, 308
social justice,
  curriculum, 154–157, 163, 164
  education, 11, 154–157, 164, 165, 330
  emotional aspects of, 160
  literacy for, 160
socially just environment, 159

Sputnik, 29, 69, 75
standardized tests, 201, 202, 204, 273, 319
standards-based education, 175
student-teacher, 9, 102, 108, 286, 287
  ratios, 286, 287
  relationships, 9, 102, 108,
success
technological determinism, 297, 298
The Republic, Plato, 226,
theatrical production, 281
thematic, 10, 91, 145, 327
  approach to curriculum, 10
  interdisciplinary unit, 145
Theory of Forms or Ideas, Plato's, 226
trust, in students, 99, 101, 102, 150, 172, 204
21st century, skills, trends, 11, 12, 15, 176, 177, 293–302, 317
Values, 9, 71, 74, 81, 84, 85, 87, 89, 101, 111, 115, 116, 131, 153, 163, 210, 230–233, 236, 241, 243, 255, 269, 272, 274, 280, 286, 296, 298, 299, 303, 306, 318, 319
  modern, 299
  postmodern, 298, 299
whole child, educating the, 175, 210
WICS model of leadership
  Sternberg's, 226, 233, 234
Williams' Plank, 245, 250
World Values Surveys, 298
Yunus, Muhammad, 311
zone of proximal development (ZPD), 133

CPSIA information can be obtained at www.ICGtesting.com
Printed in the USA
LVOW13s0253070114

368251LV00001B/30/P

9 789462 094178